AF412674

The Comparative Economics of Sport

The Comparative Economics of Sport

Stefan Szymanski

First published 2010 by
PALGRAVE MACMILLAN

Palgrave Macmillan in the UK is an imprint of Macmillan Publishers Limited, registered in England, company number 785998, of Houndmills, Basingstoke, Hampshire RG21 6XS.

Palgrave Macmillan in the US is a division of St Martin's Press LLC, 175 Fifth Avenue, New York, NY 10010.

Palgrave Macmillan is the global academic imprint of the above companies and has companies and representatives throughout the world.

Palgrave® and Macmillan® are registered trademarks in the United States, the United Kingdom, Europe and other countries.

ISBN-13: 978–0–230–23224–2 hardback

This book is printed on paper suitable for recycling and made from fully managed and sustained forest sources. Logging, pulping and manufacturing processes are expected to conform to the environmental regulations of the country of origin.

A catalogue record for this book is available from the British Library.

A catalog record for this book is available from the Library of Congress.

10   9   8   7   6   5   4   3   2   1
19 18 17 16 15 14 13 12 11 10

Printed and bound in Great Britain by
CPI Antony Rowe, Chippenham and Eastbourne

Contents

List of Figures and Graphs

Figures

Graphs

List of Tables

Acknowledgements

I have been lucky enough to work with many outstanding co-authors over the years. I wish to thank those who agreed to have our joint papers republished here: Luigi Buzzacchi, Stefan Késenne, Ian Preston, Steve Ross and Tommaso Valletti as well as those I have worked with elsewhere: Kevin Alavy, Wladimir Andreff, Giles Atkinson, Tunde Buraimo, David Forrest, Filippo dell'Osso, Pedro Garcia del Barrio, Steve Hall, David Harbord, Takeo Hirata, Tom Hoehn, Georgios Kavetsos, Tim Kuypers, Umberto Lago, Stephanie Leach, Neil Longley, Susana Mourato, Susanne Parlasca, Rob Simmons, Ron Smith and Andy Zimbalist. I have also been fortunate to work in sports economics at a time when the subject has been transformed from a minor curiosity into a genuine subfield of economics with its own journals, associations and conferences. There are now hundreds of economists who have published papers on sports economics, most of whom I have met and learnt from, and to whom I owe many thanks for advice, support, and even, on occasion, correction.

I am grateful to Taiba Batool for initiating this project, to Gemma Papageorgiou for managing it Palgrave and to Cherline Daniel for her efficient project management.

Chapter 1 was originally published as "The Economic Design of Sporting Contests" in *Journal of Economic Literature*, 2003, XLI, 1137–1187. Reproduced with kind permission.

Chapter 2 was originally published as "The Political Economy of Sport" in *World Economics*, 1, 2, 101–109. Reproduced with permission from *World Economics with permission.* © Economic and Financial Publishing Ltd.

Chapter 3 was originally published as "Antitrust and Inefficient Joint Ventures: Why Sports Leagues Should Look More Like McDonald's and Less Like the United Nations" (with Stephen F. Ross) in *Marquette Sports Law Review*, 2006, 16, 213–260. Reproduced with permission from Marquette University.

Chapter 4 was originally published as "Open Competition and League Sports" (with Stephen F. Ross) in *Wisconsin Law Review*, 2002, 3, 625–656. "Copyright 2003 by The Board of Regents of the University of Wisconsin System; Reprinted by permission of the Wisconsin Law Review."

Chapter 5 was originally published as "Equality of Opportunity and Equality of Outcome: Open Leagues, Closed Leagues and Competitive Balance" (with L. Buzzachi and T. Valletti) in *Journal of Industry, Competition and Trade*, 2003, 3, 3, 167–186. Reproduced with kind permission of Springer Science and Business Media.

Chapter 6 was originally published as "Promotion and Relegation in Sporting Contests" (with Tommaso Valletti) in *Rivista di Politica Economica* (www.rivistapoliticaeconomica.it), 2005, 95, Issue May–June, 3–39.

Chapter 7 was originally published as "Competitive Balance and Gate Revenue Sharing in Team Sports" (with Stefan Késenne) in *Journal of Industrial Economics*, 2004, LII, 1, 165–177. Reproduced with kind permission of Blackwell Publishers.

Chapter 8 was originally published as "Professional Team Sports Are Only a Game: The Walrasian Fixed-Supply Conjecture Model, Contest-Nash Equilibrium, and the Invariance Principle" in *Journal of Sports Economics*, 2004, 5, 2, 111–126. Reproduced with kind permission.

Chapter 9 was originally published as "Why Have Premium Sports Rights Migrated to Pay-TV in Europe But Not in the US?" in *The Economics of Sport and Media*, C. Jeanrenaud and S. Kesenne (eds), Edward Elgar, Cheltenham, 2006. Reproduced with kind permission.

Chapter 10 was originally published as "Seizing the Moment: A Blueprint for Reform of World Cricket" (with Ian Preston, and Stephen F. Ross), mimeo.

Introduction

Why study the economics of sport? Larry Kahn has suggested (and amply demonstrated with his own research) that the wealth of information on player performance and remuneration make sports an ideal testing ground for labour market theories. Some have argued that sports are a good way to teach economics, largely because so many economic aspects of sports are familiar to students (e.g. player wages and performance, ticket prices, broadcast rights values). A third reason is that sports are an important part of the economy, and a fourth is that sports are just plain interesting. I have some sympathy with all of these reasons, but I have never been entirely convinced. Sports are good for studying labour markets, but given the very special talents of those who perform at the highest level, and very obvious non-monetary pressures and incentives involved, it's not always clear what lessons there are for, say, setting the pay of clerks working in an insurance company. Sports are familiar to students, but they often bear little in common with other economic activities. Above all, competitors in sporting competition need their competitors in order to provide sporting entertainment—there is a shared interest in production which is different from car manufacturers or fast food franchises. Moreover, measured in purely monetary terms, sports remain a relatively insignificant part of the economy—they employ relatively few people and generate relatively low sales volumes, unless one is prepared to attribute the totality of sports shoe sales to the sports industry. Finally, it may be fun for those who work on it (and I certainly admit to enjoying what I do), but universities, like most institutions, must justify what they do to those who fund their activities, and this argument cuts little ice with funding bodies.

My own rationale for the study of sports economics is that it contributes to public policy, whether in relation to the operation of professional sports as primarily entertainment businesses, or to the funding of facilities to promote mass participation and public health. Indeed, while sports may have limited economic weight measured in pounds, dollars or euros, its impact on the day-to-day lives of most people is extraordinary; successful policy in relation to sports has the capacity to raise social welfare substantially. This volume contains a selection of chapters that relate to public policy and sports.

Most of the important papers in the field of sports economics relate to policy issues. Simon Rottenberg's original contribution in 1956 was an analysis of the labour market in professional baseball which suggested that the reserve clause provided no public benefit. The collection of readings edited by Roger Noll in 1974, Government and the Sports Business, addressed public policy in all of the American major league sports. Similarly the work of economists such as Rob Baade, Dennis Coates, Rod Fort, Brad Humphreys, Roger Noll, Allen Sanderson, Andy Zimbalist and others on the impact of public subsidies for sport stadiums has played an important role in moulding public policy on this issue. I think it is noteworthy that most of these contributions have been American, while European economists contributions to the public policy debate have been more muted. Nonetheless, Peter Sloane has over many years contributed to the debate on the financing of football, Stefan Késenne played a significant role in the Bosman case, and a number of economists across Europe have been involved in debating the merits of the collective selling of broadcast rights.

1.   Public policy and sports

Public policy in sports can be divided into a number of distinct areas.

(i)   Antitrust analysis of commercial sporting organisations

Sport first became involved with antitrust in the Federal Baseball case in 1915 which ultimately resulted in the Supreme Court's landmark decision that baseball did not involve interstate commerce and therefore the federal antitrust law did not apply. This curious decision did not prevent economists from examining the restraints imposed by baseball leagues and other sports organisations. Sports leagues in particular are special, because even if the clubs are considered to be competing businesses, they cannot effectively sell their product without entering into agreements among themselves, agreements which in any other context would almost certainly violate cartel laws. The issue has always been the precise range of agreements that should be exempt. Labour market restraints on player mobility have been the most controversial, and the most prominent argument has been the claim of leagues to the "competitive balance defence". This is the argument that if players were free to move at will, the best players would all migrate to the biggest teams, creating a predictable and therefore unappealing championship. The economic analysis of this proposition began with Simon Rottenberg and continues to this day. Economists have attacked this point both from the point of view of theory and with empirical analysis; nonetheless, this most straightforward sounding of propositions remains surprisingly controversial.

A second area of antitrust scrutiny has concerned the collective selling of broadcast rights by teams in a league. Once again, a cartel of this nature would be self-evidently illegal in other economic activities, but in professional sports collective selling has been defended on the grounds that it forms the basis for the redistribution of income among member clubs.

A third area of antitrust involvement has been in the alleged predatory practices of major leagues in the US in relation to new leagues establishing themselves. While to a large extent this issue concerns labour market restraints, as when leagues threaten blackball players who jump to rival leagues, there are a number of other potentially anticompetitive practices that dominant leagues might engage in.

A fourth area, more closely associated with the European system in which clubs and leagues are affiliated to national governing bodies that claim jurisdiction over all competitions within the sport, has been the extent of the rights of governing bodies. For example, the European Commission has challenged the basis on which the governing body of motor sport, the FIA, sanctions all motor racing competitions in Europe, and more recently the larger football clubs financed a challenge to the right of FIFA to oblige clubs to release players for international representative competition without compensating the clubs. This issue really goes further than antitrust analysis, since it is at root about the social purpose of sport, not just its commercial dimension. This is an area on which national governments tend to have widely differing policies with France at one extreme (where all sport is licensed by the state) to the anglo-saxon nations at the other extreme, where sports bodies are largely autonomous and governments have (at least until recently) refused to become involved in sport.

(ii)   Cost benefit analysis of public subsidies for commercial sports organisations

Even if government has explicitly avoided involvement in sport, sports organisations have not been reticent in demanding public subsidies. In the US major league franchises have perfected the art of extracting subsidies from local taxpayers, either from the existing host city by threatening to leave or by carrying out the threat and benefiting from the largesse of the new host. Subsidies have come in the form of partial or complete funding for a project, the offer of tax credits or soft loans, while at the same time consigning revenue streams to the franchise owner. To justify these subsidies owners have argued that they will bring substantial economic benefits to host cities, in the form of employment and increased economic activity, through the construction phase of the project and then as a result of the amenity attracting spending by customers. These propositions have now generated a substantial body of economic research most of which show that the economic benefits are limited. Estimates of employment, wage levels and sales activity tend to show only marginal gains, if there are any, from hosting sports teams. Moreover, these findings are consistent with the theory of economic impact analysis which gives good reason to be sceptical—a facility can only produce an economic stimulus if it brings new resources into the locality or prevents resources leaving the region. In reality, much of the spending is local, and would have been spent in the region anyway (on alternative forms of entertainment) while much of the income generated leaves the locality (star players tend not to spend their income in the city itself). Research in this area is ongoing, and has in recent years shifted towards the analysis of revealed preferences (hedonic models), looking at, say, the impact of a stadium on property values or contingent valuation models, surveying consumers directly on their willingness to pay for sports amenities. Similar kinds of studies have been conducted to examine the impact of hosting major events such as the Olympics or the FIFA World Cup, and some recent research has looked at the impact of these events on self-reported measures of life satisfaction, in order to capture so-called "feelgood effects".

(iii) The health and social benefits of public funding for sports participation

An under-researched but growing area of concern for sports economists is the relationship between sports participation and general well-being, either physical or psychological. In the past government has tended to be involved in sport either for purposes of military preparedness (this was especially true during the 100 years between 1850, when modern sports were becoming established, and 1950) or for purposes of promoting national prestige. Since the Second World War the first motive has been largely discredited, while the second motive is also viewed with some scepticism. However, the growing crisis of obesity in developed nations has started to make public policymakers think about sports participation in a new light. Indeed, arguably the birth of the jogging culture in the 1960s and 1970s demonstrated that individuals were increasingly aware of the health benefits of sports and private sports gyms have been one of the fastest growing sectors of the commercial sports market. Governments are increasingly advocating sports programmes as a means to reduce health risks, to promote mental health, and sports scientists have been able to measure the benefits to individuals on both dimensions. More questionably, government has also tended to see sports participation as a means to promote social cohesion and to address problems such as juvenile crime.

2.   The chapters in this volume

The chapters in this volume are primarily concerned with the first of the policy areas described above. The first chapter, The Economic Design of Sporting Contests, provides an overview of commercial and professional sports, viewed as a problem of design and regulation. From the point of view of league or championship organisers, the issue is seen as one of designing a contest to generate effort which will provide entertainment to paying fans. The chapter sets this problem in the context of contest theory, a branch of economic theory that is ideally suited to the analysis of the design of sporting competition. The chapter mostly focuses on the design of team sports leagues, and discusses in detail the issue of competitive balance, which has been the major policy preoccupation of the courts and lawmakers. The chapter also summarises briefly the major antitrust cases.

In The Political Economy of Sport, I set out to put the public policy wranglings over professional sports leagues in the context of public policy more broadly. Over and again the rules of commercial sports leagues (commercial in the sense that they generate large sums of money, and even ostensibly amateur league organisers such as the NCAA are included in this analysis) have been argued over in the courts because government has not in general been willing to give them a special status exempting them from antitrust (except in some very special cases), notwithstanding significant pressures to do so, especially from the governing bodies of sports in Europe.

The third and fourth chapters are collaborations with Steve Ross, both of which were published in law reviews and deal with the legal implications of an economic analysis of sports league rules and structures. Steve and I have collaborated over many years, and we have tended to focus on two issues: the relationship between the league as an organiser of competition and the member clubs responsible for fielding teams;

and the issue of league membership and sporting merit. Our article in the *Marquette Sports Law Review* argued that enforced legal separation between the clubs in a league and the management of the league organisation itself is desirable on the grounds of efficiency. Club-run leagues are bad decisionmakers because they essentially rely on voting coalitions to agree policy rather than an executive tasked with maximising the total value of the league output. Weak incentives give rise to weak management, which is against the interests of both owners and managers. In our *Wisconsin Law Review* article we set out one aspect of efficiency management of a sports league, namely ensuring that the teams operate competitively. In north American major leagues the absence of an entry by merit system undermines the incentives for weak teams to get stronger, and we argue that a promotion and relegation system as practised around the world, most notably in professional football (soccer), provides more effective incentives.

The promotion and relegation system is one of the most interesting features of any sports leagues, but its incentive properties have scarcely been commented upon by economists. In the two chapters with Tommaso Valletti (one of which was also co-authored with Luigi Buzzacchi) we compared the incentive properties with those of closed leagues. The first of these chapters illustrates empirically the trade-off between equality of opportunity and equality of outcome which seems characteristic of league structures. Open leagues with promotion and relegation have the potential to allow entry by many more teams than the closed franchise leagues of North America, but in practice many fewer teams tend to rise to the top of the league in the promotion and relegation system of European football. We explain this in the second chapter by the incentive to share resources—we develop a model in which sharing can enhance demand by making a competition more balanced, but that sharing also implies that teams with larger endowments (e.g. fan bases) are less likely to dominate. In a promotion and relegation system the penalty for failure is much greater, and therefore dominant teams are less likely to agree to revenue sharing. It is commonplace in Europe to hear reformers call for more sharing *and* preservation of the promotion and relegation system; our chapter explains why the big clubs are unlikely to agree to reforms along these lines.

The next two chapters deal with what has been, purely from the point of view of economic analysis, the most controversial issue I have written about. It had become an established proposition of sport economics that the sharing of gate revenues by teams in a league, on the basis that visiting teams receive a percentage share of ticket revenues on the day of the game (as operates, for instance, in the NFL), would have no effect on the competitive balance of a league (the so-called invariance principle). The reasoning behind this is as follows: sharing will redistribute revenues from strong drawing teams to weak drawing teams, but would also limit the incentive to invest in talent, since the share of the rewards to success (essentially derived through the home gate) are diminished by sharing. The key result is that the fall in the marginal return to success is equal and so offsetting for both teams, and therefore competitive balance is unaffected. I found myself repeatedly unable to reproduce this result, even though it is apparently based on the simplest algebra. The breakthrough for me came several years ago when I explained my puzzlement to Stefan Késenne, and he showed me the special assumption (which has since been called the fixed-supply conjecture) required to get the result. On replacing this conjecture with what seems to me the most natural (Nash) conjecture, standard in the related literature, I found not only that the invariance principle did not hold, but that perversely gate revenue sharing would actually reduce competitive balance. This has proved for me at least to be a most insightful discovery, since it has placed in a broader context the nature of the contest model as applied to sports leagues. The two chapters published here, from the *Journal of Industrial Economics* and the *Journal of Sport Economics*, illustrate the results in different ways (another, shorter derivation is also provided in the *Journal of Economic Literature* survey). These chapters have created within the small sports economics fraternity a flurry of papers seeking to rebut, deny or amend the results in my chapters. In many ways this has been the most satisfying research I have undertaken, largely since it has engaged the attention of colleagues, however violently some of them might disagree.

The final two chapters in the volume deal with some practical sports policy issues. The chapter on premium sports rights speculates as to why these have largely (although not quite all) migrated to pay TV in Europe while remaining largely (if not entirely) on free-to-air and basic cable in the USA. One possibility is that this is a direct outcome of public policy: the Sports Broadcasting Act in the US allows collective selling when rights are sold free-to-air, but, according to the usual interpretation, not when rights are sold to pay TV. By contrast, in Europe, there is no difference in the ability to collectively sell rights on different platforms (except where particular rights have been reserved for free-to-air broadcasting), and this may explain why rights have migrated so much more rapidly to pay TV. Lastly, the chapter co-authored with Steve Ross and Ian Preston is an attempt by two economists and a lawyer to use economic analysis to resolve a particular problem. Back in 2000 the world of international cricket was beset by match-fixing scandals; it turned out that a significant number of captains of international teams who represent the highest level of competition were accepting bribes paid out by betting syndicates. Our diagnosis was not that cricketers were irredeemably corrupt, but that the incentive system which resulted in players receiving only a tiny fraction of the income they generated and in many cases leaving them barely able to maintain a modest standard of living was exposing players to temptations that could be easily removed. Our proposal involved the creation of a new form of club cricket that would ensure higher wages and therefore reduce the profitability of match fixing. Seven years on, Steve Ross and I were lucky enough to be involved in the discussions which led to the set up of the Indian Premier League, a new competition that has significantly boosted the incomes of cricketers and produced a vibrant new competition. While not to everyone's tastes, the IPL has generated large audiences, huge excitement (especially in India) and is seen by many as the future of the game (for good or ill).

3.   The future of economic research and public policy in sport

While the subject of sports economics has expanded substantially over recent years, there are still many areas in which economics research could contribute to the public policy debate. Even in the area where contributions have been most numerous there remains much to be done. Thus the antitrust analysis of sports leagues still requires a thorough and complete analysis of the basis for restrictive agreements within a league. Even where models of the impact on league revenues and profitability exist, these models have little to say about the welfare properties. There is little consensus about the benefits of redistributive policies and rules relating to systems of entry by merit. While most of the chapters in this volume concern these issues, I would not claim to have answered the major questions that policymakers need to resolve.

Economists have perhaps had more success in the second area, offering clear advice that the economic benefits from building sporting facilities and hosting major events are quite limited; the problem is that this advice has tended to fall on deaf ears. By and large, governments want to host these events because of the political prestige they bring, and they are frequently deaf to economic arguments that do not suit their purpose.

But the third area represents perhaps the most important challenges for sports economic in the future. What is the relationship between sports participation, objectively measured indicators of health and subjective measures of well-being? If sports participation does improve health in objective terms, what can be done to persuade individuals to associate sports participation with their subjective well-being? Or is the relationship between these three concepts more complex, or even, perhaps, is there no causal link? What provision of sporting infrastructure and services should be offered by the government? How should aid best be targeted and how should the state work alongside voluntary organisations (if at all)? These issues get the heart of the relationship between sport, society and government, and it is important that economists contribute to the policy debate.

4.   Sports papers

These two volumes contain a selection of sports papers. For completeness I have added a complete list of my publications in the field of sports economics below.

(i)   Refereed journals

"National wellbeing and international sports events" (with Georgios Kavetsos), *Journal of Economic Psychology*, 2010, forthcoming.

"Teaching competition in professional sports leagues", *Journal of Economic Education*, 2010, forthcoming.

"Goal! Profit maximization vs win maximization in soccer leagues" (with Pedro Garcia-del-Barrio), *Review of Industrial Organization*, 2009, 34, 45–68.

"A theory of the evolution of modern sport", *Journal of Sport History*, 2008, 35(1), 1–48.

"Olympic games, terrorism and their impact on the London and Paris Stock Exchanges: A GARCH(1,1) Approach" (with Georgios Kavetsos), *Revue d'Economie Politique*, 2008.

"Are we willing to pay enough to 'back the bid'?: Valuing the intangible impacts of London's bid to host the 2012 Summer Olympic Games" (with Giles Atkinson, Susana Mourata and Ece Ozdemiroglu), *Urban Studies*, 2008, 45(2), 419–444.

"Governance and vertical integration in team sports" (with Stephen F. Ross), *Contemporary Economic Policy*, 2007, 25, 4, 616–626.

"The Champions League and the Coase Theorem", *Scottish Journal of Political Economy*, 2007, 53, 355–373.

"The economic evolution of sport and broadcasting", *Australian Economic Review*, 2006, 39, 428–434.

"Reply: Professional team sports are only a game: The Walrasian fixed-supply conjecture model, contest-Nash equilibrium and the invariance principle", *Journal of Sports Economics*, 2006, 7, 240–243.

"English football" (with Tunde Buraimo and Rob Simmons), *Journal of Sports Economics*, 2006, 7, 29–46.

"The financial crisis in European football: An introduction" (with Umberto Lago and Rob Simmons), *Journal of Sports Economics*, 2006, 7, 3–12.

"Antitrust and inefficient joint ventures: Why sports leagues should look more like McDonald's and less like the United Nations" (with Stephen F. Ross), *Marquette Sports Law Review*, 2006, 16, 213–260.

"Promotion and relegation in sporting contests" (with Tommaso Valletti), *Rivista di Politica Economica*, 2005, 95, 3–39.

"Incentive effects of second prizes" (with Tommaso Valletti), *European Journal of Political Economy*, 2005, 21, 2, 467–481.

"Broadcasting, attendance and the inefficiency of cartels" (with David Forrest and Rob Simmons), *Review of Industrial Organization*, 2004, 24, 243–265.

"Professional team sports are only a game: The Walrasian fixed-supply conjecture model, Contest-Nash equilibrium and the invariance principle", *Journal of Sports Economics*, 2004, 5, 2, 111–126.

"Competitive balance and gate revenue sharing in team sports" (with Stefan Késenne), *Journal of Industrial Economics*, 2004, LII, 1, 165–177.

"Football trials" (with David Harbord), *European Competition Law Review*, February 2004, 2, 114–119.

"The assessment: The economics of sport", *Oxford Review of Economic Policy*, 2003, 19, 4, 467–477.

"Cheating in sport" (with Ian Preston), *Oxford Review of Economic Policy*, 2003, 19, 4, 612–624.

"Equality of opportunity and equality of outcome: Open leagues, closed leagues and competitive balance" (with L. Buzzachi and T. Valletti), *Journal of Industry, Competition and Trade*, 2003, 3, 3, 167–186.

"The economic design of sporting contests", *Journal of Economic Literature*, 2003, XLI, 1137–1187.

"Incentives and competitive balance", *European Sport Management Quarterly*, 2003, 3, 1, 11–30.

"The negative effects of central marketing of football television rights on fans, media concentration and small clubs" (with Susanne Parlasca), *Zeitschrift fuer Betriebswirtschaft*, 2002, 4, 83–104.

"Antitrust, promotion and relegation" (with Stephen F. Ross), *Wisconsin Law Review*, 2002, 3, 625–656.

"Testing causality between team performance and payroll: The cases of Major League Baseball and English Soccer" (with Stephen Hall and Andrew Zimbalist), *Journal of Sports Economics*, 2002, 3, 2, 149–168.

"A law of large numbers: bidding and compulsory competitive tendering" (with Andres Gomez-Lobo), *Review of Industrial Organization*, 2001, 18, 105–113.

"Economics of sport: Introduction", *Economic Journal*, 2001, 111, F1–F3.

"Income inequality, competitive balance and the attractiveness of team sports: Some evidence and a natural experiment from English Soccer", *Economic Journal*, 2001, 111, F69–F84.

"Race and English Football fans" (with Ian Preston), *Scottish Journal of Political Economy*, 2000, 47, 4, 342–363.

"A market test for discrimination in the English Professional Soccer Leagues", *Journal of Political Economy*, 2000, 108, 3, 590–603.

"The Americanization of European Football" (with Tom Hoehn), *Economic Policy*, 1995, 28, 205–233. Reprinted in The Economics of Sport II, A. Zimbalist (ed.), *International Library of Critical Writings in Economics*, vol. 135, 2001, Edward Elgar.

"The English Football industry, profit, performance and industrial structure" (with Ron Smith), *International Review of Applied Economics*, 1997, 11, 1, 135–153. Reprinted in The Economics of Sport II, A. Zimbalist (ed.), *International Library of Critical Writings in Economics*, vol. 135, 2001. Edward Elgar.

(ii)   Book chapters, non-refereed articles and research reports

"Why have premium sports rights migrated to Pay-TV in Europe but not in the US?", in Jeanrenaud, C. and Kesenne, S. (eds), *The Economics of Sport and Media*, Cheltenham, Edward Elgar, 2006.

"The theory of contests", in Fizel, J. (ed.), *Handbook of Sports Economics Research*, Armonk, NY, M. E. Sharpe, 2006.

"The future of football in Europe", in Rodriguez, P., Kesenne, S. and Garcia, J. (eds), *Sports Economics after Fifty Years: Essays in Honour of Simon Rottenberg*, University of Oviedo Press, Oviedo, 2006.

"La mutation des droits de television dans le sport: une comparaison entre l'Europe et les Etats-Unis", in Bolle, G. Desbordes, M. (eds), *Marketing et football: une perspective internationale*, Voiron, France, Presses universitaires du sport, 2005.

"Is there a European model of sport?", In Fort, R. and J. Fizel (eds), *International Sports Economics*, Praeger, Westport, Connecticut, 2004.

"Why have premium sports rights migrated to pay TV in Europe but not in the US?", in Andenas, Hutchings and Marsden (eds), *Current Competition Law*, vol. II, British Institute of International and Comparative Law, 2004.

"Promotion and relegation in rent-seeking contests", in Butenko, S., Gil-Lafuente, J. and Pardalos P. (eds), *Economics, Management and Optimization in Sports*, Springer, 2004.

"Foreward" to special issue on "The Governance of Sports in Europe", *European Sport Management Quarterly*, 2003, 2, 4, 259–263.

"The economic impact of the World Cup 2002", *World Economics*, 2002, 3, 1, 169–177.

"Collective selling of broadcast rights to sporting events", *International Sports Law Review*, 2002, 2, 1.

"Up for the Cup", *World Economics*, 2001, 2, 4, 175–183.

"Promotion and relegation" (with Stephen Ross), *World Economics*, 2001, 2, 2, 179–190.

"Necessary restraints and inefficient monopoly sports leagues" (with Stephen Ross), *International Sports Law Review*, 2000, 1, 1, 27–28.

"The market for gold medals", *World Economics*, 2000, 1, 4, 1–8.

"Two cases relating to broadcasting and football in England", *Reflets & Perspectives de la vie Economique*, 2000, XXXIX, 2–3, 141–148.

"Hearts and minds and Restrictive Practices Court case", in Hamil, S., Michie, J., Oughton, C. and Warby, S. (eds), *Football in the Digital Age*, Mainstream, Edinburgh, 2000.

"The decline of the FA Cup", *The Economic Review*, 2000, 17, 4, 2–5.

"The political economy of sport", *World Economics*, 2000, 1, 2, 1–11.

"The market for soccer players in England after Bosman: Winners and losers", in Kesenne, S. and Jeanrenaud, C. (eds), *Player Market Regulation in Professional Team Sports*, Standaard Uitgeverij, Antwerp, 1999.

"The European soccer business in the 21st century", in Kantarelis, D. (eds), *Business & Economics for the 21st Century*, Vol. II, Business & Economics Society International, 1998.

"Why is Manchester United so successful?", *Business Strategy Review*, 1998, 9, 4, 47–54. Reprinted in *Vezetéstudomány*, 1999, XXX, July–August, 111–118.

"Gazza and Greenbury: Similarities and differences", *Hume Papers on Public Policy*, 1996, 3, 4, 39–58.

"Beaten in the race for the ball", *New Economy*, December 1996, pp. 212–217.

"The economics of footballing success", *The Economic Review*, 1993, 10, 4.

"Football and architecture" (with Filippo dell'Osso), *Business Strategy Review*, 1991, 2, 2, 113–30.

(iii)   Books authored

Why England Lose (with Simon Kuper), HarperCollins, London, 2009.

Playbooks and Checkbooks: An Introduction to the Economics of Modern Sports, Princeton University Press, 2009.

Fans of the World, Unite! A Capitalist Manifesto for Sports Consumers (with Stephen F. Ross), Stanford University Press, 2008.

National Pastime: How Americans Play Baseball and the Rest of the World Plays Soccer (with Andrew Zimbalist), Brookings Institution, Washington DC, 2005.

Il business del calcio (with Umberto Lago and Alessandro Baroncelli), Egea, Milan, 2004.

Winners and Losers: The Business Strategy of Football (with Tim Kuypers), Viking Books, London, 1999 (softcover Penguin Books, 2000).

(iv)   Books edited

Handbook on the Economics of Sport (with Wladimir Andreff), Cheltenham, Edward Elgar, 2006.

Transatlantic Sports: The Comparative Economics of North American and European Sports (with Carlos Barros and Murad Ibrahim), Cheltenham, Edward Elgar, 2002.

(v)   Working papers

"The J.League and the World Cup" (with Takeo Hirata) *Journal of Japan Society of Sports Industry*, 2009, 19, 1, 41–54.

"Tilting the playing field: Why a sports league planner would choose less, not more, competitive balance", *Working Papers 0620*, International Association of Sports Economists, 2006.

"Competitive balance in sports leagues and the paradox of power", *Working Papers 0618*, International Association of Sports Economists, 2006.

"On the edge of your seat: Demand for football on television and the Uncertainty of Outcome Hypothesis" (with Kevin Alavy, Alison Gaskell and Stephanie

Leach) *Working Papers 0631*, International Association of Sports Economists, 2007.

"Tilting the Playing Field (Why a sports league planner would choose less, not more, competitive balance): The case of English Football" (with Stephanie Leach), *Working Papers 0619*, International Association of Sports Economists, 2006.

1

The Economic Design of Sporting Contests

*Stefan Szymanski**

The Business School, Imperial College, London

1. Introduction

What is the optimal number of entrants in a race, or the optimal number of teams in a baseball league? What is the optimal structure of prizes for a golf tournament, or degree of revenue sharing for a football championship? How evenly balanced should the competing teams be in the NASCAR or Formula One championships? What is the maximum number of entrants per nation to the Olympic Games that should be permitted? What quota of qualifying teams to the soccer World Cup should be allocated to the developing nations?

These are all examples of design issues in sports. Sporting contests are one of the most significant branches of the entertainment industry, measured by the amount of time that consumers devote to following them. According to the U.S. Census Bureau, annual attendance at spectator sports in 1997 totaled 110 million (equivalent to 41 percent of the population), while annual household television viewing of sports events is estimated to be 77 billion hours per year.[1] One might add to this several hundreds of millions of hours spent in discussion at the water cooler. Designing an optimal contest is both a matter of significant financial concern for the organizers, participating individuals, and

*I am grateful to Jeff Borland, Braham Dabscheck, David Forrest, Bernd Frick, Philippe Gagnepain, Brad Humphreys, Erik Lehmann, Stefan Késenne, Gerd Muehlheusser, Steve Ross, Rob Simmons, Peter Sloane, Paul Staudohar, Tommaso Valletti, Andy Zimbalist, the editor, and two anonymous referees for valuable comments. I also thank seminar participants at the ESRC study group on the Economics of Sport, Arts and Leisure, the Stockholm School of Economics, and Glasgow University for their observations. Errors are of course my own.

teams, and a matter of consuming personal interest for millions of fans. Not surprisingly, many lawyers and politicians express close interest in the way that sporting contests are run.

Economists have something to offer as well. The design of a sporting contest bears a close relationship to the design of an auction. In both cases, the objective of the organizer is to elicit a contribution (a bid, an investment, or some effort) from contestants who may as a result win a prize. The analogy between an auction and a contest/tournament[2] is already well known (see e.g. Arye Hillman and John Riley 1989). Given the objective function of the organizer and the technology of the auction/contest it is possible to design an optimal prize scheme contingent on the distribution of contestant abilities/willingness to pay. While there have been a number of reviews of the economics of sports in recent years (e.g. John Cairns, Nicholas Jennett, and Peter Sloane 1986; Rodney Fort and James Quirk 1995; Lawrence Kahn 2000; John Vrooman 2000),[3] none of these has attempted to explore systematically the design of sporting contests.

The contest design approach may seem an unusual way of thinking to those who use baseball or soccer as their sporting paradigm. In these and other team sports we are accustomed to thinking of teams as independent entities that come together to agree on rules of the competition. In their review for this journal, Fort and Quirk (1995) state, "Professional team sports leagues are classic, even textbook, examples of business cartels." Members of a sports league certainly have common interests and may benefit from a reduction of economic rivalry between the teams. Many sporting contests are centrally coordinated, however, with little or no input from the teams or individual contestants; examples include the Olympic Games, the soccer World Cup, the New York Marathon, and the U.S. Open Golf Championship. What all these contests have in common is the need to provide contestants with the appropriate incentives to participate and perform. Joint decision-making through a cartel is simply one (possibly inefficient) mechanism to achieve this end.

This review attempts to systematize the contribution of economic thinking to design issues in sports, and to relate this research to the growing empirical literature on sports. This is an enterprise still in its infancy, however, and much remains to be done to understand fully the interaction of contest design and outcomes. The review will suggest new directions in which the literature may develop. A unifying theme of the chapter is that the empirical literature can do much to shed light on the issues raised by the theoretical literature.[4]

The classification of sports is a subject that has exercised the minds of sociologists and economists alike. One distinction that can be made is between modern sports that have been formalized, quantified, and regularized, on the one hand, and traditional sports that are often informal and only semi-structured on the other hand. Examples of the latter might include medieval football in Europe or the Aztec Ball Game (see Allen Guttman 1994 for further examples). This chapter deals primarily with the commercialized modern sports, almost all of which were formalized somewhere between 1840 and 1900—for example, baseball (1846), soccer (1848), Australian football (1859), boxing (1865), cycling (1867), rugby union (1871), tennis (1874), American football (1874), ice hockey (1875), basketball (1891), rugby league (1895), motor sport (1895), and the Olympics (1896).[5]

Historians (see e.g. Tony Mason 1980; Wray Vamplew 1988) have argued that the process of formalization of sports mimicked the formalization inherent in industrialization and urbanization (time-keeping, routinization). Indeed, the commercialization of sport was initially an urban phenomenon, since industrial towns and cities were capable of supplying large paying audiences. It is probably for this reason that most modern sports were formalized either in Great Britain (the first industrialized nation) or the United States (the most rapidly industrializing nation of the late nineteenth century).[6]

In this chapter we draw the distinction between *individualistic* sports (such as tennis, golf, and boxing) and *team* sports, such as soccer and baseball.[7] The distinction rests on the unit of competition and the nature of the demand for the contest. In team sports, the players act as agents on behalf of the team—which may be an actual employer (e.g. a club) or some delegated authority (e.g. a national team).[8] In individualistic sports the player acts as a sole trader; typically in these sports, the athletes/players enter competition in order to establish who is the best, because this is what interests the spectators. The relationship between the tournament organizer and the players is relatively simple. Players perform and agree to abide by the tournament rules in order to compete for a prize which is usually measured in terms of both status and money. Players make little long-term commitment to the organizers, even if it is an annual event, and select among available competitions to maximize their own utility. Likewise, the organizers make few commitments to the athletes, and typically offer places to the best players they can attract. The demand for an individualistic contest depends to a significant degree on the quality of the contestants participating and the amount of effort they contribute to winning. Thus an individualistic sporting contest conforms naturally to the standard contest model, outlined in the next section. Section 3 reviews the contribution of the empirical literature to testing the predictive power of contest models.

The demand for team sports is more complex. First, while the organizational structure of individualistic sports is fairly uniform (e.g. there is little difference between the organization of the New York Marathon and the Berlin Marathon, or that of the U.S. and the British Open Golf Championships), the organization of professional team sports differs substantially on either side of the Atlantic. Section 4 discusses the major differences and considers how these differences emerged from the different institutional settings that ruled at the foundation of baseball (the archetypal North American team sport) and soccer (the archetypal European team sport) at the end of the nineteenth century.

Second, while consumers of team sports resemble those of individualistic sports in wanting to see the best players, the nature of team sports "fandom" is that supporters tend to attach themselves to teams rather than players, and teams identify themselves with particular locations.[9] In practice this can mean that fans attach themselves to perpetually weak teams that do not hire the best players, and maintain such attachments over an entire life. However, contest organizers often express the concern that fans will lose interest in perpetually weak teams and that when this happens they will desert the sport altogether. To prevent this from happening, they argue, it is necessary to design the contest in such a way that all teams have roughly equal chances of winning, or that at least all teams win occasionally.[10] The competitive-balance issue has tended to dominate the analysis of team sports, and section 5 sets out some empirical evidence on competitive balance and related issues in North American and European team sports.

Section 6 considers possibly the most important theoretical contribution to the analysis of team sports: the so-called invariance principle. This states that (a) changes in ownership rights over player services (such as the introduction of free agency) and (b) certain types of income redistribution (such as gate-revenue sharing) will have no effect on competitive balance. Empirical evidence on the first of these propositions is discussed in section 6.1, while section 6.2 considers the theoretical basis of the second.

Section 7 discusses other mechanisms used to promote competitive balance, such as prizes, salary caps, luxury taxes, promotion, and relegation. The role of exclusive territories and its implications for optimal league size are also discussed in that section. The underlying objectives of organizers of team sports have been a consistent source of controversy over the years. Section 7 discusses the implications of the most commonly proposed alternative to the profit-maximizing hypothesis, namely win maximization. While the controversy over the proper specification of the objective function of privately owned clubs is unlikely to be settled in the near future, this section also highlights the parallel development of ostensibly not-for-profit international sporting organizations offering international contests based on national representative teams (e.g. the IOC and the Olympics; FIFA and the soccer World Cup). The section concludes with a discussion of the growing rivalry in the soccer world between club-based and national-team-based competition.

Most sports are governed hierarchically, with a committee or commissioner at the apex of a pyramid possessing the right to change rules and arbitrate disputes. As sporting governments, these have found their authority challenged by the courts when dealing with matters that have an economic or commercial dimension. Section 8 provides a brief review of antitrust issues on both sides of the Atlantic. Section 9 concludes.

2.   The design of individualistic sporting contests

It is relatively straightforward to apply contest theory to the design of an individualistic contest. Consider a simple footrace, organized by a profit-maximizing entrepreneur (e.g. the owner of a racetrack).[11] The organizer may generate a profit by selling tickets, broadcast rights, refreshments, or merchandise, or some combination of these. The organizer expects that spectators will be attracted by the quality of the field entering the race and the effort the entrants contribute. Thus the objective is to design an incentive mechanism to maximize the effort contribution of the selected entrants.

2.1.   The symmetric winner-take-all contest

The winner-take-all contest has been applied to a number of economic problems and originates with Gordon Tullock's (1980) model of a rent-seeking contest.[12]

The organizer's program can be written as

$$\underset{v}{\text{Max}}\, \pi = R\left(\sum_{i=1}^{n} e_i\right) - V \tag{1.1}$$

subject to

$$p_i(e_i^*)V - e_i^* > p(e_i)V - e_i, \text{ for all } e_i \text{ (incentive compatibility)}$$

$$p_i(e_i^*)V - e_i^* > 0 \text{ (individual rationality)} \tag{1.2}$$

where $R(.)$ is a strictly concave revenue function that depends upon the sum of contributions e_i of each contestant, which can be interpreted in a number of ways (e.g. effort, investment, bids, ability) dependent on the context—for the remainder of this section it is labeled "effort." The cost of effort is assumed to be linear with marginal cost equal to unity. Equation (1.2) states that each contestant selects their optimal effort (incentive compatibility) and that all contestants willingly participate (individual rationality). The total payoff to each contestant depends on the probability of success (p_i) multiplied by the value of the prize (V), less the cost of effort. It is assumed that the contestants are risk neutral.[13]

The probability of success is defined by the technology of winning— the Contest Success Function (CSF)—which depends on both the effort contribution of the athletes and their inherent abilities. For the time being, we assume that all contestants have equal ability (symmetry). A natural form for the CSF is the logit function

$$p_i = \frac{e_i^\gamma}{\sum\limits_{j=1}^{n} e_j^\gamma}, \tag{1.3}$$

where γ is a measure of the discriminatory power of the CSF. A high γ implies that even slightly higher effort than one's rivals ensures a high probability of winning the prize, while a low value of γ implies that differences in effort have little impact on outcomes.

This winning technology differs fundamentally from that assumed in an auction, where the highest bidder wins with probability one (the contest is perfectly discriminating). Here, the technology does not discriminate perfectly between effort levels, and the highest bidder can only be certain of winning if all other contestants contribute no effort at all, except in the limiting case as γ goes to infinity, when the logit contest becomes perfectly discriminating.[14] That contests are in fact imperfectly discriminating, yielding uncertainty of outcome, was recognized by Walter Neale (1964) in his seminal paper.

Solving the contestants' first-order conditions, we find the optimal effort level in the symmetric case:[15]

$$e_i^* = \frac{\gamma V(n-1)}{n^2} \tag{1.4}$$

from which it is apparent that

(i) individual and aggregate effort is increasing in the value of the prize;

(ii) individual and aggregate effort is increasing in the discriminatory power of the CSF;

(iii) individual effort decreases with the number of contestants;

(iv) aggregate effort increases with the number of contestants.

These results are intuitive, although perhaps the third might surprise noneconomists. Large fields of contestants are usually associated with highly prestigious contests such as the Olympics, so there may be a correlation between the value of a prize and the number of entrants, which obscures the discouragement effect of large fields on effort. However, organizers of individual race meetings typically do seek to limit the field so as not to dilute the incentives of the participants. The result is very similar to the standard Cournot-Nash oligopoly result that equilibrium output choices for individual firms decrease in the number of competitors but the aggregate output increases.[16] If the organizer is interested in obtaining the maximum winning effort then the optimal number of contestants is two (see e.g. Richard Fullerton and Preston McAfee 1999). If the organizer is interested in a specific level of performance then the reward function may look more complicated than a simple contest: for example, a bonus based on the race time plus a prize for winning.

Having identified the incentive-compatible investment level, it is then trivial for the organizer to select the prize fund to maximize the difference between revenues and costs.[17]

2.2.   Multiple prizes in symmetric contests

In practice, most organizers of sporting contests do not offer a winner-take-all prize: in addition to gold medals, there are silver and bronze. Benny Moldovanu and Aner Sela (2001) show that multiple prizes can be optimal in a perfectly discriminating all-pay auction, depending on the cost structure of the bidding technology—if the cost of bidding is linear or concave, a single prize dominates any other prize structure. If costs are convex, however, a second prize can be optimal. Szymanski and Valletti (2002) extend the analysis of the problem to an imperfectly discriminating (logit) contest. They show that if contestants are symmetric, a first prize always dominates, while if contestants differ enough in ability then a second prize can be optimal. In an imperfectly discriminating contest offering a prize fund to be divided between the first and the second prize, the return to contestant i can be written as

$$(p_{i1}k + (1 - p_{i1})p_{i2}(1 - k)) V - e_i \tag{1.5}$$

where k is the fraction of the prize fund allocated to the first prize, p_{i1} is the probability of contestant i winning the first prize, and p_{i2} is the probability of i winning the second prize (contingent on not having won the first prize). Note that when the contest is symmetric the probability of winning the second prize in equilibrium is the same whoever wins the first prize (other than contestant i). For a logit contest p_{i1} is still defined by (1.3), while p_{i2} is the equivalent expression for the probability of winning second prize, the only difference being that the contest for second prize involves $n - 1$ contestants rather than n. Hence, in general:

$$p_{i2} = \frac{e_i^\gamma}{\sum\limits_{\substack{h=1 \\ h \neq j}}^{n-1} e_h^\gamma}. \tag{1.6}$$

In the symmetric case, the first-order condition for contestant i can be rearranged to show that

$$e^* = \gamma V \left(\frac{(n-1)}{n^2} - \frac{(1-k)}{n(n-1)} \right) \tag{1.7}$$

from which it follows that an increase in the weight attached to the second prize (reducing k) will lead to a reduction in effort. In a two-person contest, effort falls to zero when $k = \frac{1}{2}$ (the second prize is identical to the first prize) but will be positive for all values of $k \in [0, 1]$ for $n > 2$.

2.3.   Asymmetric two-person contests

Although symmetric contests should only ever have first prizes, most sporting contests are in practice asymmetric: there are favorites and long shots. This complicates the issue in two ways. First, in a symmetric contest there is no trade-off between winning effort, average effort, and the variance of effort. In an asymmetric contest the organizer must decide the appropriate objective. Maximizing winning effort is often important (e.g. breaking the world record). On the other hand, a close contest (competitive balance) may be valued if consumers like to see an even contest,[18] and the organizer may be keen to maintain the overall quality of the contest (average effort). Providing greater incentive for winning effort may reduce the effort of weaker contestants and so reduce average effort. Even if average effort does not decline, the variance of effort may increase. Second, in an asymmetric contest the existence of a second prize may not only increase the average and/or reduce the variance of effort, it may also increase the winning effort.

Asymmetry has been little studied in the contest literature (two notable exceptions are Dixit 1987 and Kyung Baik 1994), even though this is a fundamental characteristic of many contests, not least in sport. Asymmetry can be modeled either as a difference in the cost of effort required to achieve a given winning probability or as a difference in the winning probability for any given level of effort. Taking the first of these approaches, the payoff functions in a two-person contest can be written as

$$\pi_1 = p_{11}kV + (1 - p_{11})p_{12}(1 - k)V - (1 - \beta)e_1$$

$$= (2k - 1)p_{11}V + (1 - k)V - (1 - \beta)e_1$$

$$\pi_2 = (2k - 1)p_{21}V + (1 - k)V - (1 + \beta)e_2. \tag{1.8}$$

Asymmetry has two effects on the contest. Most obviously, it will create a competitive imbalance—the greater the β, the larger the low-cost player's winning probability—and if asymmetry gets large enough the participation constraint of the weak contestant will be violated. Second, it can affect total effort. Faced with two asymmetric contestants, the usefulness of a second prize as an instrument of the contest organizer is relatively limited. Total effort increases in the size of the prize fund and the share awarded to the winner. The two first-order conditions for effort derived from (1.8), assuming the logit CSF (1.3), imply that the effort ratio in equilibrium is

$$\frac{e_2}{e_1} = \frac{1 - \beta}{1 + \beta}. \tag{1.9}$$

This tells us that while the contest becomes less balanced as the difference in the cost of effort increases, the prize structure has no effect on relative effort: a second prize does nothing to improve the balance of the contest. This suggests two policy options for the organizer if competitive balance matters: (a) screen for ability to ensure balanced contests and (b) handicap the strong player, that is, increase the strong player's (marginal) cost or subsidize the weak player's (marginal) cost. Fullerton and McAfee (1999) consider the case where ability is not observable and show that by both setting the prize and charging an entry fee the organizer can ensure that the best contestants enter and offer first-best effort either in a homogenous contest with fixed costs or in a heterogenous contest. This may explain, for instance, why it is common to observe that entry to races with large financial prizes is by invitation only to an exclusive group of athletes.

Defining $z = (1 - \beta)/(1 + \beta)$, total effort is given by

$$e_1 + e_2 = \frac{2\gamma V(2k - 1)z^{\gamma}}{(1 + z^{\gamma})^2(1 - \beta^2)}. \tag{1.10}$$

When $\gamma = 1$ it is clear that $e_1 + e_2 = V(2k - 1)/2$, so that total effort is independent of β and any increase in asymmetry yields offsetting increases and decreases in effort from the strong and weak players respectively. When $\gamma > 1$ (the contest is relatively discriminating) increasing asymmetry reduces total effort since the discouragement effect for the weaker player outweighs the encouragement effect for the stronger player. On the other hand, when $\gamma < 1$ the reverse is true and increasing asymmetry increases effort (when the contest is not very discriminating no one is very motivated to supply effort, but asymmetry provides an encouragement to the strong player to secure the prize). Lazear and Rosen (1981, p. 858) demonstrate similar results in a rank order labor tournament where the CSF is asymmetric, but in their model the effect on total effort depends on the concavity or convexity of costs.

2.4.   Asymmetric contests with more than two players

With more than two players a second prize can be a useful instrument for the organizer. For instance, a second prize can now be a motivational device. Szymanski and Valletti (2002) develop a formal model of a three-person contest to show that second prizes may not only improve competitive balance, but also increase total effort. The intuition is quite straightforward. Consider a three-person race with two weak contestants and one strong one. If the players are more or less evenly matched, then it pays to put all the weight on first prize as in a symmetric contest. But the motivation effect of the first prize is dulled if the two weak contestants are very weak, because however much effort they make they have little chance to win. It follows that if two out of three contestants give up then even the strong contestant is unlikely to make any effort. By introducing a second prize, the two weak contestants are given something to play for, and as a result of their effort even the strong contestant cannot coast along quite so easily and is provoked into supplying more effort.

This observation suggests that large prize spreads should be observed when contestants are relatively evenly matched but narrower spreads should be offered when there are large differences in ability.[19]

A second prize may also improve competitive balance, but at this stage a problem of definition arises. It is natural to think of balance in terms of the variance of contributions, but with three or more contestants it is possible for different combinations of effort to produce the same variance, while in reality the organizer may not be indifferent among them. For example, consider a three-person contest where only effort matters. If contestant 1 contributes three units of effort, contestant 2 contributes two units, and contestant 1 a single unit, the variance of effort (equal to one) would be the same as an alternative case where the first contestant supplied 2.732 units and the other two supplied a single unit each. In the first case there is an equal gap between each contestant, while in the second case there is a larger gap between the strong player and two equally weak players. The race for first place may be more exciting in the first case, but even then the strong player has a big lead (in terms of effort). By contrast, the second case will at least produce a close race for second place, which may compensate for a lack of tension in the race for first place. An argument can be made for either case being more attractive. The problem is that there is no natural metric for competitive balance when $n > 2$, and thus it may be difficult to rank different incentive schemes.

2.5. Match play

In many sporting contests the organizers must make a structural choice between match play and simultaneous play by many contestants. For example, a golf tournament could be organized by pairing contestants and allowing the winner from each pairing to enter the next stage until a winner emerges from the final pairing, or all players could play simultaneously and the player with the lowest score would be declared the winner. Some sports, such as tennis, cannot realistically be organized as simultaneous contests, while others, such as Olympic track and field, typically have elements of both (e.g. eight lanes of runners and the fastest go through to the next round).

Rosen (1986) specifically used the example of a tennis tournament to consider the optimal prize structure in order to maintain effort over a match play tournament. He showed that if the reward for winning increases linearly as the tournament progresses, then effort will decrease, since the added spur of reaching higher and higher prizes is diminished.

This, he argued, rationalized the observation that rewards are often heavily skewed toward the top end of a contest, since this prize structure will ensure that effort is nondecreasing.

Mark Gradstein and Kai Konrad (1999) compared simultaneous contests (which they labeled S-contests) and match play contests (which they labeled T-contests) where a single prize is awarded to the ultimate winner of the contest. They showed that in a symmetric contest where the object is to ensure dissipation of all the rents (i.e. so that total effort expended equals the value of the prize), an S-contest is preferred for $\gamma > 1$ (high discriminatory power), while for $\gamma < 1$ a T-contest is preferred, and for $\gamma = 1$ the choice makes no difference. The intuition behind this result is that when discriminatory power is high a single simultaneous contest is enough to ensure that all rents are dissipated. But when the discriminatory power of each individual contest is low a single contest cannot dissipate all rents, whereas a multistage contest, in which contestants have to put in additional effort at each stage, can dissipate rents.[20]

2.6. Dynamic contests

The contests described so far have been one-shot games or, in the case of sequential contests, it has been assumed that the contestants compete in every round until eliminated. However, if contestants acquire information about the state of play as the game progresses, they may decide to drop out altogether. There are a number of models in the economics literature that examine contests in a dynamic context, most notably the war of attrition and competition for monopoly, preemption games associated with patent races (both types of game are reviewed in Drew Fudenberg and Jean Tirole 1991) and market share attraction games in the advertising literature (see George Monahan and Matthew Sobel 1994). These have some implications for contests that involve a sequence of competitions such as the T-contests described above. Many of these types of contest are found in team sports, but individualistic contests can also involve a dynamic element, either because the contest itself is drawn out (e.g. a marathon or a five-set tennis match) or because players compete throughout a season for rankings.

In the war of attrition, competitors supply effort in the expectation of winning a prize at some future date when all rivals have dropped out of the contest. If contestants are symmetric then a pure strategy equilibrium (in which each contestant is indifferent between staying in and dropping out of the game) does not exist. A mixed strategy equilibrium does exist where each player exits with some probability and the probability equates the expected value of remaining with the expected gain from quitting. However, asymmetric pure strategy equilibria also exist, and if the contestants have different abilities the game may be degenerate with weaker contestants withdrawing instantly (see e.g. Jeremy Bulow and Paul Klemperer 2001).

In the war of attrition, contestants learn nothing from their continued participation in the game (the game is memoryless). In preemption games (e.g. Christopher Harris and John Vickers 1985; Fudenberg and Tirole 1985) the players acquire experience (e.g. know-how in a patent race), and experience increases the probability of success, so that at any point the perception that one player has an established lead may cause all the other players to withdraw. In particular, if one player is known to enter the race with an established advantage, no other contestants will enter (or, if they enter, will supply zero effort), a result known as ϵ-preemption (see Fudenberg et al. 1983). This kind of first-mover advantage can thus undermine the incentive of contestants, especially weaker ones, to supply effort, effectively handing success to the dominant players "on a plate." This extreme result is sensitive to assumptions about information sets, however, and if there is some uncertainty about the state of play then the follower might have an incentive to "leapfrog" ahead of the leader (e.g. Harris and Vickers 1987).[21]

As far as a contest organizer is concerned, these types of games are degenerate, in the sense that spectators typically expect to watch a full contest and might ask for their money back if one of the contestants pulled out.[22] However, in contests where the cost of effort is extremely high (e.g. marathon running and heavyweight boxing) it is not uncommon for an out-of-contention player to pull out. Contest organizers may try to create some uncertainty about performance levels (perhaps even changing the rules) in order to prevent this from happening.

3.   Empirical research on individualistic sports

The research agenda discussed in the previous section can be summarized under four main headings:

(i) The impact of prizes on incentives to perform (depending on discriminatory power, effort functions, and the size of the prize fund);

(ii) The impact of the distribution, or spread, of the prize fund (second prizes, third prizes, and so on);

(iii) The impact of the structure of the contest (number of contestants, simultaneous or sequential contests, and so on);
(iv) The impact of prescreening and handicapping.

Researchers in the field of contest theory have set out to explain the widespread use of prizes as an incentive device in labor and product markets.[23] The claim that sports provides a natural laboratory for testing hypotheses from the economics literature is widely made (e.g. Kahn 2000). While that paper focused primarily on team sports, it pointed out that "some of the most intriguing evidence on the links from incentives to performance comes from sports... like golf and marathon running." In these sports it is possible to gather data on individual performance and relate that data to the prize structure offered in individual tournaments. Perhaps the best-known results are those of Ronald Ehrenberg and Michael Bognanno (1990a,b) who examined scores in American and European PGA golf tours.[24] Their principal finding is that scores tend to be lower (so performance is better) when the prize fund is larger, which seems to be a striking endorsement of tournament theory. They also considered the effect on the final round score of an individual's current position in the contest. Since the prize spread decreases with rank (the difference between the first and second prize is much larger than the gap between the tenth and eleventh prize) it is predicted that effort will be higher and scores lower in the final round when a player has a higher placing at the beginning of the round (this hypothesis presumably reflects the notion that a laggard will be discouraged as in a war of attrition). This prediction is also strongly confirmed by the data.[25]

Another important issue that Ehrenberg and Bognanno address is the relationship between performance in a given tournament and entry. If larger prizes attract better contestants then the observed improvement in scores may be attributable to the "sorting" effect rather than the tournament incentive effect. In fact, they found no evidence that their prize results were due to sample selection bias. This issue has also been addressed in James Lynch and Jeffrey Zax (2000), who examine data on nearly 2000 contestants covering 135 different road races in the United States ranging between 5 km and a full marathon (42 km). They were able to construct a measure of pre-race expected rank, based on an athlete's previous history, and then to construct a measure of the incentive to supply effort based on the difference between the prize for achieving his or her pre-race rank and one rank lower than this (presumably the asymmetry of the race is thought to be large enough that multiple prizes are required to increase total effort). They find on this basis that recorded times are decreasing in the prize difference, apparently suggesting higher effort in response to larger prize spreads. However, once the pre-race ranking variable is included in the regression, to account for the quality of the field entering the race, the impact of the prize spread disappears. The authors thus attribute the impact of prize spreads to the sorting effect rather than the tournament incentive effect.

Michael Maloney and Robert McCormick (2000) use data on 115 footraces ranging between 1 mile and a full marathon involving nearly 1500 athletes. They identify the sorting effect with the total size of the prize fund and the incentive effect with the prize spread, and find that both effects are statistically significant and have the expected sign. Although on average the prizes seem quite small (about $400), their impact is significant since doubling the prize spread reduces race times by 4 percent. One weakness of these footrace studies is that the contestants do not include a significant fraction of the world's best, which is reflected in the average times of the sample. Bernd Frick, Joachim Prinz, and Alexander Dilger (2001) consider a sample of 57 marathons run worldwide and involving much larger prize money ($135,000 per race in 1993 dollars). They examine the impact of the total prize fund, its distribution, and bonuses paid for achieving a fast time. They find that (a) doubling the average prize reduces average times by 1 percent; (b) doubling the spread improves average times by 2 percent; (c) doubling bonus payments improves average times by around .75 percent; (d) increasing the prize fund, spread, and bonuses increases the closeness of the race, measured as the time difference between the winner and other finishers; and (e) race times are decreasing in the number of "in the money" ranks (i.e. the number of prizes).

Apart from footraces and golf, almost the only other individualistic sport to have produced some empirical research is horse racing.[26] Susan Fernie and David Metcalf (1999) examined the effect of a change in the compensation of British jockeys which involved replacing performance-related payments with noncontingent retainers. Their evidence shows that individual performance deteriorated.[27] Higgins and Tollison (1990) examine the impact of the number of contestants on the average distance of contestants behind the winner in the Kentucky Derby and find that larger fields tend to fall further behind the winner, which they equate with a slower race, consistent with contest theory. However, they also find that larger prizes do not appear to produce systematically faster times.

Michael Maloney and Kristina Terkun (2002) address an issue that has generally been neglected in the literature, notably the competition between prize-givers and the impact of this competition on prize spreads. They point out that if prize-givers compete to attract contestants, as is the case with motorcycle racing sponsors, who are the subject of their study, then if the prize fund offered by rival sponsors increases, all else equal, a given sponsor must reduce the prize spread in order to attract the same contestants. They find that this prediction, which they derive from Lazear and Rosen, is indeed supported by the data on prize funds and spreads in a sample of 112 sponsors of motorcycle races.

One concluding comment on individual contests concerns cheating. Thus far we have assumed that all efforts contributed are equally valid, while in reality certain kinds are proscribed (e.g. bribery and performance-enhancing drugs). Little has been written on the economics of cheating in this sense, although a recent paper by Mark Duggan and Steven Levitt (2002) illustrates the potential for research in this area. A related point, raised by Lazear (1989), is that tournaments create an incentive to undermine the performance of rivals in order to increase one's own probability of winning—i.e. sabotage. Luis Garicano and Ignacio Palacios-Huerta (2000) have examined this proposition for the case of soccer, where a change in the points system appeared to lead both to more creative effort and to more sabotage (fouls, in the case of soccer).

Despite the enthusiasm of theorists for sports as a laboratory for testing contest theory, it is apparent that there remains a great deal more work to be done in this field. Almost the only issue considered thus far has been the impact of the size and spread of the prize fund. While most research seems to confirm the most basic economic proposition that bigger prizes produce more effort, even this result is subject to dispute due to the simultaneity of sorting and incentive effects. Larger prize spreads seem to elicit more effort, but the pure winner-take-all contest appears to be a purely theoretical possibility.

Issues deserving further attention include the value of screening, the role of handicapping, contest structure (match play and simultaneous contests) and discouragement effects, the impact of penalties (e.g. failing to make the cut in golf), the impact of qualifying races, cheating, sabotage, and possibly other issues. None of the papers discussed examined in any detail the objectives of the organizer, which are clearly critical in determining the optimal design. For example, rules on qualification for the Olympic Games reflect the values of the founders of the Olympic movement, and are not simply intended to find the fastest runner or swimmer. Discrimination against stronger nations by restricting the number of athletes per nation has a significant influence on the outcome of competition.[28]

4.   The comparative economics of team sports

4.1.   Peculiar economics

The analysis of team sports has been primarily motivated by normative issues.[29] Economic analysis has been used to advise team owners and player unions when negotiating wage deals, as testimony in antitrust cases, as testimony in congressional hearings on legislation, and other proposed public interventions in the organization of sporting contests. Economists and lawyers have also used economic analysis to propose alterations to the design of sporting contests (see e.g. Quirk and Fort 1999; Zimbalist 2003; Stephen F. Ross 1989).

The analysis of normative problems in sports, as in many activities, is often made more difficult by the role of culture. A contest design that is optimal for a particular group of consumers may not be to the taste of another. A good example is the attitude toward player trading in team sports. In North America most fans seem to frown upon player mobility and place the greatest value on players who remain loyal to the same team over their entire career. In Europe, however, player trading has always been an accepted part of the soccer system. While most fans would prefer that good players remain on the team, mobility is accepted as a fact of life and fans do not seem to express opposition to player trading in principle.[30]

It is possible that different attitudes may reflect broader cultural differences, while historical accident and path dependency may also account for different practices. Clearly tradition and folk memory are an important aspect of sports fandom—but are all traditions equally likely to stick, or are some more likely to hold in some cultures than in others? For example, Americans and Europeans seem to enjoy the same kinds of individualistic sports (Olympic sports, golf, tennis, boxing, etc.) but most are attracted to quite different team sports. Moreover, as pointed out in the introduction, while the design of individualistic contests seems to be relatively similar throughout the world, there are some substantial organizational differences between North American and European team sports. It is useful therefore to begin the analysis of team sports by some comparisons in the development of the archetypal American team sport, baseball, and the archetypal European team sport, soccer.

4.2. Baseball

Harold Seymour (1960), the authoritative historian of early baseball, made it clear that the structure of the National League, created in 1876, and the foundation of organized baseball emerged as a consequence of the free-for-all that was undermining interest in the new national sport. From the end of the Civil War, interest in the game spread rapidly across the United States, with teams and competitions proliferating and vying to attract spectators. The barnstorming teams of this era crossed the country in search of opponents, relying on reputations driven by winning records to generate income. The natural equilibrium of this free-entry dynamic game is (a) barnstorming teams attract support as long as they are winning and then collapse when they lose (a rational bubble); (b) team owners dissipate all the rents in competing to hire the best talent; and (c) the opportunities for gambling on the records of individual teams generate match fixing.

The founders of the National League set out to create a new kind of equilibrium, more satisfactory for team owners. The National League was a deliberately elitist affair. Its exclusivity invested members with a stake in its long-term success (to combat short-run incentives for match fixing); its granting of exclusive territories guaranteed a local monopoly (providing an incentive to invest in the local market); and its reserve clause established monopsony rights over the players (ensuring that the income stream from matches accrued principally to the owners). The extraordinary success of this model made it not only the basis for the national sport of the United States, but also the basis for the other North American team sports (football, basketball, and ice hockey). American sports played in other countries adopted this model (e.g. baseball in Japan and Mexico, basketball in Australia), as have some other sports in other countries influenced by the United States (e.g. Australian Rules Football in the 1970s). While other team sports in the United States developed new organizing principles (e.g. the draft in football or the salary cap in basketball) these principles were largely integrated into a common framework that characterizes each of the major sports. These common elements include

1. organizational independence of the domestic major leagues;
2. a fixed number of teams;
3. entry through the sale of expansion franchises;
4. exclusive territories and franchise mobility;
5. draft rules giving teams monopsony rights in player acquisition;

6. roster limits;
7. low player mobility and limited player trading for cash, especially for top stars;
8. collective bargaining over player conditions;
9. collective sale of national broadcast rights (exempted from antitrust);
10. collective sale of merchandising;
11. restrictions preventing the stock market flotation of clubs.

Each of these arrangements has been adopted to a greater or lesser extent, but is present in all the major leagues.[31] Some other types of agreement, such as gate-revenue sharing (MLB[32] and NFL) and salary caps (NBA, NFL), have not been universally adopted, but are not inconsistent with the structure of the nonadopting leagues (which have considered adoption and may yet adopt). These structures are quite distinct from those found in sports leagues outside of the United States, most notably in the case of soccer, arguably the world's most popular team sport.

4.3.   Soccer

The creation of the Football League in England in 1888 had similarly momentous implications for the national pastime of nations that adopted the British model of league organization (see Simon Inglis 1988 for full details). The Football League was formed by a group of teams that belonged to an all-encompassing governing body, the Football Association (FA), founded in 1863. As well as laying down the rules, the FA administered its own successful club competition, the FA Cup, and organized international representative matches against other countries using club players.[33] Unlike the founders of the National League, the founders of the Football League did not break away from the existing structures, but worked inside them. This meant that (a) the Football League never attempted to become an exclusive institution, but intended from the start to admit, eventually, all the major teams into its ranks, and (b) League teams accepted from the beginning the practice of releasing star players to represent their country in international competition without compensation (although this has become increasingly controversial).

As soccer spread rapidly around the globe and other nations adopted the British system, there evolved a distinctive organizational structure involving (i) an overarching governing body responsible for the rules and organizing highly successful competitions (e.g. the World Cup, the European Championship) independently of domestic league authorities; (ii) a domestic league system incorporating promotion and relegation[34]; and (iii) a system where star players are paid employees of clubs and play for them (primarily) in league competition, and are also representatives on the national team, whose success is usually seen as even more prestigious. This system has also been applied to a number of other team sports, usually in countries where the soccer system is dominant (e.g. rugby union and basketball in Europe[35]). Common elements of the "soccer system" include

1. integrated governance structure within a global hierarchy and national leagues subordinate to national associations that participate in international competition using league players;
2. mobility of teams through the system of promotion and relegation;
3. free entry for new teams at the bottom of the hierarchy, but promotion on sporting merit only;
4. nonexclusive territories;
5. competitive labor markets at the entry stage, no draft;
6. no roster limits;
7. high player mobility and trading for cash, especially for top stars;
8. limited unionization or collective bargaining over player conditions;[36]
9. limited collective sale of national broadcast rights (no antitrust exemption);
10. no collective sale of merchandising;
11. limited restrictions on the stock market flotation of clubs.

These are material differences from the "baseball system" described above. A further institutional difference lies in the plurality of major soccer leagues compared to the North American major leagues. While competition among rival leagues has characterized part of the history of North American sports, in most cases competition at the level of the league has not survived long. Fans are drawn to the best competition; competing head to head to attract talent drives down profits to the point where either leagues have folded or the incentive to reestablish monopsony has led to mergers. The close substitutability of rival major leagues in the eyes of consumers has thus been the driving factor toward establishing dominant major leagues in each of the North American team sports, particularly in the television age. In European soccer, however, the more rigidly defined regional loyalties associated with national territories has meant that the national leagues of Italy, Spain, Germany, and England have been seen as only imperfect substitutes, and while competition for player services is intense, it has not brought about league bankruptcy or mergers (even for relatively small European nations such as Belgium, Denmark, or Greece). This issue is discussed in more detail below.

Some commentators, most notably Fort (2000), have argued that these institutional differences have given rise to structural differences that are more apparent than real. For example, he argues that the difference between the closed North American leagues and the open soccer leagues of Europe (i.e. open to new entry through promotion and relegation) has little practical effect, since both systems ensure that the best teams and talents migrate to where they are most valued, whether it be through franchise expansion or promotion. The proposition that institutional differences have no implications for the attractiveness of sporting contests is a natural starting point for both theoretical and empirical analysis of team sports, as has been shown by much of the comparative analysis of team sports inside the United States (e.g. Quirk and Fort 1992; Gerald Scully 1995).

Moreover, some proposals for the reform of North American leagues have a distinctly European flavor. For example, the proposal to break up the major leagues into competing entities (Ross 1989; Quirk and Fort 1999) would create a structure in which independent leagues competed among themselves in the regular season and came together for the play-offs. This is similar to the European model where teams compete in national leagues as well as a pan-European Champions' League. Roger Noll (2002) and Ross and Szymanski (2002) have proposed the adoption by the major leagues of the European promotion and relegation system (see section 7.5). Extending the analysis of team sports to assess the effect of the strikingly different institutions of soccer offers a rich laboratory for researchers.

5. Team sports, uncertainty of outcome, and competitive balance

The justification for the striking range of restrictions utilized in the baseball system (fixed number of teams, exclusive territories, draft rules, roster limits, limited player trading, especially in relation to cash sales, collective selling of national broadcast rights and merchandising, restrictions on ownership) has been based on the nature of competitive team sports. The argument, which has formed the basis of numerous antitrust defences in the U.S. courts, can be reduced to three core claims:

1. Inequality of resources leads to unequal competition.
2. Fan interest declines when outcomes become less uncertain.
3. Specific redistribution mechanisms produce more outcome uncertainty.

These propositions have defined both the empirical and theoretical research agenda of team sports economics. This section reviews the empirical literature on the first two of these propositions. Section 6 will consider individual measures to improve competitive balance.

5.1.   Inequality and the sensitivity of success to resources

The starting point for empirical analysis is that better players produce more success, and acquiring better players costs more money. In other words, we can substitute "cash" for "talent," and talent plays the same role as "effort" in the CSF. Implicit in this notion is a functioning labor market, notwithstanding any constraints upon initial endowments or trading rights within that market. Direct testing of this hypothesis is relatively sparse in the literature. One implicit test is contained in the literature on monopsonistic exploitation, following the methodology of Scully (1974). Even if players do not receive their full marginal revenue products, in an efficient market the rate of exploitation per unit of talent should be the same—otherwise an arbitrage opportunity exists. If the rate of exploitation is common across players, then at the level of the team, contest success should be closely correlated with player salaries.

Aggregate data for total player wage bill per team provides a more direct test of the hypothesis. Table 1.1 reports a simple regression of regular season winning percentage (wpc) upon team wage bill, expressed relative to the average of all teams' wage spending in the season (RW), for the four North American major leagues and the four leading soccer leagues in Europe. These results suggest a fairly close correlation between success and relative wage spending. Since the average of RW is unity, by construction the coefficients α and β must sum to 0.5 for a representative sample (i.e. average wpc). A larger estimate of β implies a larger pay-performance sensitivity. Thus the pay-performance sensitivity of the two baseball leagues is much smaller than that of the NFL. However, this does not make baseball more balanced, since the variance of relative wage spending is much greater. Moreover, the explanatory power of

Table 1.1 Pay-performance sensitivity estimates

League	α	β	σ_{wpc}	σ^*_{wpc}	σ_{RW}	R^2	Period	Obs
North America								
Baseball NL	.42	.08	.07	.04	.27	.11	1980–96	208
Baseball AL	.40	.10	.07	.04	.33	.26	1980–96	238
NFL	.19	.31	.19	.13	.13	.05	1989–2000	350
NBA	.21	.29	.16	.06	.22	.16	1986–2000	351
NHL	.35	.15	.10	.06	.23	.11	1990–98	218
European soccer								
Premier League (England)	.33	.19	.11	.08	.34	.34	1974–99	339
Serie A (Italy)	.34	.15	.13	.11	.63	.56	1988–99	214
Bundesliga (Germany)	.39	.12	.11	.09	.47	.28	1982–96	244
Primera Liga (Spain)	.43	.07	.11	.08	.87	.32	1997–2002	111

Notes: Estimated equation: $\text{wpc}_{it} = \alpha + \beta \text{RW}_{it} + \varepsilon$. RW is wage bill of a team relative to average wage bill for the league in that year. All estimates significant at the 1 percent level. σ^*_{wpc} is the idealized standard deviation if teams had an equal chance of winning each match they played $(=.5/\sqrt{m}$, where m is the number of matches played by each team). European data refers to the top division only.

the regression, as measured by the R^2, is also larger, most notably in the American League (home of the Yankees).[37]

The apparent explanatory power of the regression for the European soccer leagues of England, Italy, Germany, and Spain is greater than for the North American leagues, even though the pay-performance sensitivity is not significantly larger. Given a much larger variation in wage payments, the same pay-performance sensitivity can account for much more of the variation of win percentages. In that sense European leagues appear more predictable. It is striking, given the widespread concern in the United States about growing imbalance in baseball, that the variation of wages and the R^2 of the regression are only noticeably larger in the American League compared to the other North American sports and even then these do not reach the levels found in the European leagues. In more recent years, however, there may have been a trend toward increasing predictability (see Stephen Hall, Szymanski, and Zimbalist 2002).

Correlation does not imply causation. An implicit assumption in the regression specification is that wages cause performance—but it could be argued that causality runs in the opposite direction, from performance to wages. For example, it is usual for winning teams to be paid bonuses, and it is sometimes said that team owners would rather come second than win a championship in order to avoid excessive bonus payments (an example of the limited role of prizes in rewarding team, as opposed to player, performance).

Testing for the direction of causality is feasible. Hall et al. (2002) tested for Granger causality from wages to performance and from performance to wages, and found that they could reject the latter direction of causality for English soccer but not for major league baseball (MLB). One interpretation of this result is that in English soccer there is an unrestrained market for players so that there is no barrier to the operation of an efficient market (for details of its operation, see Szymanski and Kuypers 1999). In MLB, player contracts are much more restrictive, both for players and owners, and this gives rise to bargaining over team rents, the outcome of which is likely to depend on past performance. Testing this hypothesis, which requires the collection of a wider range of potential explanatory variables for MLB, is an important subject for future research, as is the nature of causality in other leagues.[38]

One feature of Table 1.1 that might strike a North American reader is the combination of relatively low standard deviation of winning percentages, often considered an indicator of competitive balance, in the European leagues, combined with relatively high standard deviation of wage payments (see also Ingo Kipker 2000; and David Forrest and Robert Simmons 2002b for detailed comparison). Given a reasonable degree of sensitivity of performance to wages (which does appear causal, at least in the English case) one might have expected a relatively high standard deviation of win percentage reflecting a high degree of competitive imbalance.[39]

The standard deviation of winning percentage, however, may be a relatively poor measure of competitive balance, largely because it only considers performance within a season. Performance in the open European leagues tends to be relatively bunched together, since teams near the bottom keep competing right to the end in order to avoid relegation (see section 7.5). Yet over a number of seasons the same big teams tend to dominate European competition, so there is little turnover at the top. Relatively little attention has been paid to measuring this notion of competitive balance, although this is clearly the aspect that figured heavily in the Blue Ribbon Panel's investigation into baseball (notably the dominance of the Yankees) and has been raised by some critics of static measures (e.g. Ross and Robert Lucke 1997; Woodrow Eckard 1998).[40]

Luigi Buzzacchi, Szymanski, and Valletti (2003) develop a dynamic measure based on estimating the number of teams entering the top k ranks of a league competition over T years (they look at the top rank and the top five ranks over the ten-year intervals from ten to fifty) relative to the idealized number of teams that would have entered these ranks under an equally balanced contest. Note that in an open system where the probability of success is identical for each team, there will be a very high turnover at the top over a twenty-year period, since so many more teams have access compared to a closed league. They compare three North American leagues (MLB, NFL, and NHL) with three national soccer leagues (Italy, England, and Belgium) and find that the number of entrants to the top ranks is slightly higher in North America, but that relative to potential entrants the number of actual entrants is very small in the European leagues. They suggest that an open system can be characterized as one that produces equality of opportunity, while closed leagues are more successful at producing equality of outcome. More research is required into the causes of these differences.

5.2.   Demand and uncertainty of outcome

Whatever the causes of inequality, the lynchpin of team sports organizers' defense of restrictive agreements has been the claim that such measures are required to combat the threat of uneven contests that will reduce the interest of the fans. This proposition was first fully enunciated in the economics literature in a celebrated paper by Neale (1964). As a testable hypothesis it has now generated a substantial literature of its own. To begin with, it is useful to differentiate three types of uncertainty:

1. match uncertainty,
2. seasonal uncertainty,
3. championship uncertainty.

The meaning of match uncertainty is obvious. Seasonal uncertainty means a close championship race within a season, while championship uncertainty means there is a variety of champions over a period of years, rather than domination by one or two teams.

Table 1.2 summarizes the research in this area. In recent years, research on match uncertainty has focused on the use of pre-match betting odds as a means of measuring uncertainty. There seems to be an emerging consensus that demand for match tickets peaks at

Table 1.2 Outcome uncertainty in the literature

Authors	Testing	Uncertainty measure	Data	Result
Noll (1974)	seasonal	—whether team in contention for play-off	ice hockey	weak support
		—whether championship race close	baseball	weak support
Hart et al. (1975)	match	log difference in league positions	4 English football clubs 1969/70–1970/71	weak support
Jennett (1984)	seasonal	championship/relegation significance of each game	Scottish League Football 1975–81	Support
Borland (1987)	seasonal	—difference in games won between first and last	Victorian Football League (Australian Rules) 1950–86	weak support
		—sum of coefficients of variation of game won		
		—average number of games behind the leader		
	championship	—number of teams in contention		no support
Cairns (1987)	seasonal	dummy of contention in championship	4 Scottish football clubs 1969/70–1979/80	support
Jones and Ferguson (1988)	match	dummy for top of the table and bottom of the table matches	NHL Season 1977/78	no support
Whitney (1988)	seasonal	average expected probability of winning	baseball 1970–84	weak support
Peel and Thomas (1988)	match	betting odds (probability of home win)	1981/82 English football league matches	weak support
Knowles et al. (1992)	match	betting odds (probability of home win)	MLB 1988	support

Peel and Thomas (1992)	match	betting odds (probability of home win)	English Football League matches	weak support
Borland and Lye (1992)	seasonal	sum of matches required to qualify for the finals	Australian Rules	no support
Kuypers (1996)	match	betting odds (difference in max and min)	1993/94 individual English	no support
	seasonal	points and games left	Premier League matches	support
Peel and Thomas (1997)	match	betting odds (points spread)	Rugby League 1994/95	support
Baimbridge et al. (1996)	seasonal	dummy when both teams in top (bottom) four positions	1993/94 individual English Premier League matches	no support
Rascher (1999)	match	betting odds (probability of home win)	MLB 1996	support
Szymanski (2001)	championship	competition type (with identical contestants)	English League and FA Cup matches 1977–98	support
Schmidt and Berri (2001)	seasonal	Gini coefficient	MLB 1903–98 (Gini only) MLB 1975–88 (Gini plus other variables)	support support for AL no support for NL
Forrest and Simmons (2002a)	match	odds ratio (accounting for favorite-longshot bias)	Football League matches 1997/98	support

the point where a home team's probability of winning is about twice that of the visiting team, that is, a probability of around .66 (see e.g. Glenn Knowles, Keith Sherony, and Michael Haupert 1992; Forrest and Simmons 2002a summarizing the work of David Peel and David Thomas [1988, 1992, 1997], and Dan Rascher 1999). Several reviewers have commented upon just how *unbalanced* a contest characterized by this probability would be, and in most datasets there are relatively few observations involving such extremely unbalanced contests. Whether this imbalance is optimal from the point of view of the league is not something that these studies address, but it seems reasonable that the optimal balance for the league may be greater than that for the home team.

Less work has been done on the issue of seasonal uncertainty. The key problem in this area is controlling for all the other relevant factors that might influence demand. For example, Martin Schmidt and David Berri (2001) find that attendance is positively affected by uncertainty, using nearly a century of MLB data, but with no other explanatory variables. When they examine a shorter panel including influences such as price data, they find that, for the National League, attendance is significantly *decreasing* in uncertainty. While it is plausible that fans prefer a close championship race, a run of success by a single team may itself spark interest (like the old barnstorming teams). It may be that the causal relationships are too complex to isolate a single influence such as uncertainty of outcome.

Finally, championship uncertainty has hardly ever been tested, although the evidence comparing the relative long-run imbalance of European soccer to the North American leagues suggests that this is an issue worthy of investigation.[41] On the face of it, European soccer is every bit as popular with Europeans as the North American leagues are with Americans, despite long-run domination by a much smaller subset of teams.

Overall, of the 22 cases cited here, 10 offer clear support for the uncertainty of outcome hypothesis, 7 offer weak support, and 5 contradict it. Given that even supportive studies on the issue of match uncertainty seem to imply that attendance is maximized when the home team is about twice as likely to win as the visiting team, the empirical evidence in this area seems far from unambiguous. This is remarkable given the weight that is placed on this argument in policy making and in antitrust cases. Given that even quite unbalanced matches, championships, and leagues can be attractive to consumers, a more nuanced approach is called for.[42]

6.   The invariance principle

In this section we turn to the consideration of specific rules and restrictions that might be designed to increase uncertainty of outcome and enhance competitive balance. Because of the cartel-like organizational structure of most team sports leagues, these rules and restrictions have often been debated in the antitrust courts. On the one hand, economists can try to shed light on whether specific restrictions achieve their stated aim (and whether they were strictly necessary to achieve it); on the other hand, they can also identify other consequences arising from a given restriction. These may be consequences for profits (the owners' interest); prices, quality, and choice (the consumers' interests); and employment conditions and remuneration (the players' interests). Economic analysis of these issues is usually both theoretical and empirical, and the balance between the two often depends on the nature of the restriction and the availability of data.

6.1.   The invariance principle and talent allocation rules

One common characteristic of team sports as they developed on both sides of the Atlantic has been the desire of the owners of teams belonging to professional leagues to control the market for players, in particular to establish monopsony rights. Thus the reserve clause of baseball (see e.g. Quirk and Fort 1992 for an explanation) functioned in much the same way as the Retain and Transfer System of English soccer (see e.g. Sloane 1969).[43] This inevitably led to challenges in the courts by the players claiming the right to move freely between employers. Simon Rottenberg's celebrated (1956) article examined this issue and presented the team owner's rationale:

> The defense most commonly heard is that the reserve rule is necessary to assure an equal distribution of playing talent among opposing teams; that a more or less equal distribution of talent is necessary if there is to be uncertainty of outcome; and that uncertainty of outcome is necessary if the consumer is to be willing to pay admission to the game. This defense is founded on the premise that there are rich baseball clubs and poor ones and that, if the players' market were free, the rich clubs would outbid the poor for talent, taking all competent players for themselves and leaving only the incompetent for other teams. (p. 246)

Rottenberg argued that (a) the reserve clause did nothing to prevent the migration of talent to the big city teams and so would not affect the distribution of talent, and that (b) by establishing monopsony power over a player throughout his career the team owners were able to hold down wages and raise profitability. Point (a) has since been identified as an example of the Coase Theorem at work: the initial distribution of ownership rights should have no impact on the efficient (here profit-maximizing) distribution of resources. El Hodiri and Quirk

(1971) and Quirk and El Hodiri (1974) took this analysis one stage further in a formal dynamic model showing that, if teams have differing revenue-generating potential, (i) profit-maximizing behavior will not lead to an equal distribution of resources (playing talent) and (ii) revenue redistribution on the basis of gate sharing will have no impact on the distribution of playing talent. Points (a) and (ii) are both examples of the well-known *invariance principle.*

There have been two significant changes in talent-allocation rules in North American sports over recent years. First, in 1976, major-league baseball players won the right of free agency after completing six years of service, and this practice rapidly spread to the other sports. Second, the draft rules of the NFL, which allocated the right to hire new talent entering the league on the basis of the reverse order of finish of the previous season's competition, were adopted by the other sports (see Paul Staudohar 1996 for more details on both of these innovations). These changes can be studied to identify the impact of changes in talent allocation rules on competitive balance.

Free Agency

The advent of free agency in MLB in 1976 for six-year veterans is a clear natural experiment.[44] The owners claimed that as a result of this limited free agency, the best veterans would migrate to the big city teams and competitive balance would be undermined. A number of studies have attempted to use this rule change to test the invariance hypothesis, and the findings from these studies are reported in Table 1.3. Most of the studies simply look at the standard deviation of win percentages before and after 1976 (Scully 1989; Balfour and Porter 1991; Michael Butler 1995; Fort and Quirk 1995; Vrooman 1995), while other measures include persistence in win percent (Balfour and Porter 1991; Vrooman 1996); entropy (Horowitz 1997); the Hirschman-Herfindahl index (Depken 1999); and analysis of variance (Eckard 2001). Most of these studies find either no change (seven cases) or an improvement in competitive balance (nine cases), contrary to the claim of the owners that free agency would reduce competitive balance (four cases only). However, this meta-data is hardly a ringing endorsement for the invariance principle, since "no effect" is reported in only seven out of twenty cases. Of course, it can be argued that many other factors have altered competitive balance (e.g. the increasing dispersion of local TV revenues), but in that case the data, without controlling for these factors, can hardly be said to represent a test at all.

Table 1.3   The impact of free agency on competitive balance in MLB

Study	Measure of competitive balance	Impact on competitive balance in NL	Impact on competitive balance in AL
Daly and Moore (1981)	Movement of free agents to large market teams	(−)	(−)
Scully (1989)	Standard deviation of win percent and Gini coefficient of pennant wins	(+)	(0)
Balfour and Porter (1991)	Standard deviation of win percent, persistence of win percent	(+)	(+)
Fort and Quirk (1995)	Standard deviation of win percent and Gini coefficient of pennant wins	(0)	(0)
Vrooman (1995)	Standard deviation of win percent relative to idealized standard deviation	(+)	(+)
Vrooman (1996)	Persistence of win percent	(+)	(+)
Butler (1995)	Standard deviation of win percent and serial correlation of win percent	(0)	(0)
Horowitz (1997)	Entropy	(−)	(0)
Depken (1999)	Hirschman-Herfindahl index of wins relative to ideal	(0)	(−)
Eckard (2001)	Analysis of variance of win percent	(+)	(+)

Some other studies have approached the invariance principle as a direct test of the Coase Theorem and tried to establish whether the distribution of talent in the league has been affected by the introduction of free agency. George Daly (1992) observes that under the reserve clause, top line players were seldom traded, a situation that has been affected by free agency, where after six years the top stars have a choice, leading to increased mobility. Timothy Hylan, Maureen Lage, and Michael Treglia (1996) in a study of pitcher movements find that these players have become less mobile since free agency, a surprising result and one that they claim does not support the Coase Theorem. However, Donald

Cymrot, James Dunlevy and William Even (2001) examine player mobility in 1980, controlling for possible selection bias and find that, for that season at least, there was no evidence that restricted players (with less than six years of service) enjoyed more or less mobility than unrestricted free agents after controlling for player characteristics.

Daniel Marburger (2002) considers a different implication of the invariance principle. If trade is possible between two independent leagues then it should be more profitable to hire a player from the same league than the rival league. Intra-league trade raises the winning probability of the buying team by more than an inter-league trade, since in the former case not only does the buyer have a larger share of talent, but the seller now has a weaker team. Under the reserve clause this effect will be built into the seller's price, but under free agency it will not, since the free agent is indifferent to the adverse effect on the team he is leaving. Thus with free agency the relative price of intra-league trades should fall and their share of total trades increase. Marburger found a statistically significant increase in the share of intra-league trades, from 60 percent to 73 percent, in MLB 1964 and 1992. This finding seems consistent with the invariance principle.

In European soccer, trading players for cash has always been an accepted part of the sport, and there have been no restrictions on trading such as those that emerged in North America in the 1970s (see Daly 1992). In England a system akin to the reserve clause operated until 1963. Restrictions remained until 1978, when a form of free agency was introduced that gave players the right to move club once their contract ended (typically contracts lasted three years), but allowed the selling team to demand substantial compensation (i.e. well in excess of any damages that would be paid for breach of contract). In 1995 the European Court of Justice, in what is known as the Bosman judgment,[45] outlawed all such compensation payments for out-of-contract players and effectively established universal free agency In 2001 FIFA reached agreement with the European Commission on a new set of transfer rules. These laid down that compensation was only payable to clubs for players under the age of twenty-three and only as a reflection of training costs. Beyond that age no transfer fee is to be paid for players out of contract and players can move clubs during one of two prescribed "transfer windows."

The rookie draft

The stated intention of the rookie draft system is to provide weaker teams with opportunities to acquire talented players by awarding them first pick. Of course, an additional consequence of this system is the creation of monopsony power. The draft system was instituted by the NFL in 1936 as a way of strengthening weak performing teams to maintain competitive balance, and has since been adopted by all the other major leagues (Fort and Quirk 1995 and Staudohar 1996 provide details).

Daly and Moore (1981) first analyzed whether the draft achieved its stated intention by examining competitive balance before and after the introduction of the MLB draft in 1965. They found a significant improvement in the balance of the National League and a smaller improvement in the balance of the American League. The Japanese Professional Baseball League adopted a draft system at exactly the same time as MLB, and a study by S. La Croix and A. Kawaura (1999) also found that competitive balance improved over time (measured by the Gini coefficient for pennants) in both the Central and Pacific Leagues.[46] As they point out, these results are "virtually identical" to Fort and Quirk's (1995) results for MLB. Kevin Grier and Robert Tollison (1994) examined the impact of the rookie draft in the NFL by running an autoregressive specification for win percentage together with the average draft order over the previous three to five seasons, and found that a low draft order significantly raises performance. These results seem to provide consistent evidence against the invariance principle and in support of the owners' stated position.

Neither with free agency nor with the rookie draft is there much convincing evidence on profits and consumer welfare. It is clear that free agency has increased the earning power of free agents, but it is not clear what the distributional effects have been on the player market as a whole. For example, it might be that increased expenditure on free agents caused by competition for their services has led to a reduction of investment in the development of rookie talent or lower salaries on average for players with less than six years service. Zimbalist (1992) reports significant differences in the rate of monopsonistic exploitation for players at different stages of their careers after the introduction of free agency. In Europe, where there are no roster limits, it does appear that the number of professional soccer players has been falling over time, and this could be associated with the trend toward free agency that was visible in England even before the Bosman judgment (i.e. teams substituting quality for quantity). Eberhard Fees and Gerd Muehlheusser (2003) compare the welfare implications of the pre- and post-Bosman transfer regimes and argue that while the new regime may increase player effort (since they can secure a larger share of the returns) investment in player development is likely to fall. These issues deserve empirical investigation.

6.2.   The invariance principle and gate-revenue sharing

Quirk and El Hodiri (1974) extended the invariance principle to gate-revenue sharing, that is they claimed that a change in the percentage of gate revenues allocated to the visiting team (between 100 percent and 50 percent) would have no effect on competitive balance. Empirical testing of this proposition is made difficult by the fact that revenue-sharing rules change infrequently within a single league, while the comparison of revenue sharing across different leagues is clouded by the interference of so many other league-specific factors. An alternative approach is to examine the theoretical basis for this proposition. This section develops a simple contest model that illustrates the basis of the invariance principle for gate-revenue sharing.

The conventional approach to the modeling of league competition (as in e.g. Fort and Quirk 1995) is to some extent supported by the empirical evidence in section 5. First, it is normally assumed that teams choose investment in playing talent that is homogeneous and perfectly divisible, so that a given level of investment translates into a predictable level of playing success. Second, it is assumed that excessive dominance by one team will lead to a fall in revenue generation by that team, although at low levels of success revenues are increasing in team performance. The main difference between the team sports model and a conventional contest model is that instead of competing for a fixed prize with some probability determined by relative investment, each team generates a revenue dependent on the share of matches won, where that revenue also varies according to the revenue-generating capacities of the teams. Thus asymmetry in team sports is not typically modeled as a difference in the cost of effort (talent investment), but as a difference in the value of the prize (revenue-generating capacity).

The nature of the prize in team sports is somewhat different than in an individualistic contest. Success is usually equated with winning percentage, which in turn depends on the outcome of a sequence of bilateral contests. However, what distinguishes league competition from the kind of barnstorming match play observed prior to the creation of the National League is that fan interest is drawn to the progress of their team in the tournament as a whole, not just the individual matches. In other words, there is also a prize for success over the competition as a whole (the league championship) rather than simply collecting income from a series of events.

A further modeling issue concerns the way that decision makers interact. Fort and Quirk, among others, support the cartel interpretation, suggesting that clubs make independent decisions subject to cartel rules (i.e. a noncooperative game), and we follow this approach below.[47] The precise legal format adopted, however, may vary. Conventionally, teams are joint owners of the league and delegate an official to manage collective negotiations.

Analysis of the invariance principle is only relevant when there are asymmetries among the teams. If teams are symmetric, competitive balance cannot be an issue if, as here, we concentrate only on pure strategy equilibria. To concentrate on asymmetry we narrow our focus to a two-team model, as has been usual in most of the literature. Assuming the CSF takes the same logit form as in an individualistic contest (1.3) and that $\gamma = 1$, we can write

$$p_1 = \frac{e_1}{e_1 + e_2}, \quad p_2 = 1 - p_1 \qquad (1.3')$$

where p_i can be thought of as the expected percentage of matches won by team i, which is increasing in the relative share of investment in talent, which is how e_i is now interpreted.[48] In a standard contest model the "adding-up constraint" requires that the probabilities sum to unity, while in a league context the constraint is that the sum of win percentages equals $n/2$. Obviously, this condition is satisfied by (1.3'). Another way of expressing the adding-up constraint is

$$\frac{\partial p_1}{\partial e_1} = -\frac{\partial p_2}{\partial e_1} \quad \text{and} \quad \frac{\partial p_2}{\partial e_2} = -\frac{\partial p_1}{\partial e_2}. \qquad (1.11)$$

Note that the CSF (1.3) is identical to win percentage for a two-team model, but not with three or more teams, since expected win percentage then depends on the sum of bilateral investment shares (1.3') rather than simply investment divided by the sum of investments. Both functions will be increasing and concave in investment, and bounded by zero when investment is zero.

It is sometimes argued that a two team model fails to capture some central features of a league championship. If $n > 2$ it is possible to specify each team's revenue function as a function of rival teams' win percentage, introducing the possibility of complementarities. Although this suggests a more complex set of interactions than is modeled here, the existence of production externalities (the success of my team increases or decreases your team's revenues) does not fundamentally change the decision problem, since even in the two-team case each team's investment produces a negative externality (my success reduces your income). The important economic issue is that private decision making will not necessarily be socially efficient when externalities, negative or positive, exist.[49]

In general, demand for attendance at or viewing of matches could be thought to depend on three main factors:

- the suspense associated with a close contest (uncertainty of outcome);
- the likelihood of the home team's success;
- the quality of the match, including the aggregate of player talent on show.[50]

The interaction of these three factors will give rise to some general revenue-generating function $R(.)$. The requirement of tractability demands some simplification and so for the moment we will ignore the impact of the demand for quality.[51] We therefore focus on the impact of success and competitive balance probabilities. In most of the literature these two aspects of demand are captured by a revenue function that comprises a CSF and the assumption that team revenues have a unique maximum (e.g. at a winning record that lies between 0 percent and 100 percent). Here we assume that revenues are simple linear functions of these variables:

$$R_{11} = [1 - \lambda(1 - \mu)]p_1 - (1 - \lambda)p_1^2 = \lambda\mu p_1 + (1 - \lambda)p_1(1 - p_1) \qquad (1.12)$$

$$R_{22} = p_2 - (1 - \lambda)p_2^2 = \lambda p_2 + (1 - \lambda)p_2(1 - p_2)$$

where R_{ii} is either the revenue generated by team i from matches played at the ground of team i or the revenue generated by championship success. $\mu \geq 1$ reflects the possibility that team 1 may be able to generate a higher revenue from a given level of success. Competitive balance can be measured by $p_1(1 - p_1) = p_2(1 - p_2)$ and λ is a parameter capturing the degree to which competitive balance matters in determining team revenues; if $\lambda = 1$ only winning matters, while if $\lambda = 0$ interest in a balanced contest dominates. Each firm's profit function is simply $\pi_1 = R_{11} - ce_1$ and $\pi_2 = R_{22} - ce_2$, where c is the constant marginal cost of talent, which is treated parametrically by the teams, but adjusts to ensure that the supply of talent equals demand. Note that if $\lambda = \mu = 1$ the problem is isomorphic to the symmetric winner-take-all contest of section 2.1.[52]

The owners of each team are assumed to be profit maximizers. Under these assumptions the first-order conditions are:

$$\frac{d\pi_1}{de_1} = \frac{\partial R_{11}}{\partial p_1}\frac{\partial p_1}{\partial e_1} - c = [1 - \lambda(1-\mu) - 2(1-\lambda)p_1]\frac{\partial p_1}{\partial e_1} - c = 0 \qquad (1.13)$$

$$\frac{d\pi_2}{de_2} = \frac{\partial R_{22}}{\partial p_2}\frac{\partial p_2}{\partial e_2} - c = [1 - 2(1-\lambda)p_2]\frac{\partial p_2}{\partial e_2} - c = 0$$

These expressions state that owners invest in talent to the point where the marginal revenue from a unit of talent equals its marginal cost. For example, for team 1 the marginal revenue of a unit of talent equals the marginal revenue of a win $[1 - \lambda(1-\mu) - 2(1-\lambda)p_1]$ multiplied by the marginal impact on win percentage of a unit of talent $(\partial p_1/\partial e_1)$.

The standard assumption in the North American team sports literature has been that this latter quantity is equal to unity. Thus Fort and Quirk (1995, p. 1271) assume, "a one unit increase in t_i yields the same increase in win-percent for any level of win-percent" and Vrooman (1995, p. 973) uses a model where teams directly choose win percent, whose marginal cost is assumed to be a constant, so that a unit of talent in the present model is equivalent to a unit of win percentage. Given identical marginal costs this implies that the marginal revenue of a win is equalized across teams. This seemingly innocuous assumption has important implications about the behavior of owners. From (1.3′),

$$\frac{\partial p_1}{\partial e_1} = \frac{(e_1 + e_2) - e_1\left(1 + \dfrac{de_2}{de_1}\right)}{(e_1 + e_2)^2}, \quad \frac{\partial p_2}{\partial e_2} = \frac{(e_1 + e_2) - e_2\left(1 + \dfrac{de_1}{de_2}\right)}{(e_1 + e_2)^2}. \qquad (1.14)$$

If we assume $de_1/de_2 = de_2/de_1 = -1$ then, normalizing the total supply of talent to unity, it will indeed be the case that $\partial p_1/\partial e_1 = \partial p_2/\partial e_2 = 1$. It should be obvious that this assumption is not the same as adding-up constraint (1.11). Since the expression (1.14) appears in the objective function of the teams de_2/de_1 is a conjectural variation, that is the expectation of team 1 (resp. 2) of the response of team 2 (resp. 1) to a unit increase in talent by team 1 (resp. 2). If we assume that this conjecture equals -1, then each team is assumed to suppose that whenever they increase their investment in talent by one unit, their rival will decrease their investment in talent by one unit.

The rationale for this assumption is that the total supply of talent is fixed, which is often thought a distinctive feature of the major leagues. It is probably true that all the best baseball players, wherever they are in the world, would prefer to play in MLB, and that all the best basketball players in the world would prefer to play in the NBA and so on. If the talent supply for each league is fixed (at least in the short term) then if one team hires an additional unit of talent there is one less unit for all other teams to hire.[53] But modeling a fixed talent supply by assuming nonzero conjectural variations has significant implications for the nature of the model's equilibrium. The normal approach to identifying a Nash equilibrium is to assume Nash conjectures, namely $de_1/de_2 = de_2/de_1 = 0$. Without Nash conjectures peculiar results may follow.

To see the implications of this, combine the two expressions in (1.13) to obtain

$$\frac{\dfrac{\partial p_2}{\partial e_2}}{\dfrac{\partial p_1}{\partial e_1}} = \frac{\dfrac{\partial R_{11}}{\partial p_1}}{\dfrac{\partial R_{22}}{\partial p_2}} = \frac{1 - \lambda(1-\mu) - 2(1-\lambda)p_1}{1 - 2(1-\lambda)(1-p_1)}. \tag{1.15}$$

Note that the left-hand side of (1.15) is the ratio of the marginal impacts on win percentage of a unit of talent and the right-hand side is the ratio of marginal revenues of a win. Under the "fixed supply conjectural variation" the LHS is unity and so the marginal revenue of a win is equalized across teams. This is not true using the Nash conjectural variation, where it is only the marginal revenue from hiring a unit of talent that is always equalized in equilibrium, while the marginal revenue of a win will only be equalized at the equilibrium of a symmetric contest $(\mu = 1)$.[54] At the asymmetric Nash equilibrium the marginal revenue of a win will be greater for the strong drawing team $(\mu > 1)$ because this team hires a larger share of talent available and therefore has a lower marginal impact on win percentage from an extra unit of talent.

Nash conjectures and fixed-supply conjectures produce very different results when it comes to the impact of gate-revenue sharing. In the standard model it is assumed that each team retains a fraction α of revenues generated by home matches and pays the remainder $1 - \alpha$ to the visiting team so that profits are now $\pi_1 = \alpha R_{11} + (1-\alpha)R_{22} - ce_1$ and $\pi_2 = \alpha R_{22} + (1-\alpha)R_{11} - ce_2$ and the first-order conditions are

$$\frac{\partial \pi_1}{\partial e_1} = \alpha \frac{\partial R_{11}}{\partial p_1}\frac{\partial p_1}{\partial e_1} + (1-\alpha)\frac{\partial R_{22}}{\partial p_2}\frac{\partial p_2}{\partial e_1} - c = 0$$

$$\frac{\partial \pi_2}{\partial e_2} = \alpha \frac{\partial R_{22}}{\partial p_2}\frac{\partial p_2}{\partial e_2} + (1-\alpha)\frac{\partial R_{11}}{\partial p_1}\frac{\partial p_1}{\partial e_2} - c = 0 \tag{1.16}$$

which, using the adding-up constraint (1.11), can be rearranged to obtain

$$\left[\alpha\frac{\partial R_{11}}{\partial p_1}-(1-\alpha)\frac{\partial R_{22}}{\partial p_2}\right]\frac{\partial p_1}{\partial e_1}=\left[\alpha\frac{\partial R_{22}}{\partial p_2}-(1-\alpha)\frac{\partial R_{11}}{\partial p_1}\right]\frac{\partial p_2}{\partial e_2}. \qquad (1.17)$$

If we now further assume fixed-supply conjectures, it should be clear that since $\partial p_1/\partial e_1=\partial p_2/\partial e_2$, (1.17) collapses to the equality

$$\frac{\partial R_{11}}{\partial p_1}=\frac{\partial R_{22}}{\partial p_2}, \qquad (1.18)$$

which is clearly independent of α, hence the conclusion that the distribution of talent and success is independent of the revenue-sharing formula. However, once we introduce Nash conjectures this result will no longer hold, and instead we obtain

$$\frac{\dfrac{\partial p_2}{\partial e_2}}{\dfrac{\partial p_1}{\partial e_1}}=\frac{e_1}{e_2}=\frac{\left[\alpha\dfrac{\partial R_{11}}{\partial p_1}-(1-\alpha)\dfrac{\partial R_{22}}{\partial p_2}\right]}{\left[\alpha\dfrac{\partial R_{22}}{\partial p_2}+(1-\alpha)\dfrac{\partial R_{11}}{\partial p_1}\right]}. \qquad (1.15')$$

It should be clear that the LHS of (1.15′) is identical to that of (1.15), but when $\alpha<1$ the RHS of (1.15′) and the middle term of (1.15) are not equal (unless revenue functions are symmetric), suggesting that the invariance principle does not hold under Nash conjectures. Using the expressions for marginal revenue in (1.15) after some manipulation it can be shown that

$$\frac{e_1}{e_2}=\frac{(1-2\alpha)(1-\lambda)+\lambda[\alpha+\mu(1-\alpha)]}{1-2\alpha+\alpha\lambda(1+\mu)}. \qquad (1.19)$$

Differentiating, we obtain

$$\frac{\partial\left(\dfrac{e_1}{e_2}\right)}{\partial\alpha}=\frac{\lambda^2(1-\mu^2)}{[1-2\alpha+\alpha\lambda(1+\mu)]^2}<0. \qquad (1.20)$$

Thus under Nash conjectures, revenue sharing will in fact make competitive balance worse. Szymanski and Késenne (2004) show that this is in fact true for any concave revenue function. The intuition is that revenue sharing discourages both teams from investing, but since the weak drawing team has more to gain from a share of the strong drawing team's revenues than the strong drawing team does from a share of the weak drawing team's revenues, the weak drawing team cuts investment by more.[55]

Because revenue sharing diminishes the incentive of both teams to invest in talent, the demand for talent must fall. If the supply of talent is fixed then the wage rate per unit of talent (i.e. the marginal cost c) will fall to restore labor-market equilibrium. However, if competitive balance is to deteriorate then it must be that the strong drawing team will in fact increase its share of total talent while the weak drawing team reduces its share. If the supply of talent were elastic, however, this result need not necessarily hold, even though competitive balance must still be reduced. The assumption of elastic supply seems more reasonable in the case of European soccer where no national league is dominant and players move freely between leagues. Whether supply is fixed or not, total expenditure on talent will fall with gate-revenue sharing and total profits will increase.

There is a fundamental problem with the assumption of fixed-supply conjectures. If teams attempt to select win percentage, only one team can be decisive, since the other team's choice is thereby fixed in a two-team model. It is like a model of market share where each firm tries to choose market share—at most one firm can succeed. More generally, in an n team model with fixed-supply conjectures only $n-1$ teams can be decisive, and the nth team must accept the allocation of talent implied by the profit-maximizing choices of all the other teams. In the two-team model with fixed-supply conjectures, every choice of winning percentage is a Nash equilibrium, since there is only one feasible response to this choice and so it is trivially the best response (see Szymanski 2004 for more detail). The way around this absurdity is to allow owners to select some variable that affects the share of total talent, such as investment, without constraining the choice of rivals by so doing. This approach will result in the Nash equilibrium described above.

It seems widely accepted in the broader economic literature that, in a static game of this type, only Nash conjectures make sense (see e.g. Xavier Vives 1999, pp. 185–87) but alternative conjectural variations are sometimes defended as reduced forms of an underlying dynamic model. The original model of Quirk and El Hodiri (1974) is indeed a dynamic model. The authors do not explain in detail the source of the invariance result but it appears to be a consequence of looking for an equilibrium where the profit of each team is maximized not only with respect to talent hired at that team, but also with respect to talent hired by every other team.[56] This kind of joint profit-maximizing program is likely to produce an optimal allocation of talent regardless of the distribution of revenues. It seems more natural, however, to examine revenue-sharing rules in the context of a noncooperative game. Fixed-supply conjectures reproduce the results of a cooperative game between the teams,[57] and therefore it is perhaps not surprising that a model based on these conjectures appears to support the Coase Theorem.

The fact that almost all models of sports leagues in the literature have been based on the assumption that the total supply of talent is fixed may be associated with the fact that most of the models have been written in the context of the North American major leagues, where arguably, at any point in time supply is fixed.[58] However, even in the relatively short term it may be possible to draft in talent from outside the league, effectively increasing total supply. The increasingly global search of the major leagues for talent suggests that in the longer term supply is elastic. It would be interesting to see some empirical attempts to measure the elasticity of supply.

Frederic Palomino and Joszef Sakovics (2000) develop a model based on competition for scarce talent to account for the common observation that revenue sharing seems more prevalent in North America than in Europe.[59] In addition to the demand for success and competitive balance, they introduce the demand for the quality of the contest (i.e. the talent of the players). Regardless of the supply elasticity, revenue sharing reduces the demand for talent, since own marginal revenue from success is reduced and marginal revenue from rival success (i.e. own failure at away matches) is increased. If the market for talent ensures that marginal revenue equals marginal cost, then revenue sharing in the fixed-supply model simply drives down total cost and so raises profits (see Fort and Quirk 1995). However, with elastic supply and competition between rival leagues for players, any reduction in the willingness to pay for players by the members of a league will reduce the quality of that league (measured by total units of talent employed) relative to its rivals, and therefore undermine its relative attractiveness.

Thomas Hoehn and Szymanski (1999) develop an elastic model of European league competition that presents a related reason why revenue sharing may adversely affect competitive balance. In European sports the leading teams typically compete in more than one championship in a season—the domestic league and European-wide league (e.g. The Champions' League[60])—and typically these competitions run concurrently. Thus the top teams have a revenue function that depends on success in both competitions, and the weaker teams have a revenue function depending only on domestic competition. Under domestic league revenue sharing, the weaker team will be more willing to reduce investment in talent to take advantage of the strong team's success than the strong team will be to reduce its own investment, since by doing so the latter reduces its expected revenue from the European-wide competition.

7.   Other design issues in team sports

7.1.   Prizes and lump-sum revenue sharing

Fort and Quirk (1995) observe that sharing of local TV revenues will tend to improve competitive balance, so that the invariance principle need not hold even with fixed-supply conjectures. This finding arises out of the independence of local TV revenue-generating functions: no adding up constraints are involved and hence the problem resembles more closely a standard Cournot-Nash model where (a) noncooperative behavior does not yield joint profit maximization, and (b) revenue sharing causes each firm to internalize the effects of its decisions on its rival and therefore leads to joint profit maximization. For example, suppose that in the two-team model each generated income only from local TV revenues, labeled L, and that these revenues are increasing in the success of the home team. With revenue sharing we can write the profit function for each team as

$$\pi_i = p_i(e_i)[\alpha L_i + (1-\alpha)L_j] - ce_i, \quad i=1,2. \tag{1.21}$$

The first-order conditions are then

$$\frac{\partial \pi_i}{\partial e_i} = \frac{\partial p_i}{\partial e_i}\left(\alpha \frac{\partial L_i}{\partial e_i} + (1-\alpha)\frac{\partial L_j}{\partial e_i}\right) = c, \quad i=1,2. \tag{1.22}$$

Taking the ratio of the two first-order conditions, we can obtain

$$\frac{\dfrac{\partial p_1}{\partial e_1}}{\dfrac{\partial p_2}{\partial e_2}} = \left[\frac{\alpha \dfrac{\partial L_2}{\partial e_2} + (1-\alpha)\dfrac{\partial L_1}{\partial e_2}}{\alpha \dfrac{\partial L_1}{\partial e_1} + (1-\alpha)\dfrac{\partial L_2}{\partial e_1}}\right]. \tag{1.23}$$

If we suppose that $\frac{\partial L_j}{\partial e_i} = -\frac{\partial L_j}{\partial e_j}$ then for fixed labor supply the LHS of (1.23) equals unity and hence local TV revenue sharing has no impact on competitive balance. However, from the point of view of TV demand, there is no reason to suppose that the marginal revenue from a unit increase in the quality of the opposition is the same as the marginal revenue from a unit decrease in the quality of the home team (because in the former case the total quantity of talent on show increases while in the latter case it decreases). In general we suppose increasing the quality of the opposition will have a higher value than reducing the quality of the home team. In the absence of symmetry, revenue sharing will reduce the marginal revenue of the large market team more than the marginal revenue of the small market team and therefore revenue sharing will improve competitive balance. Marburger (1997) suggests that this kind of asymmetry might be true for gate revenues as well, where demand for absolute quality may be important.[61]

However, revenue sharing reduces the marginal revenue to each team from hiring an additional unit of talent, driving down the wage rate per unit of talent and increasing profits in equilibrium. Revenue sharing works in the opposite way to a prize because it diminishes effort incentives. This naturally raises the question of how prizes would affect competitive balance in a team sports context. While most individualistic sports offer substantial financial prizes to the winners, this is usually not the case with team sports. The team that wins a league championship may receive a cup, and team members may receive substantial bonuses, but the owners of the team in general stand to gain little or no direct monetary gain (i.e. prize money) from winning a championship. It is true that participation in the play-off or finals stage can be extremely valuable, and also that sponsorship income and merchandising are likely to be substantially increased by winning a championship,[62] and that these factors will impact on decision making in much the same way as an explicit prize. One might hope to see future research attempt to quantify the value of prize like elements in the different team sports.

Suppose that each team in the league were to contribute some fixed sum to a prize fund awarded to the winning team. In the two team case, where gate revenue depends only on success, team 1 has a greater revenue-generating potential from success than team 2 ($\mu > 1$), and there is no local TV income, we can write the objective functions for each team as

$$\pi_1 = p_1(e_1)[\mu + V] - \frac{V}{2} - ce_1,$$

$$\pi_2 = p_2(e_2)[1 + V] - \frac{V}{2} - ce_2,$$

(1.24)

where $V/2$ is the lump tax on each team used to create the prize fund V. Taking the ratio of first-order conditions we obtain

$$\frac{\dfrac{\partial p_1}{\partial e_1}}{\dfrac{\partial p_2}{\partial e_2}} = \frac{1+V}{\mu+V} \tag{1.25}$$

from inspection the RHS of (1.25) converges to unity as V increases, implying that, for any elasticity of supply, a team-funded prize will increase competitive balance.[63] Since a prize also increases aggregate effort (as in an individualistic contest), a contest designer could maximize both competitive balance and effort incentives through the use of such prizes.[64] The intuition seems quite straightforward: when teams have differing revenue-generating potential then the large (marginal) revenue-generating team dominates. The creation of a prize fund equalizes incentives, so that small (marginal) revenue-generating teams have as much to gain from winning as their larger rivals.

While direct financial prizes are rare in team sports, European soccer leagues have adopted revenue-sharing formulas for collectively negotiated TV income on a basis that introduces the flavor of a prize, in contrast to North America where all the major leagues distribute this income on the basis of strictly equal shares. For example, in the English Premier League 25 percent of annual TV income is awarded on the basis of League rank, with the League champions receiving 20 times as much (of the 25 percent) as the team ranked last in the League.[65] Palomino and Sakovics (2001) develop a model of TV revenue sharing to show that for a joint profit-maximizing league (a) full revenue sharing is optimal when it has monopsony power in the talent market, and (b) performance-based rewards (prizes) are optimal when rival leagues compete for talent. With profit-maximizing owners, equal sharing of income from collectively sold broadcasting rights will have no effect on competitive balance, and will just feed through directly to the profits of the owners. A sharing rule that equalizes ex ante incentives (equality of opportunity) but leads to inequality ex post (rewards winners) will, in the absence of capital market imperfections (e.g. credit constraints), generate a more balanced contest. This proposition, though well founded in economic theory, attracts considerable skepticism from noneconomists. This may have something to do with beliefs about the operation of capital markets or about the true objective function of team owners.

7.2.   Win maximization and ownership rules

So far we have assumed that all teams are profit maximizers, an assumption with which sports economists have been quite comfortable in the United States,[66] but which often seems less appropriate in the case of European soccer.[67] This has to do with both cultural and institutional factors. Culturally, the men who set up soccer clubs were by and large amateurs who looked down on the pursuit of profit, just as their counterparts did in aristocratic cricket.[68] While in many cases there may have existed a gap between stated objectives and reality, real constraints on behavior existed and continue to exist in many cases. Many clubs in Europe are also "clubs" in the legal sense—operating under a club committee who are volunteers and have no powers of borrowing and no shareholders to whom to distribute surplus. At the very least, the taking of profits in these situations is likely to be discouraged. Furthermore, institutional rules often favor nonprofit objectives. In England the governing body still retains a maximum dividend rule, currently set at 15 percent of paid up share capital.[69] In France the government has legislated favorable tax treatment for clubs established as "companies with a sporting objective," on condition that profit taking is restricted.[70]

If teams have objectives other than profit maximization then the outcome of competition and the implications of adopting specific incentive structures may be quite different than under profit maximization. Vrooman (1997a) shows that, inter alia, player costs (effort) will be higher and competitive balance greater in an asymmetric league of win maximizers compared to profit maximizers. Késenne (2000a) addressed the question of gate sharing in the context of a league composed of win maximizers and shows that in general it will lead to greater competitive balance. Intuitively, if teams spend all available income on hiring talent (i.e. they face a zero-profit budget constraint), then redistributing income from wealthy teams to poor teams will tend to equalize levels of talent and thus improve competitive balance.[71]

Given that different types of owners may embrace different objective functions, and that these objectives yield different outcomes, it is open to contest designers to favor particular types of owners whose equilibrium behavior is expected to produce the desired outcome. This idea is reminiscent of the "strategic delegation" literature, where a profit-maximizing owner might choose to appoint a sales-maximizing manager in an oligopoly (Chaim Fershtman and Kenneth Judd 1987). Rules in North America that prohibit stock flotation might be deemed to encourage "sportsmen owners" whose association with success might lead them to behave more like win maximizers than profit maximizers.[72] Similarly, restrictions in Europe that have until recently limited the spread of ownership to the stock markets may have been intended to create the same effect. Whether the ends of league organizers can be achieved by means of this kind of social engineering must remain open to doubt.

7.3.   Salary caps, luxury taxes, and the unions

Since the 1970s, wage negotiations in the North American major leagues have been characterized by collective bargaining. Among the successes of the unions have been the introduction of veteran free agency, minimum wages, and improved pension provisions. The invariance proposition suggests that the unions would have limited impact on competitive balance but reduce the rents extracted by owners. Support for the first of these propositions was considered in section 6.1, while Zimbalist (1992) presents evidence on the second.

The antitrust exemption for collective bargaining agreements has bolstered the power of the unions by (a) enforcing exclusive bargaining rights and (b) enabling owners to enter into restrictive agreements that might not be permitted in the absence of the exemption. The value of the exemption to the owners has at times appeared so great that some union members have attempted to decertify the union in order to bring an antitrust suit against the league, most notably the NFL players' union at the time of the McNeil case (in 1989) and the NBA players' union following the expiry of the 1988 collective bargaining agreement (in 1994, for details see Staudohar 1996). In that case the union was aiming to get rid of the salary cap (introduced in basketball in 1984) which specified a maximum payroll equal to 53 percent of defined gross revenues, in exchange for a complex set of arrangements specifying minimum player payments and subsidies to weaker teams.

It is clear in theory that a salary cap should improve competitive balance,[73] and equally clear that making a salary cap effective has proved elusive. The NBA cap is perceived to have been ineffective because of the significant exemptions permitted (see Staudohar 1999) and Fort and Quirk (1995, pp. 1277–82) find that the standard deviation of win percent has increased since its introduction (see also Késenne 2000b). From the point of view of contest design, a salary-cap system should have an effect similar to revenue sharing when teams are win maximizers. Under win maximization an increase in revenue sharing reduces the expenditure of the large revenue-generating teams, but also increases the spending of the small revenue-generating teams, and both effects enhance competitive balance. To be fully effective a salary-cap system also needs to ensure that the small revenue-generating teams raise their spending to the level of the cap.[74]

A luxury tax works in a similar way to a salary cap, but instead of imposing a fixed limit (like a quota) it discourages acquisition of playing talent by taxing expenditure over a fixed limit (a tariff). The theoretical implications are discussed by Marburger (1997).[75] The only instance of this system in the major leagues has been the agreement between the MLB and the MLBPA following the 232-day strike in 1994–95. When the two parties agreed on a settlement, it included a complex arrangement to tax expenditures of the top five payrolls on expenditures over fixed limits. The tax operated between 1997 and 1999 at a rate of 35 percent in the first two years and 34 percent in the third year. This system raised $30.6 million over the three years for redistribution to the weaker teams, compared to the total MLB payroll spending of $3877 million over the same period. Not surprisingly the luxury tax was deemed to have little effect.[76] In 2002, MLB agreed on a new luxury tax after narrowly avoiding a strike.[77]

The roster limit, through which the number of players permitted on the payroll is fixed, is a much more venerable institution in North American sports, intended to prevent the stockpiling of top players, although there is surprisingly little academic research on its impact. In baseball it is commonly argued that the farm system has been the method by which teams have evaded the roster-limit rules, but there is a complex interaction between the rules and player contracts. The existence of roster limits is itself evidence that one of the most widely adopted assumptions in modeling team sports contests (and one adopted in this chapter), namely that talent is perfectly divisible, does not hold. This is an issue clearly meriting further research.

Schemes such as salary caps, luxury taxes, and roster limits have not been introduced into the European soccer system. One reason is that there is no collective bargaining over salaries at the European Union level, another is that such bargaining would not, even if it existed, enjoy an equivalent antitrust exemption. Nor is it likely that such agreements could be agreed among the clubs in a system of multiple leagues. A salary cap tailored to the average team in the top division of a national league would seriously handicap a leading team in that league which was also competing at the European level. Moreover, a salary cap applied only in one national league would cause the most talented players in that league to move to rival national leagues which did not operate a cap. Any European-wide system would face the obstacle of significant international differences in standards of living, tax rates, and administrative systems. Only if a closed superleague system emerged in Europe, constructed on similar lines to the major leagues, is it likely that such arrangements would become feasible (Hoehn and Szymanski 1999 explore this possibility).

7.4.   Optimal number of teams in the league

An obvious puzzle for the design of a sport's league is its optimal size. This issue has been a constant concern of league authorities in North America over time, and is also associated with the public policy concern over the relocation of franchises (or the threat of relocation) to extract subsidies from local government (Noll and Zimbalist 1997). Vrooman (1997b) addresses the issue of optimal league size directly and draws the analogy with James Buchanan's (1965) theory of clubs. If members have a joint interest in total revenues generated by the club, then the individual optimum is to agree to expansion to the point where average revenue per member is maximized, which in general involves a smaller number of members than the social welfare optimum (that maximizes total member revenues).[78]

The issue can be illustrated using a simple version of the contest model. Suppose that teams in a league compete in a symmetric contest with a CSF as defined by (1.3) and a payoff function that depends on the expected value of the prize, the cost of effort/talent, and some fixed "locational" rent or utility (U) of local citizens derived from the presence of a team.[79] To avoid underinvestment issues we assume this rent can be fully appropriated by the local team. Further, we assume that some fraction of this locational rent is allocated to a prize fund V awarded to the league champion and that $(1 - \phi)$ is retained by the owner. Thus team profits are equal to $(1 - \phi)U + p_i V - e_i$ (the marginal cost of effort is normalized to unity). Maximizing with respect to e_i yields (and assuming the supply of talent is elastic[80]) we can find the equilibrium profit of each team to be:

$$\pi = U\left[1 - \gamma\phi\frac{(n-1)}{n}\right]. \tag{1.26}$$

Since all consumer surplus is appropriated aggregate welfare is simply the sum of profits:

$$W = n\pi = U[n - \gamma\phi(n-1)]. \tag{1.27}$$

The derivatives of welfare and of profits with respect to the number of teams are:

$$\frac{\partial \pi}{\partial n} = -U\frac{\gamma\phi}{n^2} < 0 \quad \text{and} \quad \frac{\partial W}{\partial n} = U(1 - \gamma\phi). \tag{1.28}$$

Since the derivative of profits with respect to n is negative, teams will prefer smaller leagues, all else equal, while as long as either γ (the discriminatory power of the contest) or ϕ (the amount of locational utility allocated to the prize) is not too large, the derivative of welfare is positive and so expansion raises welfare. In the absence of side-payments the members of a league will expand to the point where the marginal profit from expansion equals the average profit per team, rather than where the marginal profit is zero. This problem is exacerbated further if teams cannot fully appropriate locational rents. Teams oppose expansion to optimal levels in the contest model partly because this reduces their own probability of winning the prize, even though this matters little from the social planner's perspective in the symmetric case.

In a contest model where teams value championship success, there will typically be less expansion than in the "win percent" model where teams generate revenue from their success probability against each visiting team. In the contest model teams oppose expansion since it reduces their own probability of success in the contest. In the symmetric win percent model, absent capacity constraints, the teams would favor unlimited expansion since this would imply unlimited additional revenues. With a fixed talent supply teams would only wish to expand to the point where all talent resources are fully utilized.

Quirk and Fort (1992; Fort and Quirk 1995) provide a good deal of evidence to show that in fact expansion generally occurs to meet the threat of entry of a new league. Since the expected profit required to facilitate entry by an entire league is much greater than that required for a single team, underexpansion seems inevitable. In a contest, model, efficiency requires side payments (as in the standard model of a cartel; see e.g. Kevin Roberts 1985) and, in practice, new entrants do make side payments in the form of expansion fees. If all the locational rents are appropriable (and municipal subsidies are often substantial) then efficient expansion should occur. However, this is tantamount to assuming that leagues are capable of operating as efficient cartels. Efficient side-payments would in principle be tailored to the opportunity costs of each incumbent team but the information requirements for this procedure would be both significant and subject to moral hazard and adverse selection. With large numbers cartel agreements may become unenforceable (Peter Cramton and Thomas Palfrey 1990).[81] In Europe these issues have never arisen. The hierarchy established by the promotion and relegation system ensures that all locations have a right to enter the league structure at some level, and after a period of years reach the highest level if the local willingness to pay is adequate.

7.5.   Promotion, relegation, and exclusive territories

The European Commission (1998) described promotion and relegation as "one of the key features of the European model of sport." It is the rule whereby the worst-performing teams at a given level of league competition are demoted at the end of the season to play in the immediately junior league and are replaced by the best performing teams from that league. For example, at the end of each season the three teams in the English Premier League with the lowest number of points won are demoted to the Football League Division One and are replaced in the Premier League by the three best performing teams from Division One. There is promotion and relegation at every level of English soccer, from the Premier League right down to the lowest level of amateur competition, so that in theory any English soccer team might one day reach the Premier League. This system is operated in all the major soccer nations and applies to most other team sports played in Europe (e.g. rugby union, basketball, ice hockey).[82] In economic terms, promotion and relegation represents an opportunity for teams to enter the market at every level of competition. Applied to baseball in the United States, for example, it would mean that AAA teams could one day play in the majors (and conversely, that the Yankees might one day play AAA baseball). The economic consequences seem to be fairly similar to the effects of open entry in any market.

First, there is no credible threat of franchise relocation in Europe, since every city has at least one team with the potential to enter the major league (as long as it is prepared to invest in player talent) without needing to attract someone else's team. As a result teams are unable to extract large subsidies from local government in the manner so familiar in the United States (see e.g. Siegfried and Zimbalist 2000).[83] Second, teams are motivated not only to win, but also to avoid the punishment of relegation. It was noted above that the variance of seasonal win percentages is smaller in European soccer than the North American major leagues even though the variance of team expenditure is greater. That is because teams must fight to the end of the season even if they are out of contention for the championship.[84] Promotion and relegation also undermines the value of territorial exclusivity, and while it is not theoretically inconsistent for the two to co-exist, in practice open entry in Europe has meant freedom to establish a team wherever one wishes.

Promotion and relegation also has some advantages from the perspective of contest design. Authorities in a league system with promotion and relegation can optimize the number of teams eligible for the championship each season without simultaneously having to determine the size of the league. One consequence of this is that the top divisions of European soccer leagues are in fact smaller (typically with fewer than twenty teams) than the North American major leagues have become, and this can mean a less extreme difference between the best and the worst.

On the face of it this might suggest that promotion and relegation is a superior system from the point of view of consumers, although clearly inferior for the profitability of teams. However, the welfare questions are not so clear-cut. While promotion and relegation affords an opportunity for more cities to participate in the major league, it might be argued that the relegation of the Yankees to be replaced by the home team of Boise, Idaho, would not represent a net increase in welfare. This is a fine judgment, even if in practice the major teams are almost never relegated.

A more subtle problem concerns the distribution of talent. If this is fixed, and the promotion and relegation system leads to a more even spread of talent across teams (because the incentive for the smaller teams to compete is greater) then the average quality of teams at the highest level (e.g. the 30 best teams) may fall, reducing the quality of individual matches.[85] Finally, as Szymanski and Valletti (2003) show, promotion and relegation may undermine the incentive to share revenues. The cost of revenue sharing to large drawing teams is the foregone income from current success, while the benefit is their share in a more valuable (because more balanced) contest. In a closed league every team is guaranteed to participate in that contest, while in an open league any team might be relegated in the future. This may be one factor contributing to the observation that leagues in Europe have adopted many fewer mechanisms to promote competitive balance than the North American majors.

If an open system obliges teams to supply more effort and reduces profits, why would the leading teams simply not secede from the League and set up on their own? The answer to this in practice is the fear of expulsion from the national Association and the international network. Indeed, it is this fear that inhibits the clubs from demanding compensation for release of contracted players to represent their national team (for as many as twenty matches in a season). FIFA pays no compensation to the clubs who continue to pay the full salaries of their players during international tournaments, and while players receive some appearance money, this is generally a tiny fraction of their total remuneration. This makes the World Cup Finals not only the world's most popular sporting event (33 billion viewers for a total of 64 matches[86]), but also, with turnover of $4 billion, one of the world's most profitable team sports events. Clubs fear expulsion from the Association since they know that most of the players are willing to play for their country for almost nothing either because of patriotism or because of the reputation effects and its impacts on endorsement income.[87] Thus any breakaway league would find it hard to retain players.

7.6.   Club versus country

National teams have been unimportant in the development of the major team sports in the United States, but in other sports national teams and international representative sport have been the driving force in developing the popularity of the game and providing some of the most attractive events within the sport. In individualistic sports it is clear that the Olympics has provided a showcase for the development of traditional events (e.g. athletics and swimming) as well as the development of new events (e.g. Taekwondo). In team sports the soccer World Cup has been a significant contributor to the development of the sport in countries with limited professional leagues. The competition itself has helped to bring players from particular countries to international recognition while the profits generated by the competition have been used in part to fund the development of the sport (notably, on both counts, in the case of the African countries). Most ostentatiously, the decision of FIFA to locate the 1994 World Cup in the United States was seen by many as a blatant attempt to promote the game in that country given its revenue-generating potential (see e.g. Sugden and Tomlinson 1999). The North American major league sports have pursued their own development activities abroad. In Europe the NFL has established its own league, with moderate success in Germany and Spain, MLB has made more than one attempt to enter the European market on a modest scale, and in China the NBA has established a subsidiary to develop the league in that market. However, they are all to a degree hampered by their own commercial objectives, given that they are ultimately responsible to profit-oriented team owners.

   Soccer is simply one example of international representative competition dominating domestic league competition. Other examples include cricket (the dominant sport in India, as well as a major sport in nations of the British Commonwealth including England, Australia, South Africa, Pakistan, New Zealand, Sri Lanka, and the Caribbean islands that play collectively as the "West Indies"), and Rugby Union, a sport similarly found in most Commonwealth countries and historically dominated by New Zealand. What is striking about these examples is that (a) competitive balance plays no obvious role in the popularity of these sports; (b) the dominant teams are seldom drawn from the larger or richer nations; and (c) international representative competition is used to subsidize domestic league competition.

On the first two points, consider the New Zealand rugby union team known as the "All Blacks." They have been playing in international competition since 1903 and have an all-time winning record of 72 percent, despite being dwarfed in terms of population size by many of their larger rivals. For example, the All Blacks currently have a winning record of 78 percent against England, with only 8 percent of the latter's population. Similarly, the Australians in cricket have a winning record of 56 percent against England in 209 matches over the period 1877 to 2001 (ignoring ties), despite a much smaller population.[88] The West Indies, drawing on the smallest population[89] of the ten Test Match Cricket playing nations, have the second highest all-time winning record (57 percent).[90] While this phenomenon is not unknown in the individualistic sports, where small and/or poor nations seem able to produce a disproportionate number of winners, it is easily exaggerated. Andrew Bernard and Meghan Busse (2000) show that population and GDP are remarkably reliable predictors of Olympic medal success.

In soccer, the dominant countries in the World Cup (played every four years) have been Brazil (five victories), Germany and Italy (three victories), Argentina and Uruguay (two victories). These five teams account for fifteen of the seventeen World Cup wins (88 percent), despite entry being open to the entire planet. Brazil has a 76 percent winning record in all World Cup matches played. Yet this dominance does not seem to have undermined interest in these competitions. One reason may be that these international competitions bring together the best players in the world and when combined with national fervor these factors outweigh a rational concern with competitive balance. The aspect of quality may also explain why such competitions have, at least as yet, limited appeal for the North American major league sports—all of the best players are already on show in the major leagues, so in that sense an international representative competition would not offer a higher level of competition. If baseball, for example, were played to a higher level in other national leagues then international competition would become attractive. In other words, the existence of a dominant national league in team sports seems to undermine the demand for international representative competition. By contrast, where there is no dominant national league, international competition becomes attractive.

The dominance of international competition creates some interesting problems in team sports. Most notably, international cricket has been seriously undermined by the revelation that many of the top players have been accepting substantial bribes to fix matches for gambling purposes (see Sir Paul Condon 2001). Ian Preston, Ross, and Szymanski (2001) suggest that corruption stems not merely from moral frailty but also from the remarkably low salaries paid to the players who were induced to accept as bribes what were, for world class athletes, remarkably small sums of money (e.g. as little as $10,000). Low salaries in cricket are due not to the lack of popularity of the game (an international series of five matches can generate an income of $30 million) but to the use of these funds to subsidize domestic leagues which attract no interest from paying fans due to the focus on international matches. Without the subsidy there would be no competitive environment in which to raise players to the necessary international standard. The case of cricket contrasts with soccer where there is a balance of interest in club competition (with healthy finances) and international representative competition, which means that the former can afford to supply talent at no cost to the latter. In theory this can be seen as a kind of league tax to fund the development of the sport.

In the case of rugby union the international representative game traditionally dominated, but in recent years a successful international club competition has emerged in the southern hemisphere (played between teams from New Zealand, Australia, and South Africa) and may be emerging in Europe (where the dominant teams are located in England and France).[91] This suggests three models of sporting development: a dominant national league (North America) with limited international competition, a dominant international competition and weak national leagues (cricket, Rugby Union), and a combination of powerful national leagues with strong international representative competition (soccer). Given that talent is to a degree substitutable between sports in its developmental years (i.e. early to late teens) and sports increasingly compete to find the best talents worldwide, it is tempting to suggest that only sports with a strong financial structure based on a viable model of league competition will survive as major sports (see Ross and Szymanski 2003 for an analysis of optimal league design). Already cricket is suffering from a loss of interest in some of its traditional centers (e.g. the West Indies). Culture may defend other sports more robustly, but the notion that structure may influence long-term popularity may be worthy of further research.

8.   Antitrust and public policy

In the words of Michael Flynn and Richard Gilbert (2001), "One is struck by the frequency with which the structure and rules of professional sports leagues have been the subject of antitrust challenges in recent decades." It is not intended to provide an exhaustive review of these issues, which can be found elsewhere.[92] However, given the abiding interest of the courts and legislators in the fortunes of sports leagues, the implications of both the theory and the empirical research reviewed here are worthy of brief discussion. Broadly speaking, the legal issues associated with individualistic sports have been far less numerous and weighty than those of team sports. For example, in Weiler and Roberts' exhaustive textbook, out of 1007 pages only 69 are devoted to individual sports, while most of the remainder is focused on team sports. This is perhaps because the object of competition—to find the best players/athletes—is clear-cut, and the appropriate mechanism to achieve this—contests with very large prizes and spreads—is not in question. Any restriction intended to prevent these mechanisms from working while raising profitability (e.g. excluding athletes from competition without due cause) would be unlikely to stand up in court.[93]

The focus of dispute, and in some cases legislative intervention, in team sports has been the contention of team owners and league authorities that economic restraints of one form or another are required to maintain a competitive balance which is in the interest of consumers. A natural starting point therefore is the nature of the relationship between the teams and the league. As Gilbert and Flynn observe, the antitrust analysis of agreements among business units depends to a significant degree on their ownership—subsidiaries of a holding company cannot collude among themselves, while independent entities may. In the four major leagues (MLB, NFL, NBA, and NHL) the teams are independent business entities which associate as a league to agree the rules of competition and so on. In Major League Soccer, however, the team owners have a stake in the MLS entity itself, which in turn owns all the player contracts. Moreover, it seems clear that this business structure was selected specifically to avoid the attention of the antitrust authorities.[94]

Gilbert and Flynn suggest that a natural interpretation of the economic structure of the major leagues is as a joint venture. Recognizing the "peculiar economics" of team sports—Neale's (1964) famous phrase—that production requires the cooperation of rivals, so that each team has a vested interest in the existence, and even the success, of its competitors, it is reasonable to suppose that some kinds of agreements can be legally entered into. Most obviously these include agreements on the rules of the game. This is no different from the antitrust treatment that would be accorded an agreement between two competitors entering into an agreement to bring a product to market that would not exist in the absence of the joint-venture agreement. Facilitating the joint venture may in all likelihood require the agreement of restraints among the partners. The essential legal issue is whether such ancillary restraints have the effect of significantly limiting competition, and whether such restraints are proportional to their intended benefit (see also Herbert Hovenkamp 1995 and Piraino 1999 for the legal perspective on these issues).

The types of restraints that might fall under this analysis include labor market restraints (e.g. reserve clause, draft, salary cap, roster limits, restrictions on player trading), product market restraints (e.g. revenue sharing, collective selling, exclusive territories), and capital market restraints (e.g. restrictions on ownership). Most of these issues have been the subject of litigation. The most famous litigation in sport is *Federal Baseball v. National League* (259, U.S. 200 (1922)) that reached the now widely condemned conclusion that baseball was exempt from the federal antitrust laws since it did not involve interstate commerce. See Zimbalist (2003) for an interesting analysis of the exemption. Since then the courts have set out to interpret this exemption for sporting leagues as narrowly as possible, and where possible to conduct a rule of reason analysis of challenged restraints.

In the labor market, *Flood v. Kuhn* (107, U.S. 258 (1972)) examined the reserve clause in baseball but refused to prohibit it on the grounds that it is for Congress to overturn the now venerable antitrust exemption of baseball. *Smith v. Pro Football, Inc.* (593 U.S. F.2d 1173 (1978)) considered the NFL draft and declared it an unreasonable restraint of trade. Writing contracts intended to evade salary cap restrictions was considered (*Bridgeman v. NBA* (re: Chris Dudley), 838 F. Supp. 172 (D.N.J. 1993)) and upheld in this limited context. *Mackey v. NFL* (543 F.2d 606 (8th Cir. 1976)) rejected the "Rozelle Rule" that required teams signing a free agent in the NFL to compensate the player's previous team with a draft pick, and *McNeil et al. v. NFL* (70, F. Supp. 871 (8th Cir. 1992)) rejected the NFL's subsequent plan (Plan B) to allow teams to protect up to 37 players on their roster. *Finley v. Kuhn* (569, F. 2d 1193, 6th Cir. 1978) upheld the right of the commissioner of baseball to penalize teams selling players for cash on the grounds that it might weaken the selling team and reduce competitive balance.

The relationship between collective selling of TV rights, competitive balance, and revenue sharing was considered in *United States v. NFL*, 116 F. Supp. 319 (E.D. Pa. 1953) and *NCAA v. Board of Regents*, 468 U.S. 85, 107 (1984) and in both cases competitive balance justifications were considered potentially valid reasons for the maintenance of the challenged restraints (on individual selling) and so were not *per se* illegal, but in both cases on a *rule of reason* the restraints were deemed either excessive or not tailored to achieve the stated aim.[95] In the Raiders' case (*Los Angeles Memorial Coliseum Commission v. NFL*, 726 F.2d 1381 (9th Cir. 1984)) the court upheld a jury verdict that the league's application of the NFL rule requiring a majority of three-quarters of member teams to permit a relocation (thus protecting exclusive territories) restrained competition. It rejected the claim that the rule was justified by any legitimate interest of the NFL, including maintaining competitive balance. In *Sullivan v. NFL* (U.S. Court of Appeals, First Circuit, 34 F.3d 1994) the court allowed that motives such as competitive balance might on a rule of reason justify prohibiting public ownership of a franchise.

On balance it might be argued that the courts have demonstrated some skepticism about competitive balance as a justification for restraints, although they have accepted it as a possible justification under a rule of reason. However, this state of affairs has been complicated by the nonstatutory exemption for collective bargaining agreements, which has rendered the unions in North American sports so much more powerful than their European counterparts. As discussed in the case of salary caps, above, the exemption has enabled unions to bargain away rights won in the courts and to facilitate the maintenance of labor market restraints. Moreover, Congress has intervened through the 1961 Sports Broadcasting Act to exempt collectively negotiated national sponsored broadcasting agreements from antitrust scrutiny. As a result, in practice the major leagues operate a wide range of restraints, adumbrated in much of the foregoing discussion.

In European sports the power of the courts is supplemented less by the role of the legislature, which has not interfered significantly in the operation of team sports, than by the European Commission, which acts as an executive body representing the member states (who hold a power of veto over many of its activities). The competition directorate

(DG IV) of the Commission wields considerable power and has intervened to challenge various restraints in recent years, and has in most cases reached agreement with the leagues prior to going to court. In European competition law the Commission in general only acts on the complaint of parties deeming themselves to be harmed by a challenged restraint, but in recent years, as the value of TV contracts has escalated so has the number of complaints received.

In the Bosman case (see above) the complaint was taken to the European Court of Justice. The court held that competitive balance was not a valid defence of the old transfer system, even though in other cases it could justify a restraint (such as revenue sharing). Moreover, the free movement of labor, a principle enshrined in the Treaty of Rome, overrode any specific consideration of the interests of the league. In 2000 the Commission went further and challenged the economic basis of the transfer fees being paid for players within contract on the grounds that they restricted the free movement of labor within the European Union. In 2001 it was announced that the Commission had reached agreement with the football governing bodies (FIFA and UEFA, the European governing body to which all the national governing bodies belong) on a compensation system that would allow clubs to claim significant fees for players under age 23 on the grounds of investment in training costs. Players over 23 would have the right to move clubs annually even if employed under a long-term contract, subject to an economically justifiable (presumably moderate) compensation payment.[96]

Later in 2001 the Commission issued a statement of objections[97] to the collective sale of broadcasting rights to the lucrative Champions' League competition for the top European clubs, run by UEFA. Agreement was later reached over UEFA's right to market the Championship as a whole subject to some significant restrictions. Collective selling of broadcasting rights has been challenged at the national level in a number of European countries, notably Germany (ruled illegal and then given an antitrust exemption by parliament), the United Kingdom (upheld), Denmark (upheld), the Netherlands (no decision), Italy (ruled illegal), and Spain (prohibited); see Szymanski (2002) for details.

It seems that the soccer leagues of Europe have received much less favorable antitrust treatment than the North American leagues. Given that the European leagues have maintained a high degree of public interest and structural stability over the last half century despite having fewer restraints and less competitive balance than the North American leagues, would it be correct, as the European Commission (1998) has done, to speak of a European model of sport?[98] Currently, the main issue is whether the existing structures are stable or whether the growing commercialization of the sport will lead to restructuring. Hoehn and Szymanski (1999) suggest one kind of restructuring in which the dominant clubs of Europe (who are already organized in an exclusive bargaining group called G14) break away to form their own closed super-league along North American lines. If competitive balance really matters then we should expect the European system to collapse.

9. Conclusions

It is a commonplace among economists to hold up sports as an example of contest/tournament theory in action, but in practice a lot remains to be done both to understand the relationship between tournament structures and incentives in theory, and to test theories against the data. One objective of this review has been to discuss the contest theory literature in the context of sports. While there has been a good deal of research that has direct implications for the design of individualistic contests, empirical testing remains limited despite widespread agreement that this would be a very fruitful area in which to conduct testing. Moreover, there are many aspects of the organization of individualistic sports that could be modeled more fully with a view to establishing an optimal design: for example, optimal prize spreads in asymmetric contests, competition between rival contest organizers, the entry rules for contestants and optimal handicapping, to select just a few.

The relationship between team sports and contest theory seems even less well developed. The role of prizes in providing incentives has been largely ignored in the team sports literature, where much of the policy-oriented research has focused on redistribution mechanisms such as revenue sharing, and has been preoccupied with the proposition that such sharing is likely to have a neutral impact. In this chapter that claim is shown to depend on the assumption that an inelastic supply of talent is incorporated into the conjectural variations of the owners generating an equilibrium that is not Nash. This seems a relatively unfruitful avenue for research. An alternative way forward is the analysis of incentive structures. That prizes enhance incentives is surely a fundamental proposition of economic theory, but one that has been little studied in the team sports literature. The analysis of revenue sharing has paid little attention to the different ways that revenues for sharing can be collected on the basis of their allocation. For example, even if TV rights are sold collectively, different rules for distributing that income have quite different implications for incentives (and profits). The impact of prize funds also depends on the organizational structure of a sport (e.g. with or without inter-league economic rivalry).

One weakness of much of the existing literature is that the appropriate definition of a welfare function against which the optimality of contest can be measured is not carefully specified. This chapter has not touched in detail on this issue, but it is clearly critical. A conventional IO approach would be to focus on consumer surplus, but the complex specification of consumer demand, given the role of team loyalty, competitive balance, and team quality, as well as the more mundane issue of price, makes this approach problematic. In the contest literature the convention has been to focus on the issue of rent dissipation—but is this an appropriate yardstick for sporting contests? More work remains to be done to settle this crucial issue.

Comparative institutional analysis has much to offer for our understanding of organizational issues in team sports, not just between North America and Europe, but with other countries such as Australia with developed national sports and with other multinational sports such as cricket. Rosen and Sanderson (2001) reflected on the difference between North American and European leagues thus:

> All schemes used in the United States punish excellence in one way or another. The European football approach punishes failure by promoting excellent minor league teams to the majors and demoting (relegating) poor performing major league teams back down to the minors. The revenue loss from a potential demotion to a lower class of play is severe punishment for low quality—severe enough that salary treaties, league sharing arrangements, and unified player drafts are so far thought to be unnecessary, even though star salaries are enormous. It is an interesting economic question as to which system achieves better results.

Careful consideration of the impact of institutional differences may eventually lead to a better understanding of the incentive effects of contest design.

Empirically, some fundamental issues remain unresolved. For example, the central claims of sports economists that uncertainty of outcome boosts demand for sporting contests and that inequality of economic resources leads to more certainty of outcome obtain only weak support in the literature. Given that many successful team sports are characterized by highly unbalanced competition (e.g. soccer) and that proposed balance-enhancing measures are almost always profit enhancing, there are grounds for caution. From a policy point of view it may be that the invariance principle has been unhelpful in encouraging the view that restrictive measures would at least do no harm, even if they do no good. Given the role that economists frequently play in antitrust analysis, these theoretical and empirical perspectives have important policy implications.

We are still some way from being able to fully model and test an optimal design of a sporting contest. Such a project, however, is not beyond the capabilities of the economics profession.

Notes

1. Kagan Media estimates that sports accounts for 25 percent of all TV viewing, while Nielsen Media Research estimates the average U.S. household views 2738 hours of TV per year (7.5 hours per day). This significance to consumers is not reflected in dollar spending. The Census Bureau reported in 1997 that spectator sports generate a direct income of only $14 billion domestically (0.17 percent of GDP). The annual value of U.S. major league sports broadcast rights is in the region of $4 billion (Soonhwan Lee and Hyosung Chun 2001).
2. The words "contest" and "tournament" are used interchangeably throughout.
3. See also Andrew Zimbalist (2001) for a useful collection of seminal articles in the sports literature.
4. This chapter can thus be distinguished from fields such as "sabermetrics"— the study of baseball statistics for their own sake—which has little to do with empirical testing of economic theory.
5. All of these dates, associated with early rulebooks, are subject to controversy. By contrast, golf, cricket, and horse racing had established rules and clubs from the mid-eighteenth century.
6. The other great industrial nation of the period, Germany, also developed its own sporting activity during this period, the gymnastic "Turnen" movement. This movement eschewed competition between individuals in favor of the development of a disciplined athleticism with military purposes in mind, and was ultimately ousted by the Anglo-Saxon sports (see Guttman 1994, ch. 7).
7. Like all classifications, this one is at best imperfect. For example, the competitors in motor racing are teams of mechanics, but much of the spectator interest focuses on the individual exploits of the drivers. Rowing involves teams of rowers competing in a format that is very similar to most individualistic athletic contests, and horse racing is based on a distinctive form of cooperation between horse, trainer, and jockey. One difference is that in individualistic sports each contestants marginal productivity depends only on their own effort, while in team sports it also depends on the marginal productivity of other team members. While this makes individual productivity difficult to measure, its economic significance may not be all that great. In many team sports such as baseball and cricket, team members'

marginal products are almost entirely independent. Even where interactions are more important, the economic implications are unclear and their importance unproved. For example, if interaction terms were truly of economic significance in some team sports, one might expect to see players offering themselves to the market as partnerships, as happens, for instance, with teams of bond traders or teams of consultants. Even in team sports where the labor market is open to such possibilities (e.g. soccer, rugby, or cricket), player partnerships are almost unknown. The substantial empirical literature concerning the estimation of sports team production functions (see e.g. Kahn 1993) lies beyond the scope of this review.

8. In amateur sports the team is a kind of partnership, and early professional baseball and cricket teams were also organized on this basis.

9. While it is possible to be a fan of an individualistic competition (e.g. Wimbledon tennis) or event (e.g. the Olympics), this tends to happen only in the case of a small number of elite contests.

10. The Blue Ribbon Panel on Baseball Economics (Richard Levin et al. 2000), which was formed by the commissioner to investigate whether revenue disparities among the teams in Major League Baseball were undermining competitive balance, defined a proper level of competitive balance as a state where "every well-run club has a regularly recurring hope of reaching postseason play" (p. 1).

11. In some sports it is frequently argued that profit maximization is not the objective of the organizers (most notably, see Sloane 1971). This may not make much difference to the design of a competition. For example, amateur sporting associations frequently seek to maximize income from a popular sporting event, which is then used to develop the grass roots.

12. The analysis of rent-seeking contests has been applied to, inter alia, labor markets (e.g. Edward Lazear and Sherwin Rosen 1981), competition for innovation (e.g. Glenn Loury 1979), and competition for research contracts (e.g. Curtis Taylor 1995). There is also a substantial related literature on all-pay auctions (see e.g. Michael Baye, Dan Kovenock, and Casper de Vries 1996). Theoretical research on the implications of rent-seeking contests includes Baye et al. (1999), Ani Dasgupta and Kofi Nti (1998), Avinash Dixit (1987), Jerry Green and Nancy Stokey (1983), Richard Higgins, William Shughart, and Robert Tollison (1985), Barry Nalebuff and Joseph Stiglitz (1983), Shmuel Nitzan (1994), Nti (1997), and Stergios Skaperdas (1996).

13. Risk aversion is a natural assumption in many examples of labor-market contests, but in sporting contests involving professional athletes risk neutrality seems less objectionable. The very fact of investing the time and effort from an early age to become a professional athlete, when the probability of substantial earnings is very low would seem to suggest selection in favor of those with negligible risk aversion.

14. Lazear and Rosen (1981) and Dixit (1987) use the probit model, but as yet this has not been applied to the analysis of a sporting contest.

15. Here we focus on pure strategy equilibria. A mixed strategy may exist even if a pure strategy equilibrium does not (see e.g. Baye et al. 1994). Note that the equilibrium described here will not be symmetric if there are some contestants who decide not to enter the race; we ignore this possibility here.

16. Nti (1997) shows that the result on aggregate effort is sensitive to the type of winning technology selected.
17. The first-order condition is $R' \gamma (n-1)/n = 1$.
18. Competitive balance is discussed in more detail in section 5.
19. The modern practice in schools and elsewhere of offering almost all competing students a prize of some sort for participating in sporting contests is often criticized as an excess of political correctness—but in this context it might be viewed as simple recognition of the need for motivation for all contestants when abilities are heterogenous.
20. See also Moldovanu and Sela (2002) for discussion of different contest architectures in all-pay perfectly discriminating auctions.
21. "Consider a foot race between two athletes. Assume that it is common knowledge that the two athletes are equally good, and that they prefer to reserve themselves (run at a slow pace) rather than exhaust themselves by running at a fast pace. Suppose further that the leader has eyes in the back of his head and can monitor whether the follower is catching up. Because the leader can keep his lead by speeding up if the rival does so, there is no point for the rival in even engaging in the race. The leader can thus proceed at a slow pace without fear of being leapfrogged. But the picture changes dramatically if the two athletes run on tracks separated by a wall. Suppose that the wall has holes, so that from time to time each athlete can check his relative position. Now the leader can no longer run at the slow pace; if he did, the follower could run fast, leapfrogging the leader without his noticing it, and force him to drop out of the race at the next hole. Thus lags in information (or in reaction) engender competition" (Tirole 1988).
22. Of course, if a championship is decided as a "best of n matches" like the seven-match World Series, the organizers are keen to see the contest go to the wire. This is yet another reason for wanting competitive balance.
23. This research agenda is therefore primarily positive rather than normative. However, the adoption of procurement auctions by governments has introduced a normative element to this literature.
24. "The Ehrenberg and Bognanno work is perhaps the best test of tournament theory not because it is easily generalizable to the corporation but rather because the data are so well suited to testing the model" (Lazear 1995, p. 33).
25. Michael Orszag (1994) was unable to replicate these findings using data on the 1992 U.S. PGA tour. He argues that this may be due to increased media pressure since the 1980s causing more randomness (e.g. nerves) in the relationship between effort and performance.
26. Ignoring the possibility that horse and jockey operate as a team. Team elements might also be identified in golf (player and caddie) and foot races (e.g. runner and trainer).
27. Brian Becker and Mark Huselid (1992) analyzed driver performance in NASCAR races and found that prize spread improved race times. While much of the interest of the fans is focused on the drivers in this sport, there is clearly a very strong team element in the preparation of the car. Rafael Tenorio (2000) considers the practice in boxing of providing a "purse" for title fights that depends not on current but rather on past performance. He points

out that this may lead to inadequate effort supply in these matches. However, this phenomenon has much to do with the risk attached to boxing. Because of the fragmentation of governing bodies in boxing, promoters compete to offer boxers the best terms to stage a fight. A similar situation applies in the world of chess, where payments for the appearance of champions also tend to be high and independent of performance, but in this case the personal risks are not so great and so the temptation to "take the money and run" (or rather, fall over) is not so great.

28. This is also an important issue in team sports. For example, until the 1970s, European and South American teams were awarded a disproportionate share of qualifying places in the soccer World Cup, while after that period the policy was reversed by the governing body (FIFA). Since the 1970s the African teams were given an increased share and have (therefore?) been increasingly successful in the tournament (John Sugden and Alan Tomlinson 1999).

29. Perhaps the main exception to this has been in the field of labor economics where data on earnings in team sports has been used to develop tests of discrimination (reviewed in Kahn 2000 and Sherwin Rosen and Allen Sanderson 2001).

30. Leo Kahane and Stephen Shmanske (1997) found that teams with more stable team rosters enjoyed higher attendance, all else equal. Fans appear genuinely to prefer team stability. There is no evidence of any such preference among European soccer fans.

31. Here meaning Major League Baseball (MLB), the National Football League (NFL), the National Basketball Association (NBA), and the National Hockey League (NHL).

32. In the 1990s MLB ceased sharing gate revenues only in favor of local revenue sharing (including TV income).

33. The first FA Cup final and the first international match (Scotland v. England) both took place in 1872.

34. This is a structure in which clubs affiliated with the governing body are promoted from a given league division to its immediately senior division on the basis of league ranking at the end of each season, and subject to relegation to the immediately junior division on the same grounds.

35. There are exceptions: in the United Kingdom, Rugby League has adopted many American-style restrictions. The case of Australian team sports is interesting, since these had structures resembling European sports until the 1980s but since then a number of American institutions have been adopted (see e.g. Braham Dabscheck 1989; Rob Hess and Bob Stewart 1998).

36. It is perhaps more historically accurate to say that unions were relatively weak both in North America and in Europe until the 1950s. On both continents, union power started to grow at this time, and had some notable successes in Europe (e.g. the abolition of the maximum wage and the retain-and-transfer system in England; Szymanski and Tim Kuypers 1999, ch. 4). However, in North America the role of the unions has grown significantly over the past forty years, while in Europe they remain relatively weak to this day.

37. The degree of sensitivity reported here seems much greater than that reported by other authors (e.g. James Quirk and Mohamed El Hodiri 1974; Quirk and Fort 1999); this may be in part a consequence of choice of

specification and using a larger and longer panel of data. Zimbalist (1992) reports a similar R^2 for baseball and concludes that "average team salary has been related only tenuously to team performance."

38. There have been relatively few attempts to analyze causality empirically in the sports literature. Brian Davies, Paul Downward, and Ian Jackson (1995) and Stephen Dobson and John Goddard (1998) look at the relationship between income variables (attendance and revenues) and success in English rugby league and soccer.

39. A number of authors have used the standard deviation of winning percentage relative to the idealized standard deviation (assuming winning probabilities) as an alternative measure (see e.g. Scully 1989; Quirk and Fort 1992; Vrooman 1995). Other static measures include the Gini coefficient (Quirk and Fort 1992), relative entropy (Ira Horowitz 1997), and the Hirschman-Herfindahl index (Craig Depken 1999).

40. Eckard (1998) proposes a decomposition of the variance of winning percentages into a cumulative and time-varying component. For a given total variation a decrease in the variation through time implies greater cumulative variation; in other words, from season to season there is less turnover in team standings (competitive imbalance). Brad Humphreys (2002) proposes a similar measure. Alan Balfour and Philip Porter (1991) and Vrooman (1996) have estimated first-order autoregressive processes for win percent as a way to search for possible structural breaks associated with free agency (see below). In other words, they consider the degree of persistence, which might be thought a natural measure of dynamic competitive balance. Szymanski and Ron Smith (2002) adopt this approach to compare persistence across North American and European leagues.

41. One exception is Szymanski (2001), who exploits the fact that, in soccer, teams participate in two national competitions at once, one of which contains a much less balanced selection of contestants than the other. By pairing the subset of matches in each tournament that involve the same teams he is able to infer the effect of the balance of each tournament taken as a whole.

42. Paul Downward and Alistair Dawson (2000) reach a similar conclusion: "the evidence suggests that uncertainty of outcome has been an overworked hypothesis in explaining the demand for professional sports."

43. In fact, the two systems were so similar that it is hard to believe that the Football League did not copy the National League. However, no evidence to this effect has ever been produced.

44. In this case the change was exogenous—that is, not itself motivated by a desire to affect competitive balance (see Bruce Meyer 1995 for a discussion of natural experiments).

45. Bosman was a Belgian playing for a Belgian team who refused a new contract and decided he wanted to transfer to a French club that was willing to hire him and pay a transfer fee. Under the rules of the Belgian Football Association, the Belgian club had the right to veto the transaction without appeal (and so retain Bosman's services), which it did, on the grounds that it thought the buying club could not really afford the fee. This system was outlawed by the judgment (Court of Justice of the European Communities, Case C-415/93).

46. However, the within-season measure (standard deviation of win percent) was significant only for the Pacific League.
47. Some maintain that leagues should be considered (at least for antitrust purposes) as single economic entities (e.g. Gary Roberts 1984), which could imply centralized decision making.
48. Baik (1994) models asymmetry by assuming that the sensitivity of CSF to effort differs among contestants, an assumption that implies that all teams do not have access to the same technology for transforming talent into success. The assumption of symmetry effectively implies that all teams adopt best practice. The literature on team production functions sheds some light on this issue (see note 8).
49. For $n > 3$ the CSF can be thought of as a championship success function (e.g. James Whitney 1988). In practice, the difference between the share of total matches won in a season and win percentage is small and the two measures are highly correlated. For example, in English soccer the correlation coefficient between league rank and win percent is about 0.9.
50. Following most of the literature, we abstract from price issues. In North America, monopoly pricing is plausible due to distance and territorial exclusivity (see e.g. Donald Alexander 2001). Greater urban density and the promotion and relegation system in Europe make this less likely. For example, New York has two major-league baseball teams (population 20 million) while London (13 million) hosts six teams currently in the top division of English soccer, plus another six eligible to enter if promoted on merit. In Australian Rules Football and Australian Rugby League most of the teams are located around a single city (Melbourne and Sydney respectively). The implications of population density for revenue generation remain to be explored (but see Forrest, Simmons, and Feehan 2002 on the spatial pattern of demand for English soccer).
51. Intuitively, if this enters the revenue function of each team symmetrically then it will shift out the demand for talent. Some consequences of including the interaction of quality in more complex cases are considered below.
52. In the one-shot winner-take-all model, the payoff to the contestant is an expectation of the prize dependent on relative effort but only one contestant receives the prize ex post, while in the one-shot team sports version each contestant generates an income based on the share of success so that expected income equals ex post income (there is no stochastic element in the CSF). In an infinitely repeated game with no discounting, the values of the expected and actual payoffs are identical in both cases.
53. This assumes the supply is not so great that the demand curve intersects the horizontal axis at a point to the left of the fixed supply, implying that there is more talent than the MLB or the NBA require.
54. With Nash conjectures the LHS of (1.16) equals e_1/e_2.
55. Scott Atkinson, Linda Stanley, and John Tschirhart (1988) also state that they do not obtain the invariance result (p. 33, fn. 14) but attribute this to the assumption of a more general revenue function. The key difference, however, is that they do not assume fixed-supply conjectures.
56. See Noll (1974) p. 63, equation (ii) in particular.
57. Just as a conjectural variation of -1 produces the joint profit-maximizing solution in a quantity setting oligopoly.

58. Scully (1989), referred to in Vrooman (2000), has dissented from the main-stream view on revenue sharing, and this could be interpreted as the holding of the contrary view that supply is elastic. Scully (1989, 1995) discusses the elasticity of supply and cites as evidence the large salary gap between the stars and lesser players to support the proposition that supply is relatively inelastic.

59. Thomas Ericson (2000) also points out that in a European context the supply elasticity facing each league is nonzero, and he applies this to analyzing the impact of transfer rules on the distribution of talent across large and small market leagues.

60. The "Champions" in this title being the domestic league champions of the previous season.

61. He applies his model to the case of a luxury tax (see below). Késenne (2000a) shows that if team revenues depend on the quality of visitors, proxied by their winning percentage, and that the marginal revenue from visitor quality differs across teams, then revenue sharing improves competitive balance. This is essentially the same argument as that concerning local TV revenues. See also Philip Cyrenne (2001).

62. The difference between first and second is likely to be much greater than the difference between second and third, a superstar effect of the kind identified by Rosen (1981). Unlike a prize, the value of merchandising and related opportunities tends to differ between teams (e.g. because market sizes differ) and hence this kind of incentive promotes asymmetry.

63. It should be obvious that this argument will not be affected if we introduce demand for competitive balance or team quality into the revenue functions.

64. See Szymanski (2003) for a more detailed analysis of the implications of prizes in a model of team sport contests.

65. The precise formula is $V_R = \frac{n+1-R}{\sum_{i=1}^{n} R_i}$ where V_R is the prize awarded to the R_{th} ranked team and n is the number of teams in the league.

66. Although Vrooman (1997a) considers seriously the implications of alternative objectives on the part of owners. One aspect of the North American situation that has not been considered in the economics literature is the predominance of ownership of sports teams as part of a larger business empire, for example, Ted Turner and the Atlanta Braves, Rupert Murdoch and the Dodgers. The idea that teams might be operated as part of a wider business strategy deserves some attention.

67. Dabscheck (1975) considered Australian sports teams to be revenue maximizers.

68. In English cricket, amateurs and "players" (i.e. paid professionals) were segregated, changing in different rooms even when they were on the same team as recently as 1962. However, appearances can be deceptive: as far back as the 1880s the greed of many amateur cricketers in demanding "expenses" led to the coining of the word "shamateurism," to describe ostensibly amateur players who demand kickbacks of one form or another.

69. Public corporations have managed to evade this rule by establishing the football club as a subsidiary of a holding company, which faces no such restrictions.

70. Further discussion of this is to be found in Sloane (1971), Késenne (1996), and Jean-François Bourg and Jean-Jacques Gouguet (2001). Discussion of changing behavior patterns in recent years can be found in Wladimir Andreff and Staudohar (2000).
71. As Fort and Quirk (2000) point out, this does not necessarily imply more competitive balance in a win-maximizing league for a given level of redistribution. Absent revenue sharing a win-maximizing league could be less balanced than a profit-maximizing league and a given degree of revenue sharing might be inadequate to reverse the result.
72. Brian Cheffins (1998) provides an interesting legal perspective on the different approaches in North America and Europe.
73. Pace Vrooman (1995), who makes the Coasian argument that even if teams are constrained to pay identical salaries, they still have incentives to ensure that talent gravitates to its most profitable location. A team could evade the effect of the cap through the promise of endorsements and nonpecuniary benefits.
74. Arie Gavious, Benny Moldovanu, and Aner Sela (2002) show that imposing a bid cap in the context of an all pay auction reduces the bid of low cost (high revenue) types and increases the bids of high cost (low revenue) types, suggesting that even without imposing constraints there will be a tendency for competitive balance to improve.
75. See also Gustafson and Hadley (1996).
76. Somewhat oddly the Blue Ribbon Panel (Levin et al. 2000) attributed its failure to the fact that the tax threshold was a floating one (p. 39), rather than the fact that the tax threshold was simply set too high.
77. The tax regime was set for a four-year period, the tax thresholds being $117 million in 2003, $121 million in 2004, $128 million in 2005, and $137 million in 2006. Tax rates were 17.5 percent in 2003, rising to 22.5 percent for first-time offenders and 30 percent for repeat offenders in 2004 and 2005, with third-time offenders paying 40 percent in the latter year, and then 40 percent in 2006 except for first-time offenders.
78. This same argument has been applied to the inefficiency of a labor-managed firm (e.g. Benjamin Ward 1958; James Meade 1974), which might be thought an appropriate analogy for a sports league.
79. See John Siegfried and T. Petersen (2000) for an interesting analysis of locational rents.
80. An assumption that can be justified here since the optimal league size is a long-run decision, and in the long run talent supply is elastic (e.g. talent can be attracted away from other sports).
81. Cyrenne (2001) considers a related issue, the optimal number of games in a season, and contrasts the choice of a cartel to that of a social planner.
82. Noll (2002) and Ross and Szymanski (2002) analyze the system in more detail.
83. Relocation is in general prohibited by the governing bodies in Europe. Recently, Wimbledon, a team playing in the second tier of English soccer, was permitted to relocate, after lengthy debate, but only because the team's stadium had been closed and the local government did not allow them to build a new one (even at their own expense).

84. In the closed North American leagues low ranked teams may prefer to lose toward the end of the season if this gives them a better draft pick. Beck Taylor and Justin Trogdon (2002) find empirical support for this proposition in the NBA.
85. It is a mistake to argue that there is not enough talent to support a promotion and relegation system because talent will be spread too thinly. Rather, an efficient promotion and relegation system requires player mobility, since the best talent will always migrate to the top division. In practice this often happens with extraordinary speed. Promotion and relegation is a discipline on the owners rather than the players.
86. This is FIFAs claimed viewership for the "France '98" World Cup. This implies everyone on the planet could have watched five games, around 50 billion viewing hours. The IOC claimed 36 billion viewing hours for Sydney 2000.
87. In fact, top players from weak countries with little chance of winning the World Cup are sometimes reluctant to appear. In the 2002 World Cup the captain of the Republic of Ireland walked out on his team claiming that the national Association was not prepared to spend enough money on training facilities for the players.
88. Over the last twenty years Australia's dominance has become embarrassing, with a 66 percent winning record in decisive matches.
89. The other ten are Australia, Pakistan, England, South Africa, India, Sri Lanka, New Zealand, Zimbabwe, and Bangladesh, with a combined population of 1.4 billion, compared to the Island population of around 4 million. Even excluding India, this would amount to no more than 1 percent of the population of the cricketing nations.
90. If baseball were regularly played at the international representative level, such phenomena might also emerge. For example, it is well recognized that the tiny Dominican Republic would be a competitive nation, not to mention Cuba.
91. John McMillan (1997) provides an interesting discussion on the balance between centralized coordination and decentralized decision making in the case of New Zealand rugby union. But see Dorian Owen and Clayton Weatherston (2002) for analysis of how provincial competition in that country has been subordinated to the needs of the national team.
92. The U.S. literature is particularly rich—e.g. Flynn and Gilbert (2001), Thomas Piraino (1999), Roberts (1984), Ross (1989, 1997, 1998, 2001), Ross and Lucke (1997), Paul Weiler and Gary Roberts (1998). There are also a number of European texts, e.g. Simon Gardiner et al. (1998), Alexandre Husting (1998). For an Australian perspective, see Dabscheck (2000).
93. Some issues remain, such as rules relating to eligibility, and in particular eligibility and disabilities.
94. In *Fraser v. MLS* the Appeal Court cast doubt on the credibility of the single entity claim of MLS (LLC 284 F 3d.47 (1st Circ. 2002)), describing it as "somewhere between a single company (with or without wholly owned subsidiaries) and a cooperative arrangement between existing competitors."
95. The NCAA case also considered in detail the effect of broadcasting on live gate.

96. See *FIFA Regulations for the Status and Transfer of Players,* July 2001 (see also the comments in section 6.1).
97. *European Union Official Journal,* C 169, 13.06.2001, p. 5.
98. See Didier Primault and Arnaud Rouger (1999) for a trenchant assertion of difference.

References

Alexander, Donald. 2001. "Major League Baseball: Monopoly Pricing and Profit-Maximizing Behavior," *J. Sports Econ.* 2:4, pp. 341–55.

Andreff, Wladimir and Paul Staudohar. 2000. "The Evolving Model of European Sports Finance," *J. Sports Econ.* 1:3, pp. 257–76.

Atkinson, Scott; Linda Stanley and John Tschirhart. 1988. "Revenue Sharing as an Incentive in an Agency Problem: An Example from the National Football League," *Rand J. Econ.* 19:1, pp. 27–43.

Baik, Kyung. 1994. "Effort Levels in Contests with Two Asymmetric Players," *South. Econ. J.* 61, pp. 367–78.

Baimbridge, Mark; Samuel Cameron and Peter Dawson. 1996. "Satellite Television and the Demand for Football: A Whole New Ball Game?" *Scot. J. Polit. Econ.* 43:3, pp. 317–33.

Balfour, Alan and Philip Porter. 1991. "The Reserve Clause in Professional Sports: Legality and Effect on Competitive Balance," *Lab. Law J.* 42, pp. 8–18.

Baye, Michael; Dan Kovenock and Casper de Vries. 1994. "The Solution to the Tullock Rent-Seeking Game When R>2: Mixed-Strategy Equilibria and Mean Dissipation Rates," *Public Choice* 81:3–4, pp. 363–80.

——. 1996. "The All-Pay Auction with Complete Information," *Econ. Theory* 8:2, pp. 291–305.

——. 1999. "The Incidence of Overdissipation in Rent-Seeking Contests," *Public Choice* 99, pp. 439–54.

Becker, Brian and Mark Huselid. 1992. "The Incentive Effects of Tournament Compensation Systems," *Admin. Sci. Quart.* 37, pp. 336–50.

Bernard, Andrew and Meghan Busse. 2000. "Who Wins the Olympic Games: Economic Development and Medal Totals," NBER work. paper #7998.

Borland, Jeff. 1987. "The Demand for Australian Rules Football," *Econ. Record* 63:182, pp. 220–30.

Borland, Jeff and Jenny Lye. 1992. "Attendance at Australian Rules Football: A Panel Study," *Appl. Econ.* 24, pp. 1053–58.

Bourg, Jean-François and Jean-Jacques Gouguet. 2001. *Economie du Sport.* Paris: Editions La Decouverte.

Buchanan, James. 1965. "An Economic Theory of Clubs," *Economica* (Feb.), pp. 1–14.

Bulow, Jeremy and Paul Klemperer. 2001. "The Generalized War of Attrition," *Amer. Econ. Rev.* 89:1, pp. 175–89.

Butler, Michael. 1995. "Competitive Balance in Major League Baseball," *Amer. Economist* 39:2, pp. 46–52.

Buzzacchi, Luigi; Stefan Szymanski and Tommaso Valletti. 2003. "Equality of Opportunity and Equality of Outcome: Open Leagues, Closed Leagues and Competitive Balance," *J. Indust. Comp. Trade* 3:3, pp. 167–86.

Cairns, John. 1987. "Evaluating Changes in League Structure: The Organisation of the Scottish Football League," *Appl. Econ.* 19:2, pp. 259–75.

Cairns, John; Nicholas Jennett and Peter Sloane. 1986. "The Economics of Professional Team Sports: A Survey of Theory and Evidence," *J. Econ. Stud.* 13, pp. 3–80.

Cheffins, Brian. 1998. "Sports Teams and the Stock Market: A Winning Match?" *UBC Law Rev.* 32, pp. 271–91.

Condon, Sir Paul. 2001. *Report on Corruption in International Cricket.* London: Anti-Corruption Unit, Int. Cricket Council.

Cramton, Peter and Thomas Palfrey. 1990. "Cartel Enforcement with Uncertainty about Costs," *Int. Econ. Rev.* 31:1, pp. 17–47.

Cymrot, Donald; James Dunlevy and William Even. 2001. " 'Who's on First': An Empirical Test of the Coase Theorem in Baseball," *Appl. Econ.* 33, pp. 593–603.

Cyrenne, Philip. 2001. "A Quality-of-Play Model of a Professional Sports League," *Econ. Inquiry* 39, pp. 444–52.

Dabscheck, Braham. 1975. "Sporting Equality: Labour Market vs Product Market Control," *J. Ind. Relat.* 17:2, pp. 174–90.

——. 1989. "Abolishing Transfer Fees: The Victorian Football League's new employment rules" *Sporting Traditions* Nov. pp. 63–87.

——. 2000. "Sport, Human Rights and Industrial Relations," *Australian J. Human Rights,* 6:2, pp. 129–59.

Daly, George. 1992. "The Baseball Player's Market Revisited," in *Diamonds Are Forever: The Business of Baseball.* P. Sommers, ed. Brookings Institution.

Daly, George and William Moore. 1981. "Externalities, Property Rights, and the Allocation of Resources in Major League Baseball," *Econ. Inquiry* 29, pp. 77–95.

Dasgupta, Ani and Kofi Nti. 1998. "Designing an Optimal Contest," *Europ. J. Polit. Econ.* 14, pp. 587–603.

Davies, Brian; Paul Downward and Ian Jackson. 1995. "The Demand for Rugby League: Evidence from Causality Tests," *Appl. Econ.* 27, pp. 1003–1007.

Depken, Craig. 1999. "Free-Agency and the Competitiveness of Major League Baseball," *Rev. Ind. Org.* 14, pp. 205–17.

Dixit, Avinash. 1987. "Strategic Behavior in Contests," *Amer. Econ. Rev.* 77, pp. 891–98.

Dobson, Stephen and John Goddard. 1998. "Performance and Revenue in Professional League Football: Evidence from Granger Causality Tests," *Appl. Econ.* 30, pp. 1641–51.

Downward, Paul and Alistair Dawson. 2000. *The Economics of Professional Team Sports.* London: Routledge.

Duggan, Mark and Steven Levitt. 2002. "Winning Isn't Everything: Corruption in Sumo Wrestling," *Amer Econ. Rev.* 92:5, pp. 1594–1605.

Eckard, Woodrow. 1998. "The NCAA Cartel and Competitive Balance in College Football," *Rev. Ind. Org.* 13, pp. 347–69.

——. 2001. "Free Agency, Competitive Balance and Diminishing Returns to Pennant Contention," *Econ. Inquiry* 39:3, pp. 430–43.

Ehrenberg, Ronald and Michael Bognanno. 1990a. "Do Tournaments Have Incentive Effects?" *J. Polit. Econ.* 98:6, pp. 1307–24.

——. 1990b. "The Incentive Effects of Tournaments Revisited: Evidence from the European PGA Tour," *Ind. Lab. Relat. Rev.* 43, pp. 74S–88S.

El Hodiri, Mohamed and James Quirk. 1971. "An Economic Model of a Professional Sports League," *J. Polit. Econ.* 79, pp. 1302–19.

Ericson, Thomas. 2000. "The Bosman Case: Effects of the Abolition of the Transfer Fee," *J. Sports Econ.* 1:3, pp. 203–18.

European Commission. 1998. "The European Model of Sport," consultation paper of DGX.

Fees, Eberhard and Gerd Muehlheusser. 2003. "Transfer Fee Regulations in European Football," *Europ. Econ. Rev.* 47:4, pp. 645–68.

Fernie, Susan and David Metcalf. 1999. "It's Not What You Pay, It's the Way that You Pay It, and That's What Gets Results: Jockeys' Pay and Performance," *Labor* 13, pp. 385–411.

Fershtman, Chaim and Kenneth Judd. 1987. "Equilibrium Incentives in Oligopoly," *Amer. Econ. Rev.* 77, pp. 927–40.

Flynn, Michael and Richard Gilbert. 2001. "An Analysis of Professional Sports Leagues as Joint Ventures," *Econ. J.* 111, pp. F27–F46.

Forrest, David and Robert Simmons. 2002a. "Outcome Uncertainty and Attendance Demand in Sport: The Case of English Soccer," *J. Royal Statist. Society, Series D (The Statistician)*, 51:2, pp. 229–41.

——. 2002b. "Team Salaries and Playing Success in Sports: A Comparative Perspective," *Zeitschrift für Betriebswirtschaft* 72:4.

Forrest, David, Robert Simmons and Patrick Feehan. 2002. "A Spatial Cross-Sectional Analysis of the Elasticity of Demand for Soccer," *Scot. J. Polit. Econ.* 49:3, pp. 336–56.

Fort, Rodney. 2000. "European and North American Sports Differences," *Scot. J. Polit. Econ.* 47:4, pp. 431–55.

Fort, Rodney and James Quirk. 1995. "Cross Subsidization, Incentives and Outcomes in Professional Team Sports Leagues," *J. Econ. Lit.* 33:3, pp. 1265–99.

——. 2000. "Owner Objectives and Competitive Balance," work. paper, econ. dept. Washington State U.

Frick, Bernd; Joachim Prinz and Alexander Dilger. 2001. "Pay and Performance in Professional Road Running: The Case of City Marathons," mimeo, U. Witten.

Fudenberg, Drew; Richard Gilbert; Joseph Stiglitz and Jean Tirole. 1983. "Preemption, Leapfrogging and Competition in Patet Races," *Europ. Econ. Rev.* 22, pp. 3–31.

Fudenberg, Drew and Jean Tirole. 1985. "Pre-Emption and Rent Equalization in the Adoption of New Technologies," *Rev. Econ. Stud.* 52, pp. 383–402.

——. 1991. *Game Theory.* Cambridge, MA and London: MIT Press.

Fullerton, Richard and Preston McAfee. 1999. "Auctioning Entry in Tournaments," *J. Polit. Econ.* 107:3, pp. 573–606.

Gardiner Simon; Alexandra Felix; John O'Leary; Mark James and Roger Welch. 1998. *Sports Law.* London: Cavendish Pub.

Garicano, Luis and Ignacio Palacios-Huerta. 2000. "An Empirical Examination of Multidimensional Effort in Tournaments," mimeo, econ. dept. Brown U.

Gavious, Arie; Benny Moldovanu and Aner Sela. 2002. "Bid Costs and Endogenous Bid Caps," *Rand J. Econ.* 33:4, pp. 709–22.

Gradstein, Mark and Kai Konrad. 1999. "Orchestrating Rent-Seeking Contests," *Econ. J.* 109, pp. 536–45.

Green, Jerry and Nancy Stokey. 1983. "A Comparison of Tournaments and Contests," *J. Polit. Econ.* 91, pp. 349–64.

Grier, Kevin and Robert Tollison. 1994. "The Rookie Draft and Competitive Balance: The Case of Professional Football," *J. Econ. Behav. Org.* 25, pp. 293–98.

Gustafson E. and L. Hadley. 1996. "The Luxury Tax Proposal for Major League Baseball: A Partial Equilibrium Analysis," in *Baseball Economics: Current Research.* Fizel, Gustafson, and Hadley, eds. Westport, CT: Praeger.

Guttman, Allen. 1994. *Games and Empires.* NY: Columbia U. Press.

Hall, Stephen; Stefan Szymanski and Andrew Zimbalist. 2002. "Testing Causality between Team Performance and Payroll: The Cases of Major League Baseball and English Soccer," *J. Sports Econ.* 3:2, pp. 149–68.

Harris, Christopher and John Vickers. 1985. "Perfect Equilibrium in a Model of a Race," *Rev. Econ. Stud.* 52:2, pp. 193–209.

——. 1987. "Racing with Uncertainty," *Rev. Econ. Stud.* 54, pp. 1–22.

Hart, R.A.; J. Hutton and T. Sharrot. 1975. "A Statistical Analysis of Association Football Attendances," *Applied Statist.* 24:1, pp. 17–27.

Hess, Rob and Bob Stewart. 1998. *More Than a Game: An Unauthorised History of Australian Rules Football.* Melbourne U. Press.

Higgins, Richard; William Shughart and Robert Tollison. 1985. "Free Entry and Efficient Rent-Seeking," *Public Choice* 46, pp. 247–58.

Higgins, Richard and Robert Tollison. 1990. "Economics at the Track," in *Sportometrics.* Brian Goff and Robert Tollison, eds. Texas A&M U. Press, pp. 15–34.

Hillman, Arye and John Riley. 1989. "Politically Contestable Rents and Transfers," *Econ. Politics* 1:1, pp. 17–39.

Hoehn, Thomas and Stefan Szymanski. 1999. "The Americanization of European Football," *Econ. Policy* 28, pp. 205–40.

Horowitz, Ira. 1997. "The Increasing Competitive Balance in Major League Baseball," *Rev. Ind. Org.* 12, pp. 373–87.

Hovenkamp, Herbert. 1995. "Exclusive Joint Ventures and Antitrust Policy," *Columbia Bus. Law Rev.* 1.

Humphreys, Brad. 2002. "Alternative Measures of Competitive Balance in Sports Leagues," *J. Sports Econ.* 3:2, pp. 133–48.

Husting, Alexandre. 1998. *L'Union Europeene et le Sport.* Lyon: Les Editions Juris Service.

Hylan, Timothy; Maureen Lage and Michael Treglia. 1996. "The Coase Theorem, Free Agency, and Major League Baseball: A Panel Study of Pitcher Mobility from 1961 to 1992," *South. Econ. J.* 62, pp. 1029–42.

Inglis, Simon. 1988. *League Football and the Men Who Made It.* London: Willow Books.

Jennett, Nicholas. 1984. "Attendances, Uncertainty of Outcome and Policy in the Scottish Football League," *Scot. J. Polit. Econ.* 31:2, pp. 176–98.

Jones, J.C.H. and D.G Ferguson. 1988. "Location and Survival in the National Hockey League," *J. Ind. Econ.* 36:4, pp. 443–57.

Kahane, Leo and Stephen Shmanske. 1997. "Team Roster Turnover and Attendance in Major League Baseball," *Appl. Econ.* 29:4, pp. 425–31.

Kahn, Lawrence. 1993. "Managerial Quality, Team Success, and Individual Performance in Major League Baseball," *Ind. Lab. Relat. Rev.* 46, pp. 531–47.

——. 2000. "The Sports Business as a Labor Market Laboratory," *J. Econ. Perspect.* 14:3, pp. 75–94.

Késenne, Stefan. 1996. "League Management in Professional Team Sports with Win Maximizing Clubs," *Europ. J. Sport Manage.* 2:2, pp. 14–22.

——. 2000a. "Revenue Sharing and Competitive Balance in Professional Team Sports," *J. Sports Econ.* 1:1, pp. 56–65.

——. 2000b. "The Impact of Salary Caps in Professional Team Sports," *Scot. J. Polit. Econ.* 47:4, pp. 422–30.

Késenne, Stefan and Claude Jeanrenaud, eds. 1999. *Competition Policy in Professional Sports: Europe after the Bosman Case.* Antwerp: Standaard Eds.

Kipker, Ingo. 2000. "Determinanten der Zuschauernachfrage im professionellen Teamsport: Wie wichtig ist die sportliche Ausgeglichenheit?" PhD dissert. Heinrich Heine U., Dusseldorf.

Knowles, Glenn; Keith Sherony and Michael Haupert. 1992. "The Demand for Major League Baseball: A Test of the Uncertainty of Outcome Hypothesis," *Amer. Economist* 36, pp. 72–80.

Kuypers, Timothy. 1996. "The Beautiful Game? An Econometric Study of Why People Watch English Football," *Discus. Papers Econ.* 96-01 U. College London.

La Croix, S. and A. Kawaura. 1999. "Rule Changes and Competitive Balance in Japanese Professional Baseball," *Econ. Inquiry* 37:2, pp. 353–68.

Lazear, Edward. 1989. "Pay Equality and Industrial Politics," *J. Polit. Econ.* 97:3, pp. 561–80.

——. 1995. *Personnel Economics.* MIT Press Cambridge: Mass.

Lazear, Edward and Sherwin Rosen. 1981. "Rank Order Tournaments as Optimal Labor Contracts," *J. Polit. Econ.* 89, pp. 841–64.

Lee, Soonhwan and Hyosung Chun. 2001. "Economic Values of Professional Sport Franchises in the United States," *Sport J.* 5:3 (an electronic journal: http://www.thesportJ.org).

Levin, Richard; George Mitchell; Paul Volcker and George Will. 2000. *The Report of the Independent Members of the Commissioner's Blue Ribbon Panel on Baseball Economics.* NY: Major League Baseball.

Loury, Glenn. 1979. "Market Structure and Innovation," *Quart. J. Econ.* 93, pp. 385–410.

Lynch, James and Jeffrey Zax. 2000. "The Rewards to Running: Prize Structure and Performance in Professional Road Racing," *J. Sports Econ.* 1, pp. 323–40.

McMillan, John. 1997. "Rugby Meets Economics," *New Zealand Econ. Papers* 31:1, pp. 93–144.

Maloney, Michael and Robert McCormick. 2000. "The Response of Workers to Wages in Tournaments: Evidence from Foot Races," *J. Sports Econ.* 1, pp. 99–123.

Maloney, Michael and Kristina Terkun. 2002. "Road Warrior Booty: Prize Structures in Motorcycle Racing," *Contrib. Econ. Anal. Policy* 1:1.

Marburger, Daniel. 1997. "Gate Revenue Sharing and Luxury Taxes in Professional Sports," *Contemp. Econ. Policy* 15, pp. 114–23.

——. 2002. "Property Rights and Unilateral Player Transfers in a Multiconference Sports League," *J. Sports Econ.* 3:2, pp. 122–32.

Mason, Tony. 1980. *Association Football and English Society, 1863–1915.* Brighton, UK: Harvester Press.

Meade, James. 1974. "Labor-Managed Firms in Conditions of Imperfect Competition," *Econ. J.* 84, pp. 817–24.

Meyer, Bruce. 1995. "Natural and Quasi-Experiments in Economics," *J. Bus. Econ. Statist.* 13, pp. 151–62.

Moldovanu, Benny and Aner Sela. 2001. "The Optimal Allocation of Prizes in Contests," *Amer. Econ. Rev.* 91:3, pp. 542–58.

——. 2002. "Contest Architecture," discus. paper, U. Mannheim.

Monahan, George and Matthew Sobel. 1994. "Stochastic Dynamic Market Share Attraction Games," *Games Econ. Behav.* 6, pp. 130–49.

Nalebuff, Barry and Joseph Stiglitz. 1983. "Prizes and Incentives: Towards a General Theory of Compensation and Competition," *Bell J. Econ.* 14, pp. 21–43.

Neale, Walter. 1964. "The Peculiar Economics of Professional Sport," *Quart. J. Econ.* 78:1, pp. 1–14.

Nitzan, Shmuel. 1994. "Modelling Rent Seeking Contests," *Europ. J. Polit. Econ.* 10, pp. 41–60.

Noll, Roger. 1974. "Attendance and Price Setting," in *Government and the Sports Business.* Roger Noll, ed. Washington: Brookings Institution.

——. 2002. "The Economics of Promotion and Relegation in Sports Leagues: The Case of English Football," *J. Sports Econ.* 3:2, pp. 169–203.

Noll, Roger and Andrew Zimbalist. 1997. *Sports, Jobs and Taxes.* Washington: Brookings Institution.

Nti, Kofi. 1997. "Comparative Statics of Contests and Rent-Seeking Games," *Int. Econ. Rev.* 38:1, pp. 43–59.

Orszag, Michael. 1994. "A New Look at Incentive Effects and Golf Tournaments," *Econ. Letters* 46, pp. 77–88.

Owen, Dorian and Clayton Weatherston. 2002. "Professionalization and Competitive Balance in New Zealand Rugby Union," mimeo, U. Otago.

Palomino, Frederic and Joszef Sakovics. 2000. "Revenue Sharing in Professional Sports Leagues: For the Sake of Competitive Balance or as a Result of Monopsony Power?" mimeo, CentER discus. paper 2000–110, Tilburg U.

——. 2001. "Inter-League Competition for Talent vs. Competitive Balance," work. paper, CentER, Tilburg U.

Peel, David and David Thomas. 1988. "Outcome Uncertainty and the Demand for Football: An Analysis of Match Attendances in the English Football League," *Scot. J. Polit. Econ.* 35:3, pp. 242–49.

——. 1992. "The Demand for Football: Some Evidence on Outcome Uncertainty," *Empir. Econ.* 17, pp. 323–31.

——. 1997. "Handicaps, Outcome Uncertainty and Attendance Demand," *Applied Econ. Letters* 4, pp. 567–70.

Piraino, Thomas. 1999. "A Proposal for the Antitrust Regulations of Professional Sports," *Boston U. Law Rev.* 79:889.

Preston, Ian; Stephen F. Ross and Stefan Szymanski. 2001. "Seizing the Moment, a Blueprint for Reform of World Cricket," work. paper, University College, London.

Primault, Didier and Arnaud Rouger. 1999. "How Relevant is North American Experience for Professional Team Sports in Europe" in *Competition Policy in Professional Sports: Europe after the Bosman Case.* Stefan Késenne and Claude Jeanrenaud, eds. Antwerp: Standaard Eds.

Quirk, James and Mohamed El Hodiri. 1974. "The Economic Theory of a Professional Sports League," in *Government and the Sports Business,* Roger Noll, ed. Washington DC: Brookings Institution.

Quirk, James and Rodney Fort. 1992. *Pay Dirt: The Business of Professional Team Sports.* Princeton: Princeton U. Press.

——. 1999. *Hard Ball: The Abuse of Power in Pro Team Sports*. Princeton U. Press.

Rascher, Dan. 1999. "A Test of the Optimal Positive production Network Externality in Major League Baseball," in *Sports Economics: Current Research*. John Fizel, Elizabeth Gustafson and Larry Hadley, eds. Praeger, Westport CT.

Roberts, Gary. 1984. "Sports Leagues and the Sherman Act: The Use and Abuse of Section 1 to Regulate Restraints on Intraleague Rivalry," *UCLA Law Rev.* 32: 219, pp. 286–87.

Roberts, Kevin. 1985. "Cartel Behaviour and Adverse Selection," *J. Ind. Econ.* 33, pp. 401–13.

Rosen, Sherwin. 1981. "The Economics of Superstars," *Amer. Econ. Rev.* pp. 845–58.

——. 1986. "Prizes and Incentives in Elimination Tournaments," *Amer. Econ. Rev.* 76, pp. 701–15.

Rosen, Sherwin and Allen Sanderson. 2001. "Labor Markets in Professional Sports," *Econ. J.* 111:469, pp. F47–F68.

Ross, Stephen F. 1989. "Monopoly Sports Leagues," *U. Minnesota Law Rev.* 73:643.

——. 1997. "The Misunderstood Alliance Between Sports Fans, Players, and the Antitrust Laws," *U. Illinois Law Rev.* 1997:519.

——. 1998. "Restraints on Player Competition that Facilitate Competitive Balance and Player Development and their Legality in the United States and in Europe," in *Competition Policy in Professional Sports: Europe after the Bosman Case*. Stefan Késenne and Claude Jeanrenaud, eds. Antwerp: Standaard Eds.

——. 2001. "Antitrust Options to Redress Anticompetitive Restraints and Monopolistic Practices by Professional Sports Leagues," paper delivered to 2nd Annual Amer. Antitrust Inst. Conf.

Ross, Stephen F. and Robert Lucke. 1997. "Why Highly Paid Athletes Deserve More Antitrust Protection than Unionized Factory Workers," *Antitrust Bull.* 42:3, pp. 641–79.

Ross, Stephen F. and Stefan Szymanski. 2002. "Open Competition in League Sports," *Wisconsin Law Rev.* 2002:3, pp. 625–56.

——. 2003. "The Law and Economics of Optimal Sports League Design," work. paper, Business School, Imperial College, London.

Rottenberg, Simon. 1956. "The Baseball Player's Labor Market," *J. Polit. Econ.* 64, pp. 242–58.

Schmidt, Martin and David Berri. 2001. "Competitive Balance and Attendance: The Case of Major League Baseball," *J. Sports Econ.* 2:2, pp. 145–67.

Scully, Gerald. 1974. "Pay and Performance in Major League Baseball," *Amer. Econ. Rev.* 64, pp. 915–30.

——. 1989. *The Business of Major League Baseball*. Chicago: U. Chicago Press.

——. 1995. *The Market Structure of Sports*. U. Chicago Press.

Seymour, Harold. 1960. *Baseball: The Early Years*. NY: Oxford U. Press.

Siegfried, John and T. Petersen. 2000. "Who Is Sitting in the Stands? The Income Levels of Sports Fans," in *The Economics of Sports*. W. Kern, ed. Kalamazoo: Upjohn Inst.

Siegfried, John and Andrew Zimbalist. 2000. "The Economics of Sports Facilities and Their Communities," *J. Econ. Perspect.* 14, pp. 95–114.

Skaperdas, Stergios. 1996. "Contest Success Functions," *Econ. Theory* 7, pp. 283–90.

Sloane, Peter. 1969. "The Labor Market in Professional Football," *British J. Ind. Relat.* 7:2, pp. 181–99.

——. 1971. "The Economics of Professional Football: The Football Club as a Utility Maximizer," *Scot. J. Polit. Econ.* 17, 2, pp. 121–46.

Staudohar, Paul. 1996. *Playing for Dollars: Labor Relations and the Sports Business.* Cornell: ILR Press.

——. 1999. "Salary Caps in Professional Team Sports," in *Competition Policy in Professional Sports: Europe after the Bosman Case.* Stefan Késenne and Claude Jeanrenaude, eds. Antwerp: Standaard Eds.

Sugden, John and Alan Tomlinson. 1999. *Great Balls of Fire.* Edinburgh: Mainstream Pub.

Szymanski, Stefan. 2001. "Income Inequality, Competitive Balance and the Attractiveness of Team Sports: Some Evidence and a Natural Experiment from English Soccer," *Econ. J.* 111, pp. F69–F84.

——. 2002. "Collective Selling of Broadcast Rights to Sporting Events," *Int. Sports Law Rev.* 2:1, pp. 3–7.

——. 2003. "Incentives and Competitive Balance in Team Sports," *Europ. Sport Manage. Quart.* 3:1, pp. 11–30.

——. 2004. "Professional Team Sports Are Only a Game: The Walrasian Fixed Supply Conjecture Model, Contest Nash Equilibrium and the Invariance Principle," *J. Sports Econ.* 5:2, pp. 111–26.

Szymanski, Stefan and Stefan Késenne. 2004. "Competitive Balance and Gate Revenue Sharing in Team Sports," *J. Indust. Econ.* LII:1, pp. 165–77.

Szymanski, Stefan and Tim Kuypers. 1999. *Winners and Losers: The Business Strategy of Football.* London: Viking Books.

——. 2002. "Equality of Opportunity and Equality of Outcome: Static and Dynamic Competitive Balance in European and North American Sports Leagues" in *Transatlantic Sport.* Carlos Barros, Muradali Ibrahim, and Stefan Szymanski, eds. Cheltenham, UK: Edward Elgar.

Szymanski, Stefan and Tommaso Valletti. 2002. "First and Second Prizes in Imperfectly Discriminating Contests," work. paper, Business School, Imperial College, London.

——. 2003. "Open and Closed Leagues," work. paper, Business School, Imperial College, London.

Taylor, Beck and Justin Trogdon. 2002. "Losing to Win: Tournament Incentives in the National Basketball Association," *J. Lab. Econ.* 20:1.

Taylor, Curtis. 1995. "Digging for Golden Carrots: An Analysis of Research Tournaments," *Amer. Econ. Rev.* 85, 4, pp. 873–90.

Tenorio, Rafael. 2000. "The Economics of Professional Boxing Contracts," *J. Sports Econ.* 1:4, pp. 363–84.

Tirole, Jean. 1988. *The Theory of Industrial Organization.* Cambridge, MA: MIT Press.

Tullock, Gordon. 1980. "Efficient Rent Seeking," in *Toward a Theory of Rent Seeking Society.* J. Buchanan, R. Tollison and G. Tullock, eds. Texas: A&M U. Press, pp. 97–112.

Vamplew, Wray. 1988. *Pay Up and Play the Game: Professional Sport in Britain 1875–1914.* Cambridge, UK: Cambridge U. Press.

Vives, Xavier. 1999. *Oligopoly Pricing.* MIT Press Cambridge: Mass.

Vrooman, John. 1995. "A General Theory of Professional Sports Leagues," *South. Econ. J.* 61:4, pp. 971–90.

——. 1996. "The Baseball Players Market Reconsidered," *South. Econ. J.* 62:3, pp. 339–60.

——. 1997a. "A Unified Theory of Capital and Labor Markets in Major League Baseball," *South. Econ. J.* 63, pp. 594–619.

——. 1997b. "Franchise Free Agency in Professional Sports Leagues," *South. Econ.J.* 63:July, pp. 191–219.

——. 2000. "The Economics of American Sports Leagues," *Scot. J. Polit. Econ.* 47:4, pp. 364–98.

Ward, Benjamin. 1958. "The Firm in Illyria: Market Syndicalism," *Amer. Econ. Rev.* 48:4, pp. 566–89.

Weiler, Paul and Gary Roberts. 1998. *Sports and the Law: Text, Cases, Problems.* 2nd ed. Amer. Casebook Series, West/Wadsworth.

Whitney, James. 1988. "Winning Games vs Winning Championships: Economics of Fan Interest and Team Performance," *Econ. Inquiry* 26:October, pp. 703–24.

Zimbalist, Andrew. 1992. *Baseball and Billions.* NY: Basic Books.

——, ed. 2001. *The Economics of Sport.* 2 vols. Cheltenham, UK: Edward Elgar.

——. 2003. *May the Best Team Win: Baseball Economics and Public Policy.* Washington: Brookings Institution.

2

The Political Economy of Sport

Stefan Szymanski

Senior Lecturer, Management School, Imperial College, London

The founding fathers of the United States and signatories to the Treaty of Rome were both guilty of a glaring omission in their otherwise admirable constitutions—they forgot to mention sport. This simple omission is becoming one of the biggest headaches for legislators, the judiciary and the executive, and the problem is getting worse every year. Team sports, such as soccer and baseball, have long been the principal interest of a majority of adolescent and adult males. There are signs that this preoccupation is also taking hold of the other half of the population, and the economic magnitude of these activities is becoming substantial. According to the European Commission, sport now accounts for 3% of world trade, worth around $200 billion. The broadcasting rights to major sporting events alone now trade for dollar amounts that run into billions, while a large segment of the leisurewear market is driven by sporting icons and images. During the 1980s in the US, and in the 1990s in Europe, sport took a step forward in its penetration of day-to-day life. Perhaps because of improvements in broadcasting technology, perhaps because of the enormous increase in leisure spending power, or perhaps because, with the end of the cold war, most forms of physical conflict are now discouraged, the social significance of sport seems to have risen to a level which was hitherto unknown.

As long as sports were popular, but not significant money-spinners, the politicians and judges could stand aside. Before the 1960s there were few significant interventions in the market.[1] The advent of television changed all this. Mainly because sport is one of the few reliable ways of reaching the high spending 18–33-year-old male, the appetite of TV networks for live sporting events is almost unlimited. At first, the main way of turning televised sport into money was through advertising. However, as technologies have developed, sport can be sold as a product in its own right through Pay-TV systems and more recently as a Pay-Per-View service. Broadcasting unleashed the earnings potential of sport and sports stars in the same way as recording techniques (gramophone, tape, CD) unleashed the earnings potential of musicians and film unleashed the earnings potential of actors. Recorded music and film turned top performers in these fields into millionaires in the early years of the century. Sportsmen and women had mostly to wait until the latter part of the twentieth century, since the additional ingredient necessary to make sport attractive is live broadcast—where the outcome is unknown. Artistic performance depends on the perfection of technique—which can then be played over and over again. Sporting performance relies on the uniqueness of each event, and the inherent uncertainty of outcome.

But sport has now become big money. Individual teams or clubs may not account for much: the average Premier League team in England has a smaller annual turnover than the average supermarket (store, not company). However, broadcasting contracts now amount to billions of dollars. In 1998, the National Football League (NFL) TV contracts were sold for $17.6 billion, or $2.2 billion per year. The broadcasting contracts for the four major European soccer leagues (England, Italy, Germany and Spain) are worth about $1 billion a year, and the rights to the 2002 and 2006 World Cups were sold for $2.5 billion. Companies that sell branded sports goods are among the largest clothing producers in the world. Adidas and Nike each have an annual world-wide turnover of around $10 billion.

The interest of politicians centres on two aspects of sport. As individuals courting public opinion, politicians want to be associated with those activities that interest their constituencies. Hence, every US politician has to be seen to be watching the Superbowl or the World Series, and almost every world leader wants to be at the World Cup Final. Almost since the beginning of sports, politicians have tried to free-ride on popular admiration of sporting heroes, fêting them at public functions and hoping that the glamour will rub off. Today, most sports heroes have a higher popularity rating than politicians. The logical conclusion has already been reached: many legislatures around the world include former top sportsmen and women, and an ex-basketball star (Bill Bradley) is a candidate for the Democratic nomination for the 2000 US Presidential election.

The second aspect of political interest is the price that citizens must now pay for sports. The billions of dollars generated by sports are paid by the punters through ticket prices, TV subscription costs, merchandising and the like. As revenues have grown, the clamour of consumer dissatisfaction has echoed in the political corridors. Paying more for what was once cheap, or worse still, free, irks the average citizen more than most of life's inconveniences. Sport is particularly prone to this kind of complaint, since nostalgia is part and parcel of sporting enthusiasm. Even if increased costs necessarily were associated with producing a higher quality product today, it seems unlikely that the sports organisations would be given the benefit of the doubt on prices charged. In fact, most fans appear to think that rising prices simply reflect the excessive salaries of various bête noirs—players, owners, managers, agents, middlemen and a whole host of hangers-on.

Politicians thus face a dilemma. On the one hand, they do not want to upset the apple cart, since doing so will be likely to diminish their ability to exploit attractive photo-opportunities. On the other hand, they want to respond to the groundswell of public opinion—that "something must be done". This dilemma plays out somewhat differently on either side of the Atlantic, largely because of different organisational traditions.

The American dilemma

In America, professional sports leagues have developed as entirely private business ventures. As businesses, they possess the unique characteristic that they require competitors in order to make a product at all. Whereas in most businesses, fewer competitors means more profit; in sports, fewer competitors usually means less profit. This extends not only to the number of competitors, but also to the quality of competitors. One attractive feature of a match for the consumer is that the outcome is unknown. Arguably, greater uncertainty leads to greater interest in the match, so that each team has an interest in ensuring that its rivals are neither greatly superior, nor greatly inferior, in terms of ability and therefore likelihood of winning.

This argument has been used repeatedly in the US to justify all kinds of concerted practices that would typically have been forbidden under competition law. For years, a policy which tied players to their clubs in baseball (the Reserve Clause) was justified as a means of maintaining competitive balance. Other labour market restrictions, such as salary caps and the reverse-order-of-finish draft, have been justified on the grounds that they promote competitive balance, despite the fact they are also likely to diminish the earnings capacity of players and enhance the profitability of the teams. In product markets, restrictions that tend to enhance profitability have also been justified on the grounds of competitive balance. In particular, the collective sale of broadcasting rights and, in the NFL, even the collective sale of merchandise rights have been justified in this way.

While these policies undoubtedly have promoted successful businesses, there are those who have questioned whether any of the benefits have been shared by consumers. However, the biggest issue has concerned not the internal distribution of income or expenditure, but the location of teams. The US is simply too large to operate a single top-class league which covers all the major population centres. While the major leagues have expanded significantly over the past thirty years (e.g. in Major League Baseball there were sixteen teams, now there are thirty) this still leaves some population centres unserved. This excess demand for major league sports teams has created a significant opportunity for teams to extract economic rent, by threatening to relocate franchises from one city to another. While actual cases of relocation are relatively rare (over the last 40 years the average has been around one relocation per year), the threat has been sufficient to persuade municipal authorities to build public stadia free of charge to the team owners, even permitting the owners to retain the income from car parking services and so on. While most citizens deplore what they see as extortion, politicians cannot resist the temptation to bring major league teams into their constituencies or pay to retain them.

In the home of the free market, why has competition not eradicated excess demand and eroded team rents? The answer seems to be that the scale of entry required to produce a successful rival league is simply too great for any private entrepreneur to be interested. Entry has occurred from time to time, particularly in American Football, but has never succeeded in posing a serious competitive threat. The only case where the entrant showed some signs of success was the American Football League in the early 1960s, which then agreed to merge with the NFL, to the benefit of both leagues. This might sound like a simple case of a cartel at work, but given the interest of the fans in a competition that involves all of the best players, the merger was hard to resist. In any event, in the 1960s there were enough unserved cities to make entry viable, but nowadays, with 30 teams in each major league, entry appears less attractive. To continue to extract their rents, all the teams need is one unserved city to act as an implicit threat to any recalcitrant municipal authority.

Not that imaginative solutions to this problem are lacking. One recent proposal from two leading American sports economists has been an antitrust break-up of the major leagues. By breaking the majors into three or four competing leagues there would be more competition on the supply side to meet the excess demand. In this model, the leagues could still co-operate to produce a champions' championship (like the play-offs at the end of the major league season), but restrictions, such as exclusive territories as maintained currently, would be diluted since such restrictions would not apply between leagues. Clever as this solution is, what politician would ever take on the power of the major leagues?

The European dilemma

In Europe, sport is different. US sports were built as businesses, whereas European sports have been constructed around higher ideals. The Victorians, who founded team sports such as soccer, rugby and cricket, constructed all-embracing hierarchies that offered everyone a place within the sport—as long as they knew their place. The essence of the structure of these sports is an interlocking hierarchy of leagues, where every season teams are promoted and relegated on the basis of merit. While these principles were first established in Great Britain over one hundred years ago, they have now been adopted across all team sports in Europe (even, for example, in the case of basketball which was imported from the US), and are now proudly proclaimed by the European Commission as "the European Model". At the top of the hierarchy stands the governing body. As sports have expanded, governing bodies have become international monoliths, claiming to regulate every aspect of their particular sport.

In general, these governing bodies claim three functions—regulatory, redistributive and impresario. Regulatory functions involve simple rule setting to ensure orderly competition. Redistributive functions aimed at promoting the sport at junior and amateur levels involve claiming the right to tax the income of the wealthier teams. Impresario functions involve promoting their own competitions (e.g. the FA Cup or the Champions' League). The power of the governing bodies has grown in line with the financial scale of sports. As long as these institutions are perceived to operate in the public interest, no conflict of interest arises. But who defines the public interest? Politicians have usually seen themselves as the final arbiters on such questions; however, in the international governing bodies they are facing serious rivals.

As in the US, the European national governments have generally avoided legislation on the organisation of team sports (although they have intervened in specific areas such as hooliganism, policing and safety at grounds). They have left it to the courts and competition authorities to arbitrate the fairness of league rules. These rules thus have been judged on their economic merits. While the courts have recognised the unique nature of the competitive process, they have tended to steer clear of commenting on the wider responsibilities of leagues. However, in the 1990s this approach started to reveal significant tensions. As the price of TV rights rocketed and consumers started to find that they had to pay for what had once been free, the competition authorities in Germany, the Netherlands and the UK challenged the rules by which TV rights were sold collectively. While each case was different in its particulars, the implication of the positions adopted was that economic competition among teams should be maintained, in spite of the need to act collectively in the interests of the game as a whole. In every case, the governing bodies believed they were being treated inappropriately, as if they were simply a price-fixing cartel rather than an institution with wider responsibilities to promote their sport as a whole. Following an unfavourable decision in 1998, the German Football League managed to persuade the German government to give it an antitrust exemption on the grounds of its special status.

However, the real battleground was not at the national level, but at the level of the European Union. In 1995, the European Court of Justice held that the rules of national and international football associations that imposed restrictions on the free movement of players within the European Union were in violation of Community law, the famous Bosman judgement. The case identified professional sport as a commercial activity, and thus within the scope of economic regulations such as competition policy. In other words, European sport is just as much a business as baseball. This led to an explosion of complaints and investigations by DGIV, the antitrust directorate of the Commission, which complained in 1998 of having to deal with more than 60 different cases on sport and competition law. In truth, the Commission was not happy. DGIV has an obligation to uphold competition, and many agreements within European sport have a distinctly anti-competitive flavour. There are cartels aplenty—indeed every league is a kind of cartel, or at least possesses the potential for anti-competitive collusive activity. There are also many instances where governing bodies can be accused of abusing a dominant position. For instance, the Union of European Football Associations (UEFA) decides not only on the regulations governing football matches, including the times at which its matches can be played, it also promotes its own competition, the Champions' League, which competes for air-time with national league competitions. There can be no doubt that there are genuine competition policy issues involved in European sport, but the enthusiasm of the Commission for interfering is tempered by a recognition that sport is not purely a business. Even the Advocate General in the Bosman case accepted the need for restrictive measures to maintain competitive balance in sporting competitions. However, those restrictions that would be acceptable could only be tested in court.

A deeper dissatisfaction has emerged through the medium of another Directorate General-XV, which is in charge of cultural issues. DGXV has argued that there is a specifically European model of sport—in other words, one that is not American. This model is jeopardised if sport is treated as a purely commercial operation. Under the rule of the market, the strong survive (i.e. those with the most popular product) and the weak go to the wall. However, if sporting clubs with long traditions are lost, then European culture will suffer. Worse still, European sports leagues may come to resemble the US Majors—after all, they are the products of a more or less free market.

The European Commission has recently signalled its desire to limit its role in regulating sport through competition policy. In particular, it has emphasised that non-economic functions of sports governing bodies lie outside the Commission's competence and that measures which "ensure equality between clubs, uncertainty as to results, and the integrity and proper functioning of competitions" are not covered by Treaty competition rules. However, there are bolder steps afoot. It has been suggested that the Amsterdam Treaty could be amended to include an explicit recognition of the special status of sport. Some go as far as to argue for a complete antitrust exemption. Pressure is building for a political solution, and it is widely expected that new proposals will be put forward during the French Presidency of the Commission in the second half of 2000. However, an antitrust exemption only makes sense if the ownership structure of the industry is deemed acceptable. The Commission is effectively relying on the governing bodies to limit commercialism in sport. In the UK, the Competition Commission went further and vetoed the ownership of a football club (Manchester United) by a broadcaster (Sky). Without such intervention, it is not clear how the governing bodies can ultimately prevent ownership falling into the hands of commercial interests who value the rights most. At its most stark, what would happen if a broadcaster set up an independent soccer league by hiring the two hundred best players in the world? As TV audiences become more valuable than the live gate, the day when a breakaway of this kind would look profitable is fast approaching.

A political future

Politicians in both the US and Europe in a mess. In the US, sports have developed on a purely commercial footing. The authorities have then granted significant exemptions from antitrust oversight, while allowing individual franchises to hold local communities to ransom by threatening relocation. In Europe, sports developed as social institutions with only a limited economic dimension, until the 1990s, when the economic potential was recognised by business interests in broadcasting and merchandising. Politicians saw no need to intervene in the past, but are now facing up to developments which do not please their constituents, but have not violated any specific rules or regulations.

The next stage in this process is likely to be transatlantic competition. As significant exporters, the sports industries of both the US and Europe are in competition with each other. Both compete in each other's markets, and both are competing to attract the interest of the vast, untapped Asian markets. All the major sports have carried marketing exercises in China and other far Eastern states. Soccer has an established popularity but basketball, in particular, is competing for attention. The potential for US/EU trade friction is obvious. Antitrust exemptions granted to sports on both sides of the Atlantic could be seen as anti-competitive abuses, aimed at obtaining strategic international advantages. Furthermore, since sports constitute a significant element of national identity, the potential for these disputes to become politicised is significant. Soccer v. basketball at the World Trade Organization (WTO) would be a compelling, if none too pretty, match.

Note

1. The main exception to this was the extraordinary Supreme Court judgement of 1922 that held baseball was exempt from competition law (the Sherman Act). The judgement hinged on the peculiar assertion that there was no inter-state commerce involved in baseball and hence the Federal law did not apply. Few jurists have supported this conclusion since, but the Supreme Court has refused to overturn the ruling, arguing that this issue would be better dealt with through legislation. Congress, however, has declined to legislate.

3

Antitrust and Inefficient Joint Ventures: Why Sports Leagues Should Look More Like McDonald's and Less Like the United Nations

Stephen F. Ross[a] and Stefan Szymanski[b]

[a] *Professor of Law, University of Illinois, B.A., J.D., University of California (Berkeley)*
[b] *Professor of Economics, Tanaka Business School, Imperial College (London), B.A., University of Oxford, M.Sc., Ph.D., University of London*

Abstract

Antitrust law generally favors joint ventures that allow separate firms to integrate economic functions while continuing to compete as independent entities. In evaluating the risks to competition that joint ventures could pose, insufficient attention has been paid to the risk that joint ventures with market power may be structured so that the parties, acting in their independent self-interest, will prevent the venture from providing innovative goods and services responsive to consumer demand. In these cases, it may be better if a single firm provided services rather than having them provided jointly.

We illustrate this problem by challenging the conventional wisdom that sports leagues must be organized and run by clubs participating in the sporting competition. The fastest-growing competition in the United States is organized by NASCAR, a distinct business entity that is not controlled by the drivers who participate in stock car races. We suggest that the club-run sports leagues in the major North American sports impose significant costs on sports fans in a variety of markets. If,

The authors thank Lee Fennell, Clark Griffith, Herb Hovenkamp, Leo Kahane, Kit Kinports, Andy Leipold, David Meyer, Matt Mitten, Roger Noll, Jim Pfander, Gary Roberts, Richard Storrow, Charles Tabb, and Andy Zimbalist for helpful insights in developing this chapter.

instead, relevant rules were decided by an independent Board of Directors of "NFL, Inc.," "MLB, LLC," or the like, we suggest that franchise allocation, broadcast rights, effective club management, marketing and sponsorship, and labor markets would be regulated more efficiently and more responsively to consumer demand.

Our analysis blames significant transactions costs for the inability of club owners who run leagues to reach efficient, consumer-responsive results. These same transaction costs may prevent an efficient restructuring of sports leagues. Thus, we apply conventional antitrust doctrine in innovative ways to argue that courts could view the current structure as an unlawful refusal of club owners to participate in a sporting competition that they themselves cannot control, which we argue unreasonably restrain trades and unlawfully maintain monopoly power.

I.   Introduction

For some time now, antitrust law has generally looked kindly upon joint ventures—when separate firms combine to perform some kind of economic activity.[1] The law has strived mightily to distinguish joint ventures from cartels, the latter being condemned as involving agreements to restrain trade and serving no other legitimate purpose.[2] It would be difficult to find those who would not prefer a joint venture of firms that combine for limited purposes, even if they comprise most of the firms in the market, to a merger that eliminated all competition between the formerly separate firms.[3]

To be sure, courts and commentators have recognized that some joint venture agreements can have significant anticompetitive effects, and antitrust law should intervene to protect the market and consumers from such effects. The leading commentaries synthesize the cases and the literature to focus on whether a joint venture could harm competition by (1) reducing potential rivalry between the parties to the venture, (2) facilitating collusion relating to other aspects of competition between the parties, or (3) excluding or hampering rivals to the venture parties in their access to an essential product or service necessary to compete.[4] Much less attention has been paid to another important risk of joint ventures that do not face vigorous rivalry in the marketplace—that the venture is structured so that the parties, acting in their independent self-interest, will prevent the venture from providing innovative goods and services responsive to consumer demand. In such cases, consumers and society may be better served if a single firm provided certain services instead of having them provided jointly. For example, a baseball competition would be organized by Major League Baseball, Inc. rather than participating clubs; a commodities exchange would be organized by Chicago Board of Trade, LLC rather than by participating brokers; an oil field would be operated by a single company rather than jointly by mineral rights owners.

To be sure, Judge Richard Posner has sagely cautioned that "[i]t does not follow that because two firms sometimes have a cooperative relationship there are no competitive gains from forbidding them to cooperate in ways that yield no economies but simply limit competition."[5] Yet in *National Collegiate Athletic Ass'n v. Board of Regents*,[6] the Supreme Court appears (albeit in dicta) to have overlooked the significant antitrust risks from the parties' conscious decision to operate a member-run venture; instead, the Court assumed that this choice was an indispensable part of the parties' pro-competitive cooperation. Speaking for the Court, Justice John Paul Stevens declared that the marketing of contests between competing clubs or teams "would be completely ineffective if there were no rules *on which the competitors agreed* to create and define the competition to be marketed" and that agreements among rival firms were "essential if the product is to be available at all."[7]

As a matter of antitrust doctrine, the Court's precise holding was that the degree of cooperation among those who jointly organize and participate in sporting competitions is sufficiently extensive that their agreements should not be formulaically condemned as *per se* illegal.[8] Thus, the Court's embrace of the conventional wisdom that it is *essential* to permit collusion among clubs who compete both on the field/court/ice in a sporting competition and off the field/court/ice for talent and revenue was not required for the Court's holding.

It is our thesis that this conventional wisdom is wrong. Entertainment in the form of competitive sports leagues can be produced through a structure in which coordination of the particulars of the competition (playing rules, distribution of revenues, terms for competition for players' services) is provided by a separate entity that is distinct from the clubs participating in the competition. In the United States, the fastest growing sports competition exists among stock car drivers, who not only compete in individual races but whose success in races over the course of a season determines the winner of the lucrative Nextel Cup. Here, the competition organizer is not a venture of competing drivers, but rather a separate, for-profit entity, the National Association for Stock Car Auto Racing (NASCAR), controlled by the family of Bill France, who founded the competition.[9] NASCAR, and not the participating drivers, determines the rules of competition and the location of premier races.

Moreover, when the National Basketball Association (NBA) created a women's league, they did so by explicitly giving majority control of the Women's National Basketball Association (WNBA) board of directors to owners and league executives who did *not* operate clubs in the new competition.[10] Elsewhere, Australian antitrust law has recognized that leagues and clubs are not inherently one and the same, the former competing in a distinct market for "competition organizing services."[11]

Properly recognizing that the decision to form a joint venture is a conscious rejection of alternative forms of inter-firm organization, such as merger or contract, Professor Joseph Brodley has observed that firms would not need to form joint ventures if significant transactions costs did not prevent them from reaching agreement with those with whom they need to cooperate to conduct their business.[12] Thus, for example, McDonald's Corporation is vertically separate from its franchised restaurant outlets, who do business pursuant to a detailed franchise agreement.[13] Although joint ventures allow for the reduction of transactions costs without the disadvantages of mergers, the problem of serving multiple masters raises potential problems.[14]

The traditional structure of club-run leagues imposes significant costs on consumers/sports fans in a variety of markets where sports leagues operate. Consider the following:

- Why would Major League Baseball (MLB) for years deny a team to fans in the national capital area, largely because a single owner of a neighboring franchise objected?
- Why would the NBA try to limit the number of times that the Michael Jordan-led Chicago Bulls could be shown on a national superstation, when the Bulls were willing to pay the league all revenues attributable to showing the game outside of Chicago?
- In light of the recognized interdependence of sports franchises, why do leagues tolerate years of gross mismanagement by particular owners, subjecting local fans to years of unnecessary mediocrity that would never be tolerated in a competitive business environment?
- Why do North American sports leagues centralize virtually all aspects of the marketing of team merchandise (other than retail sales), when individual owners want to pursue innovative ideas to add revenue (and in contrast, the top English soccer league seems unable to offer any significant collaborative effort in merchandising)?
- Why do sports leagues subject fans to the risk or reality of strikes and lockouts, and impose competitive restraints that actually harm competitive balance, in order to lower team payroll costs? (e.g.,

fans responded with a huge attendance increase in the seven years after the lifetime "reserve clause" was abolished in baseball in 1976, because competitive balance had actually improved during that time period, but owners were not happy because salaries more than tripled![15])

The reason for these woes, in our view, is that club-run leagues forego attractive business opportunities because they are unable to overcome the significant transactions costs involved in agreeing on how to distribute the proceeds from the opportunity. Contrary to conventional wisdom, club owners need not insist on collectively controlling the sporting competition in which they participate. If, like NASCAR, relevant rules were decided by an independent Board of Directors of "NFL, Inc.," "MLB, LLC," or the like, we suggest that (a) franchises will be more likely to be located in a manner responsive to consumer demand; (b) broadcast rights will be sold in a manner to maximize overall revenues, which often means increased viewership; (c) incompetent ownership would be more likely to be replaced; (d) marketing and sponsorship opportunities would be divided between the league and local clubs based on which entity can most efficiently sell rights and products; (e) collective bargaining agreements will be easier to reach (no approval of a super-majority of owners) and more likely to be designed in a manner to enhance the consumer appeal of the sport.

Although reorganizing sports leagues from an inefficient joint venture structure to one featuring a single firm organizing a competition among participating clubs would increase efficiency, benefit fans, and increase total profitability, there are significant reasons why sports league owners may not support such a change. All of the problems identified above exist only because transactions costs prevent agreement on side payments that would make all concerned better off. Absent transactions costs, MLB would have expanded years ago into Washington, D.C., and provided a lump-sum compensation for the Baltimore Orioles; Michael Jordan's exposure to a national television audience would have been maximized with proceeds shared between his team and the NBA; incompetent owners would have been paid off to either sell their team or place club operations in skilled hands; clubs with new ideas for marketing or sponsorship revenue would pursue them with an agreed-upon share of proceeds going to the league; players, leagues, and clubs would easily agree on a scheme to maximize revenue and then share it among league stakeholders. Suppose, echoing this chapter, an investment banker were to present a league with a proposal to acquire all assets necessary to organize the competition from the clubs. Even if the offer exceeded the aggregate value of all clubs, owners may well be unable to agree on how to divide the proceeds. Indeed, news reports have concluded that the biggest obstacle to the National Hockey League (NHL) owners' consideration of a $3.5 billion offer from investment bankers for all league assets is "disagreements among owners over how much their individual franchises are worth."[16]

Antitrust law provides a remedy for these transaction cost problems. Despite a historic preference for joint ventures as a means to maintain the independence of separate firms, courts have long implicitly recognized that joint ventures may act in ways that are less efficient than a single firm. Thus, the competing pipe manufacturers found to have engaged in *per se* illegal price fixing in the landmark 1899 *Addyston Pipe* decision were allowed to merge into a single entity.[17] The Supreme Court has held that an agreement by rivals not to compete in each other's geographic markets is illegal, even though an agreement by a supplier firm that its retailers would not compete might not be.[18] Consistent with the analysis presented in this chapter, the Court also rejected the proposition that there is no difference between a joint venture's decision to bar intra-brand competition in a local area and the decision of a major national supermarket chain to only have one of its stores in the area.[19]

The logical implication of these decisions, we suggest, is that antitrust doctrine needs to look more critically at joint ventures that possess economic power to determine whether consumer welfare is being harmed by a structure that inhibits efficient business opportunities. Our principal application of this argument is that the best way to organize and market a sporting competition is to separate the entity (we call it "The League") that organizes a sporting competition, and the clubs participating in the competition, where responsibilities are assigned in well-drafted franchise agreements between The League and each club.

In light of the importance of sporting competitions to millions of sports fans, determining the proper legal response to the choices about industry structure made by participants in major North American sports leagues has independent significance. We offer this analysis as part of a larger project on the structure of sports leagues in the United States.[20] More concretely, the issues raised by this chapter also have immediate implications for non-sports industries. Currently, a variety of stock and commodity exchanges are exploring whether their control by member-brokers may lead to inefficiencies that would be avoided by placing ownership in an independent, for-profit entity.[21] The development of antitrust and intellectual property doctrines relating to technology standards may be influenced by insights that help identify when collectively determined standards may be inefficient.[22] Efficient operation of an oil field is likely to be impaired where mineral rights are vested in different owners, and public policy that facilitates the field's unitary operation by a single operator on behalf of all owners may be welfare-enhancing.[23] Where beneficial ownership of assets is divided between a life estate and a remainder interest, trust instruments may overcome transaction costs that prevent parties with conflicting interests from agreeing on an efficient utilization of the assets.[24]

This chapter critically analyzes the legal and economic implications of the prevailing choice of sports league design and suggests an alternative more likely to promote efficiency and to avoid cartel-like inefficiencies. Our central theme is that even a single-firm monopoly may be more efficient than a joint venture when bargaining costs prevent participants, keen to pursue their own self-interest at the expense of the group's profits or consumer appeal, from agreeing on efficient, welfare-enhancing strategies that even a monopolist would adopt. Part II details our concern that bargaining costs among league members lead to inefficiencies in the determination of the number and location of franchises, the sale of broadcast, marketing, and sponsorship rights, the effective oversight of club management, and the efficient allocation of players among teams. If these key decisions were instead made by an economic entity independent of the participating clubs, a more efficient organization and marketing of the competition is likely to result. Part III notes the significant legal advantages that a vertically separate league would enjoy in operating more flexibly than club-run leagues. Part IV examines obstacles to the proposed restructuring. The same transactions costs that preclude efficiencies among club-run leagues may also inhibit the member clubs' willingness to adopt a more efficient structure. Specifically, owners may well reject a profitable restructuring because of an inability to agree on how to distribute the gains. Thus, Part V argues that proper application of antitrust principles justifies the involuntary restructuring of sports leagues along the lines discussed in this chapter.

To be sure, when a joint venture faces significant inter-brand competition, it can be expected to strive mightily to overcome any transaction costs that cause it to operate inefficiently. If it fails to do so, "market retribution will be swift."[25] But we assume for purposes of this chapter that the major North American sports leagues face neither product market competition nor a viable entry threat sufficient to force them to avoid the inefficient practices we discuss herein.[26] Thus, this chapter accepts the continuing ability of leagues to exercise market power, but suggests ways to facilitate greater efficiencies within that context.[27] In short, we suggest that both profitability and the provision of services responsive to consumer demand would improve if sports leagues looked more like McDonald's and less like the United Nations.

II.   The problem with vertical integration in dominant sports league joint ventures

In this section, we adopt the approach of Australian courts[28] and think of a sports league as product created by the combination of upstream competition organizing services and downstream clubs participating in the competition. Upstream services are those which enable the competition to take place, but do not necessarily have to be provided for by the competitors themselves. Sports leagues have conventionally recognized that the function of enforcing league rules is best done by investing broad authority with regard to "integrity of the game" issues in an independent entity—the league commissioner.[29] At the same time, common sense suggests that certain functions are best fulfilled by participating clubs, including organizing the team, training the players, organizing spectator services in the form of seating and ticketing, providing refreshments and other stadium amenities, and similar activities. The focus of this chapter is the myriad activities that traditionally have not been performed by a commissioner or by individual clubs, but rather by a governing body composed of a representative from each club, with a super-majority required for major changes or initiatives.[30] These services include the determination of the number of teams admitted to the league, the determination of player contract and trading rules, stadium facility standards, the sale of broadcasting rights, the extent of revenue sharing, and the allocation of shared revenues.

The decision to have these important business decisions be determined jointly by the participating clubs—to have, in our parlance, a "club-run league"—is, in economic terms, a conscious decision to vertically integrate. That is, clubs have decided to provide their own competition organizing services, rather than allow a separate entity, like NASCAR, run the competition. Economic theory supports the argument that decisions made by a club-controlled body subject to super-majority voting requirements are unlikely to be optimal. In any partnership where profits are shared, the marginal benefit to each partner accruing through the sharing arrangement is smaller than the total benefit, and therefore no partner has the incentive to vote in ways which maximize total payoffs.[31] Efficient allocation of resources requires the services of a "residual claimant," a separate economic actor who has the incentive to make optimal decisions, pay each member of the "team" their opportunity cost, and then retain the surplus.[32]

Sports leagues' unique features make the absence of a residual claimant (i.e., an independent competition organizer) particularly problematic. In order to preserve the integrity of the competition, an actual or potential competition organizer possesses a unique disincentive to integrate forward into the operation of participating clubs—NASCAR cannot own all the participating race car teams. (As a European court noted, the integrity of the competition is impaired if even a few of the teams are owned by the same corporation.[33]) Club-run leagues will necessarily make decisions about how to organize the league that limit the extent of economic competition; these decisions may simultaneously enhance the overall quality of league play (acceptable under antitrust law) and simply increase profits (unacceptable under antitrust law).[34] Moreover, unlike a more typical vertical integration of a single upstream firm and a single downstream firm, the "backward integration" of clubs into competition organizing services cannot resolve many of the problems that economists have identified when economic functions are performed by contract rather than integration, such as double marginalization,[35] free riding,[36] opportunistic behavior,[37] and costly contracting.[38] Because vertical integration appears less likely to achieve these predicted efficiencies in the sports context, and because of the particular potential for vertical integration to cause a welfare-reducing relaxation in inter-club competition, the general Chicago School presumption that vertical integration is efficient[39] is particularly unwarranted with regard to sports leagues.

In this part, we seek to demonstrate that significant inefficiencies in the operation of club-run leagues result from the tendency of these leagues to put the interests of individual clubs above the interest of the league as a whole, and that substantial transaction costs prevent optimal results. Not only does this reduce the potential profits available to providers of sports entertainment, but because sports leagues lack effective product market competition—this results in output that is reduced and unresponsive to consumer demand compared to that which would be provided by a sports league owned by an entity separate from participating clubs.

Consider the alternative of a vertically separate entity (The League) that would organize the competition and determine which functions are best carried out at the club or league level. This new entity would then contract with separate firms (the clubs) as franchisees, granting clubs the right to participate in the competition that The League will organize. Franchise agreements would set forth conditions for termination, rules of the game, revenue streams that would be retained by the franchisees, and revenue streams that would be reallocated by The League back to franchisees (as revenue sharing or as prizes for competitive success). Thus, well-drafted franchise agreements would assign to The League those marketing activities that can most be efficiently performed centrally, while preserving incentives for club innovation in any markets where such innovation is foreseeable. Our analysis of five important sports markets concludes that, in comparison with The League, collective action problems are likely to lead club-run leagues to adopt practices that result in a smaller "pie," because of the clubs' inability to agree on how to share the proceeds of profit-enhancing initiatives. As a result, club-run monopoly leagues are likely to produce (a) fewer franchises, (b) fewer opportunities for broadcasting or web-casting of games, (c) less effective licensing of merchandise, (d) greater tolerance for inefficient front-office management, and (e) a less efficient allocation of players among teams. As a result, consumers will benefit from receiving an entertainment product delivered more efficiently and responsively to their demand, and investors should also see profits increase from these realized efficiencies.

A.   Optimal number and location of franchises

Sports leagues that do not face competition from close substitutes will artificially suppress the number of franchises in the league.[40] Club-run leagues will necessarily reduce output by even more than a profit-maximizing single-firm monopolist would, and will avoid placing franchises in locations that, while more efficient, may hurt individual club owners' interests.

The optimal number of clubs within a league typically depends on the revenue expected from creating additional clubs, the additional costs associated with additional clubs, and any lost revenue that arises because of reduced demand for games involving existing clubs.[41] An additional club is likely to increase revenue because new fans will be attracted. At the same time, costs increase due to the overhead involved in supplying an additional team to the league, and any increase in operating costs due to an increase in the number of players hired and greater competition for services of players. Revenues to existing clubs may potentially fall, either because (a) fans will substitute watching games involving the new club for those involving an existing club, (b) the total quality of the league may be diminished by the addition of a club (e.g., because talent becomes spread too thinly and the overall quality of each game declines),[42] or (c) because the number of games between popular teams is reduced by the need for these teams to also play against expansion clubs (i.e., to make room for games with the Tampa Bay Devil Rays, the New York Yankees play fewer games against the Boston Red Sox).

A league designed to maximize overall profits will increase the number of clubs, as long as the revenues from expansion outweigh increased costs plus lost revenues to existing clubs. A club-run league, however, will not expand unless a super-majority of clubs are compensated for any lost revenue, even though the league as a whole might benefit from expansion.[43] To illustrate, any expansion in the National Football League (NFL) will modestly expand television ratings, and each club's pro-rata share of broadcast revenues is likely to shrink, even if the expansion would be profitable from a league perspective. Because each club's representative votes for the amount of expansion that maximizes *its own club's* profits, there will be fewer clubs in club-run leagues.

Depending on its strategic goals, The League might continue the practice of reaping significant monopoly profits by reducing the number of clubs and demanding public subsidies for stadia, which could be recovered by The League in the form of an entry fee. Alternatively, The League might subsidize franchisees located in under-developed areas to promote the sport and deter potential entry. Still, club-run leagues are likely to under-expand to a greater degree, as part of explicit or implicit agreements to protect local markets from competition. Many suggested, for example, that MLB's reluctance to expand to the Washington, D.C., area for many years was solely due to vigorous opposition from the Baltimore Orioles.[44] Of course, if transactions costs were zero, the members of the league would be able to agree to a set of side payments that ensured efficient expansion, because the precise cost to the Orioles from expansion could be quickly ascertained and an agreed-upon lump-sum payment would remove any objections. However, because transactions costs are not zero, efficient contracting often fails to occur.[45]

In contrast, The League would have an incentive to draw up franchise agreements that preserve the flexibility to add or relocate teams when the trade-off is favorable. We would expect that, like any other franchisor, The League would determine the number and location of franchises authorized to participate in the competition. In light of the dynamic nature of demand for a sport, we predict that The League would follow the now-typical franchisor practice of granting non-perpetual franchises, with specified terms for non-renewal,[46] and flexible provisions rather than guarantees of geographic exclusivity.[47]

To illustrate, suppose that reliable market research were to demonstrate that overall baseball profits would increase if the Montreal Expos were relocated to the Washington, D.C., area and two expansion teams were added in suburban New Jersey and Connecticut:[48] that is, the sum of increased revenues from entry fees paid by new owners to the league, live gate and stadium-related revenue at these three new locations, and increased revenues from broadcasting, licensing, and merchandise, exceeds lost revenue from Montreal-based sources, marginally lost revenue from the New York and Baltimore teams in close proximity, and increased costs of operating two new teams. The League would be expected to proceed with the expansion after compensating existing clubs for losses pursuant to carefully drafted provisions of the franchise agreement. However, under current rules the rest of the clubs would not agree unless the expansion fees exceeded the reduction in their pro-rata proportion of shared revenues from 1/30 to 1/32. Moreover, the New York Mets, the New York Yankees and the Baltimore Orioles could plausibly lobby a significant minority of owners to block the expansion out of fear that future expansion or relocation might be adverse to their interests. Thus, although absent product market competition, The League will still have an incentive to reduce the number of franchises below the optimal number in order to obtain stadium subsidies.[49] We predict that it would likely increase the number from that which prevails in most club-run leagues.[50]

B.   Sale of broadcast rights

Transactions costs also inhibit club-run leagues from maximizing profits from the sale of broadcast and internet rights. Owners have passed up profitable opportunities because, unable to agree among themselves on how to divide the proceeds, a requisite super-majority cannot agree to proceed with a valuable rights sale. In the English Premier (soccer) League, for example, rights have traditionally been sold collectively. In reviewing a government challenge to an agreement to sell television rights for only sixty of the league's 380 possible games, a tribunal found that the league's limitation on television sales actually reduced revenues.[51] However, the clubs could not agree on how to share revenue gained from additional sales, whether negotiated individually or collectively.[52] Unlike English soccer, television rights to NBA games not collectively sold by the league may be sold by each club within a team's assigned territory. However, the NBA sought to prevent the then-popular Chicago Bulls, featuring superstar Michael Jordan, from carrying their games on a leading Chicago free-to-air channel (WGN) that was shown outside of Chicago as a "superstation" by cable and satellite distributors, although the trial court found no evidence of substantial injury to the ratings or the value of broadcast rights elsewhere.[53] The league could have permitted the Bulls games to be shown on WGN and taxed the Bulls for any excess profits,[54] but the owners were unable to agree on a formula for doing so. Club sales of broadcast rights involve significant externalities. Clubs do not operate in completely independent broadcast markets. All broadcast revenues are partly attributable to individual team effort and party due to the league's overall appeal. Some out-of-market sales may harm other clubs' ratings,[55] while other sales may not.[56] Competition can be distorted because of revenue disparities based not on performance but on the relative size of local media markets.[57] These issues would be internalized if all television revenues flowed to The League as the residual claimant. Because different packages of rights can be sold at different prices (enabling rights sellers to price discriminate between different buyers), The League would have little incentive to reduce output. Currently, most clubs sell local broadcast rights to two or three programmers, so the need to identify the best local broadcaster is not a task that The League's officials will find difficult (and, indeed, since the vast majority of local cable rights in the United States are currently purchased by a handful of companies,[58] there may be efficiencies in a single negotiation).[59] The result, we predict, would be increased output in terms of number of games, and a greater responsiveness of output to consumer demand.

C.   Licensing, merchandise and sponsorships

The design and licensing of professional sports merchandise—jerseys, hats, jackets, and so on—would appear to include some functions most efficiently done on a league-wide basis and others best done by individual clubs. There are obvious economies of scale in granting licenses for a particular item to one or a few manufacturers. At the same time, merchandise design and local promotion would also appear to be essential in maximizing a product's appeal. Economists suggest that decision-making in this context should be left to those who have the best information.[60] Thus, one would expect that an efficient league would divide merchandising responsibility and income, "selling" those parts of the merchandising activities that the teams understand best back to them. Yet, virtually all licensing in North America is done centrally, while soccer clubs in the English Premier League offer little cooperative licensing of merchandise.[61] Revenue sharing could address any problems with individual club promotional activities that might free-ride on league promotion efforts or distort competitive balance, assuming that clubs could agree on the appropriate sharing formula. The inability to reach agreement has led to disputes and litigation in the United States,[62] and the lack of any central licensing in England. Thus, collective action problems on both sides of the Atlantic seem to explain the unwillingness of club-run sports leagues to achieve a balance of cooperation and local promotion that The League could achieve.

D. Accountability of club executives

Profit maximization at the club level requires considerable business acumen in varied tasks. The owner must assemble a staff to effectively deal with stadium utilization issues (including either construction or rental of facilities and management and marketing of luxury suites), marketing and promotion of local live gate, local broadcast rights, and sponsorships, not to mention the organization of on-field playing talent. Because each club's success is tied to some degree to the success of fellow owners, it is critical that the league hold each owner accountable for the stewardship of her franchise. However, in a club-run league, the club owners rarely hold a fellow owner accountable for the poor stewardship of a club. Indeed, although league officials may have privately orchestrated some ownership transfers to bring in new management, we are unaware of any cases where a league has disciplined owners for mismanagement. Despite their inter-dependence, owners would rather allow their joint ventures to modestly reduce their own profits rather than allow themselves to be judged. It is clear that incentives for efficient management are significantly reduced when we consider that owners do not face vigorous competition from substitute products, and that many clubs are owned by wealthy entrepreneurs, or corporations investing in clubs to pursue strategic advantages with affiliated businesses,[63] who are not likely to be subject through a market for corporate control to a hostile take-over by investors who believe they can improve corporate management. In a true franchise relationship that would exist between The League and club franchisees, we would not expect The

League to grant a perpetual franchise, and the franchise agreement can specify standards that franchisees must achieve.[64]

E.   Competition for players

Like all for-profit organizations, professional sports leagues seek to maximize revenues and minimize costs. With regard to structuring the market for players, this requires a series of extremely complex trade-offs. Collective action problems severely impede the ability of club-run leagues to achieve an efficient structure for labor market competition.

As applied to labor markets, revenues are maximized when the market is structured to present fans with a level of absolute quality and competitive balance that will have the greatest appeal. Costs are minimized in complex negotiations with well-organized players' unions, often incorporating revenue sharing and other agreements that significantly affect labor market competition. Determining the optimal structure is quite a tricky business.[65] A league that simply uses its muscle to negotiate the lowest cost agreement with the players' union may produce a structure that results in too much competitive imbalance (driving down overall fan interest) or a league with too much parity (losing revenues otherwise available to large market or popular teams).

The most efficient way to structure a labor market would be to calibrate the appropriate economic reward for clubs that win (in the terminology of the relevant economic literature, adjusting the "prize").[66] This calibration can be complicated, for if the prize is set too high, clubs potentially may bid themselves into bankruptcy; if the prize is based on localized revenues, teams with built-in advantages (such as large market size or a traditionally large fan base) may become so strong as to reduce the overall appeal of the league. If the prize for winning is too small, clubs lack the incentive to improve the absolute or relative quality of their rosters. Handouts to poor team owners will simply make those poor team owners richer without necessarily increasing investment in success on the field. The critical insight of contest theory is that equality of outcomes will be promoted if every contestant has an equal probability of winning the prize for a given level of effort (equality of opportunity). To optimize the investment, then, requires careful selection of the prize.

Selecting the best plan, and then negotiating a deal with the players' union that minimizes costs as well as deviations from the ideal structure, is significantly distorted when the league is run by participating clubs. To determine how to structure a prize, a league needs to determine how much locally generated revenue clubs will be permitted to keep, how much to share, and how centrally generated revenue will be distributed. In a club-run league, however, each club is primarily concerned with whether a proposed prize structure will be in its own interests, not whether the structure will maximize overall fan appeal for the entire league through improved competitive balance and by increasing club incentives to improve performance within the competition. For example, wealthier clubs are likely to block sharing of locally derived revenues like ticket sales, even if they were revenue-maximizing (and, by enhancing consumer appeal, welfare-enhancing).[67] Especially because most leagues require these arrangements to be approved by a super-majority, a minority of owners could veto a proposal that demonstrably increases fan appeal.[68] Similarly, the necessary trade-offs to secure union approval may not affect clubs equally. A trade-off may minimize overall labor costs while maximizing fan appeal, yet be contrary to the interests of a significant minority of clubs. Of course, skilled league executives may be able to overcome these objections by side payments to adversely affected clubs, but this process is not costless – especially because it is never precisely clear *how much* any club is adversely affected – and thus there is a substantial likelihood of sub-optimal behavior.[69]

The dynamics of collective bargaining present further problems for club-run leagues. A successful team with a strong fan base, an inferior large-market team, and a struggling small-market team will each have different incentives in labor negotiations: the effects of minimizing labor costs, restraining a club's ability to improve quickly, and losses caused by strikes or lockouts vary widely from team to team. Often, the most difficult task for league officials is securing owners' agreement on a bargaining offer.[70] The inability of club-controlled management negotiators to present a united front often makes it easier for union leaders to assume that management will not remain firm; in other cases, the union's perception that it needs to create a sufficiently credible threat of disruption to persuade the most militant minority of the owners to reach a compromise may result in miscalculations that also lead to inefficient labor disruptions.

Club owners—most of whom come to the sports having accumulated their wealth elsewhere—appear to be keen on attaining "cost certainty" with regard to the labor market. This seems to mean that they place a high value on avoidance of the economic consequences of making good or bad front-office player personnel decisions—even if the result is reduced fan appeal.[71] Avoiding the rigors of competition allows the owner the ability to enjoy the "quiet life,"[72] and increases the franchise's value, by making the club a potentially profitable investment for a wide variety of wealthy investors who would be unlikely to profitably operate a club where profitability turned on the owners' business acumen. From either an efficiency or consumer-welfare perspective, this emphasis on cost certainty is not desirable.

In our model, The League will select a prize structure designed to create incentives for clubs to succeed in a manner that creates the level of competitive balance that maximizes fan appeal, without driving teams into bankruptcy. The League will design its revenue sharing to induce clubs collectively to make an investment in talent equal to the aggregate return, measured by a league-awarded prize and any local revenues clubs are permitted to retain.[73] The more the league-awarded prize dominates the income stream of the teams, the more balanced the outcome of the contest is likely to be. If the only reward were a prize, every contestant would have an equal incentive to win. (Thus, if all baseball revenues were shared and the World Series champion received a $40 million prize, New York teams would have no long-term advantage over clubs from Pittsburgh or Kansas City.) Although the prize thus can correct for club dependence on local revenues, with their inevitable asymmetry, this need not imply that The League should aim to achieve a perfectly balanced contest. Because fans in each franchise location are unlikely to derive an equal amount of utility for a given level of success, and because in some instances competitions featuring dynastic teams increase fan appeal, a scheme is likely to maximize revenue and welfare if certain clubs (with a larger fan base, or where fans respond to wins by significantly greater attendance) won disproportionately, while all clubs had a reasonable opportunity to be competitive.[74] This is likely to reflect some mix of local revenue and prize money.

Labor relations executives from The League will be able to agree on a collective bargain with the union to implement the most efficient and revenue-maximizing structure for labor market competition, without the additional need to ensure that the agreement makes a super-majority of clubs better off. They will be able to offer the union incentives to agree to such a structure, or to minimize any departures from this ideal competition design.[75] Relatedly, The League will present a united front that avoids costly misjudgments concerning the resolve of management as well as the need to craft a proposal acceptable to a minority of "hard line" owners. Helpfully to the union (and to fans seeking to avoid industrial disruption), in a mature well-run league that can attract competitive levels of investment,[76] The League has no particular incentive to reduce competition for player services in ways that the union is likely to oppose (e.g., because the owners demand "cost certainty," or want to shield themselves from the risk that bad personnel decisions will require increased spending because of their club's poor record in prior seasons). We note that in the one major North American league not run by clubs, NASCAR, there are serious restraints on the compensation provided by participating racing teams for drivers, crew chiefs, or other skilled personnel.[77] Although the actual effect on player salaries is uncertain and subject to collective bargaining, we predict that The League would likely recognize that competition in the marketplace is usually the best means of allocating resources (here, players) among teams.

F.   Summary of economic comparisons between club-run and vertically separate leagues

The industrial organization of a sports competition is a complex endeavor, requiring those who develop the product for sale to fans to account for many different considerations. More franchises increase national television audiences and attract new fans, while modestly diluting playing talent and reducing the number of games between highly attractive clubs. More telecasts or webcasts increase revenues from rights purchasers and sponsors, but may affect live gate or ratings from other telecasts currently under contract. Merchandise often is sold because of league rather than club popularity and can often be efficiently sold collectively, yet individual club initiatives might allow for localized opportunities that league marketers will miss. Determining an optimal level of competitive balance and devising a mechanism to efficiently allocate players among clubs to maximize consumer appeal is enormously difficult. These trade-offs are challenging enough for skilled professionals to accomplish. However, executives of club-run leagues must not only develop a business model that optimizes these trade-offs in a way that maximizes profits for the sport, they must also obtain approval from owners whose votes are cast based on their own long-term, short-term, or other strategic interests. Although in theory side payments can be made to any owners adversely affected by a model that maximizes league profits, the difficulty in agreeing on these payments can lead to inefficient rules that reduce consumer appeal as well as league-wide profits. These problems are exacerbated in cases where a super-majority of individual clubs must approve any proposal.

Our predictions about how The League might implement its authority to maximize profits and consumer appeal are primarily illustrative. What is critical is that The League, unlike the clubs acting collectively, has the incentive to determine efficiently how sporting competitions are conducted and the business of sport is run.

III.   Antitrust treatment of sports leagues: Single entities contracting with clubs versus club-run leagues

Contracts in restraint of trade violate section 1 of the Sherman Act.[78] The Supreme Court held almost a century ago, however, that the statute's broad language precluded only agreements that unreasonably restrain trade.[79] More recently, in *Board of Regents*,[80] the Court provided guidelines to determining unreasonableness in the sports context. Because of the cooperation among clubs required to organize a sporting competition, agreements among participating clubs are evaluated under the rule of reason. According to *Board of Regents*, a "hallmark antitrust violation" occurs when these agreements result in higher prices, lower output, or output unresponsive to consumer demand compared to what would "otherwise be,"[81] even where some agreements among the defendant-rivals are considered necessary for the product to exist at all.[82]

Although this reasonableness inquiry does not apply to intra-firm agreements within a single business entity,[83] courts have overwhelmingly rejected efforts by club-run leagues to be treated as single entities.[84] Indeed, one of the principal doctrinal insights to be gleaned from Part II of this chapter is that the significant economic difference in the way that a club-run league operates, compared to a league controlled by a single entity acting as "residual claimant" for profits not distributed to clubs, provides a persuasive justification for continued close scrutiny of the former.[85] While Part II demonstrated the economic advantages of organizing a sporting competition through a single business entity, The League, this part suggests that there are significant legal advantages to organizing a vertically separate business entity as an independent organizer of sporting competitions. As explained below, The League would enjoy much greater flexibility than a club-run league in (1) the sale of broadcast rights, (2) decisions relating to entry and franchise relocation, (3) the creation of balance-enhancing or otherwise efficient rules governing clubs' competition for the services of players, and (4) the implementation of regulations relating to the structure of club ownership.

A.   Sale of broadcast rights

Under the common law, the home team has the right to telecast a ball game.[86] Thus, any rights sales by a club-run league constitutes an agreement among competing clubs to jointly sell valuable rights, which is subject to rule of reason analysis under the *Board of Regents* standard. Any sale that demonstrably raises prices, reduces viewership, or renders output unresponsive to consumer demand would be unlawful.[87]

Where sports competitions are organized by The League, we envision that the clubs' common law television rights would be transferred to the League as part of the franchise agreement. The franchise agreement's provision initially granting all rights to The League would be scrutinized under the *Board of Regents* test. However, in light of the significant pro-competitive benefits to vesting control of broadcast revenues in The League, this transfer should be upheld as reasonable because it is likely to enhance viewership and the overall appeal of the sport. Allowing The League to distribute all broadcast rights avoids the significant collective action problems when clubs individually sell rights and then—to pursue legitimate goals like competitive balance—must reach agreement as to how revenue is shared. Moreover, it provides The League with a critical base of revenue that can be used to achieve the level of competitive balance designed to maximize consumer appeal, through outright redistribution or through competitive prizes.[88] Once the initial common law rights have been vested in The League, all subsequent rights sales to programmers or networks would no longer be viewed as a collective sale for purposes of the Sherman Act. Thus, absent a demonstrable anticompetitive effect in another market (e.g., if a contract with a dominant purchaser had the effect of foreclosing competition from other broadcast companies, harming competition in the broadcast market),[89] The League would be free to do as it chose.

B.   Franchise entry and relocation

The specter of antitrust liability poses perhaps the greatest concern for club-run leagues with regard to franchise entry and relocation. The collective refusal of current clubs to permit new entry or to approve a relocation opens club-run leagues to lawsuits challenging these decisions as unreasonable trade restraints among competitors.[90] As the Supreme Court noted in *Board of Regents*, horizontal restraints among competitors are generally treated with suspicion under the antitrust laws.[91] In contrast, there will be minimal antitrust scrutiny of The League's entry and relocation decisions.

Even for club-run leagues, courts are generally deferential on questions of entry,[92] and there is even less risk if, as we predict, The League will allow entry where market dynamics so indicate.[93] As a matter of legal doctrine, while the NFL's refusal to allow the Oakland Raiders to move to Los Angeles was viewed as a restraint among competitors, any decision by The League would be considered a vertical restraint and a plaintiff would have a heavy burden under the rule of reason to show that The League's interest was not the same as fans. As noted earlier, decisions by a single firm as to where to sell its product raise fewer competitive problems and warrant less antitrust scrutiny than a collective decision by rivals.[94] As a matter of substance, it is unlikely that The League would block a relocation that enhanced overall fan appeal simply because increased intra-league competition might result; at the same time, relocations that reduce fan appeal by trampling on fan loyalty (such as the Cleveland Browns' relocation to Baltimore or the Baltimore Colts' relocation to Indianapolis) would be less likely to be permitted by The League on business grounds, and The League's commissioner would not have the same antitrust worries that the NFL Commissioner now faces.

C.   Labor restraints

In most instances, labor restraints no longer present significant antitrust concerns to any league, club-run or not. The Supreme Court has held that any restraints primarily affecting the labor market that occur in an industry where there is ongoing collective bargaining between management and a union falls within a judicially created exemption to the antitrust laws.[95] However, in the context of club-run leagues, players retain the option of decertifying their union as their bargaining representative, ceasing collective bargaining, and filing an antitrust suit to challenge jointly adopted labor market rules, alleging that clubs competing among themselves for players' services were illegally restraining trade.[96] The League would face no such threat if it centrally controlled all labor relations.[97]

As with the initial grant of television rights in the franchise agreement, the provisions granting The League central control over player assignment would initially be subject to Sherman Act scrutiny. To be sure, if the result was a centralized allocation of players among teams, eliminating any competition for players' services, this decisions would raise serious risks of antitrust liability. However, for the same reason that the most brilliant planners that Lenin could assemble were unable to centrally plan an economy, we believe that a centralized labor market is unlikely to maximize fan appeal. Whereas a club-run league may not care about maximizing fan appeal if the harm is outweighed by significant savings on salaries, The League's management will not be spending any money on player salaries: the club-franchisees will be. Just as NASCAR has no reason to limit the salaries participating racing teams pay their drivers,[98] The League is likely to create rules designed to optimally allocate players among teams via a generally free labor market.[99] For these reasons, perhaps the best solution for The League would be to assure players of their fair share of the benefits from this competition through a collective bargaining agreement, thus minimizing an antitrust challenge to the initial grant of control to The League. Indeed, the ability of The League's organizers to attract capital and investment is probably enhanced by initially securing a long-term collective bargaining agreement with the union.[100] Moreover, such bargaining may well be necessary under federal labor law, to the extent that the restructuring of a league would be considered to have such a significant effect on player wages and working conditions as to constitute a mandatory subject of bargaining.[101]

D.　Policies concerning ownership

Finally, leagues have faced antitrust litigation concerning the creation or application of policies concerning ownership. For example, applying the rule of reason under section 1, courts have found the NFL's rule against corporate ownership of its clubs to unreasonably shield owners from competition from more efficiently structured entities,[102] while the NBA's rejection of a particular buyer was upheld.[103] Antitrust liability for ownership rules is more likely when a league is club-run: plaintiffs will allege that club owners are trying to hamper rival clubs by precluding more efficient ways of organization or of obtaining capital. If The League unilaterally imposed its own rules on franchisees, it would be difficult to construct a theory of competitive harm.

Any league can persuasively argue that the overall league appeal can be affected by the ownership structure of participating clubs. Club-run leagues face a disadvantage in devising optimal policies however, because it is in the interest of each owner to tacitly agree that virtually any high bidder seeking to purchase a club from an existing owner should be able to do so, even if such an owner would not be an effective steward of the sports in their local market. Alternatively, a club-run league may prefer a less-effective steward precisely because a rival bidder may increase competition in various markets in which owners compete.[104] In contrast, The League would be much more likely to prevent clubs from being operated by those whose ownership structure was inimical to the league's best interests.

In sum, an independent entity organizing a popular sporting competition is likely to enjoy significant legal advantages over traditional club-run leagues.[105] The competition is more likely to be designed to enhance consumer appeal and operated in a manner to maximize overall profits. Because The League's business decisions will either be unilateral or "vertical" agreements with independent clubs, The League will enjoy a significant legal flexibility to make decisions that would otherwise risk serious antitrust liability. The result should be greater profitability as well as greater responsiveness to consumers.

IV.   Why current owners may be unwilling to restructure even if it is efficient to do so

In a well-functioning market, no one would design a league that resulted in a sub-optimal number and location of franchises, a sub-optimal exploitation of broadcast rights, inefficient marketing of sponsorship and licensing, labor markets that are neither cost-minimizing nor efficient in allocating players among clubs, and lack of effective oversight of each club's stewardship of its valuable franchise. Absent transaction costs, of course, the assignment of rights to club owners would not affect the ultimate structure of a league: where a revenue-enhancing alternative is available, side payments can be made to assure the desired result.[106] However, where transaction costs are significant, the allocation of control rights to club owners can significantly affect the distribution of resources.[107]

Unlike most other businesses that could profitably restructure, neither actual or potential rivals, nor a market for corporate control, constrains individual club owners' pursuit of their own interests at the expense of an efficient league operation. The same transactions costs that prevent current leagues from achieving efficient results may prevent current club owners from voluntarily embracing an efficient restructuring of the league in which their club competes. Although a solid promise of cash today and the opportunity to share in the gains from an even more profitable business operation in the future provides a significant incentive for parties to overcome transactions costs, the existence of such costs means that the inability of a league to restructure does not necessarily mean that the current system is efficient.

This part explores why vertically separate leagues have not been established already if, as we claim, the idea is so efficient. Then, this part details the transactions costs that must be overcome to achieve restructuring on a voluntary basis.

A.   Why leagues haven't done this already if it is such a good idea

Each major North American professional team sports league has always been vertically integrated. We do not believe, however, that vertical integration is inherently required in order to maximize consumer appeal or efficiently operate a team sport competition. Rather, vertical integration is the result in part of the dynamic economics of fledgling sports leagues that lack market power, and in part due to historic accident.

Vertical integration was a necessity when the first club-run league—baseball's National League—was created in 1876.[108] This model emerged as a consequence of two factors. First, interest in the rapidly growing sport was being undermined by the free-for-all existing in baseball at the time, characterized by (a) barnstorming teams attracting support as long as they were winning and then collapsing when they lost, (b) team owners dissipating profits in competing to hire the best talent, and (c) opportunities for gambling that led to significant match fixing. Second, almost all the revenues associated with baseball in the late nineteenth century were generated locally by clubs, principally through sales of admission tickets.[109] The founders of the significantly named "National League of Professional Baseball Clubs" set out to create a new kind of equilibrium: a league with stable membership. The new arrangement[110] invested members with a stake in its long-term success (to combat short-run incentives for match fixing), granted exclusive territories guaranteeing a local monopoly (providing an incentive to invest in the local market), and established a reserve clause to eliminate competition for players (ensuring that the income stream from matches accrued principally to the owners). The extraordinary success of this model made it the basis for not only the national pastime, but also for the other North American team sports.

Although the founders of the National League deemed it natural to integrate governance functions with the supply of matches, this was not really necessary but rather a direct consequence of the lack of any alternative credible supplier of these services in 1876. In England, by contrast, the Football Association (FA), established in 1863, had successfully standardized rules and maintained oversight of the development of English soccer and had also developed two important forms of competition in its own right: the FA Cup, a knock-out competition including all members, and international representative football.[111] Thus, when leading English soccer clubs found the same need as American baseball teams for a fixed and reliable playing schedule and therefore created the Football League in 1888, they did not fully integrate the competition. Although in part this may have been due to the desire to continue participating in the FA Cup, the founders also believed that it would be both in their interests and in the wider interests of soccer to maintain an independent governing body at the head of the sport.[112] The English governance model has been adopted globally in soccer.[113]

Whether an organization created for other purposes exists to develop a league competition may be a historic accident, but where a sport is just developing in the relevant market, or where a new entrant is organized to challenge an established incumbent league, vertical integration can be extremely important. There is unlikely to be a credible supplier of competition-organizing services to clubs who might join such a league, and club owners may be reluctant to participate in such a risky venture without some role in controlling the fortunes of the new competition.[114] However, today's owner of the Chicago White Sox would not find, as his predecessor William Hulbert did, that there is no one willing and able to provide competition-organizing services. The explosion in revenues from broadcasting, merchandising, and sponsorships creates huge incentives for vertically separate firms to perform these services. Unlike those seeking to organize Major League Soccer,[115] and like NASCAR's owners, competition organizers would likely find many interested in participating in the dominant professional baseball competition in the United States, even if they lacked the ability to control the league. Once a league becomes sufficiently dominant so that vertical integration is no longer necessary to attract potential franchisees, it may well retain its traditional structure simply because the potential gains from an efficient restructuring are not large enough to justify the trouble. It is only recently that the revenues (primarily from broadcasting) have exploded to such a degree that the sort of restructuring proposed in this chapter is worth the significant transaction costs involved in bringing it about.

Recent developments suggest a growing industry recognition of the benefits of vertical separation. Preventing owners from engaging in self-aggrandizing opportunistic behavior is seen as a serious problem: according to one sports executive, "if [NFL Commissioner] Paul Tagliabue could convert the NFL to a single entity, he'd do it tomorrow."[116] Although not formally as separated as The League we suggest in this chapter, the WNBA is run by a Board of Directors with each club participating pursuant to an operating agreement that designates revenues and costs for which the club is responsible. While four of the nine directors come from the group of NBA owners who operate WNBA teams, the other five include four owners without WNBA franchises and the NBA Commissioner. The Board of WNBA, LLC is ultimately responsible to the WNBA's sole owner, a corporation named NBA Development, which in turn is owned by the 29 NBA owners. Thus, while some of the problems that plague club-run leagues could rear their head, the benefits of negotiating broadcast rights and sponsorship deals without the fear that clubs may undercut the rights sold by the league is a major advantage, according to the WNBA's former chief executive.[117] As a result, while some club-run league constitutions have express terms to make clear the reality that club owners vote the interests of their own club rather than the league as a whole,[118] a WNBA owner serving on the WNBA board who put his club's interests ahead of the league's would arguably breach his fiduciary duty.

Just recently, two investment banking houses presented the NHL with an offer to acquire the entire league.[119] Although the initial proposal, unlike the proposal for The League contained in this chapter, would retain the vertical integration of competition organizing and club participation by having a single entity own both the league and all clubs, its structure is designed to take advantages of the efficiencies here.

Finally, the strongest demonstration of the viability of vertical separation in sports leagues is the tremendous success and growth of NASCAR. Historically, this centrally run giant was developed out of a chaotic industry where independent tracks set their own rules for the competition.[120] Of course, if today NASCAR were sold to a consortium of competing drivers, who agreed to henceforth operate the circuit by super-majority vote, and to limit entry to current Nextel Cup drivers and any qualified driver who bought the rights to participate, there would be a public uproar as well as an antitrust challenge, and properly so.

B. Transaction costs inhibit efficient restructuring

Corporate finance experts can offer myriad ways to implement the creation of The League as a separate business entity and the assignment of rights necessary for The League to organize a sports competition efficiently. To create a separate business entity through a voluntary transaction will require organizers to overcome substantial transaction costs. Whether the organizers are current league owners or officials[121] or outside investors,[122] securing consent of a requisite super-majority of league owners to change the league constitution would involve the difficult task of distributing the proceeds among the current owners.

This is the very problem that causes current leagues to operate inefficiently. Owners will forego potential pareto-optimal opportunities because of an inability to agree on how to divide the spoils. To illustrate, suppose that the current aggregate value of all MLB franchises were $9 billion,[123] and that a vertical separation would result in efficiencies sufficient to increase the combined value of MLB and club assets to $10 billion. The current 30 owners would then realize an average profit (realized either in cash or through increased valuation of preferred stock in The League) of $33.3 million. Even George Steinbrenner would likely approve the concept if, say, $400 million of the $1 billion increase went to the New York Yankees. Of course, the owner of the Kansas City Royals would initially insist on a pro-rata distribution, which would never be accepted. Given the potential revenue growth from an efficient restructuring, perhaps a skilled investment banking firm would be able to overcome these obstacles and secure agreement to proceed with a lucrative initial public offering. Yet, on the other hand, if owners cannot agree on how to distribute the small amounts available from increased sale of rights to out-of-market broadcasts,[124] one cannot be too sanguine about the likelihood of voluntary restructuring.

Another reason why owners may choose not to voluntarily restructure is ego. Most owners have already succeeded in other businesses and are personally wealthy. Although they would likely retain the perquisites of ownership of a club/franchisee in a competition organized by The League (owners' box, accepting the presentation of the champions' trophy), they would have to give up the power to make the rules and instead would have to accept directives from others. Even if this chapter is correct that restructuring leads to substantial efficiencies, ($1 billion in our illustration for an average payout of $33 million), those efficiencies may be insufficient when their value is divided among the owners.

Ultimately, the most important reason why club owners may choose not to surrender control of their club-run leagues to a more efficient centralized operation is that they do not have to.[125] Sports leagues do not face significant competition from actual or potential product market rivals.[126] As a result, market retribution will not be swift[127] should owners fail to achieve efficient results.[128] Even club-run leagues might face pressure for greater efficiency, if a market for corporate control existed so that outsiders who believe that the business can be operated more profitably can acquire the firm's assets.[129] But sports clubs are not publicly traded in North America, and even where a club is a subsidiary of a publicly traded corporation, the parent often has sufficient strategic interests that efficient operation of the league is not a principal concern.[130] Thus, a series of hostile takeovers of clubs is not a feasible option.[131]

Part II of this chapter lays out the argument why club-run leagues have incentives to perform inefficiently in the market vis-a-vis vertically separate leagues. This part has suggested that, while there may be growing industry recognition of the problems with club-run leagues, the transactions costs involved in dividing up the proceeds of a restructuring in a manner satisfactory to a super-majority of club owners may be too great to permit this development. If that is the case, legal intervention to effectuate an involuntary restructuring may be required. This option is considered below.

V. Involuntary restructuring: Mandatory divestiture under antitrust law

Government intervention is welfare enhancing if it can reliably require an industry restructuring to eliminate collective action problems that cause inefficient and exploitive output reductions not likely to be subject to market correction. There are several ways that this welfare-enhancing restructuring could be required. Congress could mandate restructuring through legislation enacted pursuant to its power to regulate interstate commerce.[132] Perhaps more controversially, Congress could use its eminent domain power to acquire from current club owners the property rights necessary to operate The League.[133] This part focuses on another alternative. By applying conventional antitrust principles in the unique context of sports, we justify structural antitrust relief mandating the divestiture by clubs of the competition-organizing function of a league.[134]

As noted above, *Board of Regents* holds that club owners may not enter into agreements that result in higher prices, lower output, or output unresponsive to consumer demand compared to what would "otherwise be."[135] In this regard, one of Judge Richard Posner's most profound antitrust insights is particularly relevant: "[i]t does not follow that because two firms sometimes have a cooperative relationship there are no competitive gains from forbidding them to cooperate in ways that yield no economies but simply limit competition."[136]

We suggest that the relevant anticompetitive agreement is the agreement among competing clubs to arrogate to themselves control of the organization of their sport's dominant competition. The economic analysis set forth in this chapter demonstrates that compared to what would "otherwise be" – a sporting competition organized by a separate entity – the vertical integration between competition-organizing and competition-participating raises prices, lowers output, and renders output unresponsive to consumer demand.

As noted above, club-run leagues distort competition in a number of relevant markets.[137] They are likely to set the number of teams participating in the competition at a sub-optimal level, fail to fully exploit the sale of broadcast or internet rights, and inefficiently market licensed merchandise, all of which result in reduced output that is unresponsive to demand. Compared to an entity solely concerned about the interests of the league as a whole, club-run leagues are more likely to allocate labor resources inefficiently,[138] and tolerate operational mismanagement of clubs,[139] which also results in output being unresponsive to consumer demand. As in the *Board of Regents* case, these are all hallmarks of antitrust violations.[140] The central thesis of an excellent book on the success of the NFL is that its growth was the result of Commissioner Pete Rozelle's heroic efforts to persuade owners to engage in "League Think"—that is, to put the interests of the league over the interests of their clubs.[141] Implicit in this analysis is the conclusion that, absent Rozelle's vision and talent, the NFL would not efficiently act to maximize league value or consumer appeal. If these leagues feared the swift retribution of the marketplace for these errors, they would not tolerate these inefficiencies.[142]

Of course, the claims made in this chapter are subject to proof in a court of law. Evidence that the efficiency gains we discuss are insubstantial, or that club-run leagues possess efficient properties that our analysis has failed to account for, would obviously favor a judgment for the defendant owners; evidence that the gains are substantial and that transactions costs explain the owners' unwillingness to voluntarily restructure would obviously favor the plaintiffs.

In a related antitrust area—the analysis of territorial market division arrangements—the Supreme Court has carefully and expressly differentiated between schemes imposed by a vertically separate manufacturer and those agreed to by downstream competitors. This distinction supports mandatory vertical separation in the sports industry. The Court recognizes that vertical restraints insulating a reseller from intra-brand competition have complex effects, simultaneously shielding the firm from potentially beneficial rivalry from sellers of the same product, while creating desirable incentives for promotion, quality assurance, or other investment that might otherwise be subject to free riding by rivals, potentially enhancing the brand's consumer appeal and thus promoting inter-brand competition.[143] When imposed by an upstream seller in the independent exercise of its own business judgment, the Court concluded that such a seller was sufficiently likely to balance intra-brand harm and inter-brand benefit to reach a socially optimal result that case-by-case antitrust scrutiny under the rule of reason was appropriate.[144] In contrast, an intra-brand restraint that is the result of horizontal agreement among downstream rivals carries too much risk that the restraint is intended to benefit the rivals' interest in reduced competition, and thus remains *per se* illegal.[145] The Court likewise condemned a venture that jointly promoted a single trademark and divided markets for the manufacture and sale of the trademarked product by separate firms, basing its decision on the critical fact that the so-called "principal" (the corporate entity that owned the national trademark) was controlled by the so-called "agents" (the individual manufacturing firms).[146] These precedents demonstrate why antitrust is so hostile to cartel behavior, in contrast to that of a fully integrated firm. For the latter, the whole is greater than the sum of the parts. As to the former, activity will only occur if supported by a majority of the parts. These precedents therefore support the conclusion that the agreement to organize a vertically integrated club-run league constitutes an unreasonable restraint of trade in violation of Section 1.

Section 2's condemnation of monopolization provides an additional basis for a judicially ordered restructuring of sports leagues. Leading precedents establish that competitors may not control a key upstream input where such control allows the maintenance of a monopoly and does not reflect efficiencies. Although to date the courts have not required that the upstream input (in this case competition-organizing services) be provided by an independent firm, we believe that such a remedy is justified here by the unique features of sports leagues. Two of the leading cases help illustrate this point.

In *United States v. Terminal Railroad Ass'n*,[147] the Court held that the Sherman Act barred a consortium of rival railroads from acquiring the only three means by which railroads could cross the Mississippi River at St. Louis and using crossing charges to disadvantage non-owner rivals. Because of the significant efficiencies in joint operation of the three previously independent crossing points, the Court declined to order a horizontal divestiture. Instead, the Court required open access to the venture.[148] Similarly, in *Associated Press v. United States*,[149] the Court invalidated a by-law provision that allowed AP members to veto new members within their territories. The veto was effective even if the additional members might provide stories of value to the rest of the membership. This by-law demonstrated the inefficient divergence of the interests of AP members and the entity as a whole.[150] Here, the remedy permitted presumably independent non-rivals to determine membership decisions.[151]

Where a monopoly bottleneck exists, the ability of the bottlenecked function to be captured by an open-access cooperative among buyers may, in some cases, actually have the potential to eliminate the distortion caused by monopoly profits. For example, in *Terminal Railroad*, if the company that operated the river bridges had been owned by all railroads, it would have no incentive to charge monopoly prices to its own members.[152] Thus, vertical divestiture would actually have increased the potential for monopoly pricing. A requirement that an independent firm contracts to purchase news stories from papers around the country and resell them elsewhere could have a similar effect. Moreover, complete vertical integration may be procompetitive in markets characterized by natural monopoly at several levels. Economic theory suggests that in this case of "serial monopoly," prices may be raised and welfare reduced as both monopolists seek to take monopoly profits.[153] Because it is often efficient to allow a vertical integration between the two serial monopolists, which will result in a single monopoly price,[154] open access regimes may not be welfare enhancing.[155]

Sports leagues, however, are different. Most significantly, because there is an optimal number of clubs in a top-tier league, leagues cannot really be subject to the open access regime contemplated by *Terminal Railroad*.[156] Nor can leagues avoid the serial monopoly problem discussed above simply by acquiring and operating all of the teams. Separately owned clubs form an important aspect of sport's consumer appeal.[157] Because of sports leagues' interdependence, a model where "downstream firms" (here the clubs) jointly operate the "upstream firm" (here the league), and then compete among themselves, will not work in live gate, stadium, and some television and licensing markets.[158] Hence, if we accept the assumption that each sport will continue to feature a single dominant competition,[159] the monopoly power in competition organizing will not be dissipated. The inefficient and exploitive effects of club-run monopolies can, however, be mitigated. In light of the demonstrated benefits of vertical separation, this novel remedy is justified in the specialized context of sports leagues.[160]

Conclusion

An inherent conflict exists when clubs participating in a sports league competition control the way in which the competition is organized. This conflict distorts the manner in which the league determines the number and location of franchises, how broadcast rights are sold, how merchandise, licensing, and sponsorships are marketed, how club executives are supervised, and how player talent is distributed among clubs. In each of these instances, any particular decision may make some clubs better off and some worse off, and transaction costs often prevent the most efficient result from being selected. Both profits and consumer welfare would increase if these decisions were made instead by a competition organizer independent of the clubs. Although owners and outside investors could capitalize the increased profitability of a vertically separate league by voluntarily restructuring professional sports, the same transactions cost problem could prevent current owners from agreeing on how to divide the proceeds from such a restructuring, resulting in an inefficient *status quo*. To the extent that league owners refuse to voluntarily restructure the industry, we believe that a plaintiff could establish in antitrust litigation that the continuing agreement by clubs to run their own competition constitutes both an illegal restraint of trade and monopolization in violation of the Sherman Act.

Although the operation of a sporting competition raises some unique issues, the organization of a sports league also provides an accessible illustration of a more common issue with regard to joint ventures. Cooperation among competing firms often yields substantial benefits. At the same time, joint ventures do not face the discipline of the market – either because they enjoy market power or due to the absence of an effective market for corporate control – there is a substantial risk that transactions costs will result in the operation of jointly held assets in an inefficient manner as those assets are controlled by member firms whose individual interests may differ from those of the collective whole. This chapter sets forth an argument about how the Sherman Act – our nation's "magna carta of free enterprise"[161] – can be invoked in a tailored fashion to permit the economy to reap the benefits of collective action while mitigating the effects of market power.

Notes

1. See Robert Pitofsky, A Framework for Antitrust Analysis of Joint Ventures, 74 *Geo. L.J.* 1605, 1606–7 (1986); Joseph F. Brodley, Joint Ventures and Antitrust Policy, 95 *Harv. L. Rev.* 1521, 1525 (1982).
2. See, e.g., Robert Pitofsky et al., *Trade Regulation: Cases and Materials* 378 (5th ed. 2003) ("[A] joint venture carries the positive connotation of cooperation among firms, usually accompanied by some actual integration of managerial or production resources, to achieve some useful business objective more efficiently than either (or any) could alone. It is thus distinguished from a cartel or price-fixing arrangement, for example.").
3. SCFC ILC, Inc. v. Visa USA, Inc., 36 F.3d 958, 963 (10th Cir. 1994).
4. See Pitofsky, *supra* note 1, at 1608; Brodley, *supra* note 1, at 1530–32. See also Herbert Hovenkamp, Exclusive Joint Ventures and Antitrust Policy, 1995 *Colum. Bus. L. Rev.* 1, 4.
5. Gen. Leaseways, Inc. v. Nat'l Truck Leasing Ass'n, 744 F.2d 588, 594 (7th Cir. 1984).
6. 468 U.S. 85 (1984).
7. *Id.* at 101 (emphasis added) (quoting Robert H. Bork, The Antitrust Paradox 278 (1978)). A sports league is a leading example of a business activity that "can only be carried out jointly." 468 U.S. at 101.
8. *Id.* at 103. Because of the procompetitive potential of the challenged joint selling arrangement as well as the plaintiffs' concession that the great majority of the NCAA's rules enhanced competition, a judgment about the competitive significance of the restraint required a fuller consideration of the defendants' justifications.
9. See Koszela v. Nat'l Ass'n of Stock Car Auto Racing, 646 F.2d 749, 750 (2d Cir. 1981) (stating that anyone wishing to participate in stock car racing must "join" NASCAR; however, this does not give right to participate in control of organization but merely to participate in its sanctioned events); Michael A. Cokley, In the Fast Lane to Big Bucks: The Growth of NASCAR, 8 *Sports Law. J.* 67, 70–71 (2001).
10. See Larry Lebowitz, Leagues are Forming as "Single Entities" Where Decision and Profits are Shared by All Owners, *Ft. Lauderdale Sun-Sentinel*, Apr. 20, 1997, at 1F.
11. In News Ltd. v. Australian Rugby League, 139 A.L.R. 193, 338 (Full Fed. Ct. 1996), the court recognized a market for "competition organizing services" where two rival leagues sold these services and clubs participating in competitions were buyers. See also S. Sydney Dist. Rugby League Football Club Ltd. v. News Ltd., 200 A.L.R. 157 (H.C. 2003). A merged league excluded the plaintiff from the receipt of competition organizing services, but exclusion did not meet specific standards for *per se* illegality under the Australian Trade Practices Act.

    Indeed, the evolution of a national rugby league competition in Australia demonstrates the distinct functions of clubs and leagues. The traditional competition was organized by the Australian Rugby League, an entity controlled by a board of directors representing clubs participating at the top level of competition as well as a variety of other clubs and individuals involved in the sport; the courts determined that clubs competed among themselves for the right to participate in the annual top-tier competition. *News Ltd.*, 139 A.L.R. at 318 ("the clubs were not members of the League"); *Id.* at 338–42 (detailing competition for competition organizing services).

12. Brodley, *supra* note 1, at 1527.
13. See, e.g., Marane, Inc. v. McDonald's Corp., 755 F.2d 106 (7th Cir. 1985). In rejecting antitrust and tort claims by former franchisee, court describes initial grant of franchise by defendant to plaintiff and its termination under terms of the agreement.
14. Brodley, *supra* note 1, at 1528–29.
15. Stephen F. Ross, Monopoly Sports Leagues, 73 *Minn. L. Rev.* 643, 676 (1989).
16. See, e.g., Stefan Fatsis and Dennis K. Berman, Puck Plan: NHL Explores Sale to Cure a Troubled Sport, *Wall St. J.*, Mar. 4, 2005, at B1.
17. See John Shepard Wiley Jr., Antitrust and Core Theory, 54 *U. Chi. L. Rev.* 556, 564 (1987) (citing the discussion by George Bittlingmayer, Price-Fixing and the *Addyston Pipe* Case, 5 *Res. L. & Econ.* 57, 90 (1983), of United States v. Addyston Pipe & Steel Co., 85 F. 271 (6th Cir. 1898), *aff'd*, 175 U.S. 211 (1899), and its aftermath, including the defendants' merger into the United States Cast Iron and Foundry Company).
18. United States v. Gen. Motors Corp., 384 U.S. 127, 140 (1965) (distinguishing joint action by rival dealers to exclude rivals from action General Motors might take unilaterally pursuant to franchise agreements). This distinction was reaffirmed in Cont'l T.V., Inc. v. GTE Sylvania, Inc., 433 U.S. 36, 59 n.28 (1977).
19. See United States v. Topco Assocs., Inc., 405 U.S. 596 (1972) and *id.*, 405 U.S. at 623 n.11 (Burger, C.J., dissenting). One of us has previously detailed an application of our theory that single firms are likely to make more efficient decisions about where to permit intra-brand competition, in the context of the *Topco* case. See STEPHEN F. ROSS, *Principles of Antitrust Law* 152 (1993).
20. We are currently researching a book-length comparative review of the structure of a variety of sports around the world and the appropriate governmental/regulatory response to problems raised by these structures. The general topic is one we have tackled before. See, e.g., Stefan Szymanski, The Economic Design of Sporting Contests, 56 *J. Econ. Lit.* 1137 (2003); Stephen F. Ross and Stefan Szymanski, Open Competition in League Sports, 2002 *Wis. L. Rev.* 625.
21. See, e.g., Roberta S. Karmel, Turning Seats Into Shares: Causes and Implications of Demutualization of Stock and Futures Exchanges, 53 *Hastings L.J.* 367 (2002).
22. See, e.g., Mark A. Lemley, Antitrust and the Internet Standardization Problem, 28 *Conn. L. Rev.* 1041 (1996).
23. For a helpful discussion, see Gary D. Libecap, Contracting for Property Rights, in *Property Rights: Cooperation, Conflict, and Law* 156–65 (Terry L. Anderson and Fred S. McChesney eds., 2003).
24. Compare Brokaw v. Fairchild, 237 N.Y.S. 6 (N.Y. Sup. Ct. 1929) (inflexible law of waste governing relationship between life tenant and remaindermen prevented efficient use of real property), *aff'd*, 177 N.E. 186, 1931 N.Y. LEXIS 1272 (1931), with Baker v. Weedon, 262 So.2d 641 (Miss. 1972) (court employs its equity powers in the best interests of both the life tenant and the remaindermen). Recent changes in the Uniform Principle and Income

Act recognize the need to place greater discretion in the hands of a single entity capable of efficiently utilizing assets to craft a portfolio that maximizes total return on investment. See JESSE H. DUKEMINIER ET AL., *Wills, Trusts and Estates* 828 (7th ed. 2005).

25. Valley Liquors, Inc. v. Renfield Imps., Ltd., 678 F.2d 742, 745 (7th Cir. 1982).
26. At the same time, we assume that each league's insulation from rivalry is not subject to imminent threat from antitrust intervention. One of us has previously suggested that the government intervenes to require a divestiture of monopoly sports leagues into competing entities. Ross, *supra* note 15, 733–53. We have also discussed ways that league power could be restrained through intervention to facilitate new club entry. Ross and Szymanski, *supra* note 20, 639.

    The focus of this chapter is on promoting efficiency and not reducing the market power of dominant sports leagues. Economic reasoning suggests that these other proposals would be likely to have a greater effect in enhancing overall welfare and in reducing wealth transfers from consumers to sports fans. There are costs and risks of any reform proposal, and we believe even a "second-best" alternative that significantly improves the efficiency of an important industry merits serious consideration.
27. Although more than one vertically separated leagues are possible, we assume that the ability of any dominant sports league to exercise market power makes it unlikely that multiple leagues will develop absent antitrust intervention.
28. See *supra* note 11.
29. See, e.g., Milwaukee Am. Ass'n v. Landis, 49 F.2d 298, 299 (N.D. Ill. 1931). With regard to enforcing the code, the parties' clear intent was "to endow the commissioner with all the attributes of a benevolent but absolute despot and all the disciplinary powers of the proverbial *pater familias.*" *Id.* at 299.
30. See, e.g., Chicago Nat'l League Ball Club v. Vincent, No. 92 C 4398 (N.D. Ill. 1992), excerpted in PAUL C. WEILER and GARY R. ROBERTS, *Sports and the Law* 28–32 (3rd ed. 2004) (holding Commissioner's broad power did not extend to alignment of clubs within league divisions, based on specific provisions of the league Constitution limiting power in that manner), *decision withdrawn and vacated at request of the court,* 1992 U.S. Dist. LEXIS 11033 (July 23, 1992) (following settlement by parties).
31. See, e.g., Bengt Holmstrom, Moral Hazard in Teams, 13 *Bell J. Econ.* 324 (1982); Armen Alchian and Harold Demsetz, Production, Information Costs and Economic Organization, 62 *Am. Econ. Rev.* 777 (1972).
32. Holmstrom, *supra* note 31, at 327 (Theorem 2).
33. AEK Athens and Slavia Prague v. Union des Associations Europeenes de Football, CAS 98/200 (August 20, 1999), reprinted in *XXV Yearbook of Commercial Arbitration* 393, 395–97 (2000).
34. Antitrust decisions generally treat restraints imposed by pressure from downstream firms more harshly. See, e.g., Gen. Motors Corp., 384 U.S. 127 (agreement imposed on GM by a conspiracy of dealers held illegal *per se*); Cont'l T.V., Inc. v. G.T.E. Sylvania, Inc., 694 F.2d 1132, 1137 (9th Cir. 1982) (under rule of reason, significant that vertical restraint imposed by manufacturer and not at the request of other dealers). However, intra-league

sports restraints are often tolerated because of the clubs' unique inter-dependence. See, e.g., Bd. of Regents, 468 U.S. at 103 (most agreements enhance competition); *id.* at 117 (acknowledging that rules that promote competitive balance can enhance public interest and thus be procompeti-tive); United States v. Nat'l Football League, 116 F.Supp. 319 (E.D. Pa. 1953) (interdependence of strong and weak football teams justified protections to preserve viability of weak teams).

Tribunals around the world that have invalidated sports league restraints have acknowledged that some restraints were necessary but the challenged one was overly restrictive. See, e.g., Los Angeles Mem'l Coliseum Comm'n v. Nat'l Football League, 791 F.2d 1356, 1369 (9th Cir. 1986) (league over-sight of franchise relocation permissible but rejection of specific proposed relocation found unreasonable); Mackey v. Nat'l Football League, 543 F.2d 606 (8th Cir. 1976) (restraints on competition for players to promote com-petitive balance permissible but existing plan overbroad); *Nat'l Football League*, 116 F. Supp. 319 (restraints on competition in sale of broadcast rights permissible to protect live gate but not to facilitate higher returns in rights sales); Union Royale Belge des Sociétes de Football Association v. Bosman, [1996] 1 C.M.L.R. 645 (E.C.J.) (restraint on movement of players throughout Europe could be subject to reasonable restraints to promote competitive balance and to recoup investment in players but mandatory payment of transfer fee unreasonable); Buckley v. Tutty, 125 C.L.R. 353 (H.C. 1971) (some restraints on competition for player services in Aus-tralian rugby league permissible but complete ban unreasonable); Eastham v. Newcastle United Football Club, [1963] 3 All E.R. 139 (Ch.) (same re English soccer).

35. Double marginalization occurs in some cases where both firms have market power, because the downstream firm's effort to achieve its own monopoly price will result in the price to consumers being higher than is optimal for profit maximizing by both parties. JEAN TIROLE, *The Theory of Industrial Organization* 174–76 (1988). For example, where a league adopts a revenue sharing plan that requires one-third of revenues from live gate be shared with the league as a whole, the result will be higher ticket prices for fans than if (a) all ticket revenues went to the league or (b) no revenue was shared.

36. Free-riding problems occur when firms under-invest in promoting a prod-uct because of a desire to free ride on promotional efforts of others. *Id.* at 185. For example, teams could spend less on payroll, or avoid costly public relations activities like community outreach, confident that the gen-eral appeal of their club is significantly affected by the general goodwill generated by the efforts of league officials and other clubs.

37. In some contexts, a club-run league may be thought to be less likely to engage in opportunistic behavior vis-a-vis the downstream clubs that con-trol it. However, where opportunistic behavior can be directed at a minority of clubs, the majority could well vote to engage in such behavior. Cer-tainly, individual clubs have ample incentive to engage in such behavior vis-a-vis their league "partners" in a club-run league. A franchise agreement between vertically separate competition organizers and club/franchisees can be designed to eliminate foreseeable opportunistic behavior, so it is

difficult to conclude that club-run leagues offer significant advantages in this regard.

38. Any significant policy requires league officials to navigate a costly minefield to get the requisite approval of a majority or super-majority of owners interested primarily in their own club's profitability. NASCAR can easily negotiate a new enhanced broadcast rights deal featuring greater national telecasting of its races; and opportunity for MLB to sign a lucrative national rights contract reducing the number of games available for sale by each club would require complex negotiations among owners.

39. See, e.g., ROBERT H. BORK, *Antitrust Paradox* 225–31 (1978). This approach and the competing theories discussed in text are outlined in JEAN TIROLE, *supra* note 35, 90–106.

40. See Roger G. Noll and Andrew Zimbalist, Build the Stadium-Create the Jobs!, in *Sports, Jobs, and Taxes* 1–54 (Roger G. Noll and Andrew Zimbalist eds., 1997); Ross, *supra* note 15, at 656.

41. This chapter assumes the existence of a monopoly league facing no serious threat of entry, whose teams cover the geographic breadth of the relevant market. Strategic considerations may cause a league to expand to forestall entry. Operational considerations may cause a league to decline to expand to new geographic areas if travel costs significantly increase.

42. We suspect—in the context of a modest expansion — that the "dilution" effect of league expansion is overstated—in market terms—by the general sports media. Consumers most sensitive to perceiving the reduced quality of play that comes from expansion are likely to be "hard core" fans who are not likely to significantly reduce their patronage of their favorite sports teams, much as they might like to complain about it over a beer in their favorite drinking establishment.

43. For a mathematical demonstration, see Ross and Szymanski, *supra* note 20, at 630–31 n.21. There is a close analogy between a sports league and a labor-managed firm that will choose to produce less output than a profit-maximizing firm. Benjamin Ward, The Firm in Illyria: Market Syndicalism, 48 *Am. Econ. Rev.* 566 (1958).

44. Mark Asher, *Expos' Relocation In 2004 Is '50-50', Wash. Post*, April 16, 2003, at D7. A jury similarly found that the National Football League (NFL) had blocked the relocation of the Oakland Raiders to Los Angeles principally to protect the incumbent Los Angeles Rams from competition. Los Angeles Mem'l Coliseum Comm'n v. National Football League, 726 F.2d 1381 (9th Cir. 1984).

45. ROBERT COOTER and THOMAS ULEN, *Law and Economics* 85, 111–12 (3rd ed. 2000).

46. See Andrew A. Caffey, et al., Structuring the Franchise Relationship, in *Fundamentals of Franchising* 47, 61 (Rupert M. Barkoff and Andrew C. Selden eds., 1997).

In the food service industry, newer companies may grant greater protection for franchisees than well-established firms. For example, neither Taco Bell nor Subway grants any exclusive territories, while the newer Jimmy John's firm states that it "usually" will not grant competing franchises and allows franchisees to purchase "development territories." *See* World Franchising, *Franchise Directory*, http://www.worldfranchising.com/ (last visited

Mar. 6, 2006). Unlike food service, of course, preserving the integrity of on-field competition would not allow the NFL, for example, to give the Chicago Bears the right to own a second franchise in Chicago if market circumstances warranted.

47. For truly national leagues unconcerned by the threat of entry, our prior research suggests that overall consumer appeal would be maximized by the creation of a multi-tiered competition, with entry into the major league the result of promotion from a lower tier and league size maintained by the relegation of unsuccessful clubs into lower-tiered competition. *See* Ross and Szymanski, *supra* note 20.

48. Although this assumption is purely illustrative, we note that this would give the New York metropolitan area 4 of 32 major league teams. In the English Premier League, by contrast, where market forces determine entry into the top-tier league (because good teams are promoted from lower tiers and bad teams are relegated), between five and six London-based clubs regularly participate in the twenty team elite competition.

49. Ross, *supra* note 15, at 649–66.

50. It is theoretically possible (and plausible within the context of the NHL) that a club-run league may have over-expanded due to misplaced optimism about the ability of a sport to expand into untraditional areas of fan support. A club-run league may be reluctant to contract, because owners would not want to risk having their colleagues vote to eliminate *them*, and because clubs could not agree on compensation for excluded clubs. The League is more likely to reach an efficient result, taking into consideration the likelihood that accommodations with the players' union to preserve major league jobs may lead to the preservation of these clubs.

51. In re Football Ass'n Premier League Ltd., 1996 No. 1, ¶313 (E&W) (Restrictive Practices Court, 28 July 1999), (noting that Sky Sports, the holder of the rights to broadcast 60 matches per season, had manifested a willingness to purchase 90 matches, but was turned down).

52. Stefan Szymanski and Stephen F. Ross, Necessary Restraints and Inefficient Monopoly Sports Leagues, 1 *Int'l Sports L. Rev.* 27 (2000).

53. Chicago Prof'l Sports Ltd. v. Nat'l Basketball Ass'n, 874 F.Supp. 844, 861 (N.D. Ill. 1995), *vacated and remanded on other grounds*, 95 F.3d 593 (7th Cir. 1996).

54. Chicago Prof'l Sports Ltd. v. Nat'l Basketball Ass'n, 961 F. 2d 667, 675 (7th Cir. 1992).

55. See, e.g., Richard Sandomir, Just How Super are These Stations, *N.Y. Times*, Sept. 1, 1992, at B13. Neilsen ratings dropped 30 percent for Cardinals games broadcast in St. Louis on same night as Cubs games broadcast on WGN superstation and 20 percent for games broadcast on same night as Braves games on WTBS, while ESPN ratings were 69 percent higher when not competing against any other games.

56. The *Chicago Bulls* litigation, which produced numerous trial court opinions and two opinions from the court of appeals, can perhaps be explained by the significant discrepancy between the NBA's position that the Bulls' superstation telecasts significantly affected other rights sales and evidence put forth by the Bulls that it did not.

57. Although the ability to recoup quality investments through higher fees is lost if The League captured all broadcast revenue for local broadcast rights, The League can create appropriate incentives through the prize mechanism we discuss at text accompanying note 66 *infra*.
58. See R. Thomas Umstead, Going to the Net Isn't Always Easy; Sports Teams' Start-Up Cable Channels Face Hurdles, *Multichannel News*, Apr. 29, 2002, at 36 (3 networks controlled 27 local markets).
59. In contrast, there may be marketing efficiencies in allowing clubs to sell radio rights for play-by-play of their games, building a network with a flagship local station and various other stations in smaller towns where demand warrants.
60. See, e.g., Sanford Grossman and Oliver Hart, The Costs and Benefits of Ownership: A Theory of Lateral and Vertical Integration, 94 J. *Pol. Econ.* 691 (1986).
61. For example, the league website, www.premierleague.com, features a "Shop" page that simply provides links to each club's "team shop." *F.A. Premier League Welcome Page*, http://www.premierleague.com (last visited Mar. 6, 2006). In contrast, www.mlb.com directs the consumer to a fully integrated website where each club's products are available. *MLB Welcome Page*, http://www.mlb.com (last visited Mar. 6, 2006).
62. For example, the New York Yankees were anxious to enter into a lucrative shoe contract while Major League Baseball was taking years to collectively sell this sponsorship opportunity. The lawsuit is described in Joshua Hamilton, Comment, Congress in Relief: The Economic Importance of Revoking Baseball's Antitrust Exemption, 38 *Santa Clara L. Rev.* 1223, 1235 (1998).
63. See Andrew Zimbalist, *May the Best Team Win* 55–74 (2003).
64. It is unlikely that The League (or its shareholders) will be content to allow revenues to suffer because of chronically poor stewardship of any of The League's valuable franchises. Even when a commissioner tries to get an under-performing owner to sell, the result can be complicated litigation on peripheral issues. Accountability would significantly increase if a clearly drafted franchise agreement set forth minimum goals for a club. See Caffey et al., *supra* note 46, at 47, 61.
65. Economists and judges have long accepted that labor relations in sports raise unique issues because, unlike other industries, a competitive balance among clubs in a league makes the product more attractive. See, e.g., *Nat'l Football League*, 116 F. Supp. 319; Walter C. Neale, The Peculiar Economics of Professional Sport, 78 *Q. J. Econ.* 1 (1964). The different markets in which clubs operate, and the tendency for successful teams to generate more income, suggest that a completely unrestrained labor market will result in reduced consumer appeal. See, e.g., Paul Weiler, *Leveling the Playing Field* 189 (2000) (noting the "externality" that all other clubs suffer if dominant team signs star); Ross, supra note 15, at 687–88 (same). But see Szymanski, *supra* note 20. Literature review finds mixed support for hypothesis that promoting contest or seasonal uncertainty – i.e., competitive balance – increases popularity.
66. A sports league fits naturally into models of economic contests. The original notion of an economic contest was developed in Gordon Tullock, Efficient

Rent Seeking, in *Toward a Theory of Rent Seeking Society* 97 (James Buchanan et al. eds., 1980) (suggesting that competition for political favors could be characterized as rent-seeking contests, where different lobbyists invest (e.g., time, effort, bribes) in winning a prize (e.g., the location of a new public facility such as a military base)). This model has since been applied to a number of contexts, including labor market tournaments (contests between workers for promotion), see Edward Lazear and Sherwin Rosen, Rank Order Tournaments as Optimal Labor Contracts, 89 *J. Pol. Econ.* 841 (1981), patent races (R&D spending aimed at a monopoly rent granted by the patent), see Glenn Loury, Market Structure and Innovation, 93 *Q. J. Econ.* 385 (1979), and competition for research contracts, see Curtis Taylor, *Digging for Golden Carrots: An Analysis of Research Tournaments*, 85 *Am. Econ. Rev.* 873 (1995).

67. See Stefan Szymanski and Tommaso M. Valetti, *Promotion and Relegation in Sporting Contests* (Imperial College Working Paper June 2003), available at http://www.nhh.no/omnhh/organisasjon/fag/sam/stabssem/2003/szymanski.pdf.

68. Clubs will often find it most profitable to minimize their investment in player talent and resulting roster quality, accomplished by creating a "prize structure" (i.e. revenue distribution) that minimizes the economic reward for winning. As Rosen and Sanderson observe, "All schemes used in the United States [major leagues] punish excellence in one way or another." Sherwin Rosen and Allen Sanderson, Labour Markets in Professional Sports, 111 *Econ. J.* 469, F47–F68 (2001).

69. For example, the Kansas City Royals will receive over $18 million from the league as part of new revenue sharing. If they wisely invest $10 million in increased payroll and the resulting improvement in the team's quality produces $12 million in additional revenue to the club, their revenue sharing transfers would be reduced by $9 million, resulting in a net loss to the club of over $3 million. This is illustrated in ZIMBALIST, *supra* note 63, at 103–07.

70. See, e.g., Don Pierson, Tagliabue Urges 'New' Tactics With Union, *Chi. Trib.*, Mar. 22, 2005, at C4 (detailing obstacles to NFL owners' internal agreement).

71. See generally Stephen F. Ross, The NHL Labour Dispute and the Common Law, the Competition Act, and Public Policy, 37 *U.B.C. L. Rev.* 343 (2004). See also Nat'l Baskeball Ass'n v. Williams, 857 F. Supp. 1069, 1072 (S.D.N.Y. 1994) (NBA Deputy Commissioner justified salary cap in part on grounds of "cost certainty").

72. See John Hicks, Annual Survey of Economic Theory: The Theory of Monopoly, 3 *Econometrica* 1, 8 (1935) ("best of all monopoly profits is a quiet life").

73. See Tullock, *supra* note 66. The optimal contribution to effort depends on the "discriminatory power" of the contest: the degree of sensitivity of success to effort. If discriminatory power is high, it means that if one contestant supplies only a small amount of effort more than the others, then that contestant is highly likely to win; if discriminatory power is low, then a contestant has to put much more effort in than anyone else in order to achieve a high probability of winning. If discriminatory power is high then the optimal prize may be quite small, since even this

small prize will elicit enormous effort to win. By contrast, if discriminatory power is low, then the prize will need to be quite high in order to extract effort.

74. A classic argument in this vein is RICHARD C. LEVIN ET AL., *The Report of the Independent Members of the Commissioner's Blue Ribbon Panel on Baseball Economics* (July 2000), http://www.mlb.com/mlb/downloads/blue_ribbon.pdf, attributing baseball's woes to an increasing disparity in local revenues among clubs, which the Report blames for an increasing inability of well-run "small market" clubs to have a "regularly recurring reasonable hope of reaching post-season play." *Id.* at 8. The effect of asymmetric local revenue bases on local revenue should not be overstated, however. Using the Report's data, among the top six clubs are teams located in the relatively small markets of Atlanta, Denver, and Phoenix, while Detroit and Montreal are in the bottom quartile; indeed, if half the population size for each club in metropolitan areas with two clubs are assigned to each team, the statistical correlation between media market rank and local revenue based on Report data is a modest. *Id.* at 58. Stephen F. Ross, Light, Less-filling, It's Blue-ribbon!, 23 *Cardozo L. Rev.* 1675, at 1685–86 and n.38.

75. To the extent that across-the-board salary caps improved competitive balance to such an extent that overall league revenues were really maximized, The League and the union can be expected to reach an agreement. However, salary caps often reduce consumer appeal by prohibiting inferior clubs from quickly improving by increasing payroll through the infusion of new talent. Stephen F. Ross, The Misunderstood Alliance Between Sports Fans, Players, and the Antitrust Laws, 1997 *U. Ill. L. Rev.* 519, 567–77. Moreover, the need for salary caps to address revenue disparities among clubs is reduced where The League is setting the prize.

76. A fledgling or flailing league that requires additional incentives to attract investors to operate clubs may find cost certainty to be a legitimate priority. Indeed, this was the basis on which the NBA persuaded the players' union to agree to a salary cap in return for a guaranteed share of hopefully growing revenues in 1982. See Interview with David Stern, NBA Commissioner, *Antitrust*, Summer 1987, at 27.

77. Scott Warfield, NASCAR Rules, *Sports Bus. J.*, May 23, 1994, at 20.

78. Section 1 of the Sherman Act, 15 U.S.C. §1 (2000), declares unlawful every "contract, combination in the form of trust or otherwise, or conspiracy, in restraint of trade or commerce among the several States, or with foreign nations."

79. Standard Oil Co. v. United States, 221 U.S. 1 (1911).

80. 468 U.S. 85 (1984).

81. *Id.* at 107.

82. *Id.* at 101.

83. Copperweld Corp. v. Independence Tube Corp., 467 U.S. 752 (1984).

84. Earlier cases are catalogued in Stephen F. Ross, Antitrust Options to Redress Anticompetitive Restraints and Monopolistic Practices by Professional Sports Leagues, 52 *Case W. Res. L. Rev.* 133, 146 n.35 (2001). For academic commentary in favor and opposed to the single entity defense as applied to club-run leagues, see Ross, *supra* note 75, at 549 n.136. Cf. Fraser v. Major League Soccer, L.L.C., 284 F.3d 47 (1st Cir. 2002) (the district

court's rejection of an antitrust claim based on the single entity argument was criticized and the result affirmed on other grounds).

85. See Chicago Prof'l Sports Ltd. v. Nat'l Basketball Ass'n, 95 F.3d 593, 603 (7th Cir. 1996) (Cudahy, J., concurring) (sports leagues can make inefficient decisions where individual teams can gain at the expense of the league).

Even Professor Gary Roberts, the principal academic advocate for treating club-run leagues as single entities, has recognized that

> there is a legitimate concern that the structure of a league, unlike that of other business organizations, may cause, albeit infrequently, individual club economic interest to be contrary to the interests of the league as a whole. While it is unusual for partnerships or corporations to be organized such that a proposal enhancing the efficiency or profitability of the firm as a whole is contrary to the economic interest of any partner or shareholder, the universal sports league practice of allocating all or most of the nontelevision, game-generated revenues to the home club makes the potential more likely in some sports league contexts.

Gary R. Roberts, Sports Leagues and the Sherman Act: The Use and Abuse of Section 1 to Regulate Restraints on Intraleague Rivalry, 32 *UCLA L. Rev.* 219, 295 (1984). Our principal difference is with Roberts' belief that "in the overwhelming majority of instances, the interests of the league will coincide with those of individual clubs." *Id.* at 295 n.261. Rather, we have identified a wide variety of areas where we believe that club-run leagues will behave differently than a league controlled separately. In suggesting that club-run leagues enjoy single-entity status unless a plaintiff shows that a minority of clubs actually vetoed a proposal that would benefit the league and the majority of clubs. *Id.* at 296. Roberts also ignores the distinct possibility that a majority of club owners will engage, over time, in a tacit agreement to adhere to policies that benefit each of them as club owners even if the league as a whole will suffer, or the alternative scenario where the majority agree not to pursue an efficient innovation because of an inability to agree on the distribution of profits.

86. Pittsburgh Athletic Co. v. KQV Broad. Co., 24 F. Supp. 490 (W.D. Pa. 1938).

87. Bd. of Regents, 468 U.S. at 107 (1984). See also Stephen F. Ross, An Antitrust Analysis of Sports League Contracts with Cable Networks, 39 *Emory L.J.* 463 (1990). A major exception is if a league sells a package of games to a free-to-air television network. Congress has passed a specific and limited exemption from antitrust scrutiny for such sales. Sports Broadcasting Act, Pub. L. No. 87-331, 75 Stat. 732 (1961), codified at 15 U.S.C. §§1291–94 (2000).

88. See *supra* text accompanying notes 73–74. The downside to this legal advantage that The League would have over club-run leagues is that the ongoing evolution of the market for pay television could lead The League to shift many games now shown on free-to-air television to a more expensive medium. Shifts away from free-to-air are becoming more prevalent in club-run leagues, see ZIMBALIST, *supra* note 63, ch. 7, but may be inhibited

by the inability of clubs to agree on how to divide the proceeds from collective rights sales to pay programmers. While an agreement among rivals to collectively shift the sale of their rights to more expensive tiers may constitute an unreasonable restraint of trade, Ross, *supra* note 87, at 481, the unilateral sale by The League to a satellite or pay programmer would not. We do not believe that this concern outweighs the benefits in allowing The League to control broadcast rights, but if this shift is socially undesirable Congress can follow the pattern of many other developed countries that have enacted "Listed Events" legislation that specifies that key events (championships, late playoffs, a game of the week) must be on free-to-air television. See, e.g., Broadcasting Act, 1996, ch. 55, §§97–105 (Eng.); Broadcasting Services Act, 1992 (Austl.) (authorizing minister to list events required to be available on free-to-air television).

89. See, e.g., Henderson Broad. Corp. v. Houston Sports Ass'n, 541 F. Supp. 263 (S.D. Tex. 1982) (plaintiff claimed exclusive contract monopolized competition for radio in Houston-Galveston area). See also *Monopolies and Merger Commission, British Sky Broadcasting Group PLC and Manchester United PLC: A Report on the Proposed Merger* (Apr. 9, 1999), available at http://www.competition-commission.org.uk/rep_pub/reports/1999/426sky.htm (blocking acquisition of leading British soccer team by leading pay television programmer in part based on concerns that acquisition would distort competition for lucrative soccer television rights between acquiring firm and its rivals).

90. See, e.g., St. Louis Convention & Visitors Comm'n v. Nat'l Football League, 154 F.3d 851 (8th Cir. 1998) (league requirement that Rams pay a fee for permission to relocate to St. Louis was reasonable; allegations that league agreed that Rams would be only team to negotiate with St. Louis unproven); Nat'l Basketball Ass'n v. San Diego Clippers Basketball Club, 815 F.2d 562 (9th Cir. 1987) (league relocation rules are not *per se* illegal but must be evaluated on a case by case basis); Los Angeles Mem'l Coliseum Comm'n, 726 F.2d 1381 (affirming jury verdict that NFL refusal to allow Oakland Raiders relocation to Los Angeles was unreasonable effort to protect Los Angeles Rams franchise from intra-league competition); San Francisco Seals v. Nat'l Hockey League, 379 F. Supp. 966 (C.D. Cal. 1974) (no claim of any injury to competition from bar on relocation of franchise to Vancouver); State v. Milwaukee Braves, 1966 Trade Cas. ¶71,738 (Wis. Cir. Ct., Milwaukee Co.) (National League's approval of Braves' relocation to Atlanta and refusal to expand to Milwaukee constituted monopolization in violation of state antitrust statute), *rev'd on other grounds*, 144 N.W.2d 1 (Wis. 1966) (application of state antitrust statute to league rules requiring uniformity constituted an unconstitutional burden on interstate commerce).

91. Bd. of Regents, 468 U.S. at 100.

92. In Mid-South Grizzlies v. Nat'l Football League, 720 F.2d 772 (3d Cir. 1983), the court rejected an antitrust suit by a would-be entrant to the NFL. The court reasoned that, unlike the *Raiders* case, there was no serious claim that a Memphis entrant into the league was rejected by an inefficient monopoly venture in order to protect an existing rival (the closest other franchise, the then St. Louis Cardinals, was over 250 miles away),

and that leaving markets such as Memphis open actually encouraged new inter-league rivalry by promoting entry.

93. See *supra* text accompanying notes 46–50.
94. Compare Cont'l T.V., Inc., 433 U.S. 36 ("vertical" territorial restraint imposed by television manufacturer on locations where its product could be sold at retail subject to rule of reason) with Gen. Motors Corp., 384 U.S. 127 ("horizontal" territorial restraint imposed by auto manufacturer at behest of organized group of retailers held illegal *per se*) and United States v. Sealy, Inc., 388 U.S. 350 (1967) (territorial restraint imposed by trademark owner on licensees considered "horizontal" where licensees controlled the corporation owning the trademark). This distinction was reaffirmed in Cont'l T.V., Inc., 433 U.S. at 58 n.28.

   Even if The League did not permit efficient entry in order to add to its monopoly profits, this conduct by a single dominant firm would not violate the Sherman Act. The League's liability as a single firm for monopolization is discussed *infra* at note 105.
95. Brown v. Pro Football, Inc., 518 U.S. 231 (1996).
96. Indeed, this is exactly what the NFL players did over a decade ago. See, e.g., Powell v. Nat'l Football League, 764 F. Supp. 1351, 1359 (D. Minn. 1991).
97. Although centrally controlled labor relations were subjected to close antitrust review in Fraser, 284 F.3d 47, the league was not found to be independent of rival clubs but rather was controlled by the club owners. *Id.* at 57, 57 n.5.
98. See *supra* note 77.
99. See *supra* text accompanying notes 70–77.
100. One way for current owners to profit from the restructuring we propose would be to create The League as a separate business entity and sell stock in that entity, either as an initial public offering or as a private sale to selected investors. The value of that sale would be maximized by creating The League prior to issuance of public stock, establishing a highly regarded Board of Directors and executive team, and securing a collective bargaining agreement with players. Cf. Taylor Milk Co. v. Int'l Brotherhood of Teamsters, 248 F.3d 239 (3d Cir. 2001) (describing merger where acquiring firm desired to have new collective bargaining arrangement secured before closing deal).
101. Cf. Mackey, 543 F.2d at 615 (league rules restricting inter-club competition for players affects salaries so that they constituted mandatory subject of bargaining under §8(d) of the National Labor Relations Act, 29 U.S.C. §158(d) (2000)). If the restructuring is the result of legislation or court order, the fact of restructuring would not, of course, be a mandatory subject of bargaining. Obviously, The League would then need to enter into a new collective bargaining agreement with the players.
102. Sullivan v. Nat'l Football League, 34 F.3d 1091 (1st Cir. 1994).
103. Levin v. Nat'l Basketball Ass'n, 385 F. Supp. 149 (S.D.N.Y. 1974).
104. Some have suggested that the recent highly leveraged sale of the Los Angeles Dodgers was approved, notwithstanding a fiscally superior offer in the wings from a wealthy local philanthropist, because other owners wanted a major-market team to be saddled with less aggressive ownership.

Thomas S. Mulligan, McCourt Teams Up on Land Use, *L. A. Times*, Mar. 17, 2005, D1 (purchase featuring little cash and unusual seller financing raised questions about whether buyer's pockets were deep enough to keep the Dodgers competitive). The jury in *Sullivan* was persuaded that the fear of competition from clubs owned by publicly traded corporations was more important to league owners than the chance to maximize their franchise resale opportunities. 34 F.3d at 1100.

105. Because The League would likely be the dominant provider of competition organizing services in each sport, it would potentially remain liable for attempted or actual monopolization under §2 of the Sherman Act, 15 U.S.C. §2. Courts have generally found that the dominant league in a major sport possesses monopoly power. See, e.g., Ross, *supra* note 84, at 140 n.16 (citing cases). However, The League's liability would be no greater than that faced by club-run leagues today. Antitrust law does not forbid the exercise of monopoly power, only its illegal maintenance. See United States Football League v. Nat'l Football League, 842 F.2d 1335, 1361 (2nd Cir. 1988) (upholding jury verdict that a monopolist "is free to set as its legitimate goal the maximization of its own profits so long as it does not exercise its power to maintain that power"). To prove illegal monopoly maintenance, a plaintiff must establish not only that rules are exclusionary, but also that they are unnecessarily so – that is, that they are inefficient. Rules designed to promote consumer appeal or to achieve efficiencies are lawful. Aspen Skiing Co. v. Aspen Highlands Skiing Corp., 472 U.S. 585, 605 (1985).

Like current club-run leagues, The League could not engage in blatantly anticompetitive acts without violating §2, nor could it foreclose rival leagues from essential inputs; thus, The League could neither tie up every television network (this was a principal, albeit unproven, theory in United States Football League, 842 F.2d 1335), nor structure its player contracts so that in any given year it would not be feasible for a rival to have access to a sufficient number of players to viably compete. See Philadelphia World Hockey Club, Inc. v. Philadelphia Hockey Club, Inc., 351 F. Supp. 462, 508 (E.D. Pa. 1972) (provisions reserving all major and minor league players to NHL clubs or affiliates for three years constituted monopolization by precluding rival league from entry).

Likewise, The League might be required, in the interest of maintaining the potential threat of competition, to permit clubs to retain control of their trademarks. Allowing clubs to keep their trademarks (subject to a limited assignment to The League for licensing purposes that now occurs) if they choose to join another league would enhance the opportunity for rivalry in competition organizing services and the possibility of The League's displacement by a more efficient rival. In similar fashion, although franchise agreements can reasonably be set for a sufficient duration to allow for long-term planning, unduly long franchise agreements could operate to monopolize if they precluded any ability to lure existing clubs to a new league. See *XI Herbert Hovenkamp, Antitrust Law* ¶1802g (1998).

Because even in natural monopoly markets antitrust laws favor competition for the monopoly, it could be argued that the best way to promote competition in the market for competition organizing services is to prohibit

The League's control of player contracts. If players were contracted to individual clubs, then a new entrant could compete by simply attracting the club owner, rather than develop a league of minimum viable scale by individually signing players. We do not believe that The League's control of players – assuming that after any given season a reasonable number of player contracts will expire – is sufficiently anticompetitive to constitute monopolization. There are significant efficiencies in allowing The League negotiate as a single entity with the players' union to devise an optimal scheme to allocate players among clubs participating in its competition. Collective action problems make such an agreement with club employers more difficult. Moreover, The League might allocate a player to a particular club precisely because this allocation is efficient in the context of the club's participation in the competition organized by The League. If The League feared that an individual club might take all its players and participate in another competition, The League might allocate players differently, and less optimally in the short run. Foregoing clear benefits to The League's competition in the short run, because of the possibility that entry into the presumptively natural monopoly market for competition organizing would be marginally facilitated if clubs employed players, would not seem to be reasonable.

At the same time, the Sherman Act should properly constrain clubs' ability to jointly negotiate with The League and rival competition organizers. If a rival can organize a competition more efficiently than The League, it is free to bid for individual teams to compete in its competition. A rival league could conceivably pursue a strategy of attracting clubs by offering them greater power and authority, similar to that now enjoyed in club-run leagues, and that such competition will result in a structure no different than currently exists. We believe that such a strategy is unlikely to succeed. Precisely because club-run structures are less efficient, it is difficult to see how a new entrant could make an offer sufficient to attract so many clubs that The League would not remain viable. To use two simple examples, if a new entrant made an offer aimed at attracting small-market clubs, The League would remain viable on a smaller basis focusing on its large markets; if a new entrant made an offer aimed at the top clubs in major cities, The League with its preexisting brand loyalty and infrastructure could add additional franchises in these major markets, which are likely to be capable of supporting additional teams. If we assume that The League will remain as a viable entrant in the market, then clubs considering jumping to a rival will have to weigh the more attractive package offered against the lost profits because of the usually fierce inter-league rivalry that will follow. On the other hand, a rival that develops a model that really is more efficient than The League's should be able to attract almost all the clubs through individual negotiations.

106. See Ronald H. Coase, The Problem of Social Cost, 3 *J. L. & Econ.* 1 (1960).
107. See COOTER and ULEN, *supra* note 45 at 111–12.
108. The authoritative work on the origins of baseball, from which the textual narrative is derived, is IIAROLD SEYMOUR, *Baseball: The Early Years 77–85* (1960).
109. *Id.* at 75–85.

110. To bring this about, the league's principal founder, William A. Hulbert of the Chicago Baseball Club (now the White Sox), assembled a talented team by raiding other clubs and then secured an agreement from leading clubs in a geographically balanced group of eight cities from Boston to St. Louis. *Id.*, at 77–80.
111. The early history of the game is recounted in GEOFFREY GREEN, *Soccer, the World Game: A Popular History* ch. 3 (1956).
112. In the words of William McGregor, founder of the Football League:

> The League should never aspire to be a legislating body … by the very nature things the League must be a selfish body. Its interests are wholly bound up in the welfare of its affiliated clubs, and what happens outside is, in a sense, of secondary importance only … the League has its work to do; the [Football] Association has its work to do and there need be no clashing.

SIMON INGLIS, *English League Football and the Men Who Made It* 11 (1988). See also GREEN, *supra* note 111, at 62. ("The FA on the one hand [is] the monarchy as it were, with its watchful care and authority over the whole of English football: on the other hand [there is] the Football League, with its narrower horizons, existing under the licence of the FA.")
113. Each country's domestic competition operates under the aegis of a national association modeled on the FA; an association of associations governs each continent. For example, Europe's governing body is the Union of European Football Associations (UEFA). See UEFA Welcome Page, UEFA.COM, http://www.uefa.com/ (last visited Mar. 7, 2006). An international federation, the The Fédération Internationale de Football Association (FIFA), is the world governing body. See FIFA Welcome Page, FIFA.COM, http://www.fifa.com/en/organisation/index.html (last visited Mar 7, 2006).
114. Recently, the commercial power of English football clubs has expanded dramatically, resulting in greater deference to club interests by the FA resulting in some of the same problems that exist in North America. See, e.g, JOHN WILLIAMS, *Is it All Over? can Football Survive the Premier League* 53–60 (1999). This is due in large measure to the perceived threat of the top clubs to secede from the FA and organize their own competition. We discuss why we believe a concerted secession from a competition by the leading teams should violate the Sherman Act, *supra* note 105.
115. See WEILER and ROBERTS, *supra* note 30, at 495–97.
116. See Lebowitz, *supra* note 10, at 1F.
117. *Id.* (citing Commissioner Val Ackerman).
     At the same time, several leagues that have adopted a "single entity" approach by completely integrating all competition organizing and club participation services (so the league owns all the franchises) have found the approach wanting. See *id.* (indoor lacrosse league needed to modify single entity to attract local investors); WEILER and ROBERTS, *supra* note 30, at 496 (Major League Soccer could only find investors after agreeing to grant them local rights).
118. See, e.g., NATIONAL FOOTBALL LEAGUE CONST., Art. II, §2.1(a) (purpose of NFL is to "foster the primary business of League members, each member

being an owner of a professional football club"), *excerpted in* PAUL C. WEILER and GARY R. ROBERTS, *Statutory and Documentary Supplement to Sports and The Law* 42 (2d. ed. 1998).

119. See, e.g., Stefan Fatsis and Dennis K. Berman, Puck Plan: NHL Explores Sale to Cure a Troubled Sport, *Wall St. J.*, Mar. 4, 2005, at B1.

120. See *NASCAR History*, http://www.nascar-info.net/nascar_history_1.html (last visited Jan. 20, 2006).

121. To illustrate, current owners could create The League as a separate corporate entity ("NHL, Inc.") with a relatively small percentage of outstanding shares created as voting stock and most of the shares retained by club owners as preferred non-voting stock. The return on an initial public offering of voting stock would be maximized if The League had a high-profile board of directors independent of current club owners, and if it had already entered into a new collective bargaining agreement with the players and detailed franchise agreements with existing clubs. Under this scheme, current owners would profit by receiving cash from the proceeds of the offering and by realizing potential capital gains from the appreciation of their preferred shares. Owners would retain ownership in their clubs, although obviously the franchise value of the clubs would be substantially reduced under this restructuring. Although reaping the benefits of vertical separation requires that club owners' investment in The League be non-voting, to facilitate the marketability of the preferred stock it can be made immediately convertible to voting stock if acquired by anyone not involved with club operations. Thus, once the market price had been established after the initial public offering, club owners could gradually sell off their non-voting stock and thus capture almost all of the surplus from the restructuring. Alternatively, in light of the continuing growth of the value of sports franchises, club owners could hold onto their stock, which, along with the value of their franchise (which has tripled in the last decade, see Rodney Fort, *Major League Baseball Team Values*, http://www.rodneyfort.com/SportsData/BizFrame.htm [last visited Mar. 14, 2006]), could continue to appreciate. We thank Professor Cynthia Williams and investment analyst R. J. Bukovac for assistance regarding the mechanics of the restructuring.

122. If the initiative came from outside the league, a more effective approach would probably be for a relatively small group of investors to form a new entity, The League, which would initially be closely owned, combining those with sizable assets with those knowledgeable about the sports business. The League would then tender an offer to acquire those rights necessary to organize the competition from current club owners. If an initial offer was not accepted by the three-quarter super-majority required by most league constitutions, then The League's organizers could enter into separate negotiations with individual club owners in an effort to find the sufficient number to effectuate the purchase. Once the tender was accepted, The League could then enter into franchise agreements with clubs, and a collective bargaining agreement with the union. With the new structure in place, the owners could then turn to public equity markets, both to realize a gain on their successful organizational efforts and also to refinance debt

or personal assets required to provide the initial cash payments to current owners.

123. According to Forbes magazine, in 2004 the average franchise value was $295 million, or a combined total of $8.85 billion. See *MLB Valuations* (Apr. 26, 2004), available at http://www.forbes.com/free_forbes/2004/0426/066tab.html.

124. See cases cited *supra* notes 53–54 and accompanying text.

125. Cf. *Saturday Night Live: The First 20 Years* (Michael Cader ed. 1994) (famous line by telephone operator "Ernestine" popularized by Lily Tomlin: "Next time you complain about your phone service, why don't you try using two Dixie cups with a string. We don't care. We don't have to. (snort) We're the Phone Company.") The idea that firms with monopoly power have the luxury to conduct their affairs inefficiently is widely supported. See, e.g., United States v. Aluminum Co. of America, 148 F.2d 416, 427 (2nd Cir. 1945). Monopoly power "deadens initiative, discourages thrift and depresses energy…immunity from competition is a narcotic, and rivalry is a stimulant, to industrial progress" and competition "is necessary to counteract an inevitable disposition to let well enough alone." Aluminum Co., 148 F.2d at 427; Hicks, *supra* note 72, at 8 ("best of all monopoly profits is a quiet life").

126. See *supra* note 105.

127. Cf. Valley Liquors, Inc., 678 F.2d at 745 (noting swift market retribution as a characteristic of firms lacking market power).

128. The inefficiencies engaged in by monopoly sports leagues, and an explanation for how competition would eliminate these inefficiencies, are discussed in Ross, *supra* note 15.

129. See generally WILLIAM A. KLEIN and JOHN C. COFFEE, JR., *Business Organization and Finance: Legal and Economic Principles* 191–94 (8th ed. 2002).

130. For a more detailed discussion of this point, see Ross, *supra* note 84, at 145–46.

131. Moreover, because of the strong public aversion to having different clubs owned by a single firm, the outside investors cannot realistically pursue a strategy of buying up individual teams until they can persuade the club-run league to restructure.

132. The Supreme Court's decision in Flood v. Kuhn, 407 U.S. 258 (1972), makes clear that all sports, including baseball, constitute interstate commerce subject to congressional regulation. Congress could enact special regulatory legislation prohibiting clubs from maintaining a voting interest in the operation of any league that does not face significant competition from rival leagues in the same sport. This regulatory legislation could legalize conduct that was efficient and enhanced consumer appeal while specifically prohibiting anticompetitive conduct by The League, clubs, or rivals. This would be analogous to the detailed provisions of the Telecommunications Act of 1996, Pub. L. No. 104-104, 110 Stat. 56 (1996), regulating the break-up of AT&T, which prohibited the "Baby Bells" (the local phone monopolies) from entering the market for long-distance phone calls unless the local telephone market was open to competition. See 47 U.S.C. §271 (2000).

133. A full analysis of this issue is beyond the scope of this chapter. In Berman v. Parker, 348 U.S. 26 (1954), the Supreme Court held that the power of eminent domain can be used not only to acquire property for future public ownership, but also for resale to a private party, where that sale would serve a public purpose. This holding was recently reaffirmed in Kelo v. City of New London, 125 S. Ct. 2655 (2005) (granting *certiorari* to consider this issue). In authorizing the use of eminent domain to acquire land for stadium construction, courts have recognized that the operation of professional sports competitions for the benefit of local fans constitutes a public purpose. See, e.g., City of Los Angeles v. Superior Court, 333 P.2d 745 (Cal. 1959) (upholding use of eminent domain to construct a major league baseball stadium). A leading example of the use of federal eminent domain power to remedy inefficiencies caused by transactions costs is described in Mfrs. Aircraft Ass'n v. United States, 77 Ct. Cl. 481 (1933). The decision details the government's actions just prior to World War I to pay royalties to the Wright Brothers and other holders of conflicting patents regarding aircraft construction based on a conclusion that "various companies were threatening all other airplane and seaplane manufacturing companies with suits for infringements of patents, resulting in a general demoralization of the entire trade." *Id.* at 484.

134. Major antitrust suits seeking divestitures are expensive. Although a consumer class action by a private attorney is plausible, because of the difficulty of establishing consumer damages such a lawsuit is unlikely. Such litigation would most likely be brought by a federal antitrust agency, or a collection of state attorneys general, or by a private investor or a minority of league owners interested in using the litigation as a vehicle to force owners to overcome the transactions costs identified above to effectuate a reorganization.

135. 468 U.S. at 107.

136. *Gen. Leaseways, Inc.*, 744 F.2d at 594.

137. See *supra* Part II.

138. For example, baseball fans have just witnessed the first collective bargaining agreement in 30 years that did not require industrial disruption to be achieved. For a detailed chronicle of the difficulties in securing workable collective bargains in light of management's obligation to secure agreement from owners acting in their own club's interests, see JOHN HELYAR, *Lords of the Realm* (1994).

139. The National Basketball Association has done nothing to restrain the complete mismanagement of one of their two franchises in the huge Los Angeles market. See, e.g., Richard Hoffer, The Loss Generation, *Sports Illustrated*, Apr. 17, 2000 at 58 ("[The Clippers'] helplessness, so practiced and so dependable, is clearly the work of just one man—we're thinking of Donald Sterling here.").

140. 468 U.S. at 107.

141. See DAVID HARRIS, *The League: The Rise and Decline of the NFL* (1986).

142. Cf. Valley Liquors, Inc., 678 F.2d at 745 (noting this characteristic exists where firms lack market power).

143. Cont'l T.V., 433 U.S. at 51–52.

144. *Id.* at 54–56.

145. *Id.* at 57 n.27, citing Topco Assocs., 405 U.S. at 608.
146. Sealy, Inc., 388 U.S. 350. The decision in *Fraser*, 284 F.3d 47, further supports the distinction between a separate entity organizing a competition and a club-run league. The court refused to accept the claim that a league consisting of rival owners who simultaneously invested in the league and their own clubs was an entity akin to a corporation (indeed, akin to The League that is envisioned by this chapter). Citing *Sealy*, the court of appeals emphasized that, unlike a single entity, the league was controlled by these rivals. *Id.* at 57, 57 n.5.
147. 224 U.S. 383 (1912).
148. One possible objection to any antitrust relief when firms collectively control an input essential to participating in the market is that such relief may lessen incentives for investment at either level. Where the remedy is designed to preclude monopoly profits that arise from a natural monopoly, as opposed to a monopoly resulting from "superior skill, foresight, and industry," cf. Aluminum Co. of America, 148 F.2d at 430, incentive problems should not deter antitrust relief. Stephen G. Breyer, Antitrust, Deregulation, and the Newly Liberated Marketplace, 75 *Cal. L. Rev.* 1005, 1033–34 (1987). In the case of developing sports, perhaps the only firms interested in investing in a new league would be those interested in operating clubs, and so a club-run league may well be efficient for sports that lack market power. Once a sport obtains market power, however, there should be no shortage of investors for a entity capable of organizing the competition (The League). The principle that restraints may be justified for new entrants but not after the firm has established market power has strong support in antitrust precedents. See, e.g., Jefferson Parish Hosp. Dist. v. Hyde, 466 U.S. 2, 23 (1984) (citing United States v. Jerrold Elecs. Corp., 187 F. Supp. 545 [E.D. Pa. 1960], *aff'd per curiam*, 365 U.S. 567 [1961]) (tied sale to ensure new entrant's reputation for quality would be maintained was reasonable, but after firm was established no longer necessary). Similarly, non-competition agreements are reasonable for a limited time until the promisee has been able to establish itself in the marketplace. *Restatement (Second) of Contracts* §§186–88 (1982).
149. 326 U.S. 1 (1945).
150. Hovenkamp, *supra* note 4, at 37–44.
151. Given the thousands of members of the association, the risk of reciprocal rejection of new entrants to protect local incumbents was apparently not given serious consideration.
152. Hovenkamp, *supra* note 4, at 36.
153. Joseph J. Spengler, Vertical Integration and Antitrust Policy, 68 *J. Pol. Econ.* 347 (1950).
154. David Reiffen and Andrew Kleit, *Terminal Railroad* Revisited: Foreclosure of an Essential Facility or Simple Horizontal Monopoly?, 33 *J. L. & Econ.* 419, 424 (1990). For a contrary view, see Richard D. Friedman, *Antitrust Analysis and Bilateral Monopoly, Wis. L. Rev.* 873 (1986) (arguing that firms will agree on profit-maximizing output); Peter Carstensen, Khaning the Court: How the Antitrust Establishment Obtained an Advisory Opinion Legalizing "Maximum" Price Fixing, 34 *U. Tol. L. Rev.* 241, 288 (2003) (noting that because monopoly pricing takes place on elastic portion of

demand curve, bilateral monopolists will err on the side of lower prices and increased output). The latter two articles do not, however, discuss the serial monopoly problem in the context of joint venture of independent downstream monopolists and a collectively run upstream monopolist.

155. A sports illustration cited by Reiffen and Kleit, *supra* note 154, at 414, is Fishman v. Wirtz, 807 F.2d 520 (7th Cir. 1986), where they imply that the court erred in finding a Sherman Act violation in the refusal of the owner of Chicago Stadium, who was seeking to own the Chicago Bulls basketball team, to offer a stadium lease to a rival bidder. A rival bidder would have sought to exploit the Bulls' local monopoly while paying monopoly rents to the owner of the only suitable stadium. On the other hand, the refusal to permit rivals to gain access to the stadium precludes the sort of competition for the natural monopoly that antitrust law generally encourages. Union Leader Corp. v. Newspapers of New England, Inc., 284 F.2d 582, 590 n.4 (1st Cir. 1960). Which effect predominates requires a case-by-case analysis.

156. Ross and Szymanski, *supra* note 20, at 649–50 and nn. 109–110.

157. The Court of Arbitration for Sport recognized this justification in upholding a challenge to a European soccer regulation barring clubs from participating in the European club competition if owned by the same entity. *AEK Athens*, CAS 98/200.

158. Cf. Gamco, Inc. v. Providence Fruit & Produce Bldg., 194 F.2d 484 (1st Cir. 1952) (requiring reasonable access to wholesale fruit facility advantageously located in railroad terminal was required under the assumption that rival fruit merchants would then compete with each other).

159. See *supra* note 26 and accompanying text.

160. Although there are strong arguments in favor of a finding that the maintenance of vertically integrated, club-run leagues in the major North American sports violates the Sherman Act, there are significant obstacles to judicially mandated vertical divestiture. Such an order requires a plaintiff to bear the expense and risk of a lawsuit. In the case of Major League Baseball, either a lower court would have to narrowly construe the judicially created antitrust exemption for the National Pastime or the Supreme Court would have to expressly apply the antitrust laws to the sport. See, e.g., *Flood*, 407 U.S. at 283 (Congress' "positive inaction" in refusing to overrule precedents exempting baseball's reserve clause from antitrust scrutiny justified its continued application, although it was concededly an "anomaly"); Butterworth v. Nat'l League, 644 So. 2d 1021 (Fla. 1994) (baseball exemption applies only narrowly to the specific restraint at issue in *Flood*); Henderson Broad. Corp., 541 F. Supp. at 268–69 (exemption only applies to baseball's "unique characteristics and needs"); Major League Baseball v. Crist, 331 F.3d 1177 (11th Cir. 2003) (exemption applies broadly to "business of baseball"). For these reasons, Congress may wish to consider legislative approaches that would achieve the same welfare-enhancing result.

161. *Topco Assocs.*, 405 U.S. 596, 611 (1972).

4

Open Competition in League Sports

Stephen F. Ross[a] *and Stefan Szymanski*[b]
[a] *Professor of Law, University of Illinois; B.A., J.D., University of California (Berkeley)*
[b] *Reader in Economics, Imperial College School of Management; B.A., University of Oxford, M.Sc., Ph.D., University of London*

Introduction

As this chapter goes to print [April 2002], Major League Baseball (MLB) has announced plans to contract from thirty to twenty-eight teams, refusing to permit the relocation of a financially troubled Montreal franchise to our Nation's capital and strongly hinting that the refusal of Minnesota taxpayers to subsidize a new stadium will result in the demise of the Minnesota Twins.[1] At the same time, Los Angeles has more than enough basketball fans to support two teams, but a wealthy mogul continues to steward the Clippers into new lows of mediocrity.[2] When Tennessee wanted a pro football team, they had to shell out over $292 million in taxpayer money to lure the Houston Oilers.[3] The National Hockey League has doled out American expansion franchises so artfully that the Montreal Canadiens pay more than triple the tax bills of all their American rivals combined.[4] Why does this happen?

In 1602, an English judge invalidated a monopoly in playing cards that Queen Elizabeth I had granted to a court crony, finding that the Queen must have been deceived, since monopolies so clearly led to higher prices, lower output, and lower quality.[5] The basic rules of economics recognized almost four hundred years ago remain true today in the world of sports. Facing no real competition, professional sports clubs raise prices, hold down the number of franchises in their leagues, and

For their helpful comments on earlier versions, the authors wish to thank Brian Cheffins, Kit Kinports, Roger Noll, Gary Roberts, Peter Sloane, Charles Tabb, Andrew Zimbalist, participants in a faculty workshop at the University of Illinois, and the audience at the 2000 annual meeting of the Sports Lawyers Association.

often fail to put the best possible club on the field or ice. Yet while MLB is talking about contracting, there are 20 or more cities with populations in excess of 1 million that could host a major league team in each of the major sports.[6] This amounts to a potential fan market between 25 million (for baseball) and 50 million (for football) people, most of whom are unlikely to see a major league team in their city in their lifetime.

One reason for this is that in North America, sports leagues are closed ventures. Membership in the league is a gift from the existing members, who typically grant the right of entry only in exchange for a substantial fee. (And baseball owners are prepared to pay $250 million to each owner of the teams to be eliminated by the proposed contraction,[7] an amount significantly higher than the market value of the teams.[8]) This is fundamentally different than the structure of team sports in the rest of the world. Elsewhere, sports leagues are usually open: membership in the league is contingent on success. Professional sports leagues in soccer, rugby, basketball, and cricket are organized in ascending tiers (generally called divisions), and every year the teams with the worst record are relegated to a lower division and replaced by the most successful teams from that lower division.

This structural difference has significant consequences for the conduct and performance of sports leagues. Because the leagues[9] are almost always the sole providers of the highest quality club play in each sport, and in North America the leagues do not face reasonable substitutes for consumers' patronage,[10] the closed structure also has potentially important antitrust consequences. However, perhaps owing to the ethnocentric American view that sports-related structures not known on these shores must not be relevant here, there has been very little research on the impact of openness on the organization of sports leagues.

This chapter argues that the practice of "promotion and relegation" tends to raise consumer welfare by increasing effective competition among the teams in a league. Teams that are relegated to a lower division after an unsuccessful year will play a lower standard of competition and generate less interest among fans, and therefore will reduce the revenue-generating potential for their owners. Because teams seek to avoid relegation as well as to win championships, they have a greater incentive to invest in players than teams participating in closed competitions. For lesser teams in lower divisions, the allure of promotion to the top division enhances the incentive to invest in players and provides fans with new and innovative professional league competition, distinct from and qualitatively superior to the current minor leagues. Moreover, promotion provides a market-based means of permitting new entry, which will check the power of incumbent clubs to exercise market power. These effects involve a direct gain for consumers (sports fans), since the additional efforts of their team enhance the quality of play, while at the same time the excitement of promotion and relegation struggles adds an extra dimension to league competition.

The competitive check provided by new entry is particularly significant in the sports industry, because the particular interdependence that sports teams have with other economically separate firms within the same league has led courts to be much more permissive in their antitrust scrutiny of trade restraints among members of sports leagues than in the case of most businesses. Rules involving limitations on competition for players and sharing revenue between rival clubs, as well as restrictions on entry into the league joint venture, on the sale of broadcast rights, and on the internal business structure of member clubs, are all tolerated unless demonstrably unreasonable in the sports context. Yet such rules would probably be unacceptable under the antitrust laws if employed in other industries. This legal generosity stems from the recognition that teams need to cooperate to some degree in order to produce their output[11] and that a more balanced competition requiring cooperation is more interesting to consumers.[12] Restraints that promote balance are therefore deemed justifiable, and reasonable forms of those listed above have all been accepted as legitimate.[13]

However, numerous commentators have expressed concern about the potential for abuse of market power that has been created by the permissive regime applied to sports leagues.[14] Examples of such abuses include escalating ticket prices, indifference to the interests of committed fans, exploitation of players, and racial discrimination. But perhaps the most notable abuse has involved public subsidies for new stadia. Since 1960, almost every major league team has benefited from a public subsidy of some kind.[15] In most cases, these subsidies have been the result of a bidding war between municipal authorities. Noll and Zimbalist characterize the situation thus:

> All major sports are controlled by monopoly leagues. Like monopolists anywhere, these leagues profit from a scarcity of teams. By creating a situation in which several cities that are viable franchise sites do not have teams, the leagues set up competitive bidding for any team that becomes available, whether through expansion or relocation. Cities that lack a team then become credible threats to induce an existing team to move, as well as to provide a hungry pack of suitors when a league decides to expand. This situation bids up the price for franchises and the subsidy that a city must expect to pay in order to capture or to retain a team.[16]

Presently in baseball, the only area prepared to subsidize a stadium is the Washington, D.C. area,[17] although owners are reluctant to approve a relocation because of the objections of the nearby Baltimore Orioles.[18] So, owners propose contraction in hopes of recreating the cycle of bidding for franchises among have-not municipalities.

A system of promotion and relegation places a significant limit on the monopoly power of sports leagues. The system preserves the integrity of the league itself and indeed allows leagues to legitimately expand or contract to most effectively market the product. At the same time, a club's threat to relocate without tax subsidies is diluted by the possibility that the team itself may be relegated and, more importantly, by the creation of alternative entry routes for cities that do not possess a major league team. In other words, both the expected benefit of the subsidy for the municipality and the expected benefit to the team of its other option (relocation) are diminished. As a result, the ability of teams to extract subsidies is either reduced or eliminated altogether.

Given its advantages, would a system of promotion and relegation ever be adopted in North America? We think it unlikely that clubs themselves would voluntarily introduce such a system. Thus, some form of government intervention is probably necessary to achieve this result. Promotion and relegation is in fact an ideal structure for surgical intervention to promote entry, since it involves replacing the least efficient incumbent (in terms of wins) with the most efficient entrant. Moreover, entry is only conditional on continuing success, so that a relegated incumbent has an opportunity to recapture its position in the following season.[19] Indeed, in the current controversy over baseball's contraction, government-ordered promotion and relegation seems clearly preferable either to the continued monopolistic exploitation by owners or to some court-supervised freeze on franchises, mandatory relocations, or other highly regulatory approach.

This chapter elaborates on our proposal for legislative or judicial antitrust intervention to require dominant North American sports leagues to implement a system of open competition such as that used in most of the professional sporting world. Part I provides a basic analysis of the economics of promotion and relegation. Part II outlines the way that promotion and relegation operates in English soccer, where it has existed since the nineteenth century, and the implications of the English experience for North American leagues. Part III discusses how closed leagues might be challenged under the Sherman Act, and Part IV considers the details of implementing a system of promotion and relegation.

I.   The economics of promotion and relegation

In general, a larger league is more attractive than a smaller one. A world championship title is more prestigious than a national title, which is more prestigious than winning a regional competition. The more inclusive the competition, the more gratifying the victory. However, there are limits to the optimal size of a league. If the clubs all play each other at least once during a season, there are limits imposed by the physical ability of the players to perform in a sequence of matches, and by the total supply of talent. A larger league leads to a skewed distribution of talent, creating more unbalanced contests. If expansion leads to more unbalanced contests, it can be argued that very large leagues will sacrifice quality for quantity. Finally, even if player talent were evenly spread across all clubs, the talent level for each team would be diluted. Although in many cases the value-added for the fans of the additional clubs outweighs the marginal decline in attractiveness for the fans of the existing teams, at some point this ceases to be the case. These are reasons why members of a league would want to control access in order to maintain an optimally sized league, and why society's laws should find such control to be desirable.

However, there are reasons to suppose that league members will tend to restrict access to a point below the socially optimal level. The major North American sports leagues are organized as joint ventures, where entry and other major business decisions are made jointly by clubs seeking to maximize their own profits, as opposed to a "single entity," where entry and other decisions would be made by an executive or board seeking to maximize overall league profits.[20] Thus, while a single entity league would ordinarily be expected to expand franchises until the point where marginal revenue equals zero, the objective of teams in the league will be to choose the number of franchises so as to maximize average revenue per club.[21] This is analogous to prior observations by labor economists that a labor-managed firm will not expand employment as far as a profit-maximizing firm.[22]

Even though expansion franchises can be assessed a fee to compensate the existing teams for the loss of expected income (reduced probability of winning a championship, reduced percentage of revenue from league-wide ventures), there are several reasons why leagues will still tend to engage in under-expansion. Transaction costs in estimating and agreeing upon expected losses from future entry may lead the league to set the fee too high to attract efficient entry. Most significantly, league members have an incentive to expand sub-optimally in order to provide clubs with a credible threat to move to economically viable open markets unless local taxpayers provide generous tax subsidies. Any expansion can be expected to remove the most viable markets as threatened reloca- tion sites, thus reducing the ability to acquire subsidies.[23] These points have been illustrated most vividly by the recent judgment of baseball owners that they are better off paying two of their fellow members $500 million in order to contract the number of teams.[24]

When monopoly leagues do expand, it is often not to be responsive to consumer demand but rather as a strategic move to deter entry from a rival league. As Fort and Quirk put it, "[m]onopoly profits earned by leagues invite entry, so that one critical aspect of league decision making is acting to inhibit entry."[25] The monopoly league is likely to respond to threatened entry by creating new franchises in locations most likely to be attractive to an entrant league.[26] Moreover, if and when a rival league does manage to enter the market, the incumbent can absorb all or part of the new league: "If a rival league is successful, the inevitable outcome is merger with the existing league in order to exploit the result- ing market power over players, TV networks and stations, and local governments."[27] Thus, even if strategic entry deterrence considerations lead to expansion beyond the point that maximizes average franchise revenue, it is unlikely over time to result in optimal expansion and will continue to result in significant opportunities to obtain monopoly rents.

In contrast to the closed league structure featured in North America, an open league system with promotion and relegation will significantly dissipate rents, as well as inefficient rent-seeking activity such as the cre- ation of sub-optimal entry restrictions, without causing the problems that might be associated with over-expansion. The prospects of demo- tion for teams in the major leagues and promotion for teams in the junior league both induce an increase in investment, raising the quality of competition. Not only will individual clubs have a greater incentive to improve the quality of their product by obtaining better players, but the total talent level is likely to increase as well. Even if all the best base- ball, basketball, football, and hockey players in the entire world already play in the North American major leagues,[28] the existing talent pool is likely to improve through increased expenditure on training and coach- ing. This is driven by the fact that failure would potentially involve a significantly heavier price than simply "waiting until next year." An additional advantage of promotion and relegation would be a consis- tent average talent level in the major leagues, in contrast to alternatives that rely on significant expansion.

The system of promotion and relegation will also significantly increase the quantity as well as the quality of competition. The system will introduce an entirely new level of competition available for mid-sized cities, suburban areas, and growing metropolitan areas, which is qualitatively distinct from and superior to that provided by minor league farm teams, where young players compete solely to develop skills to be used at the discretion of the parent club.

Another advantage of promotion and relegation is a significant increase in the attractiveness of the second half of each season for fans of teams not in contention for the championship, by creating a new aspect of competition: avoiding relegation. The problem of end-of-season ennui has become even more acute in recent years, as teams that have lost hope rush to trade players whose contracts are expiring to pennant contenders in return for young prospects, thus rendering the remainder of their season even less interesting for fans.[29]

One of the most significant economic implications of the system of promotion and relegation is its effect on the opportunity for incumbent clubs to obtain rents because of franchise scarcity.[30] It is arguably efficient to extract the quasi-rents associated with maintaining a team of high quality through some form of public subsidy (like the fixed fee of a two-part tariff), to the extent that teams cannot extract, through conventional means of ticket pricing, broadcasting rights sales, and merchandising, the consumer surplus associated with reading about the local team in the newspaper or talking about it with friends.[31] However, it is socially wasteful to extract pure economic rents by threatening to relocate unless a heavily subsidized facility is provided. This wasteful extraction is possible only because of franchise scarcity, and the amount of the rent extracted matches the willingness to pay of the unserved location (and if this is larger than the willingness to pay of taxpayers/voters in the current location, the team moves). The existence of an unserved location enables all of the teams to extract economic rents from their existing location, whether or not any of them actually move.

Once a system of promotion and relegation is instituted, all credible locations will be served, even if only by teams competing in a lower tier. The threat of relocation would then have limited value. The only credible relocation scenario in the open system would arise when a team in a small drawing location currently in the top tier offers to relocate to a large drawing area. However, the amount of rent would be much smaller, because (a) second-tier competition has a value; (b) a second-tier team can be promoted in the future (and will be likely to do so if it is from a large drawing area that will generate revenue sufficient to support investment in a major league payroll); and (c) a team currently in the top tier might end up getting relegated at some point in the future. All of this suggests that relocation is quite unlikely with a system of promotion and relegation.

Compare the economic choices facing civic officials wishing to obtain a major league franchise under the two systems. In a closed system, the government will likely have to construct a new stadium at public expense and provide it to an existing or expansion franchise on heavily subsidized terms. Even then, a local owner will have to be found who is willing to invest a significant amount of capital in paying an expansion fee or purchasing an existing franchise. In an open system, several local owners anxious to eventually enter the major leagues may well compete for the local land development rights to build a new stadium (or, if civic officials choose to build a public stadium, to pay market-based rent). The winning owner's investment will not be used to pay a huge fee to other owners, but rather to acquire the front-office and on-field talent necessary to succeed in the junior league and secure promotion to the major league.

An open system also provides the proper incentives for owners in a monopoly league to efficiently, and without the need of government regulation, determine the optimal number of teams playing at the top level. For example, if baseball owners believed that competitive balance could be enhanced or the quality of pitching improved by reducing the number of teams, fans would be assured that this judgment was not pre-textual. Competition on the field, rather than willingness to subsidize new stadia, would identify those teams to be relegated.

The foregoing analysis also suggests that promotion and relegation is a more efficient and consumer-responsive means of allocating franchises than allowing the owners of a fixed league to accept or reject requests for individual franchises to relocate. Teams would be optimally located in markets where consumer demand for major league sports is most intense. With closed leagues, relocating to reflect a change in demand requires (a) an owner's ability to identify the change; (b) the owner's willingness to incur transaction costs to make the change; and (c) the other owners' willingness to agree to the change. With open leagues, local entrepreneurs who may have better information about their market's ability to support a major league team, and who may have ancillary reasons for wanting to bring a major league club to their town, can do so at a lower cost.[32] Modern architectural techniques permit the construction of modest-sized stadia viable for junior league competition that can, without prohibitive expense, be expanded to accommodate major league capacities.[33]

Indeed, relocation is almost unheard of in Europe, where the promotion and relegation system operates. As detailed below, the economic performance of professional soccer clubs in Europe, and in England in particular, provides further support for the welfare-enhancing and rent-dissipating effects of promotion and relegation.

II.   Promotion and relegation in English soccer

When the twelve-team English Football League was founded in 1888, it was agreed that the four worst-performing teams should have to seek re-election by a vote of the remaining members, a system borrowed from county cricket.[34] From the beginning it was intended that a second division should be created, but its provisional title—the "second class" —clearly indicated its status.[35] Five years later, the second division came into being and potential aspirants could apply to join either division.[36] In 1898, the system of automatic promotion and relegation from Division One to Division Two was introduced for the two best/worst performing teams in each Division.[37] This basic principle of hierarchical openness has been adopted throughout the soccer-playing world and in most other team sports played in Europe. Indeed, the "system of promotion and relegation is one of the key features of the European model of sport."[38] In theory teams can start at the lowest rung of the ladder in a regional competition and by dint of sporting merit alone they reach the top.

English soccer provides a case study to evaluate the impact of promotion and relegation on league structure and performance. A full financial evaluation is uniquely possible in England because of a legal requirement that all limited companies file standard financial accounts that contain details of revenues, wages, and profits, and make them available for inspection by the general public.[39]

Mobility between the divisions is more than a theoretical possibility. In any one year, there are ninety-two league clubs, and over the seasons 1976–77 to 1997–98 there have been ninety-nine teams participating in four professional divisions (there have been a small number of demotions to the lower semi-professional divisions).[40] Of these ninety-nine teams, only five were never relegated or promoted over the period.[41] Furthermore, over the same period, more teams have moved between three divisions (forty-three) than have played only in two (thirty-two), while twelve teams managed to visit all four divisions over the space of twenty-two years.[42] Moreover, many promoted teams become championship contenders even in their first year after promotion. Between 1991 and 2000, three newly promoted teams finished third in the Premier League and two finished fourth (also giving these teams a lucrative entry into European competition)—accounting for 17% of all promoted teams over the decade.[43] In all, 50% of all promoted teams succeeded in surviving at least one season in the top division over the decade, with 27% of these teams finishing in the top half of the table.[44]

Expenditure on players represented the largest single cost item for all teams.[45] In the Premier (top-tier) League, salaries accounted for 52% of total income, while wages in the second-tier league (confusingly called the Football League First Division) averaged 68% of income.[46] In the Second and Third Divisions, teams traded at a loss, spending respectively 84% and 97% of their income on salaries.[47] Only three Premier League teams reported an average operating surplus in excess of $10 million per year over the five seasons between 1993 and 1998.[48] Of the seventy-two teams comprising the top four tiers of English soccer, only eight reported an operating surplus at all.[49] Of all the English clubs, only Manchester United can be considered to have reported significant and consistent profits.[50]

These figures, representing modest profitability, were reported not against a background of relative decline, but one of considerable growth. Between 1990 and 1998, aggregate attendance at league matches rose by 27% to 24.7 million.[51] In 2001, capacity utilization averaged nearly 93% in the Premier League[52] and almost 69% in the First Division.[53] Ticket prices rose at an annual rate of around 15% in the 1990s, well in excess of the rate of inflation, and by the late 1990s the average ticket price for a Premier League match (when tickets were available) was around $40.[54] Television broadcasting income rose from less than $10 million per year (for the entire league) in 1983 to a more plausible figure of around $250 million per year in 2001.[55] Furthermore, low profit figures are explained in part not only by high levels of player spending, but also by significant increases in stadium expenditure made by the clubs themselves, which has in part made possible the increasing levels of match attendance.[56]

American economists have documented the many ways in which teams can understate their true profitability,[57] and skeptics of profit figures issued by sports teams on this side of the Atlantic point to the very large values attached to franchises when they are sold.[58] Such sales are infrequent in England, but in the mid-1980s around twenty English clubs floated at least part of their equity on the financial markets.[59] According to financial markets theory, the market value of a stock should reflect the net present value of anticipated earnings.[60] In mid-1999, only three teams had a market capitalization in excess of $100 million (Manchester United, Newcastle, and Chelsea).[61] Of the remaining Premier League teams, those that seldom fall into the bottom of the division had capitalizations just under the $100 million mark (Tottenham, Leeds, and Aston Villa).[62] Three teams that have recently moved between divisions or repeatedly faced the threat of relegation (Sunderland, Leicester, and Southampton) had market capitalizations of $50 million, $20 million, and $17 million respectively, which is little different from comparable teams in the (lower tier) First Division.[63]

The relatively low market value of teams at the bottom of the Premier League does not simply reflect the fact that England is a smaller market than North America. Since 1998, Manchester United has been valued at over $1 billion, making it the most valuable sports team franchise in the world.[64] The income of clubs at the bottom of the Premier League is between five and ten times smaller than that of Manchester United, but in 1998 still amounted to around $30 million per year, whereas the average baseball club's income approached $80 million in the same year.[65] Yet the least valuable baseball franchise would sell for well in excess of two and a half times the market value of an English club threatened with relegation.[66] Conversely, there can be little doubt that if Leicester City or Southampton were promised perpetual membership in the Premier League, their market values would rise sharply.

Finally, it is worth observing that while all English soccer clubs have increased their investment in stadium facilities, and several teams have moved to entirely new stadia, none of these investments have been supported directly by local government and no team has moved out of the local area.[67] Even if a local authority had the power to fund such a move, it would make little sense to invest money in this way, since every local authority of any size has at least one local team and could plausibly invest in developing its existing team with a view to promotion up through the divisions.

In sum, despite the strong monopoly position of English soccer,[68] a brief overview of the economic performance of English soccer teams supports the economic theory that promotion and relegation will dissipate monopoly rents and increase relative spending on players. An industry where profits are plowed back into improving the quality of the product for sports fans would appear to be better for overall economic welfare than one where profits are pocketed by owners. In the United States, arrangements that permit economic actors who face no meaningful market competition to pocket excess profits instead of making their products more responsive to consumer demand are normally thought to violate federal antitrust law. A promising means to secure the implementation of a promotion and relegation scheme in North America would be to consider an antitrust challenge to the very structure of a closed league.

III.   An antitrust challenge to the structure of a closed league

Because clubs forming sports leagues must, of necessity, reach agreements on a variety of rules and regulations, the U.S. Supreme Court recognized in *NCAA v. Board of Regents* that these agreements should not be summarily condemned as conspiracies in restraint of trade in violation of the Sherman Act, as they might be in other industries.[69] Where rivals' collaboration has efficiency-enhancing potential, the proper legal framework to analyze their joint venture is the doctrine of "ancillary restraints." The doctrine, which originated in the English common law on restraint of trade, was imported into American antitrust law by William Howard Taft's landmark decision in *United States v. Addyston Pipe & Steel Co.*[70] This decision remains today the most coherent explanation of Supreme Court decisions in this area of antitrust law.[71] The ancillary restraints doctrine requires courts to evaluate whether challenged agreements among competitors are ancillary to an efficiency-enhancing collaboration and, if so, whether the restraints are reasonably necessary to achieve the benefits of the lawful collaboration.[72]

The Supreme Court effectively incorporated the ancillary restraints doctrine into its analysis of sports league conduct in the *NCAA* decision. Having rejected the plaintiff's claim that an agreement to restrain output of televised games was illegal per se, the Court examined the restraint to determine its effect on price, output, and the responsiveness of output to consumer demand.[73] Finding adverse evidence on all three counts, the Court nevertheless proceeded to consider the defendants' arguments that the agreement was justified. In doing so, the Court in effect examined whether the challenged restraints were ancillary to the lawful purposes for which the NCAA was organized.[74]

The economic analysis detailed above suggests that the decision by member clubs to operate as a closed league bears these hallmarks of an unreasonable restraint of trade. The closed league structure allows the league to restrict the number of franchises below an efficient level, and this scarcity allows the league to increase the prices paid by consumers (in areas where exclusive territories bar competition) and taxpayers (in terms of stadium subsidies). Local taxpayers would have no reason to provide substantial subsidies to attract or retain sports franchises if there were reasonable substitutes. Similarly, clubs guaranteed the permanent protection of a closed league would not enjoy their immunity from new entry if fans in their communities had reasonable substitutes.[75] The saga of the Houston Oilers/Tennessee Titans illustrates this point. The Oilers were founded in 1959 as part of the maverick American Football League.[76] At the same time, the incumbent NFL had awarded one of its own franchises to Houston.[77] Because the market was insufficient to support two teams, the Oilers prevailed by offering to spend money to refurbish a local stadium (the NFL franchise went to Minnesota).[78] Four decades later, with no rival league to engage in bidding, the same team owner relocated the franchise to Tennessee for nearly $300 million in subsidies.[79]

The guarantee of permanent presence in a dominant sports league renders output unresponsive to optimal consumer demand in two respects. First, it allows firms to pocket profits, rather than using them to improve the quality of their teams, as fans would prefer. Second, to the extent that fans in another market place greater value on having a major league team, the permanence of major league franchises renders the allocation of franchises among locations in North America unresponsive as well,[80] thus rendering output unresponsive to optimal consumer demand. Where, as in North America, the dominant league in each sport has expanded to the point that entry by a new league is unlikely because of the scarcity of remaining viable markets,[81] the potential for new entry is not sufficient to prevent the exploitation of economic power. Under *NCAA*, therefore, it would appear that the closed league system could be successfully challenged as an unreasonable restraint of trade.[82]

Although North American sports leagues have faced numerous legal challenges over the years, the decision by member clubs to operate as a closed league has never been subjected to judicial scrutiny. The leading case concerning entry is *Mid-South Grizzlies v. NFL*.[83] In that case, the plaintiff sought entry into a closed league.[84] The court concluded that this was not a case of rivals conspiring to eliminate other competitors, because the new entrant did not propose to compete with the incumbents.[85]

The court's rationale would be inapplicable if, instead, the plaintiff had challenged the NFL's refusal to create an open league structure that would give it the opportunity to enter the top-tier league through promotion. Viewed in this light, the existing clubs in the NFL *are* in competition with each other in two important respects. First, by agreeing to a closed league structure, existing clubs are excluding potential rivals for stadium subsidies now obtained through threats of relocation. For example, such a structure effectively excluded other firms who might have been willing to pay a higher rent to play in Tennessee Stadium in return for the chance to build the team up and secure promotion to the NFL.[86]

Second, in an open league structure all teams would be competing with each other to remain in the top tier; the decision to operate as a closed league thus constitutes an agreement to foreclose competition among existing clubs. Because this challenge has never been considered by a court in the United States, there are no American precedents directly on point. Obviously, an agreement among firms that have never competed against each other in a relevant market not to do so in the future is as much a horizontal agreement in restraint of trade as an agreement by current rivals to cease competition.[87]

The foregoing analysis is consistent with Professor Herbert Hovenkamp's general approach to the antitrust evaluation of the exclusion of rivals from joint ventures.[88] Applying *Addyston Pipe*'s ancillary restraint doctrine to this issue, Hovenkamp's approach first dictates that the rule of reason, rather than per se illegality, should apply because leagues have legitimate efficiency-based reasons for imposing *some* limits on entry.[89] Under the rule of reason, the economic analysis in Part I above shows that the major league's exclusion of entrants who are willing to qualify by demonstrating success in junior league competition does indeed threaten to reduce output, raise prices, and render output unresponsive to consumer demand. The analysis also demonstrates that, comparing the venture's output when the league is closed with the output after applicants are admitted, including the output from new entrants, it is promotion and relegation rather than a closed league structure that will increase venture-wide output.[90]

Like Hovenkamp, we acknowledge the general principle that compulsory access rules invite legitimate concerns that firms may underinvest in risky ventures, either because the advantage of innovation will be lost to latecomers whom they must admit to their ultimately successful venture, or because firms themselves will wait for others to innovate and then seek mandatory access.[91] However, we do not believe that these "free riding" concerns are substantial in the case of dominant sports leagues facing no reasonable substitutes. Free riding is solely an *ex ante* concern that legal rules requiring firms to do business with others will lead to inefficient output reduction through lack of investment. In the case of any specific sport, however, our analysis suggests that promotion and relegation will lead to more efficient output through *increased* investment.[92] There is also the theoretical possibility that our proposal could create a disincentive to new investment in new sports—the argument might be that people will be less willing to invest in a new cricket league if they knew that, once established and highly profitable, they will be subject to promotion and relegation rules and thus be deprived of monopoly rents.

We are unpersuaded for three reasons. First, antitrust law does not allow collaborators to exclude others from the market for the purpose of recouping initial investment.[93] Suppose the United States Cricket League was formed in eight cities, and with a huge promotional investment the sport proved wildly successful. The antitrust laws would still prevent the owners from engaging in boycotts or other conduct designed to prevent the formation of a rival American Cricket League, and antitrust judges would reject the argument that—absent congressionally recognized protection akin to a patent or copyright—maintenance of the incumbent league as the only cricket league was necessary to permit the owners to recoup their investment in promoting the sport.[94] Second, because the incumbent league could not use anticompetitive means to forestall a rival league, its original investors could be assured of rents only if the league carried out a successful strategy of entry-forestalling expansion. Leagues are not always so prescient. Third, the first-mover advantages in sports, like in many other businesses where new products are developed and promoted, are likely to provide sufficient incentive to warrant investment where the market is likely to support it. Thus, there is no significant likelihood of investment-chilling free riding from this proposal. To the extent that a portion of a club's prior investment in the major leagues can be considered as capital specific to membership in that league, a reasonable fee might be imposed when clubs are promoted to the major league, to be paid to those clubs being demoted (similar to the capital fees paid by and to attorneys or accountants upon admission to and exit from partnership at their firms).[95]

The Supreme Court's decision in *United States v. Terminal Railroad*[96] provides further support for a finding that the closed league structure violates the Sherman Act. In that case, the Court held illegal an agreement by a number of leading railroads to invest in a corporation that acquired control of the only two bridges and one ferry providing railroad transportation across the Mississippi River at St. Louis.[97] The Court stated that the "fact that the Terminal Company is not an independent corporation at all is of the utmost significance."[98] While an independently owned company—even one with a monopoly—would make its facilities available to all, albeit at a profit-maximizing price, the defendant made access to a means to cross the Mississippi available on a preferred basis to those railroads that were stockholders, and new railroads could be added only by unanimous consent.[99] The Court emphasized the unusual "topographical condition peculiar to the locality" that prevented new entrants from constructing their own bridge across the river.[100] As a remedy, the Court ordered that new entrants be permitted access on "just and reasonable terms and regulations" that would put them "upon as nearly an equal plane" with the defendants.[101]

Although the barriers to entry in baseball, basketball, football, and hockey at the major league level may be based more on economics than on topography, it is clear that for those wishing to compete against current major league clubs, the option of creating their own major league is no more feasible than the option in *Terminal Railroad* of building a new bridge across the Mississippi.[102] Similarly, access to the major leagues is not determined by an independent corporation, but by an entity (the sports league) controlled by rival clubs. Not only would an independent corporation have less incentive to artificially depress the number of clubs below the socially optimal level,[103] but it would also have an incentive to ensure that the clubs in the top-tier league reflect the best possible markets and management available. Therefore, the independent corporation would be willing to replace an inefficient incumbent club with a more efficient new entrant.

There appear to be a few significant, but ultimately non-material, differences between the Terminal Railroad's denial of access and monopoly sports leagues' similar exclusion. In the former case, the facilities were owned by a variety of separate corporations, while sports leagues have no independent stock ownership. Thus, the Court's requirement in *Terminal Railroad* of non-discriminatory access to ownership seems inapplicable. More significantly, the Court seemed to assume that the bridges and ferries had sufficient capacity to accommodate all who might seek to use them. If the optimal use of these facilities required rationing, presumably it would have to be done on reasonable and non-discriminatory terms. In the railroad context, this could occur through open competition for access (perhaps by charging higher bridge tolls). In the sporting context, one could imagine a circumstance where membership in the NFL each year was determined by auction, but the open competition plan we propose here would appear to be more directly responsive to consumer demand. It is literally true that new entrants are not placed on *immediately* equal terms by a system of promotion and relegation, since initially they would have to compete in a junior league; however, within two years, it is fair to say that any team with sufficient and sound investment to earn promotion could be competing at the major league level. In terms of overall antitrust policy, this seems substantially compliant with the *Terminal Railroad* precedent.

In sum, proper application of antitrust doctrine relating to joint ventures among competitors should lead to the conclusion that the closed league structure maintained by the clubs comprising the four dominant North American sports leagues constitutes an unreasonable restraint of trade.[104] Similarly, an agreement among owners to contract the size of their league without reasonable access back into the league for excluded or new franchises warrants condemnation under the Sherman Act. Antitrust tribunals should enjoin the operation of closed leagues and require them to establish a system that grants new entrants reasonable access to top-tier competition. Such access must allow a new entrant who makes skillful business and sport-related decisions to be in a position to meaningfully compete with the existing clubs in the top-tier league within two years.[105] How sports leagues might comply with the mandatory access order contemplated in this Part is considered below.

IV.   Promotion and relegation as a legal remedy

Once the agreement among teams in a dominant league to maintain their closed structure is found unlawful under the Sherman Act, the defendant teams should be given the opportunity to propose a remedial plan that maximizes their legitimate efficient goals while complying with the law's requirement to provide reasonable access. An antitrust tribunal should not mandate the form that reasonable access should take absent an unwillingness to cooperate on the part of the defendant leagues. Without presuming to design a reasonable access requirement, we offer in this Part a brief discussion of why we think it likely that sports leagues would select a model roughly maintaining the existing major league as the top-tier league and adding one or two junior leagues, the lowest tier featuring easy entry. We also discuss some implementation issues that would arise in designing such a structure.

A. Structure

The dominant leagues could maintain their closed structure and comply with the antitrust laws in two quite different ways. First, the dominant league could divide itself into two or more closed leagues that would act as economic competitors, while collaborating on rules and a final champion. Assuming that each league made its own intra-league decisions about labor market restraints, expansion, and relocation, a challenger to the closed structure of any individual league would probably be unable to demonstrate that the league's rules had any substantial competition-lessening benefits.[106] Although this result would have a number of pro-competitive effects,[107] we believe it unlikely that a dominant league would choose such an approach. The clubs would lose whatever economic power they currently enjoy in the broadcast and souvenir markets. Moreover, although one of us has previously analyzed the viability of competition between rival leagues,[108] we suspect that many clubs fear that their particular league might be perceived as inferior, with disastrous results, if it were then excluded from the dominant, closed league.

Second, a league would be unlikely to face antitrust liability if it voluntarily admitted any minimally qualified entrant that could establish a viable plan for success in a new market. There are a variety of reasons why we believe clubs in a dominant league would find this remedy unattractive as well. Overall output might well decline as fans found it difficult to follow all the teams in the league. Because this alternative would require the admission of new clubs on relatively equal terms, existing dominant clubs would play each other fewer times. Easy entry into a closed league would exacerbate competitive imbalance, which would result in either a loss of fan interest or the need to substantially increase the amount of revenue sharing from the wealthier clubs, a prospect they are likely to oppose. Clubs in local geographic markets potentially capable of supporting additional teams would face immediate competition (while under promotion and relegation new entrants in their area would have to first earn entry into the top tier).[109]

Thus, we believe the most likely scenario would see the current leagues comply with the antitrust laws by facilitating the creation of a junior league that has no significant obstacles to entry and that allows successful teams in that league to gain promotion to the higher-tier league.[110] Such an approach is, we suggest, the most acceptable method to the clubs, because it minimizes the effect on the wealthy and powerful teams in the current dominant leagues. The likelihood that these teams would be relegated is rather remote. It is also the most efficient way to identify those clubs that should participate in the top-tier league.[111] Promotion and relegation allows the clubs to maintain their current schedule of contests against traditional rivals and ensures that revenues shared by the wealthy teams with the poorer ones actually are spent on improving competitive balance rather than simply enhancing the profits of the weak teams' owners.[112]

In order to meet the standard of meaningful entry within two years, open entry must be available at no lower than the "third division" within each sport. Leagues can be expected to determine whether to have one or two junior leagues, and to determine the size of each league, based on their own assessment of the net gains and costs for larger leagues.[113]

B.   Issues of implementation

Under the antitrust laws, joint ventures are permitted to impose entry limits that result in lower prices, higher output, or output more responsive to consumer demand.[114] This standard provides guidance as to whether a variety of ancillary rules are reasonably necessary for the efficient operation of the joint venture.

Currently, closed leagues periodically choose to expand, and then as a separate and secondary consideration they take steps to ensure that a new franchise is acquired by an owner who meets acceptable criteria. Reasonable access—with an eye toward maximizing the ability of the public to reap the fruits of competition, rather than protecting specific competitors—means that objective limits to ensure that new owners possess personal integrity and have structured new clubs on a financially sound basis would be permissible. Rules requiring that entrants play in stadia with capacities likely to generate income sufficient to compete at the lower level would also be reasonable. These rules are likely to make the sport more attractive to fans and are unlikely to eliminate so many would-be entrants as to harm competition. Limits must be fair and non-pretextual, however. Thus, for example, rules limiting indebtedness must apply to existing clubs as well as potential entrants, and standards dictating the criteria for stadia and facilities required for entry must not be so high as to preclude meaningful entry.

The benefits from open competition would be lost if incumbent firms were able to forestall entry by depriving rivals of the inputs necessary for success—primarily players. Although the player talent available to a club that seeks, or has just achieved, promotion to the major league varies with each sport, each major league currently has rules, embedded in the collective bargaining agreement with its players' union, that limit the ability of clubs to bid for the services of most players, even at the expiration of their contracts.[115] Moreover, virtually all minor league baseball players sign contracts that are renewable by their major league employer for up to seven years.[116] If new entrants were subject to these agreements, it could well foreclose their ability to compete meaningfully. For entry to be likely, timely, and effective, new clubs must have reasonable access to existing talent so that incumbent teams cannot simply sink costs in player contracts and thereby re-establish entry barriers.

Under the Sherman Act, a standard player contract that bound players to their current employer for at least three years was held to unlawfully foreclose competition with a rival league.[117] Under the common law, a good argument can be made that, for teams that are not part of the major leagues, the lengthy contractual right to renew that exists, for example, in minor league baseball is simply unenforceable.[118]

One acceptable remedy to this problem would be to follow the international practice (and one that prevailed in MLB prior to World War II) of allowing the sale of players for cash. Cash sales are rare in all sports and were seemingly prohibited by the Commissioner of Baseball once veteran players were free to seek competitive bids for their services.[119] With approximately thirty teams in each league, new junior league clubs should not have difficulty acquiring necessary player talent, if cash sales of minor league players are permitted, and the major league teams do not collude.[120]

Cash sales of players play an essential element in a system of promotion and relegation for at least three reasons. First, the ability to purchase key players for cash is critical to the ability of junior league clubs to achieve—through increased investment—success at the lower levels and thus secure promotion to the major league. Second, once promoted to the major league and thus eligible for the vastly increased revenue accompanying major league sports, a club must be able to significantly increase the quality of its roster in order to compete at the top level. The only way to do this quickly is by spending its new-found income on additional player talent.[121] Third, the sale of players is essential to allow clubs relegated from the major league to avoid bankruptcy and remain viable pending their return to the top tier in later years.

Similarly, incumbent firms should not be able to foreclose access to markets necessary to gain revenue. Under the doctrine of *Hecht v. Pro-Football, Inc.*,[122] a club that controls access to an essential facility must grant reasonable access to the facility if it would not interfere with its own use.[123] Although modern techniques of stadium construction would ordinarily preclude a finding that use of an existing stadium is essential, short-term use might well be necessary in specific cases to permit effective entry in two years.

Exclusive contracts regarding the local broadcast rights for games have many legitimate purposes but can potentially foreclose access to new entrants in certain markets. Here, the key issue would be the length of the contract. Unduly long contracts, or contracts that required the broadcaster to maintain exclusivity even if the incumbent club were relegated, may be unreasonably foreclosing in markets where there are no realistic alternatives.[124]

Another key issue of implementation concerns the need to modify existing collective bargaining agreements with players' unions to accommodate promotion and relegation. Although the labor exemption removes most matters agreed to by clubs and players from antitrust scrutiny,[125] unions and dominant firms cannot use the collective bargaining process to agree to exclude rival firms from the market.[126] The precise contours of the limits on a hostile union's ability to frustrate promotion and relegation would require case-by-case analysis, with pathmarking litigation likely. However, we do not believe this scenario is probable, for the likely way that promotion and relegation would be implemented—by maintaining the current number of major league teams and introducing a new tier of junior league competition—would be highly attractive to players. Current major league players would see an increase in the demand for their services from teams that need talented players to forestall relegation. The demand, and the consequent salaries, for junior league players would vastly exceed the paltry sums now paid in the minor leagues.

Although the need for continuing supervision of the operation of a promotion and relegation system would be minimal, antitrust tribunals would ensure that incumbent clubs are not retaining economic power by imposing unduly restrictive criteria on club ownership or stadium size. In addition, standard application of the antitrust proscriptions on foreclosing agreements is necessary to ensure that new clubs can obtain necessary personnel and have access to markets in order to make their entry timely, likely, and effective.

V.   Conclusion

An economic model comparing incentives for professional sports teams demonstrates that a structure of open competition, whereby new entrants have an opportunity to displace existing clubs in the top-tier league, is likely to increase incentives to invest in player talent. Further, this model would decrease the ability of clubs to extract monopoly rents from state and local governments by threatening to relocate. Media interests and sponsors should generally welcome the increased attention that end-of-season races for relegation attract. Competition for promotion from the lower tier would also generate new programming that would likely be much more exciting than the current minor leagues because the rewards for successful teams will be so much greater. Indeed, open competition is likely to benefit almost everyone besides the current owners, who would have to spend more of their monopoly profits on improving their product and would lose much of their leverage over local taxpayers.

But, after all, the Sherman Act is a "consumer welfare prescription,"[127] and the most relevant conclusion we draw is that open competition appears to be good for sports fans. We predict that sports leagues would respond to an antitrust tribunal's finding that their closed league structure violates the Sherman Act by creating one or more lower-tiered leagues. Sports leagues would also promote the top teams from the second-tier league into the major league each season, while relegating the worst teams from the major league. Whether this system was implemented in response to a consent decree or to express legislation, potential fans in unserved cities would have a realistic prospect of having their own team appear in the majors. Fans of existing teams are also likely, on balance, to be more satisfied. While supporters of mediocre teams currently have little to root for after mid-season, fans of teams that successfully stave off relegation are treated to more exciting seasons, not to mention the increased investment in the quality of their teams. Whether or not the teams with the highest payrolls increase their investment further because of fears of relegation, their fans would benefit from the overall improvement of competitive balance due to other teams' increased investment. Even fans of doormat teams are potentially better off with an occasional relegation and the consequent excitement of success at the lower level, as well as increased investment in the quality of the team. This would be in contrast to perpetual mediocrity with no chance of success in a closed league. Taxpayers surely will benefit as well: instead of completely subsidizing a relocation, a public–private partnership with minimal public investment can, using new architectural techniques, build a smaller stadium to support a second-tier team that can then be expanded if and when the team is promoted. Finally, sports fans in unserved cities who currently have the option of seeing only minor league sports, where players are simply there to train for "the Show," would now be able to watch a new, exciting level of professional sports, with young talent and some aging stars vigorously competing for a shot *next year* at the major leagues.

To be sure, a requirement of open competition for monopoly sports leagues does occasion a government-mandated restructuring of sports leagues. Right now, however, consumers pay billions of dollars in tax subsidies, and fans continue to suffer through too many games played by teams with no real prospect for a championship and no real incentive to improve. There ought to be a better way, and an economically sound application of established antitrust principles provides one.

Notes

1. Mark Asher & William Gildea, *Selig's Economic Recovery Pitch Elicits Few Takers*, WASH. POST, Dec. 7, 2001, at D1.
2. *See* Richard Hoffer, *The Loss Generation*, SPORTS ILLUSTRATED, Apr. 17, 2000, at 56.
3. Gordon Forbes, *Oilers Ready to Pull Trigger on Move*, USA TODAY, Nov. 2, 1995, at 4C.
4. *See* James Deacon, *Faded Glory*, MACLEAN'S, Feb. 5, 2001, at 40.
5. Darcy v. Allen, 77 Eng. Rep. 1260 (K.B. 1602).
6. Data on population is based on metropolitan area data published by the Census Bureau and is available at http://eire.census.gov/popest/archives/metro/ma99-02.txt (last visited May 20, 2002).
7. *See* Mark Asher & Dave Sheinin, *Union and MLB Talk Over Plans*, WASH. POST, Nov. 13, 2001, at D3.
8. The Minnesota Twins, for example, have been valued at $99 million. *Braves No. 3 in Total Value Behind No. 1 Yankees, Mets*, ATLANTA J. CONST., Mar. 31, 2001, at 3E. A detailed list of all franchise estimates is available at http://www.forbes.com/basesball/free_forbes/2002/0415/092tab2.html (last visited Apr. 29, 2002).
9. This chapter focuses on the four dominant sports leagues in North America—the National Football League (NFL), Major League Baseball (MLB), the National Basketball Association (NBA), and the National Hockey League (NHL).
10. A variety of courts have concluded that the sports leagues that are the topic of this chapter are sufficiently different from other forms of entertainment and that the dominant league exercises market power. *See, e.g.*, Fishman v. Wirtz, 807 F.2d 520, 531 (7th Cir. 1986) (NBA); L.A. Mem'l Coliseum Comm'n v. NFL, 726 F.2d 1381, 1393 (9th Cir. 1984); U.S. Football League v. NFL, 644 F. Supp. 1040, 1042 (S.D.N.Y. 1986), *aff'd*, 842 F.2d 1335 (2nd Cir. 1988); Mid-South Grizzlies v. NFL, 550 F. Supp 558, 571 (E.D. Pa. 1982), *aff'd*, 720 F.2d 772 (3rd Cir. 1983); Phila. World Hockey Club, Inc. v. Phila. Hockey Club, Inc., 351 F. Supp. 462, 500-02 (E.D. Pa. 1972) (NHL). The authoritative Supreme Court case on point is *International Boxing Club of N.Y., Inc. v. United States*, which held that world championship bouts were in a separate market from other major professional boxing fights. 358 U.S. 242 (1959). This reasoning supports the lower court cases cited *supra* as well as a finding of MLB's market power.
11. NCAA v. Bd. of Regents of the Univ. of Okla., 468 U.S. 85, 102 (1984).

12. *Id.* at 117–20; Mackey v. NFL, 543 F.2d 606, 621 (8th Cir. 1976); United States v. NFL, 116 F. Supp. 319, 323 (E.D. Pa. 1953).
13. *See generally* Stephen F. Ross, *The Misunderstood Alliance Between Sports Fans, Players, and the Antitrust Laws,* 1997 U. ILL. L. REV. 519, 537–49.
14. For example, JAMES QUIRK & RODNEY FORT, HARD BALL: THE ABUSE OF POWER IN PRO TEAM SPORTS (1999); GERALD W. SCULLY, THE MARKET STRUCTURE OF SPORTS (1995); ANDREW ZIMBALIST, BASEBALL AND BILLIONS (1992); Thomas A. Piraino, Jr., *The Antitrust Rationale for the Expansion of Professional Sports Leagues,* 57 OHIO ST. L.J. 1677 (1996).
15. *See* Roger G. Noll & Andrew Zimbalist, *"Build the Stadium—Create the Jobs!",* in SPORTS, JOBS, AND TAXES 2 (Roger G. Noll & Andrew Zimbalist eds., 1997).
16. *Id.* at 26–27.
17. *See* John Henderson, *Contraction on Deck for Baseball,* DENVER POST, Nov. 6, 2001, at D4.
18. Richard Justice, *No Easy Answers; Owners' Contraction Plan Means Questions, Controversy, Legal Issues,* HOUSTON CHRON., Nov. 8, 2001, at 10B.
19. In this sense, promotion and relegation is analogous to a rule developed by leading economists for contestable markets—the so-called Baumol-Willig efficient components pricing rule—which requires incumbents to grant access on terms that ensure that only entrants more efficient than the incumbents can enter the market. *See, e.g.,* William J. Baumol et al., *Parity Pricing and Its Critics: A Necessary Condition for Efficiency in the Provision of Bottleneck Services to Competitors,* 14 YALE J. ON REG. 145, 151–53 (1997).
20. *See* Ross, *supra* note 13, at 549–55.
21. The point is easily made with a simple model. Suppose each team in a league has a profit function of the form $\pi_i = V + w_i(t_i) - t_i$ where $W_i = \dfrac{t_i}{\sum\limits_{j=1}^{n} t_j}$

    is the success of the team (expressed in the form of win percent), *t* is the playing talent that produces success (at a constant marginal cost normalized to unity), and *V* is some fixed utility associated with the presence of a sports team in a particular location (which the team is assumed to extract through stadium subsidies or other means). Social welfare in this model is simply $n\pi$, where *n* is the number of teams. The symmetric profit-maximizing talent investment for each team $t^* = (n-1)/n^2$, and hence $\pi^* = V + 1/n$. Clearly, profits are decreasing in *n*. However, total welfare is simply $nV + 1$ and so social welfare is increasing in *n*. This is the basis of the under-expansion result.
22. For example, J.E. Meade, *Labour-Managed Firms in Conditions of Imperfect Competition,* 84 ECON. J. 817 (1974); Benjamin Ward, *The Firm in Illyria: Market Syndicalism,* 48 AM. ECON. REV. 566 (1958).
23. *See, e.g.,* Stefan Fatsis, *Seven Strikes and Still Swinging: St. Petersburg Still Hopes to Get a Major-League Team,* PLAIN-DEALER (Cleveland), July 14, 1993, at 5F, *available at* 1993 WL 4300853 (listing five existing franchises that threatened to relocate to the St. Petersburg-Tampa area alone, only to remain in their current city after receiving tax subsidies).
24. *See supra* note 7 and accompanying text.

25. Rodney Fort & James Quirk, *Cross-Subsidization, Incentives, and Outcomes in Professional Team Sports Leagues*, 33 J. ECON. LIT. 1265, 1292 (1995).
26. This observation is illustrated by MLB's experience in the period from 1959 to 1962. Despite a huge population growth and a major population shift away from the northeastern United States, the American and National Leagues had remained constant at eight teams each since the turn of the century. In 1960, legendary baseball executive Branch Rickey sought to create a new "Continental League" with franchises in New York (which at the time had only one club, the Yankees), Houston, Minneapolis—St. Paul, and five other locations without any established major league team. *See* Stephen F. Ross, *Monopoly Sports Leagues*, 73 MINN. L. REV. 643, 719 (1989). Many felt this league would have been viable, but the two established leagues responded by adding additional teams in New York (the Mets) and Los Angeles (the Angels) as well as new teams in Houston and Minneapolis—St. Paul. *See id.* This move deprived Rickey of sufficient markets to operate at minimum viable scale and thus forestalled entry. *See id.; see also* Jay Weiner, *Baseball Contraction; The Rise, and Then the Fall*, STAR-TRIB. (Minneapolis—St. Paul), Nov. 11, 2001, at C1.
27. Fort & Quirk, *supra* note 25, at 1294. As one of us has argued elsewhere, the outcome is "inevitable" only in the sense that it is the clearly preferred option for owners seeking to regain monopoly power, and one that society has in the past permitted by allowing the Supreme Court to create a special antitrust exemption for baseball and via special congressional legislation authorizing the NFL to merge to monopoly. *See* Ross, *supra* note 26, at 715–33.
28. This assumption is questionable in light of the increased globalization of sport.
29. *See* Ross Newhan, *Giants Masters of All Trades*, L.A. TIMES, Aug. 1, 2001, at D1. In contrast, in the final week of the 2000 English Premier League season, for example, Manchester United had long since clinched the league championship and the other meaningful places at the top were settled (in England, the top four-to-five finishers are eligible for invitation to European club tournaments), but sports fans followed with interest as the two highlighted games selected for telecast featured the two teams on the verge of relegation. *See, e.g.*, Simon Barnes, *Kitchen-Sink Drama Gives Me Double Vision*, TIMES (London), May 15, 2000, at 30, http://www.times-archive.co.uk/news/pages/tim/2000/05/15/timfoofoo01002.html.
30. The repeated use of this threat is well documented in Noll & Zimbalist, *supra* note 15, at 4.
31. In other words, it is efficient for teams to extract revenues from fans even if they pay in excess of marginal cost, if these excess revenues pay to produce a team of a quality responsive to what consumers demand (what appear to be economic rents are dissipated in the costs of production, hence the term "quasi-rent"). One way to extract these quasi-rents is through a club membership fee, which is independent of the cost of going to the game, so that fans pay a two-part tariff: membership fee plus entry fee. One could imagine treating public subsidies as similar to a membership fee, only paid out collectively by the municipality.

32. *See* Roger G. Noll, *The Economics of Promotion and Relegation in Sports Leagues: The Case of English Football*, 3 J. SPORTS ECON. 169 (2000).

33. *See, e.g.*, Erik Spanberg, *Knights Take Swing at Building Ballpark Uptown*, BUS. J. OF CHARLOTTE, Feb. 11, 2000, at 1 (describing design of proposed stadia in Charlotte and Buffalo), *available at* 2000 WL 14788227.

34. The Football League, *The History of the Football League*, at http://www. football-league.co.uk/club/view/third_feature/0,,10794,00.html (last visited May 23, 2002).

35. *Id.*

36. *Id.*

37. *Id.* For further history of the league's evolution, see STEFAN SZYMANSKI & TIM KUYPERS, WINNERS & LOSERS (1999).

38. EUROPEAN COMM'N, DIRECTORATE GEN. X, SPORT UNIT, THE EUROPEAN MODEL OF SPORT 4 (n.d.), http://europa.eu.int/comm/sport/doc/ecom/ doc_consult_en.pdf (last visited Apr. 29, 2001).

39. The usefulness of these accounts is enhanced by the fact that all of the companies that operate English soccer clubs have virtually no other business interests separate from soccer. SZYMANSKI & KUYPERS, *supra* note 37, at 23.

40. The data reported in this paragraph are compiled from *id.* app. at 340–78.

41. Four of these teams have remained in the top division (Arsenal, Coventry, Everton, and Liverpool) while one has remained in the lowest division (Rochdale). *See id.*

42. *See id.*

43. *See id.*

44. *See id.*

45. *See id.*

46. *See id.*

47. *See id.*

48. *See id.*

49. *See id.*

50. *See id.*

51. *See id.* at 43 fig.2.5, 52 tbl.2.4.

52. *See* Soccer-Stats.com, *Premier Attendances, at* http://www.soccer-stats.com/ divisions/attendances.asp?divno=1&orderby=8 (last visited May 24, 2002).

53. *See* Soccer-Stats.com, *Division 1 Attendances, at* http://www.soccer-stats.com/divisions/attendances.asp?divno=2&orderby=8 (last visited May 24, 2002).

54. *See* Jennie James, *The Money Game*, TIME EUROPE, June 5, 2000, http://www. time.com/time/europe/magazine/2000/0605/football.html. *Cf.* John Reid, *Reclaim the Game: Ten Seasons of the Premier League Swindle* (stating that it would cost £100 for a family of four to attend a premier league match), http://www.socialistparty.org.uk/ReclaimTheGame/ReclaimtheGame.htm.

55. *See* SZYMANSKI & KUYPERS, *supra* note 37, at 57.

56. *See id.* at 55.

57. *See, e.g.*, ROGER G. NOLL, THE ECONOMIC VIABILITY OF PROFESSIONAL BASEBALL: REPORT TO THE MAJOR LEAGUE PLAYERS ASSOCIATION (1985). The profitability of sports teams is an issue that has sparked particular controversy in North America given the disputes between owners and player

unions about the clubs' ability to finance wage increases. *See, e.g.,* Richard Justice, *Labor Pains: With Owners and Players Locked in Another Collective Bargaining Dispute, Strike Clouds Are Hovering over the 2002 Season,* HOUS. CHRON., May 22, 2002, at 1.

58. *Cf.* Justice, *supra* note 57. The Boston Red Sox sold for $670 million in 2001. Leonard Shapiro, *O's Future Programming May Start at Home Base,* WASH. POST, May 7, 2002, at D1.

59. *See* SZYMANSKI & KUYPERS, *supra* note 37, at 18, 72–75.

60. ROBERT COOTER & THOMAS ULEN, LAW & ECONOMICS 39 (3rd ed. 2000).

61. SZYMANSKI & KUYPERS, *supra* note 37, at 289 tbl.8-2.

62. *Id.*

63. *See* DELOITTE & TOUCHE, ANNUAL REVIEW OF FOOTBALL FINANCE (2000).

64. Peter Finney, *Yankees Getting World Serious; Champs Unite with England's Manchester United Soccer Franchise in Global Marketing Venture,* TIMES-PICAYUNE (New Orleans), Feb. 26, 2001, at 1 Sports.

65. *Compare* SZYMANSKI & KUYPERS, *supra* note 37, at 289 tbl.8-2 (English soccer), *with* Michael K. Ozanian, *Selective Accounting,* FORBES, Dec. 14, 1998, at 124, 126 (baseball).

66. *See* QUIRK & FORT, *supra* note 14, at 212 (showing that the Phoenix and Tampa expansion baseball franchises sold for $135 million each in 1997). This is about seven times the market value of Southampton and Leicester.

67. *Cf.* Peter Ferguson, *Plans Won't Sink Us, Says Everton Chief But Fans Are Left Feeling Relegation Issue,* DAILY MAIL (London), July 24, 2001, at 75 (describing Liverpool-based Premier League club's plan to privately finance new £155 million stadium).

68. For example, expenditure on soccer broadcast rights accounts for about 50% of all sports broadcasting expenditure in the UK; no other sport accounts for more than 10%. *See* KAGAN EUROPEAN SPORTS (2000).

69. 468 U.S. at 102.

70. 85 F. 271, 282–83 (6th Cir. 1898), *aff'd,* 175 U.S. 211 (1899).

71. This analysis is detailed in STEPHEN F. ROSS, PRINCIPLES OF ANTITRUST LAW 121–43 (1993). Across the spectrum of antitrust ideology, the *Addyston Pipe* decision has been described as the "true precursor" of the per se rule and "a rational and useful way of distinguishing lawful and unlawful restraints," LAWRENCE A. SULLIVAN & WARREN S. GRIMES, THE LAW OF ANTITRUST 191–92 (2000), and "one of the greatest, if not the greatest, antitrust opinions in the history of the law," ROBERT H. BORK, THE ANTITRUST PARADOX: POLICY AT WAR WITH ITSELF 26 (1978).

72. *See, e.g., Addyston Pipe,* 85 F. at 284; FED. TRADE COMM'N & U.S. DEP'T OF JUSTICE, ANTITRUST GUIDELINES FOR COLLABORATION AMONG COMPETITORS § 3.36(b) (2000), http://www.ftc.gov/os/2000/04/ftcdojguidelines.pdf.

73. *See NCAA,* 468 U.S. at 114–15.

74. *Id.*

75. Virtually no teams in the recent history of major sports have folded, in contrast to the experience of sports leagues in earlier years when they did not have monopoly power, and in contrast to minor sports leagues like the Continental Basketball Association, which have experienced constant instability.

76. *See* Ross, *supra* note 26, at 655 n.52 (citing HOUSTON POST, Oct. 30, 1959, §5, at 2).
77. *Id.*
78. *Id.*
79. Gordon Forbes, *Oilers Ready to Pull Trigger on Move*, USA TODAY, Nov. 2, 1995, at 4C.
80. Allocating franchises entirely on market-based principles might be socially undesirable if the result was a concentration of all the best teams in a few major cities. The European experience, however, does not bear this out. London has five of the twenty teams in the Premier League, but is only slightly overrepresented with twenty percent of the national population. *See* Planet Football, *English Barclaycard Premiership, at* http://www.optasoccer.com/table.asp?cpid=8 (last visited May 23, 2002); World Gazetteer, *United Kingdom: Top Cities, at* http://www. gazetteer.de/t/t_gb.htm (last visited May 23, 2002). Only Manchester and Liverpool (the eighth and fourth largest cities in England) have had multiple teams recently (actually, Manchester City was relegated last year). *See English Barclaycard Premiership, supra; United Kingdom: Top Cities, supra.* Sixteen Italian and Spanish cities host the eighteen teams of the Seria A and La Liga, with only Rome, Milan, Madrid, and Barcelona having two entries. *See* Planet Football, *Italian Serie A, at* http://www.optasoccer.com/table.asp?clid=&cpid=21 (last visited May 21, 2002); Planet Football, *Spanish La Liga, at* http://www.optasoccer. com/table.asp?cpid=23 (last visited May 23, 2002).
81. QUIRK & FORT, *supra* note 14, at 136.
82. Regarding the closed league system in MLB, the textual analysis assumes that a plaintiff could successfully argue that the antitrust laws should apply to baseball. The current application of the theory espoused in this chapter and other potential antitrust challenges to baseball practices is detailed in Stephen F. Ross, *Antitrust Options to Redress Anticompetitive Restraints and Monopolistic Practices by Professional Sports Leagues*, 52 CASE W. RES. L. REV. 133 (2001).
83. 720 F.2d 772.
84. *Id.* at 775.
85. *Id.* at 779, 787.
86. *Cf.* Piraino, *supra* note 14, at 1687–88 (arguing that teams now engage in intense competition to obtain the most favorable stadium packages). Piraino suggested that one of the reasons Browns/Ravens owner Art Modell left Cleveland even before a vote was taken in an Ohio referendum proposing tax subsidies to build a new football stadium was to beat other teams to Baltimore. *Id.* at 1688 & n.46.
87. Palmer v. BRG of Ga., Inc., 498 U.S. 46, 49–50 (1990). Competition among clubs to remain in a top-tier league has been recognized as a relevant market for rivalry under Australian competition law. News Ltd. v. Austl. Rugby Football League Ltd., 139 A.L.R. 193, 338–39 (1996).
88. Herbert Hovenkamp, *Exclusive Joint Ventures and Antitrust Policy*, 1995 COLUM. BUS. L. REV. 1.
89. Hovenkamp's analysis initially asks courts to determine whether exclusion should be considered per se illegal because its only rational purpose is price

fixing or similar trade restraints. *Id.* at 122. As demonstrated in Part I, *supra*, unlimited entry is not optimal for sports leagues, and per se condemnation is therefore inappropriate. In any event, *NCAA*'s language about the need to evaluate all sports restraints under the rule of reason given the close need for some cooperation among club members, probably forecloses this analysis in the sports context. 468 U.S. at 103.

90. *Cf.* Hovenkamp, *supra* note 88, at 123.
91. *Id.* at 96.
92. *See supra* Part I.
93. *Mackey*, 543 F.2d at 621.
94. *See* Fashion Originators' Guild of Am., Inc. v. FTC, 312 U.S. 457, 464 (1941).
95. Such a fee would also have the desirable effect of cushioning the impact of relegation and providing the team with cash to help it maintain viability while it works to return to the major league.
96. 224 U.S. 383 (1912).
97. *See id.* at 410–11.
98. *Id.* at 398.
99. *Id.* at 399–400.
100. *Id.* at 405.
101. *Id.* at 411.
102. Unlike the situation in earlier days, when a new league could form because of the availability of viable markets without any teams belonging to the dominant league, *cf. Am. Football League*, 323 F.2d 124 (4th Cir. 1963), each of the dominant leagues now includes thirty or more franchises, covering the entire continent. Direct competition within a market is especially difficult: new entrants would have to compete against entrenched clubs awash in tax subsidies, and local governments are not likely to be eager to subsidize additional teams. *See* Noll & Zimbalist, *supra* note 15, at 27–28.
103. This is because the transactions costs involved in determining whether the net income from the new team is greater than the net losses caused to existing teams are likely to be lower when the determination is made within a single firm. For a general discussion of why a horizontal agreement is more likely to reduce output than a single dominant firm controlling the same dominant share of the market, see Ross, *supra* note 71, at 152; Hovenkamp, *supra* note 88, at 59–61.
104. A common argument raised by sports leagues defending against allegations that their anticompetitive conduct violates section 1 of the Sherman Act is that the leagues are like corporations—they are single economic entities, so that intra-league agreements cannot constitute a contract, combination, or conspiracy in restraint of trade. This issue has been exhaustively rehearsed in the literature. *See* Ross, *supra* note 13, at 549 n.136 (collecting citations). Our analysis comparing the output of a single firm and a joint venture demonstrates why sports leagues whose policies are established by member clubs are not single entities. *See supra* notes 20–22 and accompanying text. Moreover, even if a closed league's decisions on how to allocate labor inputs or how to sell broadcasting rights were to be considered the decisions of a single entity, the decision to form the league as a closed league, and to maintain that structure, ought to be subject to scrutiny under section 1.

In *Fraser v. Major League Soccer, L.L.C.*, the trial court found that Major League Soccer (MLS) was organized differently from the conventional major leagues and was in fact a single entity for purposes of labor restraints. 97 F. Supp. 2d 130, 139 (D. Mass. 2000), *aff'd on other grounds*, 284 F.3d 47 (1st Cir. 2002). Additionally, the court held that the decision to organize MLS as a single entity could not have lessened competition in violation of section 1 of the Sherman Act and section 7 of the Clayton Act, because there was no league in existence prior to formation. *Id.* at 140. In contrast with this holding, the First Circuit's decision affirming the judgment for the defendant on other grounds poses no obstacles to the imposition of open competition as a remedy for the major North American sports that are the subject of this chapter. *See* Fraser v. Major League Soccer, L.L.C., 284 F.3d 47 (1st Cir. 2002). Most importantly, the court of appeals correctly reaffirmed the significant focus on who controls the operation of the league, finding that MLS decisions were not necessarily exempt from section 1 scrutiny because the club owners "are not mere servants of MLS; effectively, they control it, having the majority of votes on the managing board." *Id.* at 57. Next, the court concluded, as we do, that the determination of access to a sports league is sufficiently related to the economic integration of the collaborative venture to preclude attack on per se grounds. *Id.* at 59. Further, the court found that in the particulars of that case the plaintiff players, challenging MLS formation on grounds that it lessened competition in the labor market, had failed to demonstrate that the relevant market was for major league players in the United States. *Id.* (The defendants produced evidence, believed by the jury, that in competing for player talent, the MLS faced competition from minor league U.S. clubs and foreign clubs.) We do not believe that juries would reach similar conclusions about baseball, basketball, hockey, or football.

In the course of rejecting the plaintiffs' contention that the designation of MLS by the United States Soccer Federation as the sole major soccer league in the United States constituted a conspiracy to monopolize, and that the MLS's formation was a sham for price fixing, the court emphasized that the league was "formed as a risky venture against a background of prior failure." *Id.* (citing United States v. Jerrold Elecs. Corp., 187 F. Supp. 545, 566–68 (E.D. Pa. 1960), *aff'd*, 367 U.S. 567 (1961)). The citation to *Jerrold* is significant, for in that case the court held that a tying arrangement was justified in the early years of a firm's existence, but was no longer justifiable once the firm was well established. *Jerrold*, 187 F. Supp. at 557–58. Clearly, whatever justification may have existed in 1993 for the creation of a single, closed soccer league does not justify the continuation of single, closed leagues in the four major North American sports. Indeed, the Supreme Court has suggested that, to justify an otherwise unreasonable closed league structure, owners of monopoly sports leagues would have to demonstrate that they would lack the economic incentive to compete if their leagues were open. *See* Jefferson Parish Hosp. Dist. No. 2 v. Hyde, 466 U.S. 2, 23–24 n.39 (1984) (justification inapplicable where record showed that desired service would be provided without a tying arrangement).

105. The federal antitrust agencies use a two-year time frame in determining whether new entry will be sufficiently timely to prevent existing firms from

substantially lessening competition through a merger. *See* U.S. DEP'T OF JUSTICE & FED. TRADE COMM'N, HORIZONTAL MERGER GUIDELINES § 3.2 (1997), http://www.usdoj. gov/atr/public/guidelines/horiz_book/32.html.
106. *NCAA*, 468 U.S. at 115 n.55.
107. *See generally* Ross, *supra* note 26.
108. *Id.*
109. The first three reasons stated in the text are also sufficient to reject an argument that this sort of open entry, rather than the open competition we propose, is required by the antitrust laws. Advocates of open entry would likely fail in an effort to demonstrate that output would be higher and more responsive to consumer demand under such a structure. In two thoughtful articles, Thomas A. Piraino, Jr., argued that application of the essential facilities doctrine would require open entry. *See* Thomas A. Piraino, Jr., *A Proposal for the Antitrust Regulation of Professional Sports*, 79 B.U. L. REV. 889, 948 (1999); Piraino, *supra* note 14, at 1692–93. Indeed, he suggests that restrictions on the total number of franchises are illegal per se because they are not justified by any legitimate efficiency objective. *See* Piraino, *supra*, at 944. Piraino concedes that leagues operating at "full capacity" could legitimately limit new franchises, but he seems to define that concept too broadly, based on whether scheduling effectively is "impossible" or whether the number of franchises exceeds the pool of available players. *Id.* at 944–45. Rather, the efficient "capacity" of a sports league, measured properly in terms of optimal consumer demand, is much smaller. Indeed, it is arguable that with the type of open competition we propose here, overall consumer demand would increase if the number of clubs in the major leagues were reduced.
110. The so-called "essential facility" cases cited by Piraino would not support a finding of liability if a monopoly sports league permitted entry via promotion from a junior league. *See* Piraino, *supra* note 109, at 946–48; Piraino, *supra* note 14, at 1690–92, 1707–08. In each of these cases, the courts found, either on the facts or in theory, that granting access to the new entrant would not affect the ability of the existing firms to service their customers. Many of the cases also involved situations where otherwise open entry could be blocked by particular incumbents. For example, in *Associated Press v. United States*, the "essential facility" was membership in a joint venture with unlimited capacity, and the government did not seek unlimited access but only elimination of by-law provisions giving local competitors the right to veto requests for admission. 326 U.S. 1, 3–4 (1945). (This case would be applicable, for example, if the NBA had a rule permitting anyone who paid a fixed fee to join the league, but gave an individual veto to each existing franchise so they could keep out local competition.) Similarly, in *Silver v. N.Y. Stock Exchange*, membership in the defendant stock exchange did not have a consumer-optimal capacity, and therefore exclusion from the exchange's services was unreasonable. *See* 373 U.S. 341, 347–48 (1963). *Radiant Burners, Inc. v. Peoples Gas Light & Coke Co.* involved a group boycott of those lacking a company's "seal of approval." 364 U.S. 656, 658 (1961) (per curiam). Because the boycott was unrelated to any efficiency, it was per se illegal. *See id.* at 659. Here, it is clear that excluding a potential entrant from a sports league cannot be considered to be unrelated to any

efficiency. *Cf.* N.W. Wholesale Stationers, Inc. v. Pac. Stationery & Printing Co., 472 U.S. 284, 297 n.7 (1985) (finding that joint venture's exclusion of rival was unreasonable where the exclusion was "not substantially related to the efficiency-enhancing or procompetitive purposes that otherwise justify the cooperative's practices").

Two lower court cases apply the essential facilities doctrine to sports, but neither is directly on point, and their holdings tend to support a remedy of open competition rather than a remedy of open entry. In *Hecht v. Pro-Football, Inc.*, the court found that Washington D.C.'s RFK Stadium was an essential facility and therefore concluded that the prospective owner of a franchise in the rival American Football League should have been allowed to share the use of the stadium with the NFL's Washington Redskins. 570 F.2d 982, 992–93 (D.C. Cir. 1977). The court emphasized that the essential facilities doctrine "must be carefully delimited: the antitrust laws do not require that an essential facility be shared if such sharing would be impractical or would inhibit the defendant's ability to serve its customers adequately." *Id.* To support its proposition, the court cited the Supreme Court's decision in *Otter Tail Power Co. v. United States. Id.* (citing 410 U.S. 378, 381 (1973)). In *Otter Tail*, the Court made clear that the essential facility in question there—wholesale power transmission lines subject to regulation by a federal agency—need not be opened to new entrants "if to do so 'would impair [the utility's] ability to render adequate service to its customers.' " *Otter Tail*, 410 U.S. at 381 (quoting 16 U.S.C. § 824a(b)). However, because another team could use RFK Stadium in the Redskins' absence, a denial of access was held illegal in *Hecht. Hecht*, 570 F.2d at 993.

Unlike the situation in *Hecht*, Piraino's proposal for open entry in league competition would indeed impair the league's ability to render adequate service to its existing fans, because such entry would lower overall quality. On the other hand, our open competition plan meets the *Hecht* test: (1) membership in MLB, the NFL, NBA, or NHL is essential to operate a club at the major league level; (2) this membership cannot be practicably duplicated through creation of a new league; (3) entry will not impair the league's ability to serve customers; and (4) the closed league structure prevents "equitable" sharing of league membership by potential competitors. *See* 570 F.2d at 993.

Another case Piraino cites is *Fishman v. Estate of Wirtz. See* Piraino, *supra* note 109, at 948 (citing 807 F.2d 520 (7th Cir. 1986)). This decision is complex and somewhat troubling analytically. The court held that a bidder for the Chicago Bulls should have been offered a lease for the Chicago Stadium because the stadium "could not feasibly be duplicated." *Fishman*, 807 F.2d at 539. The reason that the plaintiff was not offered a lease was that the defendant, who controlled the Stadium, also had an ownership interest in a rival investment group seeking to purchase the Bulls. *Id.* at 529. Consumers presumably benefit when different firms compete to be the local monopolist because the result is that service is provided by the most efficient monopolist. *See id.* at 534–35 (quoting Omega Satellite Prods. Co. v. City of Indianapolis, 694 F.2d 119, 127 (7th Cir. 1982) (antitrust laws protect "competition to be the firm to enjoy a natural monopoly")). But *Fishman* does not support a claim for open access where such access would impair the quality of the product for other customers. Indeed, to the extent that membership in a league can be seen as a natural monopoly (*but see* Ross, *supra* note 26, at 715–33), *Fishman* supports the argument that open competition for a sport among the optimal number of franchises, not unlimited access, is the preferred antitrust result.

111. One of the doctrinal difficulties with applying the essential facilities doctrine to sports league entry is that the most likely plaintiffs are not government enforcers seeking a macro-remedy in the public interest, but private plaintiffs simply seeking their own entry into a dominant league. Especially before a sympathetic local judge, each plaintiff may well establish that (1) the league is a monopoly; (2) it has artificially limited the number of franchises; and (3) the plaintiff can viably operate a club in the local market. Thus, relief ordering the mandatory entry of the plaintiff club would be sought. The problem with this approach is that it ignores the very real possibility that, assuming the addition of another franchise would be welfare-enhancing, the franchise should be located elsewhere. *See* Ross, *supra* note 26, at 709–11 (discussing State v. Milwaukee Braves, Inc., 1966 Trade Cas. (CCH) ¶71,738 (Wis. Cir. Ct., Branch 5, Civ. Div., Milwaukee County), *rev'd on other grounds*, 31 Wis. 2d 699, 144 N.W.2d 1 (1966)).

112. For example, the Montreal Expos maintain profitability by pocketing shared revenues and maintaining a low payroll. T. R. Sullivan, *Upstairs, Downstairs; With Arizona's Ordination into the Upper Crust, It's Easy to See Baseball Has Its Favorites and Outcasts*, STAR-TELEGRAM (Fort Worth), Sept. 20, 1999, at 5C.

113. The clubs would recognize that additional second-tier teams will increase revenues. Each expansion, though, modestly dilutes the quality of talent available for the remaining second-tier clubs and modestly reduces the attractiveness of the product to fans of the other clubs by decreasing the number of contests between top rivals and by lessening the chance that each team will be promoted.

114. *See NCAA*, 468 U.S. at 103 (sports league rules analyzed under the rule of reason). The hallmark of this analysis is the effect of the challenged rule or practice on output, price, and responsiveness of output to consumer demand. *Id.* at 106–109.

115. *See generally* HOWARD L. GANZ & JEFFREY L. KESSLER, 1 UNDERSTANDING BUSINESS & LEGAL ASPECTS OF THE SPORTS INDUSTRY 13-148 (2001) (NBA and NFL collective bargaining agreements); *Basic Agreement Between the American League of Professional Baseball Clubs and the National League of Professional Baseball Clubs and Major League Baseball Players Association*, *reprinted in* Jeffrey S. Moorad, *Negotiating for the Professional Baseball Player*, *in* 1 LAW OF PROFESSIONAL AND AMATEUR SPORTS § 5.05 & app. 5A (Gary Uberstine ed., 2001); Nat'l Hockey League & Nat'l Hockey League Players Ass'n, Collective Bargaining Agreement (on file with authors).

116. *See* Moorad, *supra* note 115, § 5.04.

117. *Phila. World Hockey Club*, 351 F. Supp. at 467. In many industries, concerns about how truly "unique" talented employees are, and the desire to allow individuals to work where they please, may well trump antitrust concerns

that the hiring of a particular individual may contribute to monopolization. *See* PHILLIP E. AREEDA & HERBERT HOVENKAMP, ANTITRUST LAW 141–44 (2nd ed. 2000). But the systematic refusal by all clubs to sell the rights to players' services more closely resembles the exclusionary practice of raising rivals' costs—the strategy of sacrificing short-term profits (in this case through higher payrolls) in order to impose higher costs on rivals, so that the rivals' ability to effectively compete is significantly impaired. *See generally* Thomas G. Krattenmaker & Steven C. Salop, *Anticompetitive Exclusion: Raising Rivals' Costs to Achieve Power over Price*, 96 YALE L.J. 209 (1986).

118. *See, e.g.*, Am. League Baseball Club of Chi. v. Chase, 149 N.Y.S. 6 (N.Y. Sup. Ct. 1914) (monopoly enjoyed by National and American Leagues precluded injunction preventing White Sox star from jumping to Buffalo club of rival Federal League).

119. *See, e.g.*, Finley & Co. v. Kuhn, 569 F.2d 527, 536 (7th Cir. 1978). At a recent conference, however, Major League Baseball General Counsel Thomas Ostertag suggested that *Finley* was a more limited precedent, and that the Commissioner would consider approving cash sales that demonstrably improved competitive balance among the clubs—as would certainly be the case with a sale to a recently promoted team. This topic is discussed in detail in Stephen F. Ross, *Light, Less-Filling, It's Blue Ribbon!*, CARDOZO L. REV. (forthcoming 2002).

120. To the extent that prohibitions on cash sales to clubs that are wealthy and successful are perceived as improving competitive balance, league rules that maintained the limit on sales from existing major league clubs to the league's top teams pose no obstacle to effective entry as outlined in this chapter.

121. *See, e.g.*, Anne Hyland, *Charlton Has £10m to Spend; Relegation Cuts £4.5m from TV and Gate Receipts*, GUARDIAN (London), June 24, 2000, at 25, http://www.guardian.co.uk/Archive/Article/0,4273,4033083,00.html.   The Charlton soccer club, upon promotion to the English Premier League, raised £5.74 million to acquire two or three top quality players in order to compete at the higher level. *Id.* The strategy worked: the team finished tenth among the twenty teams in the league and can still obtain further financing for continued improvement. *See* David Bond, *The Grass Isn't Always Greener on the Other Side of the River*, EVENING STANDARD (London), May 10, 2001, at 83. The complete 2001–2002 English soccer table is available at http://www.fl.net.au/~steve/table.htm (last visited May 24, 2002).

122. 570 F.2d 982.

123. *Id.* at 992–93.

124. Local affiliates of major television networks are disinclined to broadcast local sporting events in prime time because of the conflict with regular series programming, and in many local markets there may be only one independent over-the-air station and one cable sports station interested in providing local programming. *See, e.g.*, Steven Herbert, *KTLA Channel 5 Calls Its New Identity a Hit*, L.A. TIMES, July 12, 1993, at 6F (explaining that TV station that had carried Dodger baseball games since the team arrived in Los Angeles in 1958 gave up rights because of conflict with network programming).

125. *See, e.g.,* Brown v. Pro Football, Inc., 518 U.S. 231 (1996); Wood v. NBA, 809 F.2d 954 (2nd Cir. 1987); McCourt v. Cal. Sports, Inc., 600 F.2d 1193 (6th Cir. 1979); *Mackey,* 543 F.2d at 606.
126. Connell Constr. Co. v. Plumbers & Steamfitters Local Union No. 100, 421 U.S. 616 (1975); Allen Bradley Co. v. Local Union No. 3, Int'l Bhd. of Elec. Workers, 325 U.S. 797 (1945).
127. Reiter v. Sonotone Corp., 442 U.S. 330, 343 (1979) (quoting BORK, *supra* note 71, at 66).

5

Equality of Opportunity and Equality of Outcome: Open Leagues, Closed Leagues and Competitive Balance

Luigi Buzzacchi,[a] *Stefan Szymanski*[b] *and Tommaso M. Valletti*[c]

[a]*Politecnico di Torino*
[b]*Imperial College London*
[c]*The Business School, Imperial College London*

Abstract

This chapter compares conventional static measures of competitive balance with measures that take account of the mobility of teams into the upper ranks of professional leagues, which we call dynamic competitive balance. We use this measure to compare the open soccer leagues that permit entry by the process of promotion and relegation, to the closed leagues of North America where there is no automatic right of entry. We also identify the theoretical distribution of entrants to the top k ranks assuming that all teams have equal probabilities of winning. We find that the open leagues (OL) we study are less balanced, dynamically, than closed leagues (CL), and also that OL lie much further away from the theoretical distribution than CL.

Keywords: sports leagues, competitive balance

1. Introduction

All schemes used in the United States punish excellence in one way or another. The European football approach punishes failure by promoting excellent minor league teams to the majors and demoting

We thank the editor and an anonymous referee for helpful comments.

(relegating) poor performing major league teams back down to the minors. The revenue loss from a potential demotion to a lower class of play is severe punishment for low quality—severe enough that salary treaties, league sharing arrangements, and unified player drafts are so far thought to be unnecessary, even though star salaries are enormous. It is an interesting economic question as to which system achieves better results.

Rosen and Sanderson (2001)

Since Superbowl I in 1967 the NFL has expanded from a league of 16 teams to one of 32. During this period 17 different franchises have won the Superbowl. In Serie A, the top division of Italian soccer, 48 different teams have participated since 1967, but there have been only 11 different winners.[1] Serie A has had more teams not because it is a larger league—in most seasons only 18 teams compete for the championship title. However, the institution of promotion and relegation permits new teams to enter the league each year. Nonetheless, despite having more competitors, fewer teams seem to have a chance of winning—less than quarter of the teams in Serie A over the period have one, compared to half of the current NFL franchises. Moreover, a similar story emerges if any of the North American leagues are compared to the national soccer leagues of Europe.[2] In other words, soccer leagues tend to be much less balanced than the major leagues. However, this is not true when measured in the way that has been conventionally adopted in the sports literature. This chapter proposes a way of measuring competitive balance that permits comparison between the North American closed leagues (CL) and the open leagues (OL) of Europe.

This enables us to address some important policy issues. It is a long-standing proposition in sports economics that "better" means "more balanced" results (*e.g.* Rottenberg, 1956). Competitive balance refers to the expectations of fans about who will be the winner. In a perfectly balanced contest fans believe all outcomes are equally possible so there is complete outcome uncertainty. In a perfectly unbalanced contest the winner is known *ex ante* with probability 1. It seems reasonable to suppose that without at least some degree of competitive balance, fans will loose interest in a competition. A stronger proposition would be that, all else equal, a more balanced contest is a more interesting one. This proposition is widely accepted (see Szymanski, 2003, for a survey of the evidence). Most importantly, it has frequently been accepted by the courts as a justification for restrictive agreements concerning the sharing of revenues or restraints in the player market (*e.g.* salary caps and roster limits).

Measuring the extent to which a competition is balanced, therefore, is a critical issue. However, this is no simple issue. The measure widely cited in the existing literature (see *e.g.* Quirk and Fort, 1992) is the standard deviation of winning percentages in a season. According to this measure, the greater the variance in outcomes in a season, the less balanced is the contest. The principal weakness of this measure is that it takes no account of the identity of the teams across seasons. Applying this measure to North American and European leagues produces the seemingly perverse result that European leagues are if anything slightly more balanced than North American leagues. This is an artifact of the European system of promotion and relegation, by which the worst performing teams in a league in each season are demoted to the immediately junior league—so that no team can afford to give up once it is out of contention for the title.

The novel measure of competitive balance that we develop in this chapter permits a comparison to be made between different sports leagues across time, in particular taking the account of the promotion and relegation system. This measure focuses on the identity of teams, and the frequency with which they approach the possibility of winning the title. What we show is that the North American major leagues (we consider Major League Baseball, the National Football League and the National Hockey League) are much more balanced than the dominant soccer leagues of Europe (we compare the top divisions of the English, Italian and Belgian leagues) in the sense that a greater proportion of teams in the league are likely to experience any given level of success within a given period of time. However, the North American leagues are more or less closed to entry by new teams, whereas European leagues have a system of promotion and relegation which gives many more teams access to the highest level of play (the top division). In other words, we find equality of outcomes in the closed North American leagues while in Europe, we find equality of opportunity within a system that is dominated by a small number of teams.

Previous studies of competitive balance have measured either "match uncertainty" or "seasonal uncertainty," and both of these measures can be compared across leagues. Match uncertainty refers simply to expectations about a particular game, and this can be measured, *e.g.* by studying pre-match betting odds.[3] However, interest in a league competition goes beyond uncertainty about a particular match and many fans are attracted by uncertainty about the overall outcome of the championship. Seasonal uncertainty, the closeness of an overall championship race, can be measured in a number of ways, *e.g.* the number of games behind the leader that the following k teams are as the season ends, the date at which at the championship outcome becomes known with certainty, or more generally, the standard deviation of success (*e.g.* win percentage) among the teams.

These measures tell us something about competitive balance in a "static" sense—the balance of a particular match or season, but for many fans there is also interest in competitive balance in a "dynamic" sense: do particular teams dominate the championship over time? This chapter proposes a natural basis for comparing dynamic competitive balance among leagues and a theoretical benchmark.[4] The natural basis is to consider the cumulative frequency of teams entering the top k ranks of a league (ranked by some measure such as win percentage). By analogy we can think of dynamic competitive balance like the spread of an epidemic—the more balanced a league, the more rapidly teams enter the ranks of the top k.

This raises an important additional consideration. In a "closed" league of, say, 20 teams, the top k can only ever be drawn from that 20 teams.[5] The more teams, the greater the potential for entry into the top k, just as the absolute number of people succumbing to a disease must be increasing in the total population. Leagues in North America are typically closed in the sense used above (although there can be some new entry from the sale of additional franchises and league mergers). By contrast, in most other countries leagues are "open" in the sense that at the end of each season the worst performing teams are demoted to the immediately junior league and replaced by the best performing teams from that league. The European Commission (1998) has gone so far as to suggest that "the system of promotion and relegation is one of the key features of the European model of sport." Given this hierarchical structure it is apparent that the population of potential entrants into the major league is, over time, much larger (and possibly unlimited) compared to a closed league.

One central concern of this chapter is whether this "equality of opportunity" translates into equality of outcome, as measured by competitive balance. Our theoretical benchmark approaches this issue by asking how many teams would be expected to enter the top k ranks in a league system where resources were so distributed that each match played were perfectly balanced. In other words, if success were purely random (because all sources of systematic variation, such as resource inequality, had been removed) how much mobility would there be in a given league structure? Calculating this benchmark for a CL with a fixed number of teams is relatively straightforward, but as we show the case of an OL is more complex. However, by deriving these values we can compare actual with theoretical mobility and derive a kind of Gini coefficient, measuring the closeness of league outcomes to a perfectly balanced ideal. It turns out that North American leagues are far closer to the theoretical ideal than their European counterparts, a phenomenon that can be accounted for by the much greater extent of resource equalization measures in North America, *e.g.* gate revenue sharing, collective merchandising, draft rules, salary caps and so on.

The chapter is set out as follows. In Section 2, we survey the literature comparing North American leagues and European soccer leagues. In Section 3, we compare measures of static and dynamic competitive balance for North American major league sports and the dominant national sports leagues in Europe for soccer. In Section 4, we derive our theoretical benchmark for CLs and OLs. In Section 5, we consider the difference in mobility comparing theoretical and actual measures. Section 6 concludes.

2. North American and European sports leagues

As the quote at the beginning of this chapter indicates, there are substantial differences in the organizational framework of North American and European sports leagues and many of these are illustrated in Table 5.1.[6] First, in North America, there are four significant team sports competing for market share compared to a single dominant team sport in Europe soccer. However, in North America, there is a single league that dominates competition in each sport, whereas in Europe the national league of each country is normally dominant in its own territory, with limited penetration elsewhere (in some ways the regional conferences of the NCAA bear some resemblance to this). Four leagues currently dominate Europe due to their large populations, wealth and traditional obsession with soccer: England, Germany, Italy and Spain. Another significant difference is that North American teams and players typically play in only one league or competition in any one season. In Europe, however, teams can compete in two national competitions (the league and the knock-out Cup[7]), an international league or cup competition for European clubs, while in addition the players can be selected to represent the national team[8]—and national representative competition is in most cases even more popular than club competition.

Economic arrangements in North American and European team sports also differ significantly. On the revenue side there is a much lower

Table 5.1 Differences in structure of U.S. and European sports leagues

	U.S. Sports	Football in Europe
League system	Closed, no promotion or relegation Teams compete in single league competition	Open, annual promotion and relegation Teams may compete simultaneously in many competitions
League functions	Collective sale of TV rights Centralized marketing	Collective sale of TV rights
Competition between clubs	Limited substitution by consumers	Significant potential for substitution
Competition between leagues	Numerous cases of entry by rival leagues	All leagues contained within the established hierarchy
Player market	Rookie draft Salary caps (NFL, NBA) Collective bargaining	Active transfer market
Revenue sharing	Equal division of national broadcast income Gate sharing (NFL 40%, Baseball average 15%, NBA 0%)	Sharing of television income Little or no sharing of league gate revenues Some sharing of gate from cup competitions
Competition policy	Antitrust exemption for baseball Sports Broadcasting Act exempts national TV deals from antitrust	Centralized sale of TV rights under attack Selected interventions (ticket allocation FIFA)

incidence of revenue sharing in Europe. On the expenditure side there are almost no restrictions in the player market and trading for cash is the accepted norm (more than 10% of players move team each season) compared to the U.S. where rules and custom inhibit player mobility.

The principal difference that this chapter focuses on is the existence of promotion and relegation. In Europe leagues are typically organized in an ascending hierarchy by a governing body vested with responsibility for the development of sport as a whole. At the end of each season the worst performing teams in each division are demoted to the immediately junior division and replaced by the best performing teams in the junior division. Hence, it is in principle possible for team to rise from the lowest to the highest level of competition, and vice versa. The existence of this system in Europe and not in North America is essentially an accident of history (see Ross and Szymanski, 2001, for a description of the historical underpinnings), and while the discussion in this chapter focuses primarily on soccer, this system has been adopted even in sports imported into Europe from North America, such as basketball.

A further difference between North American leagues and European leagues has been the subject of some controversy, and this is the widely held belief in Europe that North American clubs are run by profit maximizers whereas European clubs embrace purely sporting objectives, such as win maximization subject to a budget constraint (the locus classicus is Sloane (1971)), and many of the implications of these assumptions for league rules have been analyzed by Kesenne (see *e.g.* Kesenne, 2000). However, it is also clear that until recently there was limited financial return to be gained from team sports in Europe, a situation which has been transformed dramatically in the 1990s—and some authors see a shift toward more commercially oriented policies and the increasing pursuit of profit (see *e.g.* Andreff and Staudohar, 2000).

While it is clear that there are many differences, the comparative study of North American and European leagues is still at an early stage.[9] In two recent papers, Noll (2002) and Ross and Szymanski (2002) consider what impact the promotion and relegation system would have on North American leagues if introduced there, but further research is required to understand the consequences of institutional differences. By focusing on competitive balance, this chapter aims to provide a starting point for a theoretical analysis of the properties of these institutions.

3.   Static and dynamic competitive balance

Most measures of competitive balance in the literature are essentially static—they analyze the equality of winning opportunities for individual matches or for a championship season taken as a whole.[10] For example, Fort and Quirk (1995) hypothesize that if seasonal win percentages become less dispersed then a league has become more competitively balanced. They review some allegedly balance-enhancing reforms in the North American professional leagues (*e.g.* the introduction of the salary cap in the NBA in 1984, the NFL rookie draft introduced in 1936 and the beginning of free agency in baseball in 1976). In general, they find no significant change in the standard deviation after the reforms and therefore conclude that there is no evidence that competitive balance was in fact enhanced.

Horowitz (1997) uses an entropy index to measure changes in competitive balance over time in Major League Baseball (and finds that there is underlying trend toward increasing balance over the period 1903–95). Applying the concept of entropy to a CL seems natural enough, but it is less clear how one might extend this to a league with promotion and relegation. Quirk and Fort (1992) look at balance over time by adopting another measure based on seasonal variance. If a given league were perfectly balanced, the winning probability for each team in each match would be 0.5, which would also be the expected value of the seasonal win percentage. The standard deviation of this win percentage would then be $0.5/\sqrt{m}$ where m is the number of matches played. This can be used as an "idealized" measure of the standard deviation for a particular league. Expressing the actual standard deviation as a ratio of the idealized standard deviation thus provides a basis for comparing the degree of competitive balance of different leagues.

In this chapter, we have chosen to compare three North American leagues (Major League Baseball (MLB), The National Football League (NFL) and the National Hockey League (NHL)) to three national soccer leagues in Europe (Italy, England and Belgium). In terms of revenues and broadcast audiences the first two in each region are somewhat larger than the third, but within both regions the basic league structures are comparable. Above all, the North American leagues are all closed and the European soccer leagues all open. In Table 5.2 we compute the ratio of actual to idealized standard deviation for North American major league sports and European soccer leagues. As Quirk and Fort have noted, the data for the North American leagues indicate a trend toward competitive balance over time in baseball, but no trend in the NFL or NHL. On this measure the NFL has tended to be the most balanced of the North American leagues and the NHL the least balanced. As has been

Table 5.2 Actual standard deviation of win percentages divided by idealized standard deviation

Decade	MLB (1950–99)	NFL (1950–99)	NHL (1949–98)	England (1949–98)	Italy (1949–98)	Belgium (1953–2000)
1950s	2.23	1.48	2.04	1.15	1.33	1.26
1960s	2.05	1.63	1.93	1.33	1.50	1.45
1970s	1.88	1.60	2.61	1.44	1.47	1.54
1980s	1.66	1.46	2.08	1.48	1.34	1.67
1990s	1.68	1.51	1.83	1.40	1.61	1.67

Note: Ties (draws) are treated as half a win. European leagues refer to the top division of the national soccer league.

noted in the work of Kipker (2000), the European soccer leagues seem by comparison to be more balanced (although the European trend is toward less balance). Thus, in the 1950s each of the three European leagues had lower standard deviations than any of the North American leagues, and in the case of England the actual standard deviation was only 15% higher than the idealized standard deviation. However, by the 1990s the gap had narrowed considerably, and for instance, the NFL seemed more balanced than either Italian of Belgian top divisions.

The principal weakness of a static measure of competitive balance such as this is that it takes no account of the identity of the successful teams.[11] So *e.g.* according to the data the NFL was less balanced than the top soccer division in England, but in between 1990 and 1999, 6 different teams won the Superbowl whereas in England only 5 different teams won the League Championship. Moreover, in England one team won the title on 5 occasions (Manchester United), whereas the biggest winner in the U.S. won only 3 times (Dallas).[12] To consider the dynamics more fully we have looked at the number of different teams winning the league title and the number of teams entering the top ranks.[13]

We conjecture that fans care about balance in the sense that they want a reasonable prospect that the identity of the winners will change from time to time (although they may also care about the variance of success among the teams within the season). "Turbulence" at the top increases the interest of fans of a greater number of teams. If, say, each team experiences diminishing returns to success in terms of fan interest, then a league that is more balanced in this dynamic sense will be more successful. This point has been made elsewhere, see *e.g.* Ross and Lucke (1997) and Szymanski (2001) who find some empirical support for the conjecture. In this chapter, our aim is to compare dynamic competitive balance across open and closed league. To do this, we have looked at the number of entrants into the ranks, first over the full 50 years of data, then over 40 years, 30 years, 20 years and 10 years. The data is reported in Tables 5.3 and 5.4.

Table 5.3 shows the number of different teams with the highest win percentage in each season. The North American leagues have developed the post season play-off season over the period in question in order to involve more teams in the championship race for longer. The play-off system introduces more randomness in outcomes and therefore adds to uncertainty even if the teams are not well balanced competitively. Since we are interested in competitive balance rather than uncertainty itself in this chapter we have restricted ourselves to considering win percentages during the regular season only (see note to Table 5.3).

Table 5.3 Teams that had the highest winning percentage or were winners of the league championship

Period	MLB	NFL	NHL	England	Italy	Belgium
1950–99	16	20	13	16	12	10
1960–99	16	18	13	13	12	8
1970–99	14	14	12	9	10	8
1980–99	12	9	10	7	7	7
1990–99	6	7	7	5	4	4

Note: North American teams selected on the basis of regular season win percentage. European teams selected on the basis on actual championship wins. Traditionally, 2 points were awarded for win, 1 for a draw (tie). Tied winning percentages were then decided on goal difference. However, from the 1980s onward leagues introduced the award of 3 point for a win and 1 for a draw. In the data, the champions always had the highest win percentage, but in 9 out of the 150 championships considered the champions were tied in win percentage with the team ranked second (on goal difference). In 1995, Blackburn Rovers won the English championship on the basis of the new points system but would have tied on the old points system (which is the same as our measure of win percentage) and had an inferior goal difference to the team ranked second.

Table 5.4 Teams that entered the top 5 ranks

Period	MLB	NFL	NHL	England	Italy	Belgium*
1951–2000	28	31	21	34	19	32
1961–2000	28	30	21	27	18	28
1971–2000	28	29	21	24	18	24
1981–2000	28	28	21	22	14	21
1991–2000	23	26	18	16	12	18

*1953–2000 only.
Note: All teams selected on the basis of regular season win percentage.

For the North American leagues the NFL had the greatest number of teams entering the top rank for 4 out of the 5 periods considered, although in the last decade the performance of all the 3 leagues looks remarkably similar on this measure (notwithstanding the recent dominance of the New York Yankees in baseball).

For any of the 5 ranges considered, both the Italian and Belgian leagues had less variation in the number of teams appearing in this rank than any of the North American leagues. Only when the last 40 or 50 years are considered did the English league have as many teams entering the top rank, and for both of these ranges the NFL had more teams achieving the highest win percentage. Thus, despite the greater opportunity through promotion and relegation for teams to reach the highest rank, there seems to be relatively less turnover at the very top in the open European leagues than in the closed North American leagues. On average over the last 30 years there have been 50% more teams achieving the highest rank in North America compared to Europe.[14]

The story told by Table 5.4 is slightly different. Looking at the last 10 years, a very large fraction of all teams in each of the North American leagues managed a top 5 finish in term of win percentage. Forty-six percent more teams in the CLs achieved this feat on average than in the open European leagues. However, as we go back further the number of teams entering the top ranks does not increase significantly for the North American case, but does in the European case. Clearly, once all the members of a closed league have entered the top 5, the population of entrants can only increase through franchise expansion. In an OL, however, there need be no limit to the increase in the population. Thus, in the case of England there were only 16 teams entering the top 5 ranks over the last decade, but 34 teams entered over the entire 50-year period, more than for any league in the sample (during this period the top division was restricted to 22 or fewer members in each season). Over this lengthy period the number of teams entering the top 5 in North America and Europe is almost identical. Thus, openness in Europe seems to give roughly similar opportunities over a very long period time, even if there are fewer opportunities over relatively short timespans. Whether this is enough to make an open European league as competitively balanced as a closed North American league in the eyes of the fans must be doubtful at least.

In order to set this picture in a proper perspective, we now consider the theoretical probability of teams entering the top k of ranks for open and closed leagues, under the hypothesis that in each season each contestant in a division has an equal probability of winning each match.

4.   Entry in the top k ranks

4.1.   Closed leagues

We consider first the case of n teams that are grouped together and compete in a CL with no system of promotion and relegation. Under the hypothesis that the outcome of the championship in a given year is purely random, each team has the same probability $1/n$ of being ranked 1st, 2nd, …, n-th. The probability that a team is ranked in the top k

places in a generic year is then $w(k) = k/n$. After T years, the probability that a given team has been placed at least once in the top k places is $w(k, T) = 1 - [1 - w(k)]^T = 1 - [(n - k)/n]^T$. Finally, the expected number of teams that has won one of the top k positions in the first T years is

$$y^{\mathrm{CL}}(k, T) = nw(k, T) = n - \frac{(n - k)^T}{n^{T-1}} \tag{5.1}$$

Equation (5.1) represents our benchmark for a CL. In particular, the expected number of teams that has won the title at least once after T years is simply $y^{\mathrm{CL}}(1, T) = [n^T - (n - 1)^T]/n^{T-1}$, increasing at a decreasing rate over time, from 1 when $T = 1$, to n when T tends to infinity.

4.2. Open leagues

We now consider the typical European way of organizing a team contest. There are L leagues ordered from the top division to the lowest one: league 1 is the "premier" league that awards the championships while league L is the lowest league. League l consists of n_l teams, $l = 1, \ldots, L$. In a generic period, a team in league l can either remain in the same league, or go to an "adjacent" league. We denote respectively by $p(l)$ and by $r(l)$ the total number of promotions to the league above and the total number of teams relegated to the league below league l.[15] If the outcome of each league is random, the probability that a team is in division l at time t is

$$d(l, t) = d(l, t - 1)\frac{n_l - r(l) - p(l)}{n_l} + d(l - 1, t - 1)\frac{r(l - 1)}{n_{l-1}}$$
$$+ d(l + 1, t - 1)\frac{p(l + 1)}{n_{l+1}} \tag{5.2}$$

where $l = 1, \ldots, L$ and $r(L) = p(1) = 0$, $d(0, t) = d(L + 1, t) = 0$.[16] It can be verified that

$$\sum_{l=1}^{L} d(l, t) = \sum_{l=1}^{L} d(l, t - 1) = 1$$

since a team starts at $t = 0$ in some league with probability 1, *i.e.* $d(l, 0)$ is 1 for only one value of l and 0 otherwise. In order to take into account the initial distribution of teams, we denote with a subscript l the league where a team starts at the beginning, $d_l(j, 0) = 1$ if $j = l$ and 0 if $j \neq l$.

The probability that a team is ranked in one of the top k places of the premier division in a generic year t is given by the joint probability

$d_l(1,t)k/n_1$. We are now in a position to calculate the probability that, after T years, a team that started in league l in the initial period $t=0$ has been placed at least once in the top k places of the top division. This probability depends on initial conditions and corresponds to the complement to 1 of the probability that such team has never been placed in the top k positions, *i.e.* the team was either in a lower division or in the top one but never "picked" one of the top placements:

$$w_l(k,T) = 1 - \prod_{t=0}^{T}\left[\sum_{l=2}^{L} d_l(l,t) + \frac{n_1 - k}{n_1} d_l(1,t)\right]$$

$$= 1 - \prod_{t=0}^{T}\left[1 - \frac{d_l(1,t)k}{n_1}\right] \tag{5.3}$$

The expected number of teams that has been placed in the top k positions after T years is

$$y^{OL}(k,T) = \sum_{l=1}^{L} n_l w_l(k,T) \tag{5.4}$$

Equations (5.2), (5.3) and (5.4) represent the benchmark for an OL and it is the counterpart to Equation (5.1). Once it is known the number of teams in each league, as well as the number of teams promoted and relegated to adjacent leagues and the initial conditions, it is immediate to obtain the value of the expected number of teams observed in the top positions after T years. For instance, if a total number n of teams is split equally among L leagues, the teams are ordered in a way such that $d_1(1,0)=1$ for the first group of n/L teams, $d_2(2,0)=1$ for the second bunch of n/L teams and so on, and if 1 team is promoted and 1 team is relegated in any period, the expected number of teams that has won the premier league at least once after T years is given by[17]

$$y^{OL}(1,T) = \left(\frac{n}{L}\right)\sum_{l=1}^{L}\left(1 - \prod_{t=0}^{T}[1 - d_l(1,t)L/n]\right)$$

$$d_1(l,t) = [d_l(1,t-1)(n/L-1) + d_l(2,t-1)]L/n$$

$$d_l(l,t) = [d_l(l,t-1)(n/L-2) + d_l(l-1,t-1) + d_l(l+1,t-1)]L/n$$

$$l = 2,3,\ldots,L-1$$

$$d_l(L,t) = [d_l(L,t-1)(n/L-1) + d_l(L-1,t-1)]L/n$$

5.   Mobility in theory and in practice

In the previous sections, we have looked at the actual number of entrants into top ranks and derived the theoretical distributions of teams appearing in top positions in closed and open leagues under the assumption of equal winning probabilities. In this section, we compare the difference between the actual and theoretical distributions.

We apply the theory of the previous section to the precise structure of each league. Table 5.5 shows the number of teams that would have been expected to achieve the highest seasonal win percentage (if all teams had equal win probabilities) over the same periods considered in Table 5.3. Table 5.6 shows the theoretical prediction of entrants into the top 5 of win percentages (if all teams had equal win probabilities), analogous to the actual data of Table 5.4.[18]

In general, there are two conflicting effects that produce differences in the theoretical predictions for the closed North American and open European leagues. First, in recent decades the expansion of North American leagues to around 30 teams has increased the number of potential winners relative to the European leagues where the size of the top division varies in size between 16 and 22 teams. The second effect is that promotion and relegation gives more teams an opportunity to enter the

Table 5.5   Theoretical number of teams with highest seasonal winning percentage under equal playing strength

Period	MLB	NFL	NHL	England	Italy	Belgium
1951–2000	22	23	18	37	40	39
1961–2000	21	21	18	32	33	31
1971–2000	18	19	17	26	26	24
1981–2000	14	15	14	18	18	17
1991–2000	9	9	9	9	9	9

Table 5.6   Theoretical number of teams with top 5 seasonal winning percentage under equal playing strength

Period	MLB	NFL	NHL	England	Italy	Belgium
1951–2000	28	29	25	82	104	100
1961–2000	28	29	25	78	94	84
1971–2000	28	29	25	70	78	67
1981–2000	28	29	25	57	58	48
1991–2000	25	25	24	32	33	28

major league. With equal winning probabilities it can be seen that these two effects would have canceled each other out over the last decade and the CL would have produced as many winners as the open leagues. Over time, however, the promotion and relegation effects increasingly dominate the expansion effect and over a 50-year period the open leagues should have produced around twice as many winners as the closed leagues.

In all cases, the actual number of winners in each cell of Table 5.3 is smaller than the theoretical prediction, but the shortfall is much more pronounced for the open leagues.

Table 5.6 illustrates a sharper contrast between the OLs and CLs. Even in a relatively short period of time the promotion effect dominates the expansion effect so that under equal win probabilities the OLs could have been expected to see more entrants into the top 5 ranks. This contrasts with Table 5.4 where it was shown that in reality the situation was the reverse—more teams entered the top 5 ranks in the CLs compared to the OLs. Even within a 10-year period most teams in a CL should enter the top 5 ranks—so over a longer period of time the theoretical number of entrants does not increase by much. However, for open leagues the theoretically possible number of entrants increases rapidly, so that over 50 years the number of entrants under equal win probabilities is around one hundred. Once again, the gap between theory and reality is much greater for the open leagues.

To illustrate the size of the gap Figures 5.1 and 5.2 show the relationship between theoretical and actual entry to the top for NFL while Figures 5.3 and 5.4 offer the same comparison for Serie A, the top soccer division of Italy. In each figure, the broken lines represent the theoretical number of entrants for each of the 5 time ranges, while the solid lines illustrate the actual rate of entry. The figures also provide some perspective on the expected and actual entry on a year-by-year basis. Figures 5.1 and 5.2 show that actual entry is quite close to theoretical entry assuming equal playing strengths, suggesting that in dynamic terms the NFL is a fairly balanced competition (particularly looking at entry into the top 5 win percentages). On the other hand, Figures 5.3 and 5.4 demonstrate a large gap between theoretical and actual entry in Italy. Actual entry increases only very slowly, both for into the group of champions and into the top 5, and there is no evidence of convergence toward the theoretical limit. This suggests that equality of opportunity in open leagues in Europe has not translated into any equality of outcomes.

While these charts paint a very clear picture, it is desirable to quantify the differences between the OLs and CLs in some way. We propose

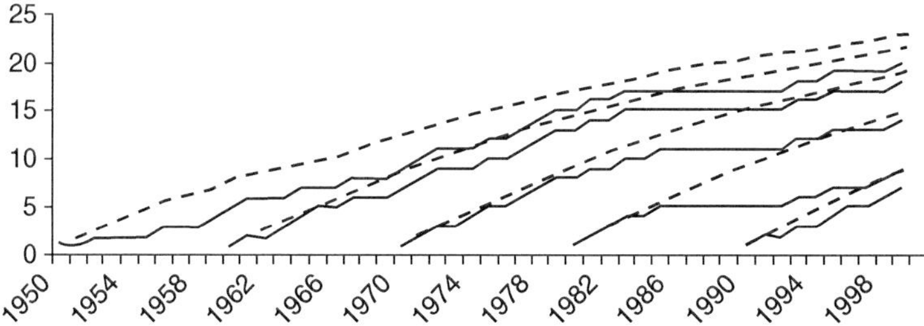

Figure 5.1   Entry to the highest rank in the NFL

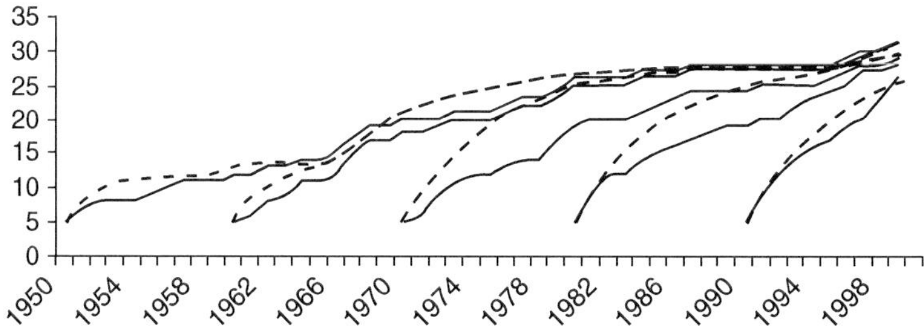

Figure 5.2   Entry to the top 5 ranks in the NFL

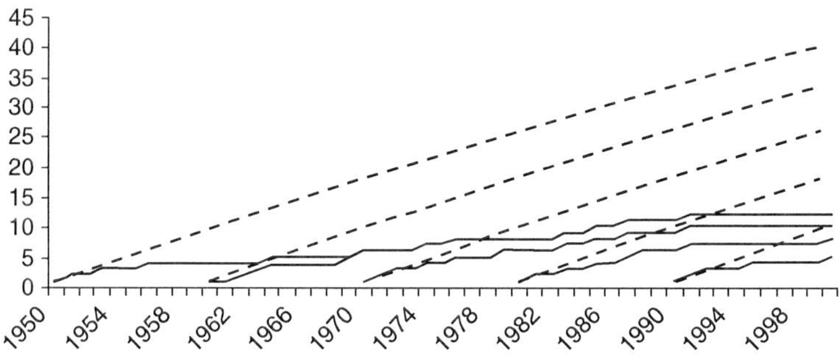

Figure 5.3   Entry to the highest rank in Italy

a Gini-type index that relates theoretical to actual entry. Thus, we calculate an index G where

$$G(T^*) = \frac{\sum_{T=1}^{T^*} y^L(k, T) - \sum_{T=1}^{T^*} y_a^L(k, T)}{\sum_{T=1}^{T^*} y^L(k, T)} \qquad (5.5)$$

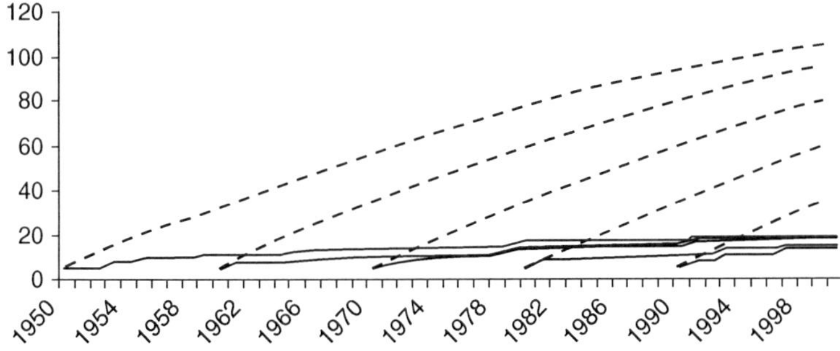

Figure 5.4   Entry to the top 5 ranks in Italy

where T^* is the range of years considered and $y^L(k, T)$ and $y^L_a(k, T)$ are respectively the theoretical and the actual number of teams appearing in rank k or higher in a given league $L = \{CL, OL\}$ over a period of T years. Thus a value of G close to zero indicates a perfectly balanced league while a value of G close to unity indicates a perfectly unbalanced league.[19] Table 5.7 reports the G-index for the highest seasonal win percentage across the leagues.

For every period considered the G-index for the closed leagues is lower than the G-index for the OLs, suggesting that the closed leagues were closer to the theoretical distribution under equal winning probabilities. In fact, the G-index for the CLs never rose above 0.5, while for the OLs value is either above or close to 0.5 for almost all periods. Looking at the individual leagues, there is some indication that baseball has become more balanced over the last 20 years while there is no obvious trend in the NFL or NHL. For the open leagues Belgium was generally furthest away from the theoretical distribution under equal win probabilities, but for the individual leagues there was no clear trend over time.

Table 5.7 G-index for teams with highest seasonal winning percentage

Period	MLB	NFL	NHL	England	Italy	Belgium
1951–2000	0.34	0.19	0.42	0.44	0.66	0.70
1961–2000	0.30	0.15	0.36	0.44	0.55	0.70
1971–2000	0.30	0.21	0.40	0.54	0.48	0.62
1981–2000	0.05	0.39	0.39	0.57	0.44	0.51
1991–2000	0.19	0.24	0.12	0.24	0.38	0.54

Table 5.8   *G*-index for teams with top 5 seasonal winning percentage

Period	MLB	NFL	NHL	England	Italy	Belgium
1951–2000	0.16	0.04	0.18	0.54	0.78	0.64
1961–2000	0.18	0.08	0.20	0.60	0.77	0.59
1971–2000	0.17	0.17	0.23	0.58	0.70	0.59
1981–2000	0.09	0.15	0.17	0.53	0.67	0.53
1991–2000	0.11	0.07	0.14	0.35	0.51	0.37

As far as the top 5 are concerned, the *G*-index scores for the CLs are all very similar and close to 0. Comparing Tables 5.7 and 5.8 this suggests that the CLs have been more successful at creating contenders rather than sharing out the most successful slot. However, since the ultimate Championship winners have been determined by play-offs that are more random than the regular season, this is probably not a problem. By contrast, the *G*-index for the OL suggests that entry into the top 5 has been more or less as difficult as into the top rank, and without a system of play-offs this suggests both little mobility at the top and considerably less competitive balance than in the closed leagues.

6.   Conclusions and policy implications

This chapter has proposed a measure of competitive balance that is dynamic, taking into account the turnover of teams at the top over time, rather than conventional measures that tend to emphasize *within-* but not *between-season* competitive balance. We have shown that by a conventional measure the open soccer leagues of Europe are, if anything, more balanced than the North American closed leagues. However, by the dynamic measure of competitive balance the OLs appear significantly less balanced than the closed leagues. We believe that the dynamic measure presents a better picture of competitive balance than the static measure.

One reason for believing that this is a better picture is that we have calculated the theoretical distribution of winning teams under the null hypothesis of equal winning probabilities for the teams, and shown that the open leagues deviate far more from the theoretical distribution than the OLs. The hypothesis that the Europe's open leagues are competitively balanced is far harder to support than the hypothesis that North America's CLs are balanced.

It is important to ask why the European pattern should be so different from the North American one. In general, successful teams draw more support, so that the greater concentration of success in Europe suggests more concentrated support. For example, clubs from Milan (AC and Inter) and Turin (Juventus) have dominated the championship with relatively few other population centers. For example, Rome (population 3.5 million) can boast only four championship titles since the start of the Serie A in 1929, compared to Turin's 28 (population 1.5 million).[20] However, it is by no means clear that fans of Roma and Lazio are less interested or less willing to pay for success than their more successful northern rivals. Moreover, while in many countries the most successful teams have been located in the largest cities (most notably in the case of Spain with Real Madrid and Barcelona) in many other countries this is not clear. In England, *e.g.* league competition has for the last 30 years been dominated by teams from Liverpool (3rd largest population,[21] 13 titles) and Manchester (7th largest, 7 titles) while London-based teams have won only 4 titles and Birmingham (2nd largest) have won only a single title.

If concentration is not a product of population endowments, it may be a product of hysteresis. Dynasties are not unknown in North American sports, most notably the Yankees in baseball.[22] But dynasties are usually seen as a significant source of competitive imbalance needing to be counteracted with redistributive measures either in the labour market (*e.g.* salary caps, roster limits) or in the product market (revenue sharing).[23] Such measures are much less widely adopted in Europe. Labor markets operate almost entirely free of any constraints while revenue sharing is rare and limited in extent. But if competitive balance promotes interest in the sport why wouldn't European leagues take on the kind of extensive redistribution seen in North America?

Two possible answers suggest themselves. One is that competitive balance in the sense described here does not matter to the fans. There certainly does not appear to be less interest in European soccer than in North American sports. But as long as the contest within each season is close (*e.g.* measured by standard deviation of win percent) then fans may be indifferent to dominance by a small number of teams over many seasons. This suggests one way in which the study of competitive balance should develop, *i.e.* to focus on the number of teams that need to be in contention to make the contest interesting.

A second possible explanation is that the promotion and relegation system itself mitigates against welfare-enhancing redistribution schemes. Szymanski and Valletti (2003) compare the incentive to redistribute income in closed and open league systems (*i.e.* with promotion and relegation). They argue that the cost of revenue sharing to large drawing teams is the foregone income from current success, while the benefit is their share in a more valuable (because more balanced) contest. In a closed league every team is guaranteed to participate in that contest, while in an open league any team might be relegated in the future. Thus a strong team has a weaker incentive to share its revenues in an open system.[24] From a policy point of view, perhaps the most interesting topics for further debate are (a) whether the alternative sources of interest in European soccer compensate fans for the relative lack of competitive balance and (b) returning to the Rosen and Sanderson quotation at the beginning of the chapter, whether the choice of balance-enhancing measures are hindered by the promotion and relegation system itself.

Annex

In this annex, we propose an indicator alternative to the G-index. As a first step, we calculate—as with the G-index—$y^L(k, T)$, *i.e.* the theoretical number of teams appearing in rank k over a period of T years. This number takes into account all the precise details of a certain league that may have changed over time. Then, we calculate $n(k, T)$, *i.e.* the equivalent dimension of a closed league with a constant structure that would have generated then the same number of teams appearing in rank k over the same period. In the third step, we consider the actual number $y^L_a(k, T)$ and then construct $n_e(k, T)$, *i.e.* the theoretical dimension of a closed league with a constant structure that would have generated the same number. Finally, our indicator is given by the ratio $n_e(k, T)/n(k, T)$. Results are reported in Table 5.A1. A league is balanced, the closer is the

Table 5.A1 E-index for teams with highest seasonal winning percentage

Period	MLB	NFL	NHL	England	Italy	Belgium
1951–2000	0.65	0.83	0.67	0.21	0.12	0.11
1961–2000	0.67	0.75	0.65	0.15	0.12	0.09
1971–2000	0.61	0.58	0.58	0.10	0.12	0.13
1981–2000	0.62	0.36	0.49	0.07	0.11	0.15
1991–2000	0.29	0.41	0.36	0.13	0.09	0.13

Table 5.A2 E-index for teams with top 5 seasonal winning percentage

Period	MLB	NFL	NHL	England	Italy	Belgium
1951–2000	1.00	1.06	0.84	0.39	0.16	0.29
1961–2000	1.00	1.02	0.84	0.31	0.16	0.29
1971–2000	1.00	0.99	0.89	0.29	0.18	0.31
1981–2000	1.01	0.97	0.83	0.28	0.18	0.37
1991–2000	0.91	1.06	0.70	0.34	0.23	0.51

E-index to 1, *i.e.* to the equivalent theoretical benchmark. Notice that this exercise allows to construct an indicator that is homogeneous both for open and for closed leagues. This indicator gives a snapshot of competitive balance at the end of a given period, without concentrating on how a particular configuration is reached over time—contrary to the G-index. Results illustrate once again the sharp contrast between open and closed leagues.

Notes

1. In fact, going back to 1945 only 12 different teams have won Serie A.
2. Soccer is by far the dominant team sport in Europe. Sports such as Rugby, cricket, basketball and ice hockey trail a long way behind in terms of popularity.
3. A review of these studies is provided by Szymanski and Kuypers (1999).
4. Humphreys (2002) and Koop (2002) have proposed alternative methods for evaluating the evolution of competitive balance over time, but in both the cases the method is not naturally adapted to inter-league comparisons.
5. Abstracting, for the moment from franchise expansion.
6. Adapted from Hoehn and Szymanski (1999) who review the differences between North American and European soccer.
7. Play-offs are not widely used. A league competition followed by play-offs can be thought of as an integrated League and Cup competition.
8. Clubs are obliged as part of their obligations to their national federation to release their players and receive no compensation. Secession from the federations is seldom considered an option. In France, *e.g.* the national federation has a statutory monopoly over the organization of league competition.
9. Hall *et al.* (2002) attempt a limited comparison of the economics of Major League Baseball and English soccer.
10. An exception is Szymanski (2001) who compares the competitive balance of two different competitions.
11. This fact may also produce uninformative information within a given period. For instance, the standard deviation of winning percentages tends to put too much weight among weaker teams. To give an example, imagine 10 teams

competing in a league in a given year. In the first scenario, there is a team much stronger than everybody else that wins every single match, while the remaining teams have identical strength and win 50% of the matches. In the second scenario, there are 5 slightly stronger teams and 5 slightly weaker teams, where a team has 50% chance of winning a match among "equals," while a stronger team has 80% probability of winning against a weaker team. Despite it would be natural to describe as more balanced the second scenario, the normalized standard deviation of win percentages would yield the same numerical value in both cases.

12. Rolling the data two years further forward would highlight the point even more clearly: only 4 winning teams in England, one of which won 7 of the 10 titles, while in the NFL there were 7 different winners.

13. League rank is the standard measure of performance in Europe. For North American leagues we have ranked teams according to their regular season win percentage.

14. In writing this chapter we have looked at some of the descriptive statistics for other European leagues such as Germany, Portugal, Scotland and Spain. In all cases, a similar pattern emerges to that described here.

15. In principle, both $p(l)$ and $r(l)$ should depend on t; however, we can drop the dependency from time under the hypothesis of random ranking as long as the number of teams in a given league is constant over time. In practice, the number of promotions and relegations can change between periods and this feature can be easily accommodated in our framework.

16. To ensure that the number of teams in a given league is constant overtime, we assume $p(l) = r(l - l)$.

17. With a simple spreadsheet it is immediate to confirm that with the same total number of teams $y^{OL}(1, T) < y^{CL}(1, T)$ for any $T > 1$. The difference between the two expected numbers of winning teams becomes smaller as T grows, or if "turbulence" is increased by increasing the number of teams promoted/relegated in any period.

18. Numbers in Tables 5.4 and 5.5 are rounded. They were obtained taking into account entry and exit of teams, as well as variations in the number of promotions and relegations over time. For instance, in England the third division was split in 1959 into a third and a fourth division. Our calculations do take into account all such institutional features and are available on request.

19. This indicator depends on the starting year; moreover the longer the time series, the less informative is the more recent data.

20. Tommasi (2000).

21. Source: www.citypopulation.de, Thomas Brinkhoff.

22. See Levi *et al.* (2000) for a discussion of baseball's competitive balance problem.

23. These measures are reviewed in detail in Szymanski (2003).

24. A third reason, suggested by a referee, is that the wider range of competitions on offer in Europe may offset the lack of dynamic competitive balance. For example, in one season the top teams compete in a domestic league, a domestic (knock-out) Cup competition, the European Champions' League, and in addition the top players are selected to play for their national team in international competition. There is certainly a greater array of competition

in Europe, but this does not explain why the fans would not find a more balanced league competition more interesting or why the league authorities would not choose to try to make it so. Moreover, Szymanski (2001) provides evidence that lack of competitive balance in the English FA Cup is leading to declining interest in that competition.

References

Andreff, W. and Staudohar, P., "The evolving model of european sports finance," Journal of Sports Economics, vol. 1 no. 3, pp. 257–276, 2000.

European Commission, The European Model of Sport. Consultation paper of DGX, Brussels, 1998.

Fort, R. and Quirk, J., "Cross subsidization, incentives and outcomes in professional team sports leagues," Journal of Economic Literature, vol. XXXIII no. 3, pp. 1265–1299, 1995.

Hall, S., Szymanski, S. and Zimbalist, A., "Testing causality between team performance and payroll: the case of major league baseball and english soccer," Journal of Sports Economics, vol. 3 no. 2, pp. 149–168, 2002.

Hoehn, T. and Szymanski, S., "The Americanization of European football," Economic Policy, vol. 28, pp. 205–240, 1999.

Horowitz, I. "The increasing competitive balance in major league baseball," Review of Industrial Organization, vol. 12, pp. 373–387, 1997.

Humphreys, B., "Alternative measures of competitive balance in sports leagues," Journal of Sports Economics, vol. 3 no. 2, pp. 133–148, 2002.

Kesenne, S., "Revenue sharing and competitive balance in professional team sports," Journal of Sports Economics, vol. 1 no. 1, pp. 56–65, 2000.

Kipker, I., "Determinanten der zuschauernachfrage im professionellen teamsport: Wie wichtig ist die sportliche ausgeglichenheit?" Unpublished chapter of Ph.D. dissertation, 2000.

Koop, G., "Modelling the evolution of distributions: an application to Major League Baseball," University of Glasgow Discussion Paper, 2002.

Levi, R., Mitchell, G., Volcker, P. and Will, G., The report of the independent members of the commissioner's blue ribbon panel on baseball economics. Major League Baseball, NY, 2000.

Noll, R., "The economics of promotion and relegation in sports leagues; the case of English football," Journal of Sports Economics, vol. 3 no. 2, pp. 169–203, 2002.

Quirk, J. and Fort, R., Pay Dirt: The Business of Professional Team Sports. New Jersey: Princeton University Press, 1992.

Rosen, S. and Sanderson, A., "Labour markets in professional sports," Economic Journal, vol. 111 no. 469, pp. F47–F68, 2001.

Ross, S. and Lucke, R., "Why highly paid athletes deserve more antitrust protection than unionized factory workers," Antitrust Bulletin, vol. 42 no. 3, pp. 641–679, 1997.

Ross, S. and Szymanski, S., "Promotion and relegation," World Economics, vol. 2 no. 2, pp. 179–190, 2001.

Ross, S. and Szymanski, S., "Open competition in league sports," Wisconsin Law Review, vol. 2002 no. 3, pp. 625–656, 2002.

Rottenberg, S., "The baseball players' labor market," Journal of Political Economy, vol. 64, pp. 242–258, 1956.

Sloane, P.J., "The economics of professional football: the football club as a utility maximizer," Scottish Journal of Political Economy, vol. 17 no. 2, pp. 121–146, 1971.

Szymanski, S., "Income inequality, competitive balance and the attractiveness of team sports: some evidence and a natural experiment from English soccer," Economic Journal, vol. 111 no. 469, pp. F69–F84, 2001.

Szymanski, S., "The economic design of sporting contests," Journal of Economic Literature, vol. 56, p. 1137, 2003.

Szymanski, S. and Kuypers, T., Winners and Losers: The Business Strategy of Football. London: Penguin Book, 1999.

Szymanski, S. and Valletti, T., "Promotion and relegation in sporting contests," Imperial College Business School Discussion paper, 2003.

Tommasi, R., Storia della Serie A. Edizioni Marchesi Grafiche, Rome, 2000.

6
Promotion and Relegation in Sporting Contests

Stefan Szymanski[a] *and Tommaso M. Valletti*[b]

[a] *Imperial College London*
[b] *Imperial College London & CEPR, London*

Abstract

The conventional model of a team sports league is based on the North American major leagues which have a fixed number of members, entry is rare and only granted by permission of the incumbents (the closed system). European soccer leagues operate a system of promotion and relegation, effectively permitting entry on merit to all-comers (the open system). This paper examines the impact of openness on the incentive of teams to invest (expend effort) and share resources (redistribution) in the context of a Tullock contest. The main conclusion of the paper is that openness tends to enhance effort incentives, but diminishes the incentive to share income.

JEL Codes: L83, P51.

1. Introduction

The structure, conduct and performance of professional sports leagues have been the subject of vehement criticism on both sides of the Atlantic in recent years. In the US the major leagues in baseball, basketball and American Football have been described as "classic, even textbook, examples of business cartels"[1] and several articles have enumerated abuses of local monopoly power, in particular the extraction of public subsidies

---

We thank Gustavo Piga and seminar audiences at Bergen and the AEA meetings (Washington) for useful comments.

for the construction of stadiums and their facilities (see e.g. Noll and Zimbalist, 1997; Siegfried and Zimbalist, 2000). A key factor in these abuses is the monopoly nature of the dominant league and the failure of entry by rival leagues which have either folded (possibly due to predation) or been co-opted (see e.g. Quirk and Fort, 1992). One solution is the enforced break-up of the majors into competing leagues, proposed by, *inter alia,* Ross (1989) and Quirk and Fort (1999). An alternative is to adopt a system that generates entry, not at the level of the league, but at the level of the team. Noll (2002) analyzes in detail the European system of promotion and relegation, by which the worst performing teams at the end of each season are demoted to the immediately junior league, to be replaced by the best performing teams in the junior league. Ross and Szymanski (2002) go further, and argue that the promotion and relegation system would be welfare enhancing for US consumers and taxpayers.

At the present time, however, the dominant European soccer leagues that have long operated the system of promotion and relegation are not in the best of health. Several teams in England have fallen into administration, the UK equivalent of Chapter 11.[2] So frequent has this become that the league authorities have introduced penalties for teams that go into administration.[3] In Germany the government has agreed to underwrite the losses of the leading clubs due to losses of broadcast income[4] and in Italy the lower house of the Parliament passed the *salva calcio* law enabling the clubs to write off losses over a longer period than is available to ordinary corporations.[5] Critics of the soccer administrators who have overseen the financial crisis in Europe point to the extent to which redistributive measures, so common in the US majors, are lacking in Europe.[6] In the European leagues there is no reserve clause, no draft, no roster limit, no salary cap, no luxury tax, no gate sharing and no collective merchandising agreement. The only form of revenue sharing in European leagues relates to the collective selling of broadcast rights, but even this is absent in many leagues (e.g. Italy and Spain) and limited in others (e.g. only 50% of broadcast income is shared in England). These restraints, claim the owners of franchises in the US majors, are desirable precisely because they promote a degree of competitive balance in league competition and prevent rival teams from falling into bankruptcy. Even critics in the US who complain that these restraints are unnecessarily restrictive accept that sports teams are special kinds of businesses in that the bankruptcy of rivals, so welcome in most lines of business, is in fact harmful to the remaining teams in the league.[7]

In this chapter we examine the relationship between rent dissipation and the incentive to share revenues in closed and open (i.e. open to promotion and relegation) league structures.[8] We model league competition in the context of an infinitely repeated logit (Tullock, 1980) contest.[9] The standard contest model involves competition for prize every period (season) among a fixed number of teams (as in a closed league). We extend this model to include a penalty for coming last: relegation. In our model the teams are divided into two groups (division one and division two). The teams in division one compete in the current period for the main prize as in the closed league (only with half as many competitors) while the teams in division two compete for the opportunity to compete in division one in the next period. In the next period the winner of division two replaces the worst performing team in division one in the current period (and this team then competes in division two).

Using this model we examine two main issues: first, which system gives the greatest incentive to invest in effort, and second which system provides the greatest incentive to promote competitive balance, meaning the closeness of the competition between the teams in the league. We find that under plausible conditions open leagues with promotion and relegation tend to promote more effort than closed leagues, but undermine incentives to share resources. Both of these issues lie at the heart of public policy in relation to professional sports leagues. Antitrust authorities have traditionally adopted a very lenient approach to collective agreements between league members on the grounds that a competitive balance is in the interest of the fans. However, collective agreements can also undermine effort incentives and this can be a particular problem in closed leagues.[10] On the other hand, the cost of extracting higher effort through promotion and relegation may be a reduction in competitive balance compared to a closed league.

Aside from its significance for the organization of sports leagues, the idea of promotion and relegation has implications for the optimal design of tournaments in general, e.g. procurement auctions. It is well known that in most contest structures individual effort is decreasing in the number of contestants (see e.g. Fullerton and McAfee, 1999), but reducing the number of eligible bidders makes collusion easier. If a principal holds regular auctions (as in of the case with government agencies) it may make sense to create an "A" list and a reserve "B" list and to allow promotion and relegation between the two. This can ensure that bidders supply optimal effort while minimizing the incentive to collude.

In the next section we discuss in more detail some comparisons between Major League Baseball and English Soccer, the archetypal North American and European sports leagues. Section 3 analyzes effort incentives in a symmetric model and Section 4 examines revenue sharing in asymmetric contests. Section 5 concludes.

2.   Some comparisons between Major League Baseball and English Soccer

The National League of baseball, founded in 1876, is the oldest surviving team sports league in the world, and the English Football League, founded in 1888, is the oldest surviving soccer league. Each of these leagues became the template for the organization of professional team sports on their continent. While rival leagues and team sports have generated organizational innovations and differences, the similarities within North America and Europe are much greater than those between the two continents.[11] North American leagues have many mechanisms for the maintenance of competitive balance (e.g. roster limits, draft rules, salary caps, luxury taxes, gate and broadcast revenue sharing), most of which are either unused or implemented in less egalitarian ways in Europe. By contrast, European leagues promote rivalry not only through competition for the championship, but also through competition to avoid relegation.

This can make comparisons difficult. For example, the most widely used measure of competitive balance in North America is the standard deviation of winning percentage (wpc) relative to the idealized standard deviation (see e.g. Fort and Quirk, 1995).[12] On this basis European Leagues can in fact look more balanced than their American counterparts. Graph 6.1 compares the standard deviation ratios for National and American Leagues (the two leagues that comprise Major League Baseball and whose champions contest the World Series) with the English Premier League[13] over the period 1980–1999.

In 15 out of the 20 seasons the Premier League had a lower standard deviation ratio than either the National or American Leagues, suggesting that competition within the season was more balanced. Comparing the means, the average standard deviation ratios for the National and American Leagues were 1.68 and 1.70 respectively, while that of the Premier League was 1.43, significantly lower than either baseball league at the 1% level.

However, this measure tells us little about the dominance of particular teams across seasons. Buzzacchi *et al.* (2003) examine the theoretical

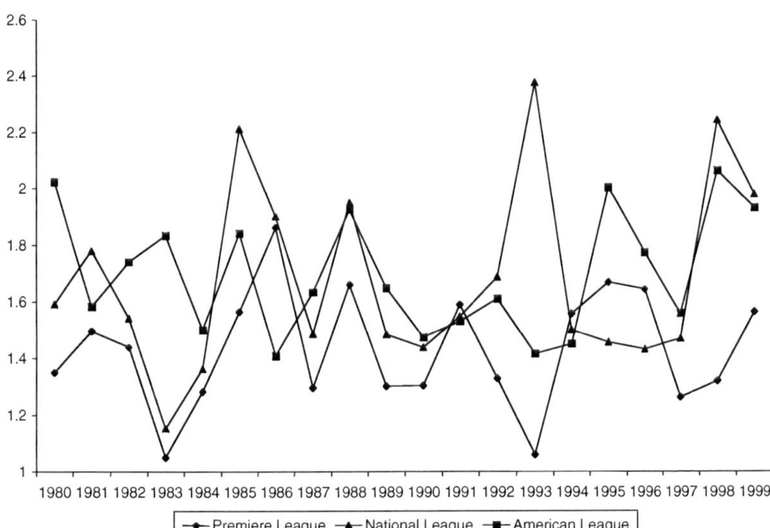

Graph 6.1   Ratio of actual standard deviation of wpc to idealized, 1980–1999, National League, American League and Premier League

number of teams that would be expected to reach a given rank at least once by the end of a given number of seasons and compare it to the actual numbers. For example, in any one year only one team can have the highest wpc, but in a perfectly balanced repeated contest among a fixed number of teams the expected number of teams reaching this rank expands, until eventually all teams will be expected to have reached it at least once. In an open league with promotion and relegation this number expands quite rapidly over time, given that more and more teams have the opportunity to compete. Buzzacchi *et al*. therefore calculated these expectations for Major League Baseball, taking account of franchise expansion, and for the English Premier League taking account of the rules of promotion and relegation, for a database covering the period 1950–2000. Graphs 6.2 and 6.3 compare the results.

The dotted lines in these figures tell us the expected number of teams that would have ever entered the top five ranks of wpc under perfect balance, starting from five different arbitrary dates, while the unbroken lines show the actual numbers. In the case of baseball, these lines are quite close together, indicating that almost every team that could have reached the highest ranks has actually done so, even if we consider the most recent period, starting from 1990.

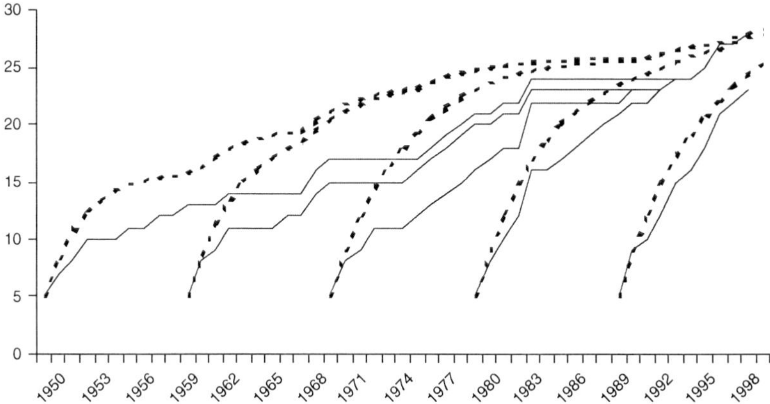

Graph 6.2   Expected (dotted line) and actual (unbroken line) number of teams ever entering the top five ranks of wpc in Major League Baseball starting from 1950, 1960, 1970, 1980 and 1990

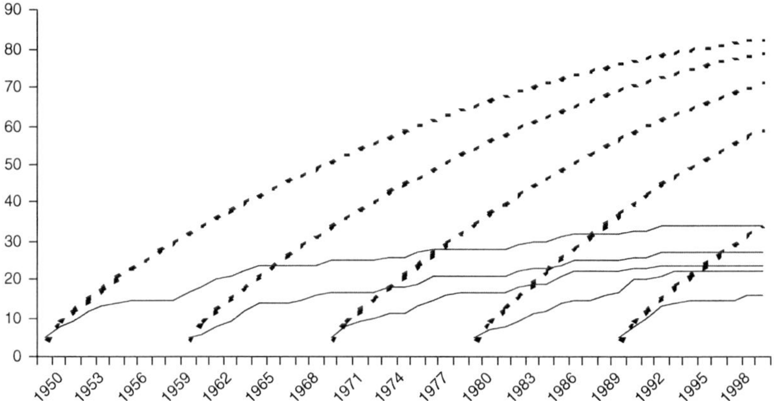

Graph 6.3   Expected (dotted line) and actual (unbroken line) number of teams ever entering the top five ranks of wpc in English Premier League starting from 1950, 1960, 1970, 1980 and 1990

If we compare the English Premier League, the gap between statistical expectation based on equal chances and actual performance is much greater. While similar numbers of teams have entered the top five ranks as in baseball, openness through promotion means that many more teams would have entered these ranks if competition was truly balanced. For example, since 1950 over eighty teams would have achieved a top five placing in the Premier League at least once, compared to just over thirty that have in fact done so. Buzzacchi *et al.* show that a similar pattern is observed in other North American major leagues and other European soccer leagues.

One way in which we can account for these findings is that the threat of relegation makes teams compete much more intensively throughout the season, even if they are out of contention for the title leading to a smaller ratio of standard deviations within the season. However, over the longer term only a small group of teams have access to the resources necessary to mount a credible challenge for the title. Redistributive measures in the major leagues ensure that more teams have the potential to reach the highest levels, but for some reason European soccer leagues are unable to implement such redistributive measures.

To explore further the question of access to resources it is useful to look at some economic financial performance data. Table 6.1 provides data for Major League Baseball teams for the 1999 season on wpc, attendance, payroll, revenues and estimates of franchise values. One indicator that captures both the relative inequality of resources and the struggle of the weaker teams to survive under promotion and relegation is the share of income devoted to payroll. The three teams with the poorest winning records in both the American and National Leagues spent less than the league average of 54% of total revenues on the payroll. In the Premier League only one out of the seven worst performing teams spent less than the league average of 60% on salaries. Blackburn Rovers, who were in fact relegated in this season, spent more than 100% of their income on payroll. Perhaps most striking is the following contrast: the top 15 clubs in baseball by wpc devoted 58% of their aggregate income to payroll, compared to only 49% for the bottom 15 clubs; in the Premier League the top 10 clubs devoted only 53% of their aggregate income to payroll, compared to 68% for the bottom 10.

The greater inequality of resources in the Premier League is illustrated by the fact that aggregate income of the bottom 10 clubs equaled 35% of league income, compared to 43% for the bottom 15 in Major League Baseball. However, this difference in inequality is not sufficient to explain the widely divergent pattern of franchise values. The estimated franchise values for the bottom 15 in baseball equaled $2.7bn in 1999, 41% of the total for the league. Franchise valuations are not available for all English clubs, but by the late 1990s 20 English clubs had obtained a stock exchange listing and therefore we have data on their market capitalization, and in 1999 five of these teams finished in the top half of the Premier League and five in the bottom half. Those in the

Table 6.1 Major League Baseball 1999

Team	wpc	Attendance m	Player payroll $m	Revenues $m	Franchise value $m
Atlanta Braves	0.63	3.28	79.8	128.3	357
Arizona Diamondbacks	0.61	3.02	70.2	102.8	291
New York Yankees	0.6	3.29	92.4	177.9	491
Cleveland Indians	0.59	3.47	73.3	136.8	359
New York Mets	0.59	2.73	72.5	140.6	249
Houston Astros	0.59	2.71	58.1	78.1	239
Texas Rangers	0.58	2.77	81.7	109.3	281
Boston Red Sox	0.58	2.45	75.3	117.1	256
Cincinnati Reds	0.58	2.06	38.9	68.4	163
San Francisco Giants	0.53	2.08	46.0	74.7	213
Oakland Athletics	0.53	1.43	24.6	62.6	125
Toronto Blue Jays	0.51	2.16	50.0	73.8	162
Baltimore Orioles	0.48	3.43	78.9	123.6	351
Seattle Mariners	0.48	2.92	47.0	114.2	236
Pittsburgh Pirates	0.48	1.64	24.5	63.2	145
Los Angeles Dodgers	0.47	3.10	76.6	114.2	270
Philadelphia Phillies	0.47	1.83	32.1	77.2	145
St Louis Cardinals	0.46	3.24	46.3	101.8	205
Chicago White Sox	0.46	1.35	24.5	79.5	178
Milwaukee Brewers	0.46	1.70	43.6	63.6	155
San Diego Padres	0.45	2.52	46.5	79.6	205
Colorado Rockies	0.44	3.24	72.5	102.8	311
Anaheim Angels	0.43	2.25	53.3	86.1	195
Tampa Bay Devil Rays	0.42	1.75	37.9	75.5	225
Detroit Tigers	0.42	2.03	37.0	78.1	152
Montreal Expos	0.42	0.77	18.1	48.8	84
Chicago Cubs	0.41	2.81	55.5	106.0	224
Florida Marlins	0.39	1.37	16.4	72.9	153
Kansas City Royals	0.39	1.51	17.4	63.6	96
Minnesota Twins	0.39	1.20	15.8	52.6	89
Total	0.50	70.10	1507.0	2773.7	6605

Payroll and revenue data from the Blue Ribbon report. Franchise values from Forbes.

top half accounted for 78% ($1.1bn) of the Premier League market capitalization and those in the bottom half accounted for only 22%, a much more uneven distribution of market valuation than that of revenues. This can be accounted for by the fact that teams in the bottom half are much more likely to face the threat of relegation (as Noll, 2002, observes "demotion usually causes teams to be worse off financially"), while

Table 6.2 Premier League 1998/1999 season

Team	Rank	wpc	Attendance m	Payroll $m	Revenues $m	Market cap $m
Manchester United	1	0.75	1.05	59.1	177.5	776
Arsenal	2	0.74	0.72	42.4	77.8	
Chelsea	3	0.72	0.66	48.3	94.5	171
Leeds United	4	0.64	0.68	29.7	59.2	88
West Ham United	5	0.54	0.49	28.3	42.5	
Aston Villa	6	0.53	0.70	26.6	55.8	90
Liverpool	7	0.51	0.82	58.0	72.4	
Derby County	8	0.51	0.55	22.8	35.2	
Middlesbrough	9	0.51	0.65	31.1	44.8	
Leicester City	10	0.49	0.39	25.6	38.1	21
Tottenham Hotspur	11	0.47	0.65	34.7	68.1	102
Sheffield Wednesday	12	0.43	0.51	21.7	30.6	
Newcastle United	13	0.46	0.70	39.2	71.5	152
Everton	14	0.42	0.69	32.4	40.7	
Coventry City	15	0.41	0.39	21.1	30.2	
Wimbledon	16	0.42	0.35	18.4	23.5	
Southampton	17	0.39	0.29	18.2	21.5	18
Charlton Athletic	18	0.37	0.38	13.2	26.0	21
Blackburn Rovers	19	0.37	0.49	35.9	34.0	
Nottingham Forest	20	0.30	0.46	18.9	27.2	27
Total		0.50	23.2	625.4	1071.4	1466
First Division quoted teams						
Sunderland (promoted)	2	0.80	0.74	16.0	38.5	64
Birmingham	4	0.63	0.40	10.0	13.5	27
Bolton	6	0.61	0.35	16.1	20.2	43
Sheffield United	8	0.53	0.31	12.1	10.3	11
West Bromwich Albion	12	0.47	0.28	7.3	10.8	13

Payroll and revenue data from company accounts (reported in Deloitte and Touche Annual Review of Football Finance). Market capitalization at end of the playing season.

even if they avoid relegation, they are much more likely to overextend themselves financially in order to avoid the drop.

3. Effort contribution in symmetric contests with and without promotion and relegation

In this section we look at the value of the league and compare the amount of effort that teams will choose to contribute in open and closed leagues. Throughout we will assume that leagues are essentially contests, where teams compete to win a single prize at the end of each season. In a closed league, all teams have a chance of winning the prize in the season. In open leagues, however, only the teams present in the highest ranked division can win the prize in the current season, and that the only incentive in lower divisions is the prospect of promotion to the highest division.[14]

To fix ideas we begin by comparing the present value of a team in an open and closed system assuming that each team always faces an equal probability of success in their division. This implies that teams have no choice in the level of effort or investment they supply and that all such contributions are equal and normalized to zero. In the second model, we make effort endogenous, although again all teams are assumed to be symmetric in the sense that equal spending produces an equal probability of winning the prize and the prize is equally valuable to all teams. Asymmetries are analyzed in Section 4.

3.1   Model 1: Symmetric teams with equal winning probabilities (no effort)

3.1.1   *Closed system*

Imagine n is the total number of teams. Every period there is a contest and $\delta < 1$ is the discount factor between periods. In every period a team has a probability $1/n$ to win. The value of winning the championship title (the prize) is normalized to 1. The present discounted value of being in a closed league (C) is then simply

$$V(C) = \frac{1}{n(1-\delta)}.$$

Thus the value of participating in the closed league is decreasing in the number of teams, since the probability of winning the prize falls, and increasing in the discount factor.

3.1.2   Open system

Imagine the total number of teams is divided among k hierarchical divisions, with $n_1 + n_2 + \cdots + n_k = n$. Also, imagine one team is promoted/relegated in every period. Call V_i the NPV of being in division i. Then

$$V_1 = \frac{1}{n_1} + \delta\left(\frac{n_1 - 1}{n_1}V_1 + \frac{1}{n_1}V_2\right)$$

$$V_2 = 0 + \delta\left(\frac{n_2 - 2}{n_2}V_2 + \frac{1}{n_2}V_1 + \frac{1}{n_2}V_3\right)$$

$$\cdots$$

$$V_k = 0 + \delta\left(\frac{n_k - 1}{n_k}V_k + \frac{1}{n_k}V_{k-1}\right)$$

It is immediate to verify that $\sum_{i=1}^{k} n_i V_i = 1/(1-\delta) = nV(C)$, i.e. the total value of an open league (O) coincides with that of a closed league, as long as the same total number of teams is involved.

On the other hand, the distribution of the total value changes quite dramatically. For instance if we have 4 hierarchical divisions, with a total of 40 teams and $\delta = 0.8$, then the above system can be solved to obtain: $V_1 = 0.383$, $V_2 = 0.0898$, $V_3 = 0.0213$, $V_4 = 0.00609$, while $V(C) = 0.125$. Equivalently, a team in the top division has the same value "as if" it were in a closed league with approximately only 13 teams (rather than 40). The equivalent number of teams in a closed league increases to 56 for a team in the second division, 235 for a team in the third division and 821 for a team in the fourth division! Obviously, the differences between the V_i's decreases as the discount factor gets bigger, and it disappears for δ equal to 1.

In this simple benchmark model the only effect of promotion and relegation is to change the distribution of team values.

3.2   Model 2: Symmetric teams with endogenous effort

Endogenizing effort requires us to specify a "contest success function". We use here the standard logit formulation adopted in much of the literature (see e.g. Nti, 1997). If a team spends x_i, the probability of winning the contest for team i is $s_i = x_i^\gamma / \sum_{j=1}^{n} x_j^\gamma$. The parameter γ is called "discriminatory power" and it defines the sensitivity of win probabilities to differences in effort. If it is zero, everybody wins with the same probability, no matter how much effort is spent. Conversely, if it tends to infinity, the team that spends more than its rivals wins with probability

1 (the contest in this limiting case is equivalent to an "all-pay" auction). In an open league system, the probability of winning is easily reinterpreted as the probability of being promoted. However, for open systems we also need a rule in order to assign a probability of being relegated as a function of effort/investment relative to the other contestants. For this purpose, we introduce a "contest losing function" that gives the probability of arriving last in a contest:

$$l_i = \frac{x_i^{-\gamma}}{\sum_{j=1}^{n} x^{-\gamma}_j}$$

Notice that the proposed losing function has a series of desired properties:

- If γ is zero, the probability of arriving first or last is independent from the effort put in the contest, $s_i = l_i = 1/n$ for all 1s;
- If γ tends to infinity, the team that puts the highest effort wins with probability 1 and loses with 0 probability;
- For intermediate values of γ, if all the rivals of team i spend the same amount, while team i outspends (respectively underspends) the individual amount spent by rivals, then $l_i < 1/n$ (respectively $l_i > 1/n$);
- If team i puts zero effort, and all the rivals put some positive effort, then $s_i = 0$, $l_i = 1$ and $l_{-i} = 0$;
- If $n > 2$, then $s_i + l_i < 1$.[15]

3.2.1 Closed system

There is no relegation. In a generic period, a team maximizes $\pi_i = s_i - x_i$ with respect to effort. This is a standard model, and it can be verified that, at a symmetric equilibrium, per-period team effort, per-period team profits and discounted team profits are respectively:

$$x = \frac{\gamma(n-1)}{n^2}$$

$$\pi = \frac{\gamma + n(1-\gamma)}{n^2} \tag{6.1}$$

$$V(C) = \frac{\gamma + n(1-\gamma)}{n^2(1-\delta)}$$

3.2.2 Open system

The model is as in Section 3.1.2, with the difference that team i in a division j that contains n_j teams now spends effort x_{ij}, in which case its probabilities of winning the league and of being relegated are respectively $s_{ij} = x_{ij}^{\gamma} / \sum_{h=1}^{nj} x_{hj}^{\gamma}$ and $l_{ij} = x_{ij}^{-\gamma} / \sum_{n=1}^{nj} x_{ij}^{-\gamma}$:

$$\max_{x_{i1}} V_{i1} = s_{i1} - x_{i1} + \delta \left[(1 - l_{i1}) V_{i1} + l_{i1} V_{i2} \right]$$

$$\max_{x_{i2}} V_{i2} = 0 - x_{i2} + \delta \left[(1 - s_{i2} - l_{i2}) V_{i2} + s_{i2} x V_{i1} + l_{i2} V_{i3} \right] \qquad (6.2)$$

$$\cdots$$

$$\max_{x_{ik}} V_{ik} = 0 - x_{ik} + \delta \left[(1 - s_{ik}) V_{ik} + s_{ik} V_{ik-1} \right]$$

We concentrate for simplicity on a league with only two divisions. It is then possible to obtain the value functions from (6.2), maximize with respect to effort taking as given the rivals' effort and so on to find at equilibrium:

$$x_1 = \gamma (n_1 - 1) \frac{n_1 n_2^2 - \delta \left[\gamma n_1 (n_2 - 1) + n_1 n_2 (n_2 - 1) - 2 n_2^2 \right]}{n_1 \left\{ n_1^2 n_2^2 - \delta \left[n_1 (n_2 - 1) - n_2 \right] \left[\gamma (n_1 - n_2) + n_1 n_2 \right] \right\}}$$

$$x_2 = \gamma (n_2 - 1) \delta \frac{n_1 - \gamma (n_1 - 1)}{n_1^2 n_2^2 - \delta \left[n_1 (n_2 - 1) - n_2 \right] \left[\gamma (n_1 - n_2) + n_1 n_2 \right]}$$

$$V_1 = \frac{\left[\gamma + n_1 (1 - \gamma) \right] \left[n_2^2 - \delta (\gamma + n_2) (n_2 - 1) \right]}{(1 - \delta) \left\{ n_1^2 n_2^2 - \delta \left[n_1 (n_2 - 1) - n_2 \right] \left[\gamma (n_1 - n_2) + n_1 n_2 \right] \right\}}$$

$$V_2 = \frac{\delta \left[\gamma + n_1 (1 - \gamma) \right] \left[\gamma + n_2 (1 - \gamma) \right]}{(1 - \delta) \left\{ n_1^2 n_2^2 - \delta \left[n_1 (n_2 - 1) - n_2 \right] \left[\gamma (n_1 - n_2) + n_1 n_2 \right] \right\}}$$

To ensure existence of equilibria in pure strategies it can be shown that it suffices the restriction $0 < \gamma \leq \min \left[n_1/(n_1 - 1), n_2/(n_2 - 1) \right]$. The effort in each league is strictly positive unless there is only one team in that league. With the exception of the case $n_1 = 1$ (no effort in the top league since the title is won with probability 1), a team always spends more effort in the top league than in the lower league, *independently* of the number of rivals it faces.[16] Also, if teams are distributed symmetrically, the difference between efforts is independent of the discount factor and it amounts to $\gamma (n_1 - 1)/n_1^2 > 0$. Despite spending more on effort, for $\delta < 1$, the value of a team in the top league is always higher than the value of a team in the bottom league. The two values converge as the discount factor gets closer to 1.

3.2.3   *Welfare analysis of model 2*

One question we might want to address is how to distribute a total number n of teams between the two leagues. Welfare analysis of sports leagues is in general problematic. Standard consumer theory suggests that we should concentrate on the utility of fans, but to reach any conclusions this would require us to quantify the utility of competitive balance, own team success and the quality of a tournament. It seems unlikely that policy makers could agree on any unambiguous ranking of outcomes on this basis. In the contest literature, welfare has generally been identified with rent dissipation, meaning the extent to which the profits from participation in the contest are consumed by the effort contributions of the contestants, a measure we will consider. In addition, we will consider the total amount of effort/investment exerted in the contest. However, it is not obvious that aggregate effort (which we might identify with the total quality of the contest) is the right measure of welfare either. The whole point of the competitive balance literature is that it is the higher moments of the effort distribution that count. In some contexts, moreover, it may be that only the effort of the winning contestant really matters.[17] However, in a symmetric contest we can at least abstract from the issue of inequality within each division, an issue to which we will return in the next section.

We can illustrate the kinds of trade-off involved in promotion and relegation by looking at total effort and effort levels per team and in each division as the total number of teams increases. Graphs 6.4 and 6.5 illustrate the case where the discriminatory power of contest success function is moderate ($\gamma = 1$). Along the horizontal axis is shown the total number of teams in the league as a whole (e.g. 20 refers to either 20 teams in a closed league or 20 teams in an open league with two hierarchical divisions—labeled Serie A and Serie B[18]—of 10 teams each).

Total effort in the open and closed leagues are almost identical for most league sizes, but inspection shows that this is because teams make almost no effort in Serie B, while the 10 teams of Serie A contribute about as much effort as the 20 teams of the closed league. This is quite clear in Graph 6.5, which shows that the effort per team in Serie A is almost double that of the effort per team in the closed league, while in Serie B effort contributions are negligible unless there are a very small number of teams in the division. Thus in this case the promotion and relegation system seems to produce a contest of relatively high quality among the elite of teams, while the closed system produces lower average quality but spreads more evenly among a larger range of teams. Intuitively, relegation creates greater inequality between the teams, so that for a fixed prize, the privileged (Serie A) contribute more effort and the underprivileged (Serie B) do not try very much, but the total effort is roughly the same as in a closed competition.

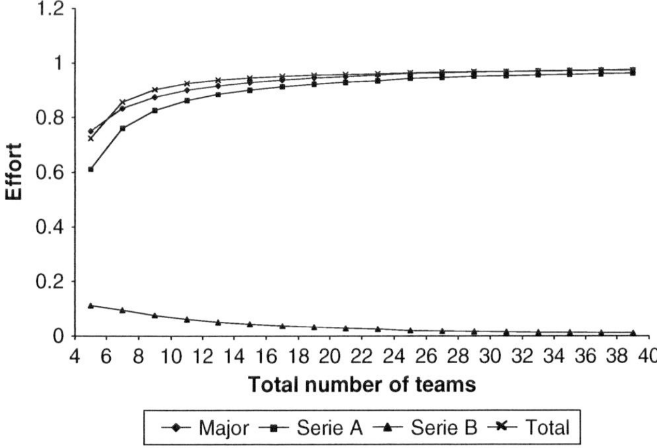

Graph 6.4 Total effort in a major league and a two division hierarchy (gamma = 1)

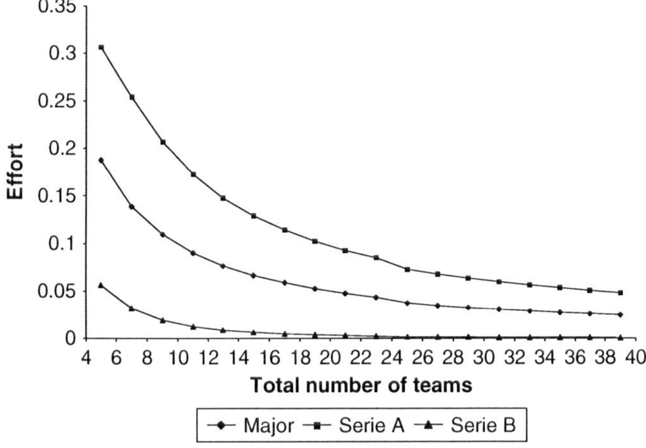

Graph 6.5 Effort per team (gamma = 1)

Graphs 6.6 and 6.7 illustrate the case where the discriminatory power of the contest is low ($\gamma = 0.1$). First, note that this discourages effort (and rent dissipation) since the marginal returns to effort are low. Graph 6.6 shows that total effort is now significantly higher in an open league system and Graph 6.7 makes it clear that this is because effort per team in the closed league is not much higher in the closed league than in Serie B.

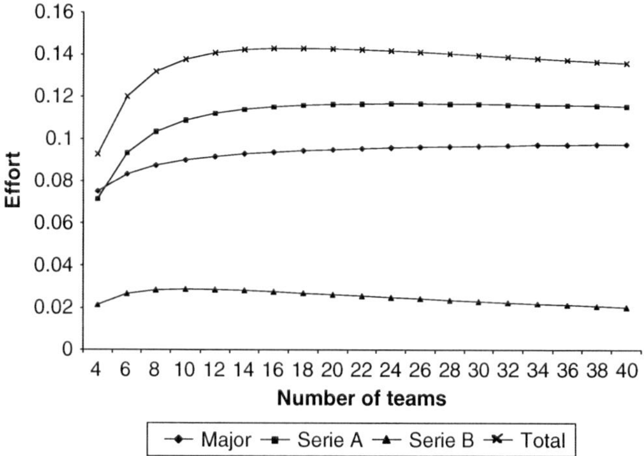

Graph 6.6   Total effort in Major League and two hierarchical divisions (gamma = 0. 1)

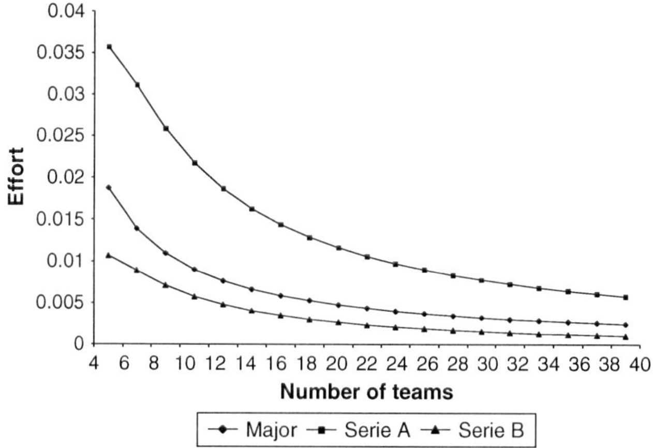

Graph 6.7   Effort per team (gamma = 0. 1)

Because the contest is not very discriminating, there is little incentive to make an effort to win, which is the only instrument providing incentives in the closed league. In the open league, however, teams in Serie A are also competing to avoid the drop, and this extra incentive keeps effort levels per team much higher than in the closed league.

Clearly, the objective of the teams (to minimize rent dissipation) conflicts with the social objective of maximizing rent dissipation. Thus, if the league members jointly determine league policy,[19] they will opt for closed leagues when the discriminatory power γ of the contest is low (recall that γ defines the sensitivity of win probabilities to differences in effort) and open leagues when the discriminatory power is high.

4.   Asymmetric teams with endogenous effort

In the previous section we focused on the incentive to supply effort, in this section we focus on the incentive to share revenues. The justification for revenue sharing in sports leagues is competitive balance—by creating a more balanced contest the league will become more attractive to fans and will generate larger league-wide profits (and welfare). This analysis presupposes asymmetry in revenue generation between the teams—i.e. for a given wpc some teams will generate a larger income, either because the club draws on a larger fan base or is more intensely supported than other teams. However, revenue sharing requires agreement among the teams. In particular, teams that enjoy a larger income absent revenue sharing must consent to a redistribution scheme that will see their income fall relative to weaker rivals. Another effect of revenue sharing that has been widely commented on in the literature is its tendency to blunt incentives (see e.g. Fort and Quirk, 1995), a factor which can make revenue sharing attractive for the strong teams. In our analysis we look for conditions where the larger revenue clubs would willingly share income.[20]

Suppose there existed four feasible locations (e.g. cities) for a sports team, based on the drawing power of those teams. We assume that each location can support only one team, while two locations possess a greater drawing power than the others. In such a universe a number of league configurations are possible. We suppose either that all teams compete in the same championship each year (the closed system) or that there are two divisions of two teams each with promotion and relegation of one team from each division each season (the open system).

For tractability we assume that in the "no sharing" case this means that the two weak teams have a zero probability of winning any match against a strong team. Moreover, we assume that whenever "sharing" occurs the teams competing with each other have an equal probability of winning in that particular contest. Our notion of sharing implies a significant restriction of the strategy space of the teams (in the Appendix we develop a model where more of the teams' choices are endogenized).

The weaker teams will always want to share. We focus on the potential benefit for the strong teams from sharing under closed and open systems.

4.1   Closed league with four teams, no sharing

A single prize is awarded to the winner of each contest. Since weak teams never win in a contest against strong teams, they can never win at all and so never contribute effort. Thus the four team case is indistinguishable from a symmetric two team league. Normalizing the value of the prize to unity the effort levels and payoffs to the strong teams (superscript S) in a closed league (C) with no sharing (N) will be

$$e^s = \frac{\gamma}{4}, \quad V^s(CN) = \frac{2-\gamma}{4(1-\delta)} \tag{6.3}$$

4.2   Closed league with four teams, sharing

Now all four teams have an equal probability of winning every season regardless of the effort they supply and so no team supplies any effort. We assume that because the contest is now perfectly balanced, this also enhances its attractiveness and therefore the value of the prize, which is now assumed to be $z > 1$. Thus the payoff to each player in a closed league (C) with sharing (S) is

$$V(CS) = \frac{z}{4(1-\delta)} \tag{6.4}$$

Clearly, the total value of the league is increased by sharing, but in the absence of side payments the strong teams will only consent to sharing as long as (6.4) is greater than (6.3), which happens when $z \geq z^C = 2 - \gamma$. This is true by assumption for $\gamma \geq 1$, and may be true even for smaller values of γ. Note that, as is true in many contest models of this type,[21] a necessary condition for the existence of pure strategy equilibrium is $\gamma \leq 2$. What this section has shown is that the incentive to share revenues depends on the potential gain from a balanced competition (z) and the discriminatory power of the contest. The latter matters because it affects effort in the no-sharing case. In a highly discriminating contest, strong teams will choose to expend high effort and thus dissipate rents, making the sharing alternative attractive.

4.3   Open league with two two-team divisions, no sharing

We assume that the worst performing team is relegated from each division in each season and replaced with the best performing team from the lower division. Again, with no sharing, the weak teams can never win against the strong teams, can never win the prize and so contribute no effort. The two strong teams never meet in the lower division, but meet every other season in the top division, and are then assumed to compete for the prize.

To calculate the optimal amount of effort, we need to identify the value of each possible state for a strong team:

$$\max_{e} V_1^{SS} = p - e + \delta\left[pV_1^{SW} + (1-p)V_2^{SW}\right]$$

$$V_1^{SW} = 1 + \delta V_1^{SS}$$

$$V_2^{SW} = \delta V_1^{SS}$$

$$p = \frac{e^{\gamma}}{e^{\gamma} + e^{\gamma}_{-i}}$$

where V_1^{SS} is the present value of a strong team currently located in the top division with another strong team, V_1^{SW} is the present value of a strong team currently located in the top division with a weak team and V_2^{SW} is the present value of a strong team currently located in the second division with a weak team. Solving for V_1^{SS} we find

$$V_1^{SS} = \frac{(1+\delta)p - e}{1 - \delta^2} \tag{6.5}$$

Maximizing (6.5) with respect to e we find the equilibrium effort level when the two strong teams are in the top division, $e^S = \gamma(1+\delta)/4$. The present value of the payoffs in the three states are

$$V_1^{SS} = \frac{2-\gamma}{4(1-\delta)}, \quad V_1^{SW} = \frac{4-\delta(2+\gamma)}{4(1-\delta)}, \quad V_2^{SW} = \frac{\delta(2-\gamma)}{4(1-\delta)} \tag{6.6}$$

Given that a strong revenue-generating team is always promoted when in the second division and is relegated with probability 1/2 when in the top division, in the steady state each of these teams obtains V_1^{SS} with probability 1/2, and V_1^{SW} or V_2^{SW} with probability 1/4. Thus the steady state payoff to strong team in an open league with no sharing is

$$V^S(ON) = \frac{4 - \gamma(1+\delta)}{8(1-\delta)}$$

The difference between $V^S(ON)$ and the closed league payoff with no sharing ($V^S(CN)$ from (6.3)) is $\gamma(1-\delta)$, which is always positive. Intuitively, the benefit to the strong teams of an open league arising from the fact that they get to win easily 25% of the time is exactly offset by the cost arising from not being in the top division 25% of the time. However, in a closed league the strong teams meet every season and so have to contribute effort every season if they want to win, whereas in our stylized model a strong team meets weak opposition only 50% of the time and on the occasions have to make no effort at all. More generally, we might expect that as long as the strong teams need to try less hard to win when they play weak teams, then they will prefer the open league system. The greater the discriminatory power of the contest, the more effort is required when strong teams compete, and the greater the benefit to the strong teams of the open system (without sharing).

The setting for this result is somewhat extreme, given the small number of teams involved and the assumed gap in capabilities. However, our result would generalize to the case where the league divisions are larger and the gaps in abilities are smaller as long as the weak drawing teams will contribute less effort. In such cases relegation is always a cost to the strong team that is relegated but a benefit to the remaining strong teams amongst whom competition is relaxed.[22] However, as we show in the Appendix there can exist equilibria in an open system where the weaker teams contribute more effort than the strong teams (in order not to be relegated), and under these conditions the strong teams may prefer a closed league.

4.4   Open league with two two-team divisions, sharing in the top division

We begin by assuming that sharing only occurs in the top division (competitive balance concerns are likely to be greatest in the top division, and gaining the consent of the strong clubs will be easier to obtain than when there is equal sharing across all divisions). With sharing the present value of a strong team is reduced compared to the closed league case, since relegated teams miss an opportunity to win the prize. However, the strong teams are always certain to be promoted in the season following relegation. Thus:

$$V_1^{SS} = V_1^{SW} = V_1^{S} = \left[z + \delta\left(V_1^{S} + V_2^{SW}\right)\right]/2, \quad V_2^{SW} = \delta V_1^{S}$$

These lead to

$$V_1^S = \frac{z}{(2+\delta)(1-\delta)}, \quad V_2^{SW} = \frac{\delta z}{(2+\delta)(1-\delta)}$$

At the steady state the strong team is at the top with probability 2/3 and at the bottom with probability 1/3.[23] Hence the payoff to a strong team in an open system (O) with top division sharing ($S1$) is

$$V^S(OS1) = \frac{z}{3(1-\delta)} \tag{6.7}$$

Note that this payoff is larger than in a closed division and equal sharing since the strong teams have the advantage of always being immediately promoted whenever they are relegated, and hence win the prize more frequently (i.e. one third of the time rather than one quarter of the time).

If we now compare the strong team's payoff to sharing in the open system ($OS1$) to no sharing in the open system (ON), the necessary condition for sharing to be preferred is found by comparing (6.7) with (6.6), leading to

$$z \geq z^O = 3/2 - 3\gamma(1+\delta)/8$$

Recall that the equivalent condition for sharing to be preferred in a closed league was $z \geq z^C = 2 - \gamma$. For high discount rates the critical value for z will be smaller in the open league, implying a greater willingness to share on the part of the strong teams. However, for lower discount rates it can happen that the critical value to make sharing attractive in the closed league would not be large enough to make sharing attractive in the open league. For example, when $\gamma = 1$, sharing will be preferred in a closed league for all $z > 1$, while if $\delta = 0.25$ sharing is preferred only if $z > 21/16$.

Equivalently, the comparison between the threshold values of z tells us that revenue sharing is a more stringent condition in an open league ($z^O > z^C$, i.e. revenue sharing is less likely to happen) if $\gamma > 4/5(5 - 3\delta)$, i.e. to say if the contest is sufficiently discriminatory.

This result is intuitive as the discriminatory power affects profits only without revenue sharing (under our assumptions firms do not react to z with any form of sharing, both in open and in closed systems). Without sharing, the higher the discriminatory power, the lower the equilibrium profits. Under CN a firm is competing 100% of its time, while under *ON* effort is exerted only 50% of the time. It is thus clear that a higher value of γ, while making sharing less appealing both in open and in closed systems, reduces profits by more in the latter than in the former.

Our assumption, however, is very restrictive. In the Appendix we show that, once we endogenize effort choices in an open league with revenue sharing, the threshold that makes revenue sharing attractive in an open league (z^O) increases, so that the range of values of γ for which revenue sharing is attractive in a closed league but not in an open league expands. If weak teams can end up contributing more effort than strong teams (this can happen because the penalty of relegation is higher: weak teams tend to find it harder to get promoted again) then one of the main attractions of the open system to the strong teams (namely weaker opponents) has vanished and they resist sharing.

4.5 Open league with two two-team divisions, sharing in both divisions

Each team has an equal probability of winning in each division and no team contributes effort. Thus for any team,

$$V_1 = \frac{z + \delta(V_1 + V_2)}{2}, \quad V_2 = \frac{\delta(V_1 + V_2)}{2}$$

so that

$$V_1 = \frac{(2 - \delta)z}{4(1 - \delta)}, \quad V_2 = \frac{\delta z}{4(1 - \delta)}$$

and the average payoff in an open system with sharing in both divisions (*S2*) is

$$V^S(OS2) = \frac{z}{4(1 - \delta)} \tag{6.8}$$

This is the same as the payoff to sharing in a closed division, since teams compete for the top prize half as frequently but with twice the probability of winning. As might be expected, this is lower than the payoff to the strong teams when there is no lower division sharing, so that strong teams will be less willing to share if sharing is applied to both divisions. Comparing (6.8) with (6.6), in an open league sharing in both divisions is preferred to no sharing when $z > 2 - \gamma(1 + \delta)/2$. Recalling that the equivalent condition for a closed league is $z > 2 - \gamma$, it is clear that the critical value of z is always lower in a closed league. In other words, strong teams will be less willing to agree to full sharing in an open league than in a closed league.

Thus in this section we have shown that under some circumstances sharing can be more attractive in an open league, but only when that sharing is limited to participants in the top division. When there is sharing across all divisions, revenue sharing is always less attractive in an open league than in a closed league.

5.   Conclusions

One of the most striking but least analyzed differences between the (closed) American and (open) European models of professional sport is the system of promotion and relegation. This chapter applies contest theory to the analysis of open and closed league systems.

We find that a promotion and relegation system typically enhances the incentive to contribute effort and hence to dissipate rents, which may be considered an enhancement of social welfare. On the other hand, promotion and relegation is also likely to inhibit incentives to share resources. Redistribution in team sports is frequently considered beneficial not only for the owners, since the incentive to compete is weakened, but also for consumers, who are said to prefer more balanced contests. To the extent that this is true, promotion and relegation may reduce social welfare.

Whatever the welfare implications, we argue that the effects of promotion and relegation on incentives are broadly consistent with what we observe on either side of Atlantic. In Europe, where the system is applied, teams compete intensively—to the point of bankruptcy in fact—and seem unwilling to share resources. In the US, where the system does not apply, economic competition is less intense and teams do share resources. While this chapter cannot be said to be the final word, we believe it points to a potentially fruitful avenue for both empirical and theoretical research.

Appendix

Consider an open league with four teams (two weak and two strong) and two divisions. In this annex, we allow the weak teams to be able to beat the strong teams in the top division, but only if there is revenue sharing. We suppose that in the lower division, where there is no sharing, the strong team always wins against a weak team but has to supply some minimum amount of effort to achieve this result.

(a)   No sharing

As weak teams never win against a strong team, we can concentrate on the effort choice for the strong team. This is derived from the following optimization problem:

$$\max_{e} V_1^{SS} = p - e + \delta \left[p V_1^{SW} + (1-p) V_2^{SW} \right]$$

$$V_1^{SW} = 1 - e_H + \delta V_1^{SS}$$

$$V_2^{SW} = -e_L + \delta V_1^{SS}$$

$$p = \frac{e^\gamma}{e^\gamma + e^\gamma_{-i}}$$

This is basically the same problem as in Section 4.3, with the only difference that the strong team has to supply some (exogenous) minimum level of effort to win against a weak team both in the top division (e_H) and in the low division (e_L). The only endogenous effort is the one supplied against an equally strong rival. At a symmetric equilibrium ($e_{-i} = e$) one gets

$$e = \gamma \frac{1 + \delta(1 - e_H + e_L)}{4}$$

$$V^S(ON) = \frac{2V_1^{SS} + V_1^{SW} + V_2^{SW}}{4} = \frac{4 - \gamma - \delta\gamma(1 - e_H + e_L) - 2(e_H + e_L)}{8(1 - \delta)}$$

which is a simple generalization of (6.6).

(b)   Sharing in the top division

The problem is considerably extended here compared to Section 4.4. We now denote by z the gross value of the prize. Team i of type $h = \{S, W\}$ competing against a team of type $k = \{S, W\}$ in division $d = \{1, 2\}$ puts effort e_{id}^{hk} and wins that division with probability $p_{id}^{hk} = \left(e_{id}^{hk}\right)^\gamma / \left[\left(e_{id}^{hk}\right)^\gamma + \left(e_{-id}^{hk}\right)\gamma \right]$. The maximization problem for the strong team is

$$\max_{e_{11}^{SS}} V_1^{SS} = z p_{11}^{SS} - e_{11}^{SS} + \delta \left[p_{11}^{SS} V_1^{SW} + (1 - p_{11}^{SS}) V_2^{SW} \right]$$

$$\max_{e_{11}^{SW}} V_1^{SW} = z p_{11}^{SW} - e_{11}^{SW} + \delta \left[p_{11}^{SW} V_1^{SS} + (1 - p_{11}^{SW}) V_2^{SW} \right] \tag{6.A1}$$

$$V_2^{SW} = -\tilde{e}_L + \delta \left[p_{21}^{SW} V_1^{SS} + (1 - p_{21}^{SW}) V_1^{SW} \right]$$

We are still assuming that, if relegated, a strong team wins with probability one since it plays against a weak team, but has to put in some effort $\tilde{e}_L$ to do so. On the other hand, the endogenous efforts are those exerted in the top division against an equally strong or a weaker team. Although there is sharing, and teams in the top division are all competing for the gross prize z, the efforts are not symmetric since firms are taking into account the probability of getting to other states that do not give the same payoffs to strong and weak teams. Hence we have to characterize also the effort supplied by the weak teams:

$$\max_{e_{11}^{WS}} V_1^{WS} = z\left(1 - p_{11}^{SW}\right) - e_{11}^{WS} + \delta\left[\left(1 - p_{11}^{SW}\right) V_1^{WS} + p_{11}^{SW} V_2^{SW}\right]$$

$$V_2^{WS} = \delta\left[p_{21}^{SW} V_2^{WW} + \left(1 - p_{21}^{SW}\right) V_2^{SW}\right] \qquad (6.A2)$$

$$V_2^{WW} = -\tilde{e}_W + \delta\left(V_1^{WS} + V_2^{WS}\right)/2$$

Hence we are endogenizing only the effort that a weak team puts to win the title, while it puts zero effort when relegated and competing without sharing against a strong team. To simplify calculations, we also assume that, when in the lower division, weak teams facing each other put an effort $\tilde{e}_w$ and win with probability 1/2.

We have solved the problems represented by (6.A1) and (6.A2) with respect to the three endogenous efforts. The expressions are rather cumbersome and therefore we show only some numerical examples below. Once the efforts are known, the expected value of a strong team can also be calculated and compared to the expected value it would get without any sharing. A strong team can be found in one of the three following states: (a) against a strong team in the top division with absolute probability p^{1S}, (b) against a weak team in the top division with absolute probability p^{1W}, (c) against a weak team in the bottom division with absolute probability p^{2W}. Taking into account the transition probabilities between states, the absolute probabilities in a steady state must satisfy

$$p^{1S} = p_{11}^{SW}\left(p^{1W} + p^{2W}\right)$$

$$p^{2W} = \left(1 - p_{11}^{SW}\right)p^{1W} + p^{1S}/2$$

$$p^{1S} + p^{1W} + p^{2W} = 1$$

These can be solved to get

$$p^{1W} = p^{2W} = \frac{\left(1 - p^{1S}\right)}{2} \qquad\qquad (6.A3)$$

$$p^{1S} = \frac{p^{SW}_{11}}{1 + p^{SW}_{11}} = \frac{\left(e^{SW}_{11}\right)^{\gamma}}{\left[2\left(e^{SW}_{11}\right)^{\gamma} + \left(e^{WS}_{11}\right)\right]^{\gamma}}$$

It can be checked that these values satisfy $p^{1W} \ldots \left(1 - p^{SW}_{11}\right) p^{2W} + p^{1S}/2$. Finally, having obtained the equilibrium efforts and thus the probability of each state, the expected value of a strong team is

$$V^{S}(OS1) = p^{1S} V^{SS}_{1} + \left(1 - p^{1S}\right)\left(V^{SW}_{1} + V^{SW}_{2}\right)/2$$

Graph 6.A1 plots the solution for the following parameterization: $\gamma = 1$, $\delta = 0.8$, exogenous efforts e_H, e_L, e_W all set to 0. The left panel reports the expected value for the strong team against the value of z: the dotted line corresponds to revenue sharing (OS1), while the continuous line refers to the no sharing case (ON). Unless z is very high, a strong team will never want to adopt revenue sharing. In the right panel we compare efforts. Revenue sharing corresponds again to the dotted lines: in particular the highest one is the effort spent by the weak team, the middle and bottom lines plot the effort spent by the strong team against a weak and a strong team respectively. We can thus tentatively conclude that, for low values of z, revenue sharing does not occur despite the effort spent is still quite limited compared to no sharing: without sharing the strong team benefits from zero effort to win against a weak team at the top (this happens with probability 25%). Now, despite the "collusive" effect of lower efforts with sharing and low values of z, when it

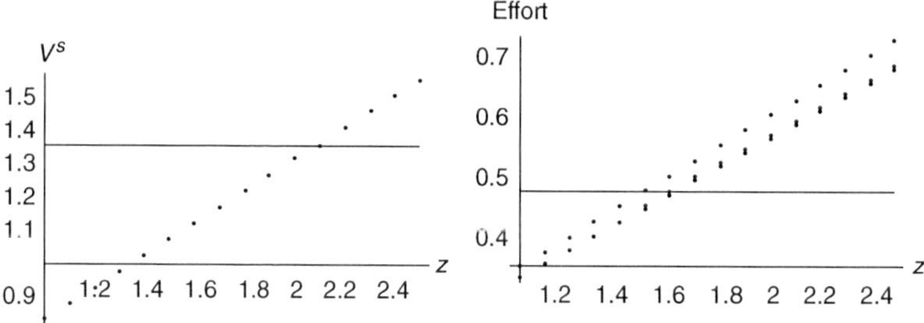

Graph 6.A1   Expected value of a strong team (left panel) and effort (right panel) in an open league with and without sharing in the top division. Parameters: $\gamma = 1$, $\delta = 0.8$

competes against a weak team at the top it has to put effort. This effect of costly effort prevails and makes sharing dominated by no sharing.[24] Only when z is sufficiently high, the higher expected gross value of the prize compensates for the higher effort and revenue sharing would be preferred by the strong team.

Another interesting observation from the graphs is that, under revenue sharing, the highest level of effort is actually put by the weak team (although in the only state where it puts an endogenous effort). The threat of relegation to the bottom, where the weak team is not competitive when it meets a strong team, means that it will fight very hard to remain at the top when it happens to be there.

Recall that the equivalent condition for sharing to be preferred in a closed league was $z > 2 - \gamma$. Given the parameterization in the figure ($\gamma = 1$), this means that, in a closed league, revenue sharing would always happen ($z^C = 1$) On the contrary, in an open system, z has to be sufficiently high ($z^O \approx 2.15$). Hence, once we endogenize the effort of the weaker teams it becomes *more likely* that the strong teams will *reject revenue sharing in an open system* when they would accept it in a closed system.

By looking at other parameterizations, we can describe the following tendencies:

(a) When the comparison is *between* an open league and a closed league, the range of γs that make sharing less likely in an open league is now considerably expanded. For instance, under the parameterization of Graph 6.A1, the threshold value of z is always more stringent in an open league ($z^O > z^C$) for $\gamma > 0.3$; on the other hand in the main text the limiting condition reduced to $\gamma > 4/(5 - 3\delta) \cup 1.54$ in this case;

(b) Similar results are obtained by putting reasonable values for the various exogenous efforts; for instance, if $\tilde{e}_W$ is positive (i.e. the effort put by the weak teams when they are both in the bottom division), then the likelihood of revenue sharing in an open league decreases even further. This is the intuition: the weak team—when at the top—competes even harder to avoid relegation that becomes a worse state; as a consequence the strong team has to face a tougher rival when it shares at the top.

Notes

1. FORT R. and QUIRK J. (1995, p. 1265).
2. Barnsley, Bournemouth, Bradford, Carlisle, Chesterfield, Crystal Palace, Ipswich, Leicester, Lincoln, Luton, Millwall, Notts County, Oxford, QPR,

Swansea and Swindon have all gone into administration in the last 5 years. *http://foot-ball.guardian.co.uk/clubsincrisis/story/0,11737,816711,00.html.*
3. *http://www.terrier-bytes.com/articles.php/news/145.*
4. *http://football.guardian.co.uk/clubsincrisis/story/0,11737,679178,00.html.*
5. *http://news.bbc.co.uk/2/hi/europe/2749673.stm.*
6. See e.g. HAMIL S. *et al.* (1999).
7. This observation, first noted in the economics literature by NEALE W. (1964), has been acknowledged by all writers on sports economics since. Indeed, it is arguable that the sports economics as a distinct field of research rests primarily on this point.
8. THE EUROPEAN COMMISSION (1998) has identified the promotion and relegation system as "one of the key features of the European model of sport". In the European system, all teams belong to a governing body that oversees a strictly defined hierarchy of divisional competitions. At all levels a limited number of the worst performing teams (usually between one and four) in any given division are demoted at the end of each season to the immediately junior division, to be replaced by the equivalent number of top performing teams from the junior division. This seamless hierarchy connects the lowest levels of amateur competition to the highest levels of European competition.
9. Models based on Tullock contest success functions are standard to analyze the properties and design of alternative contest structures (e.g. GRADSTEIN M. and KONRAD K.A., 1999). See SZYMANSKI S. (2003) for a review of the application of contest theory to sporting competition.
10. TAYLOR B. and TROGDON J. (2002) provide evidence that weak teams in the NBA have in fact attempted to lose matches toward the end of the season, since losing offers the chance of a better draft pick. Note that not only does the threat of relegation makes this strategy unrealistic for weak teams, but also that agreement to implement a draft system is less likely to be feasible under promotion and relegation. It is worth noting that there is some loss of incentives to compete in a promotion and relegation system if the bottom teams are not allowed to enter a play-off for relegation—we are grateful for the editor for this point.
11. See HOEHN T. and SZYMANSKI S. (1999) for a comparison of the main institutional differences.
12. The idealized standard deviation is calculated on the assumption that each team has an equal chance of winning, and is therefore equal to $.5/\sqrt{m}$ where m is the number of matches played by each team in the season. The extent to which the actual standard deviation exceeds the idealized value thus gives some indication of the extent of competitive imbalance during the season.
13. The Premier League is the top division of English Soccer; it consists of 20 teams and was formed by a breakaway from the English Football League in 1992. Crucially, however, it retained the promotion and relegation relationship with the First Division of the surviving English Football League. Currently, three teams are relegated and promoted between the two divisions each season. Seasons up until 1992 refer to the old First Division of the Football League.
14. Note that this (European) concept of a division as part of the hierarchical structure is therefore distinct from the American concept of a division. In

the European system the concept of inter-divisional play within the League makes no sense, since it violates the hierarchical ordering.

15. This can be seen by noting that both s_i and l_i decrease with the number of rival teams. Hence, the sum $s_i + l_i$ is bounded above by the value it takes when there are only two teams, in which case $l_i = x_j^\gamma / (x_i^\gamma + x_j^\gamma)$ and $s_i + l_i = 1$.

16. The difference is decreasing in δ, hence it takes a minimum for δ approaching 1, in which case it is easily shown to be positive. Recall that we assume no prize at all in the lower league, which is probably not quite accurate. However, it is true to say that, in practice, teams in lower divisions typically spend far less on players than teams in higher divisions, but the gap is not quite so large as in our model.

17. SZYMANSKI S. (2003) points out that this is more likely to be true in individualistic contests such as foot races, where great weight is attached to record breaking, than in team sports.

18. These are the names of the top two divisions in Italy. This at least avoids the somewhat confusing English situation where the second ranked division is now called the Football League First Division, from which teams are promoted to the Premier League.

19. In the next section we examine redistribution policies in an asymmetric model, where we assume league policies require the consent of the strongest teams.

20. We suppose that smaller revenue-generating teams could never compel the larger revenue-generating teams to share, otherwise they would simply quit the league and start a rival competition. In England, this is approximately what happened in the early 1990s—the top 5 teams led a breakaway from the Football League (a venerable institution which had recently celebrated its centenary) on the grounds that it no longer wanted broadcasting income, largely derived from their own matches, to be shared with the other 87 members of the League. Having failed to negotiate a significant increase in the share of the top teams, they persuaded 15 other teams to secede with them to form the FA Premier League.

21. BAYE M. *et al.* (1994) developed the analysis of mixed strategies when $\gamma > 2$.

22. While the very best teams will not be relegated very frequently in a league made up of a larger number of teams, it must be expected to happen at least occasionally.

23. To see this note that $p_1^S + p_2^{SW} = 1$, while the transition probabilities in the steady state must satisfy $p_1^S = p_1^S/2 + p_2^{SW}$, and $p_2^{SW} = p_1^S/2$.

24. To be more precise, one has to take into account also the probabilities of realization of each of the three possible states, which are not shown in the graphs. Since efforts under revenue sharing are not "too" different from each other, it turns out that they are in the range of 1/3—see eq. (6.A3).

Bibliography

BAYE M., KOVENOCK D. and DE VRIES C, "The Solution to the Tullock Rent-Seeking Game When R > 2: Mixed-Strategy Equilibria and Mean Dissipation Rates", *Public Choice*, vol. 81, 1994, pp. 363–80.

BUZZACCHI L., SZYMANSKI S. and VALLETTI T., "Equality of Opportunity and Equality of Outcome: Open Leagues, Closed Leagues and Competitive Balance", *Journal of Industry, Competition and Trade*, vol. 3, no. 3, 2003, pp. 167–86.

EL-HODIRI M. and QUIRK J., "An Economic Model of a Professional Sports League", *Journal of Political Economy*, vol. 79, 1971, pp. 1302–19.

EUROPEAN COMMISSION, The European Model of Sport. Consultation Paper of *DGX*, Brussels, 1998.

FORT R. and QUIRK J., "Cross Subsidization, Incentives and Outcomes in Professional Team Sports Leagues", *Journal of Economic Literature*, vol. 33, no. 3, 1995, pp. 1265–99.

FULLERTON R. and MCAFEE P., "Auctioning Entry in Tournaments", *Journal of Political Economy*, vol. 107, no. 3, 1999, pp. 573–606.

GRADSTEIN M. and KONRAD K.A., "Orchestrating Rent Seeking Contests", *Economic Journal*, vol. 109, no. 458, 1999, pp. 536–45.

HAMIL S., MICHIE J. and OUGHTON C., *The Business of Football: A Game of Two Halves?*, Edinburgh, Mainstream, 1999.

HOEHN T. and SZYMANSKI S., "The Americanization of European Football", *Economic Policy*, vol. 28, 1999, pp. 205–40.

NOLL R. and ZIMBALIST A., *Sports, Jobs and Taxes*, Brookings Institution Press, 1997.

NOLL R. "The Economics of Promotion and Relegation in Sports Leagues: The Case of English Football", *Journal of Sports Economics*, vol. 3, no. 2, 2002, pp. 169–203.

NEALE W., "The Peculiar Economics of Professional Sport", *Quarterly Journal of Economics*, vol. 78, no. 1, 1964, pp. 1–14.

NTI K., "Comparative Statics of Contests and Rent-seeking Games", *International Economic Review*, vol. 38, no. 1, 1997, pp. 43–59.

QUIRK J. and FORT R., *Pay Dirt: The Business of Professional Team Sports*, Princeton (N.J.), Princeton University Press, 1992.

——, *Hard Ball: The Abuse of Power in Pro Team Sports*, Princeton University Press, 1999.

ROSS S., "Monopoly Sports Leagues", *University of Minnesota Law Review*, vol. 73, 1989, p. 643.

ROSS S. and SZYMANSKI S., "Open Competition in League Sports", *Wisconsin Law Review*, vol. 3, 2002, pp. 625–56.

ROTTENBERG S., "The Baseball Players' Labor Market", *Journal of Political Economy*, Vol. 64, 1956, pp. 242–58.

SIEGFRIED J. and ZIMBALIST A., "The Economics of Sports Facilities and Their Communities", *Journal of Economic Perspectives*, vol. 14, 2000, pp. 95–114.

SZYMANSKI S., "The Economic Design of Sporting Contests", *Journal of Economic Literature*, vol. 41, no. 4, 2003.

SZYMANSKI S. and VALLETTI T., "Incentive Effects of Second Prizes", *European Journal of Political Economy*, vol. 21, no. 2, 2005, pp. 467–81.

TAYLOR B. and TROGDON J., "Losing to Win: Tournament Incentives in the National Basketball Association", *Journal of Labor Economics*, vol. 20, no. 1, 2002, pp. 23–41.

TULLOCK G., "Efficient Rent Seeking", in BUCHANAN J., TOLLISON R. and
   TULLOCK G. (eds.), *Toward a Theory of Rent Seeking Society*, Texas A&M University
   Press, 1980, pp. 97–112.
VROOMAN J., "The Economics of American Sports Leagues", *Scottish Journal of
   Political Economy*, vol. 47, no. 4, 2000, pp. 364–98.

7
Competitive Balance and Gate Revenue Sharing in Team Sports

Stefan Szymanski and Stefan Késenne
[a] *The Business School, Imperial College, London*
[b] *UFSIA, University of Antwerp, Prinstraat, Belgium*

Abstract

This chapter shows that under reasonable conditions, increasing gate revenue sharing among teams in a sports league will produce a more uneven contest, i.e. reduce competitive balance. This result has significant implications for antitrust authorities and legislators, who have tended to assume that revenue sharing arrangements will necessarily promote competitive balance.

I. Introduction

It is a widely held belief that a sporting competition such as a soccer or baseball league will be more successful the greater the degree of competitive balance among the teams, because the matches will be more uncertain and therefore more entertaining. Owners of teams have consistently used this argument to justify revenue sharing schemes. The idea, they claim, is to equalise resources so that 'weak drawing' teams can compete with 'strong drawing' teams. This argument has been accepted by competition authorities and legislators in North America, Europe and elsewhere and agreements to share revenues are generally considered to be pro-competitive.[1]

Critics have pointed out that revenue sharing will also blunt the incentive for profit-maximising team owners to compete, since for

We thank Tommaso Valletti, Gerd Muehlheusser, Wilfried Pauwels, the editor and an anonymous referee for useful comments. Errors remain our own.

each team the returns to winning are reduced. This may mean less competition to attract players, lower salaries and a lower standard of competition. In this chapter we analyse a specific form of revenue sharing – gate revenue sharing[2]– and show that under reasonable assumptions, it will not only blunt incentives but will also produce a more uneven distribution of talent in a league and therefore reduce competitive balance. While this does not imply that all revenue sharing agreements reduce competitive balance, it does suggest that such arrangements require more careful economic analysis.

II. Revenue sharing in contest models

Many commentators on sporting issues, not least the team owners themselves, have drawn attention to the collective action problem facing the members of a league. Suppose that some large market teams have the potential to draw a significant following from a given level of success while smaller teams will draw only a relatively small following. Self-interested behaviour, they claim, will cause the large market teams to dominate the competition to the point where it becomes too predictable and demand will fall below the level that maximises joint profits (and consumer interest). One widely advanced solution to this perceived problem is to share revenues and so provide relatively equal opportunities for all the teams.

Analysis of this problem requires a contest model. A sporting contest is a type of all-pay auction in which the players or teams make bids in the form of effort or investment in talent. A contest success function (see, e.g., Skaperdas [1996]) defines each agent's probability of success as a function of that agent's share of the total contribution of all agents to the contest. Here we think of the teams as the agents but instead of competing for a fixed prize, teams have their own revenue generating functions which depend on the degree of success of the team. All-pay auctions are typically 'perfectly discriminating' so that the highest bidder wins with probability 1 (see, e.g., Hillman and Riley [1989]). A sporting contest is always imperfectly discriminating since the most expensive team or the player who makes most effort can never be certain of winning. The most widely used contest success function in sports, as in a number of other applications, is the logit[3] (e.g., El Hodiri and Quirk [1971] and Fort and Quirk [1995]).

In the contest literature the main issues have been the amount of effort/investment that can be elicited and the degree to which any rents to be earned in the contest are dissipated by competition. To analyse this issue, researchers have mainly focused on symmetric contests.[4] In sports, unlike most other contest situations, demand exists for the contest itself, rather than its consequences. Moreover, most people believe that consumers have a preference for more balanced contests.[5] Hence the sports literature's main concern is with the distribution of effort/investment,[6] which clearly requires a model of an asymmetric contest.

In its most general form we can define the logit contest success function for n contestants as

$$w_i = \frac{h_i(t_i)}{\sum_{j=1}^{n} h_j(t_j)} \tag{7.1}$$

where w is the probability of success, t is the effort contribution of the contestant and $h' > 0$ and $h'' \leqslant 0$ with $h_i(0) = 0$.[7] In the context of a team sports league, we take w to be the probability of winning the league championship and t the investment in playing talent by the team owner. Given that the probabilities must sum to unity for any contest we have the useful adding up constraint that

$$\frac{\partial w_i}{\partial t_i} = -\sum_{\substack{j \neq i \\ j=1}}^{n} \frac{\partial w_j}{\partial t_i} \tag{7.2}$$

In what follows we shall adopt a common assumption from that literature that the h functions are identical for each team (Baik considers asymmetry in the h functions). Symmetry of the h functions implies that if all contestants invested the same amount of resources in trying to win the contest, then each contestant would have an equal probability of winning. This amounts to assuming that teams share the same production technology, so a unit of talent is expected to be equally productive of wins, for a given level of team talent, as at any other team. This might seem a controversial assumption, but in markets as competitive as professional team sports where player salaries are counted in the millions of dollars, it seems hard to believe that managers do not all adopt best practice.

Assuming symmetric h functions is not the same as assuming the contest itself is symmetric. Even with symmetric h's, teams can have asymmetric objective functions. This might be due to larger revenue generating opportunities (e.g., a larger local market, a greater reputation, a more media-friendly team) or a lower cost base (e.g., due to some distinctive capability in team management, closeness to a rich source of talent or a location that was more attractive to players).

We consider a two team model where each team is a profit maximiser and profits consist of gate revenues less the cost of talent investment. In this case the probability of winning the championship can also be interpreted as the expected percentage of matches won (win percentage). The gate revenue function from success (winning) can be asymmetric and the marginal revenue from winning can be constant or decreasing. We also allow that excessive dominance by one team can lead to a fall in revenues for the dominant team as well as the weaker team. Thus the gate revenue function for each team in the contest is defined as $R_i = R_i(w_i)$ where either $R_i' > 0$ and $R_i'' \leqslant 0$ for all w_i in $[0,1]$ or there exists a w_i^* $[0,1]$ such that if $w_i \geqslant w_i^*$ then $R_i' < 0$ otherwise $R_i' > 0$, and $R_i'' < 0$ everywhere. We assume that $w^* \geqslant 1/2$ for at least one team, otherwise both teams would prefer to win fewer than 50% of their matches and no equilibrium would exist.

The impact of gate revenue sharing on both the quantity of talent hired in the market and competitive balance is a standard problem in the sports literature (see, e.g., Quirk and El Hodiri [1974], Fort and Quirk [1995] and Vrooman [1995]). The principal difference between these models and the model presented here is that they treat the total supply of talent to the league as fixed (since they have in mind a major league where all the best players want to play), whereas here, we allow that the supply of talent may be fixed or elastic, the latter case having more in common with the situation in European soccer leagues (see Szymanski [2003] for a more detailed discussion of differences).

For the purposes of our model, we assume that each team retains a fraction $\alpha > 1/2$ of income generated from home matches and pays $1 - \alpha$ to their opponents. In line with most of the existing literature, we assume that talent can be hired in the market at a constant marginal cost c. We can write the profit function for either team (here team 1) as

$$\pi_1 = \alpha R_1[w_1(t_1, t_2)] + (1 - \alpha)R_2[w_2(t_2, t_1)] - ct_1 \tag{7.3}$$

The first-order condition for team 1 is

$$\frac{\partial \pi_1}{\partial t_1} = \alpha R_1' \frac{\partial w_1}{\partial t_1} + (1 - \alpha)R_2' \frac{\partial w_2}{\partial t_1} - c = 0 \tag{7.4}$$

(In equation (7.4) and in what follows, the equivalent conditions for team 2 can be obtained by simply switching the subscript 1 for 2, and vice versa). In our analysis of the general case, we shall assume that the marginal revenues in equilibrium are large enough to ensure that an interior solution to (7.4) always exists. Note that even if an interior solution exists for $\alpha = 1$, gate revenue sharing may introduce the possibility of corner solutions. This possibility is considered using an example below.

Given that in a two team model $\partial w_1/\partial t_1 = -\partial w_2/\partial t_1$ (this is the adding up constraint (7.2)), using the contest success function (7.1) we obtain

$$\frac{\partial \pi_1}{\partial t_1} = [\alpha R_1' - (1-\alpha)R_2']\left(\frac{w_2 h_1'}{h_1 + h_2}\right) - c = 0 \tag{7.5}$$

What distinguishes the approach of this chapter, and the contest literature in general, from the established sports economics literature, is the way the contest success function (7.1) is differentiated to produce (7.5). This is discussed in the conclusion and in Appendix 2, which explains the approach that has been used in the sports literature. Since marginal costs are identical, equation (7.5) says that in equilibrium the marginal revenue from the hiring of talent is equalised across teams. This is not the same as saying the marginal revenue of a win is equalised.

We can also see from (7.5) that if there is no revenue sharing ($\alpha = 1$) in equilibrium, both teams must choose a quantity of talent such that marginal revenue is positive (otherwise marginal profit is always negative). For $\alpha \in (1/2, 1)R_1'$ could only be negative and satisfy (7.5) if R_2' is also negative. But this cannot be an equilibrium since the teams could raise profits by hiring no talent at all. Hence marginal revenues must be positive for both teams in equilibrium. If we take the difference of the two first-order conditions, we obtain

$$R_1' - R_2' = \frac{c(h_1 + h_2)(w_1 h_2' - w_2 h_1')}{w_1 w_2 h_1' h_2'} \tag{7.6}$$

from which it is apparent that in equilibrium the team with the higher expected winning record ($w_1 > w_2$) will always have the larger own marginal revenue from winning ($R_1' > R_2'$). A natural interpretation of this is that the 'stronger drawing' dominates competition, which is true in the sense that a team whose support values an additional win more than its rivals for any given win percentage will dominate in equilibrium. While in many cases, this is likely to be true for large city teams competing against small city teams, it is also possible that a small city team could dominate a larger rival city if its fans are sufficiently sensitive to the success of the team.[8] However, despite dominating the contest, the stronger team will still have a greater marginal revenue from a win than the weaker team (but not from hiring an additional unit of talent) in equilibrium.

To make further progress, we need to simplify the problem. We want to examine the properties of the revenue sharing equilibrium for the most general revenue functions possible, and to do so, we restrict our analysis to the simplest and most widely used contest success function by assuming $h(t_1) = t_1$ so that $w_1 = t_1/(t_1 + t_2)$ and $w_2 = 1 - w_1$.

Our principal interest is in the impact of a change in the revenue sharing parameter α on the level of competitive balance. This can be measured by the ratio of winning percentages, which now also equals the ratio of talent units hired by each team, that is, $w_1/w_2 = t_1/t_2$, and so

$$\frac{\partial(w_1/w_2)}{\partial\alpha} = \frac{t_2\,dt_1/d\alpha - t_1\,dt_2/d\alpha}{t_2^2} = \frac{1}{t_2}\left(\frac{dt_1}{d\alpha} - \frac{w_1}{w_2}\frac{dt_2}{d\alpha}\right) \qquad (7.7)$$

PROPOSITION. *Assuming that a stable solution to the teams' optimisation problem exists, increased revenue sharing*

(a) *Causes competitive balance to deteriorate.*
(b) *Reduces the number of units of talent hired by each team for a given wage rate per unit of talent.*

PROOF. See Appendix 1.

What is the intuition for these results? The result that revenue sharing reduces talent investment is long established and follows simply from the dulling of incentives to win. However, part (a) also shows that the dulling effect is greater for the weak drawing team. This is because a higher probability of own success leads to a greater loss of gate revenue generated by the opponent for the weak drawing team. It is worth noting that this result depends on the logit formulation which ensures that the marginal impact on the dominant team's winning probability of an increase in the investment of the weaker team is greater than the marginal impact on the weaker team's winning probability of an increase in the investment of the dominant team. If the contest success function were specified such that there were increasing returns to talent investment, even over a relatively limited range, this result might no longer hold.[9]

It is also important to note that part (b) is derived under the condition where the marginal cost of talent (the wage rate) is treated as a parameter, that is, there is no price adjustment in the labour market. This is appropriate if the supply of talent is perfectly elastic. However, if we assume that the supply of talent is fixed, then increased revenue sharing will create an excess supply of talent and its marginal cost must fall to restore labour market equilibrium. Since competitive balance must worsen, the dominant team must increase the number of units of talent hired while the weaker team reduces its demand (but by less than in the case where marginal cost is fixed). Total investment in talent falls. To illustrate this possibility and the possibility of corner solution, it is useful to look at an example.

III.   An example

$R_1 = \sigma w_1, R_2 = w_2, \sigma > 1$. Here marginal revenue is a positive constant and $\sigma > 1$ implies that team 1 is the strong drawing team. From the first-order conditions we obtain

$$\frac{w_1}{w_2} = \frac{\alpha\sigma - (1-\alpha)}{\alpha - \sigma(1-\alpha)}$$

and

$$\frac{\partial(w_1/w_2)}{\partial\alpha} = \left\{ \frac{(1-\sigma)(1+\sigma)}{[\alpha - (1-\alpha)\sigma]^2} \right\} < 0$$

Note also that the expected win percentages are

$$w_1 = \frac{\alpha(\sigma + 1) - 1}{(2\alpha - 1)(1+\sigma)} \quad \text{and} \quad w_2 = \frac{\alpha - \sigma(1-\alpha)}{(2\alpha - 1)(1+\sigma)}$$

so that an interior solution requires $\sigma < \alpha/(1-\alpha)$. Note that this is satisfied no matter how great the inequality in drawing power when there is no revenue sharing, but can never be satisfied if there is equal revenue sharing. Because revenue sharing has a negative effect on competitive balance, there is a narrower and narrower range of initial inequality that will sustain an interior solution as the degree of sharing increases.

If $\sigma > \alpha/(1-\alpha)$ then the weaker drawing team's profit function is decreasing in its own success and therefore would choose zero units of talent. In this case an equilibrium does not exist since the best response for team 1 is to purchase a negligible quantity, implying that zero is no longer a best response for team 2.

We can also derive the investment in talent by each team:

$$t_1 = \frac{[\alpha(1+\sigma) - 1]^2[\alpha(1+\sigma) - \sigma]}{c[(2\alpha - 1)(1+\sigma)]^2}$$

and

$$t_2 = \frac{[\alpha(1+\sigma)-1][\alpha(1+\sigma)-\sigma]^2}{c[(2\alpha-1)(1+\sigma)]^2}$$

so that total demand for talent in the market is

$$t_1 + t_2 = \frac{\sigma - \alpha(1-\alpha)(1+\sigma)^2}{c(2\alpha-1)(1+\sigma)}$$

This implies the further restriction that $\sigma/(1+\sigma)^2 > \alpha(1-\alpha)$ in order for total demand to be positive. Once again, the constraint is not binding when $\alpha = 1$ but becomes increasingly restrictive as α approaches 1/2.

If the total supply of talent is fixed at some value T, then there exists a market clearing marginal cost of talent (which we can call the wage rate per unit of talent) that ensures that supply equals demand. Given that $T = t_1 + t_2$ in equilibrium we obtain the usual inverse relationship between the wage rate and the demand for talent, but changes in the wage rate will not affect the talent shares of the two teams (marginal cost does not enter the expression for the win ratios). We can also show that total expenditure on talent will be increasing in α (revenue sharing diminishes total investment).

$$\frac{\mathrm{d}(cT)}{\mathrm{d}\alpha} = 1 + \sigma - \frac{2(\sigma - \alpha(1-\alpha)(1+\sigma))}{(2\alpha-1)^2(1+\sigma)}$$

which is positive for α and σ within their permissible ranges.

IV. Conclusions

This chapter has shown that under reasonable assumptions, gate revenue sharing will not only reduce total investment in talent by teams in a league but also diminish the degree of competitive balance. This has important implications for competition authorities and legislators who have generally taken a permissive view of revenue sharing schemes on the grounds that they favour competitive balance.

The main result of this chapter contrasts sharply with the well-known 'invariance principle' which states that gate revenue sharing will have no effect on competitive balance (Quirk and El Hodiri [1974], Fort and Quirk [1995], Vrooman [1995]).[10] As the example of the previous section shows, this is not the result of assuming that the supply of talent is fixed. In the original paper of Quirk and El Hodiri, it seems to emerge as a consequence of assuming that each team maximises profit with respect to the talent choices of all other firms, so that the final allocation of talent ensures joint profit maximisation[11] (in contrast to the model here, which is noncooperative and whose equilibrium is not joint profit maximising). In the models of Quirk and Fort and Vrooman, the result stems from a different assumption about the derivative of the contest success function (see Appendix 2).

While gate revenue sharing is known in team sports, it is by no means the only sharing mechanism used. Pool revenue sharing, adopted in 1997 Major League Baseball, where teams contribute a fixed percentage of revenues which is then redistributed according to another formula, is sometimes equivalent to gate revenue sharing, but more work remains to be done to analyse the properties of different pooling schemes. Another form of revenue sharing that deserves detailed consideration is the division of revenue generated from the collective sale of broadcast rights.

In North America, this is distributed on the basis of equal shares for all teams. However, in European soccer leagues, the distribution formula (when collective sale is permitted) typically entails a prize-like element.[12] Prizes can, in principle, create balanced contests by evening up the ex ante incentives to invest. Moldovanu and Sela [2001] consider the distribution of prizes in the context of an all-pay auction (a perfectly discriminating contest) while Szymanski and Valletti [2002] have looked at this issue for the case of an imperfectly discriminating contest. The optimal distribution of prizes in asymmetric contests is an important area of research with applications wider than the sports literature.

Appendix 1: Proof of proposition

To prove part (a) it is sufficient to show (from (7.7)) that $dt_1/d\alpha - w_1/w_2 dt_2/d\alpha < 0$ if team 1 is dominant team when $\alpha = 1$ (recall that $R_1' > R_2'$ in equilibrium is a sufficient condition for team 1 to be dominant).

To sign (7.7) we need to conduct a comparative statics exercise on the decision making of the two teams. Totally differentiating the first-order conditions (7.5) for each team we can write

$$\begin{pmatrix} \pi_{11} & \pi_{12} \\ \pi_{21} & \pi_{22} \end{pmatrix} \begin{pmatrix} dt_1 \\ dt_2 \end{pmatrix} = \begin{pmatrix} -\pi_{1\alpha} \\ -\pi_{2\alpha} \end{pmatrix} d\alpha \qquad (7.\text{A}1)$$

where

$$\pi_{11} = \frac{\partial^2 \pi_1}{\partial t_1^2} = [\alpha R_1' - (1-\alpha)R_2'] \left[\frac{-2w_2}{(t_1+t_2)^2} \right] + [\alpha R_1'' + (1-\alpha)R_2''] \left[\frac{w_2^2}{(t_1+t_2)^2} \right]$$

$$\pi_{12} = \frac{\partial^2 \pi_1}{\partial t_1 \partial t_2} = [\alpha R_1' - (1-\alpha)R_2'] \left[\frac{w_1 - w_2}{(t_1+t_2)^2} \right] - [\alpha R_1'' + (1-\alpha)R_2''] \left[\frac{w_1 w_2}{(t_1+t_2)^2} \right]$$

$$\pi_{22} = \frac{\partial^2 \pi_2}{\partial t_2^2} = [\alpha R_2' - (1-\alpha)R_1'] \left[\frac{-2w_1}{(t_1+t_2)^2} \right] + [\alpha R_2'' + (1-\alpha)R_1''] \left[\frac{w_1^2}{(t_1+t_2)^2} \right]$$

$$(7.A2)$$

$$\pi_{21} = \frac{\partial^2 \pi_2}{\partial t_1 \partial t_2} = [\alpha R_2' - (1-\alpha)R_1'] \left[\frac{w_2 - w_1}{(t_1+t_2)^2} \right] - [\alpha R_2'' + (1-\alpha)R_1''] \left[\frac{w_1 w_2}{(t_1+t_2)^2} \right]$$

$$\pi_{1\alpha} = \frac{\partial^2 \pi_1}{\partial t_1 \partial \alpha} = [R_1' + R_2'] \frac{w_2}{t_1 + t_2}$$

$$\pi_{2\alpha} = \frac{\partial^2 \pi_2}{\partial t_2 \partial \alpha} = [R_1' + R_2'] \frac{w_1}{t_1 + t_2}$$

Each of these expressions can be simplified by observing that for team 1 in equilibrium

$$[\alpha R_1' - (1-\alpha)R_2'] = \frac{c(t_1 + t_2)}{w_2}$$

(and using the equivalent expression for team 2). Applying Cramer's Rule to (7.A1) we can write

$$\frac{dt_1}{d\alpha} = \frac{\pi_{12}\pi_{2\alpha} - \pi_{22}\pi_{1\alpha}}{\pi_{11}\pi_{22} - \pi_{12}\pi_{21}} \quad \text{and} \quad \frac{dt_2}{d\alpha} = \frac{\pi_{21}\pi_{1\alpha} - \pi_{11}\pi_{2\alpha}}{\pi_{11}\pi_{22} - \pi_{12}\pi_{21}} \tag{7.A3}$$

We assume that the denominators of (7.A3) are positive, which is a standard stability condition in the literature (see, e.g., Dixit [1986]). It is clear from (7.A2) that the second-order conditions π_{11} and π_{22} are negative given our assumptions about revenues. A sufficient condition for stability therefore is that the expressions π_{12} and π_{21}, which are the slopes of the reaction functions, have opposite signs. It is also clear from (7.A2) that $\pi_{12} > 0$ if team 1 is the stronger team (the reaction function of the dominant team slopes upward). However, the sign of π_{21} is ambiguous. If we assume it to be negative (as, for example, it must be if marginal revenue is constant) then stability is guaranteed. Stability is also ensured under the less restrictive assumption that $\pi_{11}\pi_{22} > \pi_{12}\pi_{21}$.[13]

We can conclude that the sign of (7.7) depends on the sign of the weighted difference of the numerators of (7.A3), i.e.

$$\text{sgn}\left(\frac{dt_1}{d\alpha} - \frac{w_1}{w_2}\frac{dt_2}{d\alpha}\right) = \text{sgn}\left[\pi_{2\alpha}\left(\pi_{12} + \frac{w_1}{w_2}\pi_{11}\right) - \pi_{1\alpha}\left(\pi_{22} + \frac{w_1}{w_2}\pi_{21}\right)\right]$$

$$(7.A4)$$

After some manipulation we can reduce the RHS of (7.A4) to

$$(R'_1 + R'_2)\left(\frac{w_1 - w_2}{t_1 + t_2}\right)\left[\frac{-c}{w_2(t_1 + t_2)}\right]$$

$$(7.A5)$$

This expression is negative if $w_1 > w_2$. Hence, win percentage of the dominant team increases as revenue sharing increases and competitive balance deteriorates. This proves part (a). Part (b) follows quite simply: from (7.A2) and (7.A3) it is clear that $dt_1/d_\alpha > 0$ (given that $\pi_{12} > 0$). But if increased revenue sharing causes the dominant team to reduce its investment and competitive balance worsens then it must also be the case that $dt_2/d_\alpha > 0$. QED

Appendix 2: Derivation of the invariance principle in Fort and Quirk (1995) and Vrooman (1995)

Given the contest success function $w_1 = t_1/(t_1 + t_2)$, its derivative (in (7.4)) can be written as

$$\frac{\partial w_1}{\partial t_1} = \frac{t_1 + t_2 - t_1(1 + dt_2/dt_1)}{(t_1 + t_2)^2}$$

$$(7.A6)$$

In this chapter, it is assumed that $dt_2/dt_1 = 0$, which we interpret to be the usual Nash conjecture, since this derivative appears in the first-order condition of the team owner's objective function (7.5). However, Fort and Quirk and Vrooman assume that $dt_2/dt_1 = -1$, which has a similar consequence as assuming joint profit maximising conjectures in a standard oligopoly model (see, e.g., Vives [1999]). They account for this assumption by arguing that the supply of talent is fixed, and that therefore a one unit increase in talent hired at one team necessarily leads to a one unit reduction of talent at another team. As a consequence of their assumption we can rewrite (7.5) as

$$\frac{\partial \pi_1}{\partial t_1} = [\alpha R'_1 - (1 - \alpha)R'_2]\left(\frac{1}{t_1 + t_2}\right) - c = 0$$

$$(7.A7)$$

Given that the win percentage derivatives are identical for each team, these cancel out when taking the ratio of the two first-order conditions and so we are left with the equilibrium condition:

$$\alpha R'_1 - (1-\alpha)R'_2 = \alpha R'_2 - (1-\alpha)R'_1 \Rightarrow R'_1 = R'_2 \qquad (7.A8)$$

Thus team marginal revenues are equalised for any value of α, and we obtain the invariance result that the extent of gate revenue sharing has no impact on the equilibrium distribution of playing talent. When $dt_2/dt_1 = -1$ the choice of one team automatically constrains the other in a two team model, and so every possible choice of talent is a Nash equilibrium, because the other team has only one feasible response, which is therefore 'best.' However, this clearly makes little sense as an economic model.

In this context, adopting t as the choice variable is inappropriate. However if we allow the share of talent employed by each team to be determined by independently selected investment levels, then the fixed supply model with conjecture $dt_2/dt_1 = -1$ conforms to the one described in the rest of this chapter. For example, suppose $t_1 + t_2 = 1$ and $t_1 = I_1/(I_1 + I_2)$ where I is the investment level, normalising marginal cost to unity we obtain team 1's objective function as

$$\pi_1 = \alpha R_1 \left\{ w_1 \left[t_1 \left(\frac{I_1}{I_1 + I_2} \right) \right] \right\} + (1-\alpha)R_2 \left\{ w_2 \left[t_2 \left(\frac{I_2}{I_1 + I_2} \right) \right] \right\} - I_1 \quad (7.A9)$$

with first-order condition

$$\frac{\partial \pi_1}{\partial I_1} = [\alpha R'_1 - (1-\alpha)R'_2] \left(\frac{w_2}{I_1 + I_2} \right) - 1 = 0 \qquad (7.A10)$$

which is essentially the same as equation (7.5) and implies that our gate revenue sharing proposition holds. See Szymanski [2004] for more details.

Notes

1. In North America, most revenue sharing agreements have not been challenged in the courts. The collective selling of national broadcast rights, which team owners claimed was intended to promote revenue sharing but which was deemed anti-competitive by the courts, has been exempted from antitrust law by Congress (Weiler and Roberts [1998]). In Europe, the European Commission has encouraged redistributive agreements aimed

at maintaining 'solidarity' between the professional and amateur levels of sport, and has also recognised the need to maintain competitive balance. While the specific issue of revenue sharing between members of the same league has not been addressed, it is widely presumed that it would not be deemed anti-competitive (see, e.g., European Commission [1999]).

2. Gate revenue sharing is most notably practised in the National Football League in the US, where 40% of designated gate revenues go to the visiting team. There is more limited gate sharing in Major League Baseball, and none in NBA (basketball) or NHL (hockey). European soccer leagues have practised various forms of gate sharing in their history. In England, visiting teams in League matches received up to 20% of the gate until the early 1980s. Gate sharing is relatively rare in European league soccer, but quite common in most Cup (knock-out) competitions.

3. For example, Loury [1979], Tullock [1980] and Nti [1997]. The principal alternative is the probit function explored, inter alia by Lazear and Rosen [1981] and Dixit [1987].

4. Dixit [1987] and Baik [1994] are notable exceptions.

5. The uncertainty of outcome hypothesis goes back at least as far as Rottenberg [1956] in the sports economics literature and is its most resilient theme. There is a small empirical literature testing the validity of this hypothesis; see, for example, Schmidt and Berri [2001] and Forrest and Simmons [2002].

6. For team sports contests of the type considered in this chapter, it is more natural to think of the contribution of each team as an investment in playing talent rather than the effort of the players onthefield.We suppose that individual players supply optimal effort. This is consistent with the belief that top players are highly motivated and therefore financial incentives are largely irrelevant to the effort supply decision or that effort is observable so that first best contracts can be written and enforced.

7. If $h_i(0) = 0$ for all contestants we define $w_i = 0$ ('no contest').

8. In practice, the phenomenon is seldom observed.

9. We are grateful to the editor for this point. One example of such a function might involve increasing returns for low levels of success but then decreasing returns at high levels of success.

10. Several writers have identified exceptions to this rule, notably Atkinson et al. [1988], Marburger [1997], Hoehn and Szymanski [1999] and Késenne [2000].

11. Quirk and El Hodiri [1974] p. 62.

12. For example, in the English Premier League, 25% of the money distributed to clubs is awarded on the basis of league rank.

13. Atkinson *et al.* [1988] use the result that $\partial t_i/\partial\alpha > 0$ (p. 33, fn. 14) to conduct their comparative static exercise. This seems to rest on a confusion of the partial derivative, which must indeed be positive from inspection of (7.A2), and the total derivative which is required for the comparative statics and can only be signed using the second-order conditions and the cross partials, which are neglected by Atkinson et al. This would not be a problem if marginal revenues were constants, but in fact they assume total revenues to be strictly concave (p. 29).

References

Atkinson, S.; Stanley, L. and Tschirhart, J., 1988, 'Revenue Sharing as an Incentive in an Agency Problem: An Example from the National Football League,' *Rand Journal of Economics*, 19, 1, 27–43.

Baik, K., 1994, 'Effort Levels in Contests with Two Asymmetric Players,' *Southern Economic Journal*, 61, 367–378.

Dixit, A., 1986, 'Comparative Statics for Oligopoly,' *International Economic Review*, 27, 1, 107–122.

Dixit, A., 1987, 'Strategic Behavior in Contests,' *American Economic Review*, 77, 891–898.

El Hodiri, M. and Quirk, J., 1971, 'AnEconomic Model of a Professional Sports League,' *Journal of Political Economy*, 79, 1302–1319.

European Commission, 1999, *The Helsinki Report on Sport.* Brussels 10.12.99 COM (1999) 644 final. http://europa.eu.int/eur-lex/en/com/rpt/1999/com-1999_0644en01.pdf.

Forrest, D. and Simmons, R., 2002, 'Outcome Uncertainty and Attendance Demand in Sport: The Case of English Soccer,' *Journal of the Royal Statistical Society, Series D (The Statistician)*, Vol. 51, No. 2.

Fort, R. and Quirk, J., 1995, 'Cross Subsidization, Incentives and Outcomes in Professional Team Sports Leagues,' *Journal of Economic Literature*, XXXIII, 3, 1265–1299.

Hillman, A. and Riley, J., 1989, 'Politically Contestable Rents and Transfers,' *Economics and Politics*, 1, 17–39.

Hoehn, T. and Szymanski, S., 1999, 'The Americanization of European Football,' *Economic Policy*, 28, 205–240.

Késenne, S., 2000, 'Revenue Sharing and Competitive Balance in Professional Team Sports,' *Journal of Sports Economics*, 11, 56–65.

Lazear, E. and Rosen, S., 1981, 'Rank Order Tournaments as Optimal Labor Contracts,' *Journal of Political Economy*, 89, 841–864.

Loury, G., 1979, 'Market Structure and Innovation,' *Quarterly Journal of Economics*, 93, 385–410.

Marburger, D., 1997, 'Gate Revenue Sharing and Luxury Taxes in Professional Sports,' *Contemporary Economic Policy*, XV, April, 114–123.

Moldovanu, B. and Sela, A., 2001, 'The Optimal Allocation of Prizes in Contests,' *American Economic Review*, 91, 3, 542–558.

Nti, K., 1997, 'Comparative Statics of Contests and Rent-Seeking Games,' *International Economic Review*, 38, 1, 43–59.

Quirk, J. and El Hodiri, M., 1974, 'The Economic Theory of a Professional Sports League,' in Noll (ed.), *Government and the Sports Business* (Brookings Institution).

Rottenberg, S., 1956, 'The Baseball Players' Labor Market,' *Journal of Political Economy*, LXIV (3), June, 242–258.

Schmidt, M. and Berri, D., 2001, 'Competitive Balance and Attendance: The Case of Major League Baseball,' *Journal of Sports Economics*, 2, 2, 145–167.

Skaperdas, S., 1996, 'Contest Success Functions,' *Economic Theory*, 7, 283–90.

Szymanski, S., 2003, 'The Economic Design of Sporting Contests,' *Journal of Economic Literature*, XLI, December, 1135–1185.

Szymanski, S., 2004, 'Professional Team Sports Are Only a Game: The Walrasian Fixed Supply Conjecture Model, Contest—Nash Equilibrium and the Invariance Principle,' *Journal of Sports Economics*, 5, 2, 111–126.

Szymanski, S. and Valletti, T., 2002, 'First and Second Prizes in Imperfectly Discriminating Contests,' mimeo.

Tullock, G., (1980), 'Efficient Rent Seeking,' in J. Buchanan, R. Tollison and G. Tullock, (eds.), *Toward a Theory of Rent Seeking Society* (Texas A&M University Press), 97–112.

Vives, X., 1999, *Oligopoly Pricing* (MIT Press).

Vrooman, J., 1995, 'A General Theory of Professional Sports Leagues,' *Southern Economic Journal*, 61, 4, 971–990.

Weiler, P. and Roberts, G., 1998, *Sports and the Law: Text, Cases, Problems*, 2nd edition (American Casebook Series, West/Wadsworth).

8

Professional Team Sports Are Only a Game: The Walrasian Fixed-Supply Conjecture Model, Contest-Nash Equilibrium, and the Invariance Principle

Stefan Szymanski

Tanaka Business School, Imperial College London

Abstract

This chapter explores the standard 2-team model of talent choice in a professional sports league and argues that the application of Nash concepts leads to a different equilibrium than that which is normally identified. In particular, it is shown that the invariance principle for gate-revenue sharing no longer holds. Because the standard model, which is here called the Walrasian fixed-supply conjecture model, is widely taught in sports management and economics programs, these finding have important implications for teachers as well as researchers.

Keywords: contests; revenue sharing; competitive balance

One of the most important developments in the modeling of decision-making problems in a competitive environment in the past 30 years has been the widespread adoption of game theoretic concepts. The most important of these is probably the concept of *Nash equilibrium*, reflected in the award of the Nobel Prize to John Nash in 1994. In the citation for his award, the Nobel Committee said, "John F. Nash introduced the distinction between cooperative games, in which binding agreements can be made, and non-cooperative games, where binding agreements are not feasible. Nash developed an equilibrium concept for non-cooperative games that later came to be called Nash equilibrium" (Royal Swedish

Academy of Sciences, 1994). In their textbook on game theory, Dixit and Skeath (1999) state, "Nash equilibrium is indeed the fundamental solution concept for noncooperative games" (p. 82).

It is natural to think of the choice of playing talent by teams in a professional sports league as a noncooperative game. Teams choose independently how many players to hire and how much to pay them, subject to the rules and bylaws of the league. Few papers in the team sports literature, however, refer to game theory or the Nash concept.[1] This chapter shows that the Nash solution to the noncooperative game of talent choice in a professional sports league (hereafter called the Contest-Nash solution) is inconsistent with the standard representation of the competitive equilibrium (which I here call the *Walrasian fixed-supply conjecture model* for reasons I will make clear in the next two sections). Moreover, I show that the Contest-Nash equilibrium is inconsistent with the invariance principle for gate-revenue sharing (Fort & Quirk, 1995; Quirk & El Hodiri, 1974; Vrooman, 1995). A general proof is provided in Szymanski and Késenne (2004). The purpose of this chapter is to show how the Nash concept implies a different solution for the simple 2-team diagram than that which is commonly offered in most sports economics and management classes.

The Walrasian fixed-supply conjecture model

The standard approach to modeling equilibrium in a sports league, using a 2-team model and a diagram in which linear marginal revenues are superimposed together with a market-clearing marginal cost of talent, seems to have been first used by Quirk and Fort (1992, p. 272). In this section, I describe the model and explain the sense in which it is Walrasian. The solution to the model requires the identification of the profit-maximizing quantity of talent t_i for each owner. This quantity translates, depending on the investment in talent by other teams, into a winning percentage, which is in turn assumed to determine revenues.

Figure 8.1 illustrates the standard assumption that the marginal revenue of winning percentage is negatively sloped and linear. Here, team 1 is assumed to have a greater marginal revenue for any value of team winning percentage (w). We can write these linear marginal revenue functions as

$$a_i - b_i w_i, \quad i = 1, 2; \ a_i, b_i > 0, \text{ and } w_i + w_j = 1. \qquad (8.1)$$

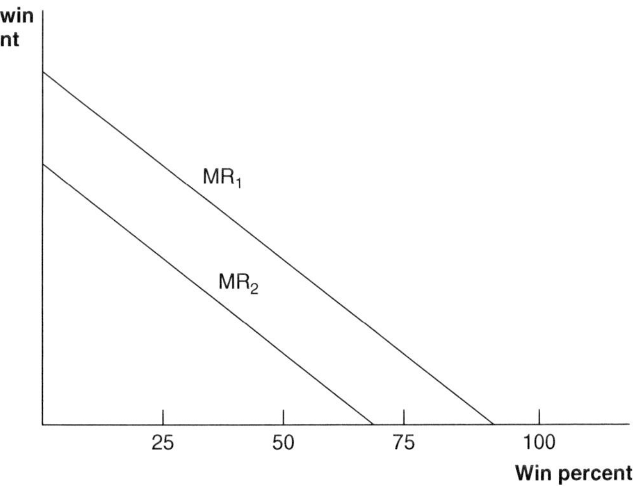

Figure 8.1   The marginal revenue of a win

These then imply a quadratic revenue function

$$(a_i - b_i/2\, w_i)w_i + k_i. \tag{8.2}$$

The implication of (8.2) is that a team's revenue initially increases with winning, but then peaks and starts to decrease as the team achieves a high level of dominance in the league. This is a reflection of the uncertainty of outcome hypothesis (Neale, 1964; Rottenberg, 1956) that consumers in aggregate prefer a close match to one that is unbalanced in favor of one of the teams.[2] This model has been widely adopted in the literature, and various elaborations have been added to the model by later writers.[3]

Given the adding-up constraint for winning percentages ($w_i = 1 - w_j$), it is possible to redraw Figure 8.1 with the winning percentage of team 1 reading from right to left. Each winning percentage for team 1 implies a unique winning percentage for team 2, and hence its marginal revenue function can be plotted against the winning percentage of team 1. This is shown in Figure 8.2.

Marginal revenues are equal at the point of intersection of the two curves, implying a win percentage of $w_1{}^M$ for team 1. In the standard model, it is now argued that this must be the profit-maximizing equilibrium for the two teams. For this to be an equilibrium in the market for players, the marginal cost curve must intersect at the same point so that MR = MC for each firm. Typically, this is shown for a constant

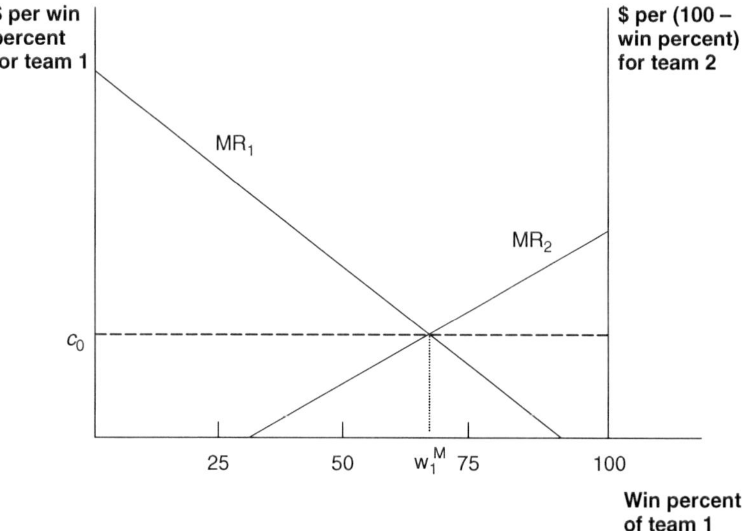

Figure 8.2   Walrasian fixed-supply conjecture equilibrium

marginal cost of talent (c_0), which is a horizontal line passing through the intersection of the two marginal revenue curves. Most writers seem to think of this as a "competitive" model so that the marginal cost of talent/win percentage is a price vector that equilibrates supply and demand.[4] The equilibrium is Walrasian in the sense that the market-clearing price vector must be identified by some kind of "invisible hand" or "auctioneer," which is disembodied from the specific actions of any agent in the market. In the next section, I will explain why this Walrasian equilibrium is also characterized by a fixed-supply conjecture.

The invariance proposition can now be derived from these assumptions. First, suppose that we shift down each marginal revenue curve by the same vertical distance. The consequence must be that the two curves intersect at the same winning percentage as before (w_1^M). The vertical shift of the marginal-revenue curve is the reduction in own marginal revenue attributed to the introduction of gate-revenue sharing, and the invariance proposition is the result that the two new marginal curves intersect at an unchanged winning percentage for each team, illustrated in Figure 8.3. Moreover, if marginal revenues shift down, then marginal cost must also shift downward to ensure MR = MC in equilibrium, and so the wage rate per unit of talent falls (from c_0 to c_α). Hence, gate sharing has no impact on competitive balance but raises profits at the expense of players.

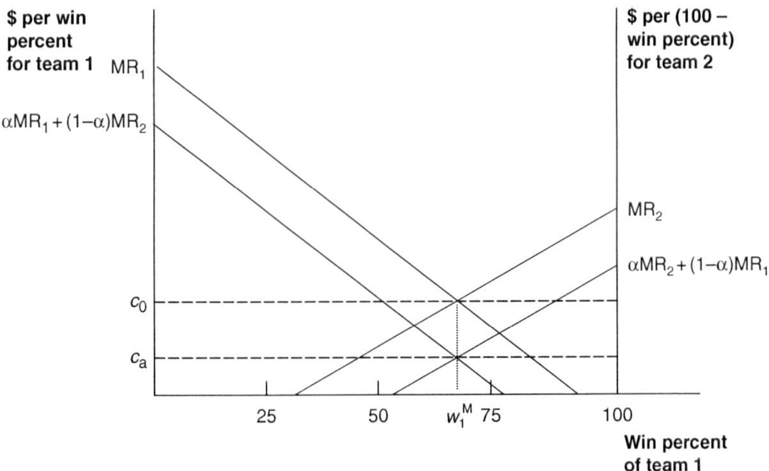

Figure 8.3 The invariance principle and Walrasian fixed-supply conjecture equilibrium

It is not, however, geometrically obvious that gate sharing shifts each of the marginal revenue curves by the same amount, and hence an algebraic "proof" is usually supplied. Consider a revenue-sharing agreement in which each team keeps a fraction α of the revenue generated from its own wins (usually taken to be gate revenue) and gives $(1 - \alpha)$ of these revenues to the other team, assuming $\alpha > 1/2$. In this case, we can write the revenues of team i as $\alpha R_i + (1 - \alpha)R_j$. If we now think of the marginal revenue of a win for team i, it will be

$$\alpha MR_i - (1 - \alpha)MR_j = \alpha(a_i - b_i w_i) - (1 - \alpha)(a_j - b_j w_i). \qquad (8.3)$$

Note that the negative sign before MR_j reflects the fact that team j's marginal revenue of a win for team i is simply equal to minus team j's marginal revenue of a win for team j. If we now consider the marginal revenue for each team owner and set them equal, we obtain

$$\alpha(a_1 - b_1 w_1) - (1 - \alpha)(a_2 - b_2 w_2) = \alpha(a_2 - b_2 w_2) - (1 - \alpha)(a_1 - b_1 w_1), \quad (8.4)$$

which reduces to the condition that $a_1 - b_1 w_1 = a_2 - b_2 w_2$, that is, that own marginal revenues are equalized in equilibrium, implying the same distribution of winning percentages as observed with no revenue sharing.

The contest success function

The key to understanding the nature of the equilibrium in the Walrasian model is the relationship between investment in talent t and winning percentage w. Central to the analysis is the assumption that the marginal revenue of a win is equal to the marginal revenue from hiring an additional unit of talent. Fort and Quirk (1995) consider this to be a normalizing assumption: "Assume that talent is measured in units such that an additional unit of talent increases win percent by one unit. Under this convention

$$\frac{\partial w_i}{\partial t_i} = 1" \text{(p. 1271).}$$

First, note that this is not the same as the adding up constraint $w_i + w_j = 1$, which can equally well be expressed as

$$\frac{\partial w_i}{\partial t_i} = -\frac{\partial w_j}{\partial t_i}.$$

The adding-up constraint simply says that the sum of win percentages must be unity. The normalization "convention" goes much further, assuming that for any distribution of win percentages, an additional unit of talent at team i raises its win percentage by one unit and reduces the win percentage of the rival team by one unit. In fact, this assumption is not based on convenience alone but also reflects a particular perception of the labor market and the league.

The relationship between investment in talent and winning percentage is generally known as the contest success function (e.g., Skaperdas, 1996), a concept that has been applied to a variety of rent-seeking games in the literature, such as political lobbying (Tullock, 1980), patent races (e.g., Loury, 1979), and labor-market tournaments (Lazear & Rosen, 1981). Contest-success functions define payoffs to players that are dependent on relative contributions to the contest, and the most widely used functional form is the logit, which simply defines the probability of success or win percentage as a ratio of the contestant's effort/investment relative to the sum of efforts/investments supplied by all contestants, that is, in the 2-team model

$$w_i = \frac{t_i}{t_i + t_j}$$

(for examples of alternative functional forms, see Nti, 1997). The logit contest-success function is explicitly adopted in the work of El Hodiri and Quirk (1971; Quirk & El Hodiri, 1974) and seems to be implicit in most of the literature on the Walrasian fixed-supply conjecture model. The "convention" that

$$\frac{\partial w_i}{\partial t_i} = 1$$

can be derived directly from differentiating the logit contest success function $w_1 = t_1/(t_1 + t_2)$:

$$\frac{\partial w_1}{\partial t_1} = \frac{t_1 + t_2 - t_1\left(1 + \dfrac{dt_2}{dt_1}\right)}{(t_1 + t_2)^2}. \tag{8.5}$$

The assumption in the Walrasian fixed-supply conjecture model is that $dt_2/dt_1 = -1$. This is accounted for by the argument that the supply of talent is fixed for the league as a whole (all talent wants to play in the major league) and that therefore a one-unit increase in talent hired at one team necessarily leads to a one-unit reduction of talent at another team. This is the fixed-supply conjecture that characterizes the Walrasian equilibrium of the standard model. Taking this assumption, we obtain

$$\frac{\partial w_1}{\partial t_1} = \frac{1}{(t_1 + t_2)}.$$

And now it is straightforward to make the normalization $t_1 + t_2 = 1$ so that we can conclude that

$$\frac{\partial w_1}{\partial t_1} = 1.$$

The critical step in this process, therefore, is the assumption that $dt_2/dt_1 = -1$. By making this assumption, it is possible to collapse a choice about the quantity of talent hired by each team into a choice about the level of win percent.

Nash Conjectures and Contest-Nash equilibrium

The idea that each team can independently choose win percentage makes no sense in equilibrium, however many teams there are. If there are n teams, at most $n - 1$ teams can choose win percentage, so that the choice of the nth team is fixed due to the adding-up constraint. In a 2-team model, the implication is that only one team can be decisive in equilibrium. Interpreting the model as a noncooperative game, this cannot be a unique Nash equilibrium.

In the Walrasian model, the market-clearing price vector identifies the equilibrium and, strictly speaking, agents have to do nothing. By contrast, in a non-cooperative game, each player must choose a (feasible) action from some nonempty set, and each player is assumed to have a best response function that depends on the actions of rivals.[5] A Nash equilibrium is defined to be a set of actions (best responses), such that no player would choose a different action given the actions of every other player. If one team in a 2-team model is able to select win percentage, then there is only one response by the other team consistent with this choice. Hence, every value of win percentage for either team is a Nash equilibrium, because one minus this win percentage is the unique and therefore best response of the other team.[6] This is a somewhat degenerate game, because typically we expect players in a game to have more than one feasible response from which to choose. If we made it a requirement of the game that each team should have at least two responses from which to choose, then by definition a Nash equilibrium does not exist.[7]

If we define a game in which each team is able to choose some variable independently of all other teams, then it is possible to find a unique Nash equilibrium. The natural way to achieve this is to model team choice in terms of a target quantity of talent or a level of financial investment in talent, which then jointly determines the relative share of talent and hence winning percentage. In this formulation, it is possible that the set of feasible responses to a given action by the other team is more than a singleton.[8]

It is the fixed-supply conjecture assumption of the Walrasian model ($dt_2/dt_1 = -1$) that leads to the degeneracy of the game theoretic interpretation. First, note that we can identify an equilibrium price vector (i.e., a Walrasian equilibrium) for any value dt_2/dt_1. For each value, there will be a marginal cost of talent that ensures that supply equals demand, and hence there are an infinite number of equilibria each dependent on a different value of dt_2/dt_1. When a quantity such as dt_2/dt_1 appears in the first-order condition of an objective function, it is generally known in mainstream industrial economics as a conjectural variation. Conjectural variations refer to the expected response of rivals to decisions taken by each player of the game. For example, in the standard quantity-setting oligopoly model, it can be shown that a conjectural variation of $+1$ conforms to the model of joint profit maximization, a conjectural variation of -1 conforms to the Bertrand model (marginal cost pricing), and the conjectural variation of zero conforms to the Cournot model. In the contest model, dt_2/dt_1 means the expected change in the talent choice of team 2 when team 1 changes its own choice of talent.

In the late 1970s and early 1980s, there was some discussion in the IO literature about the appropriate conjectural variation. It was argued during this period (e.g., Bresnahan, 1981) that each of these assumptions was faulty in the sense that in general these conjectures would be incorrect, and instead it was argued that conjectures should be consistent (i.e., the conjectural variation should always equal the rivals' best response). This approach has not, however, been widely adopted. Because the underlying model is a static one-shot game, it makes no sense to talk of any conjectural variation other than zero.[9] When each player makes its choice, its rivals will have no opportunity to respond (for a discussion, see Vives, 1999). In other words, it is appropriate for each player to choose his or her best response to what he or she believes is the profit-maximizing choices of the other players, assuming that once these choices are revealed, there will be no further opportunity to act (otherwise, it is necessary to spell out the dynamic game precisely). In the context of the oligopoly model, zero-conjectural variations in a quantity-setting game are said to be *Cournot-Nash*, as is the resulting equilibrium. In the current static model of a league contest, the appropriate conjecture is that $dt_2/dt_1 = 0$, and this conjecture can be labeled *Contest-Nash*. Only with Contest-Nash conjectures will it be possible for one team to have more than a singleton response to the choice of the other.

To compare the implication of the different assumptions about conjectural variations, consider the derivative of the revenue function (8.2) with respect to the amount of talent hired (i.e., the marginal revenue of talent rather than of winning). In general, we can write this as

$$(a_i - b_i w_i)\frac{\partial w_i}{\partial t_i}. \tag{8.6}$$

Assuming $dt_2/dt_1 = -1$ and normalizing total talent to unity, we obtain (8.1). If, however, we adopt Contest-Nash conjectures, we instead obtain

$$(a_i - b_i w_i)w_j. \tag{8.7}$$

To see this, note that Contest-Nash conjectures imply that $dt_2/dt_1 = 0$ in (8.5), so that when the total supply of talent is normalized to unity, the derivative of (8.5) is simply w_2. This means that the marginal

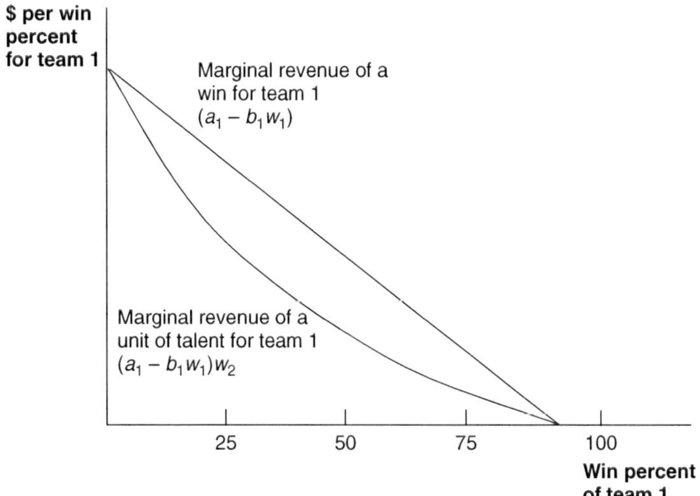

Figure 8.4   The marginal revenue of a win and the marginal revenue of a unit of talent

revenue of talent is no longer linear. Figure 8.4 sketches the marginal revenue function compared to the marginal revenue function of the Walrasian fixed-supply conjecture model, and Figure 8.5 illustrates the difference between the equilibria as shown on the standard diagram.

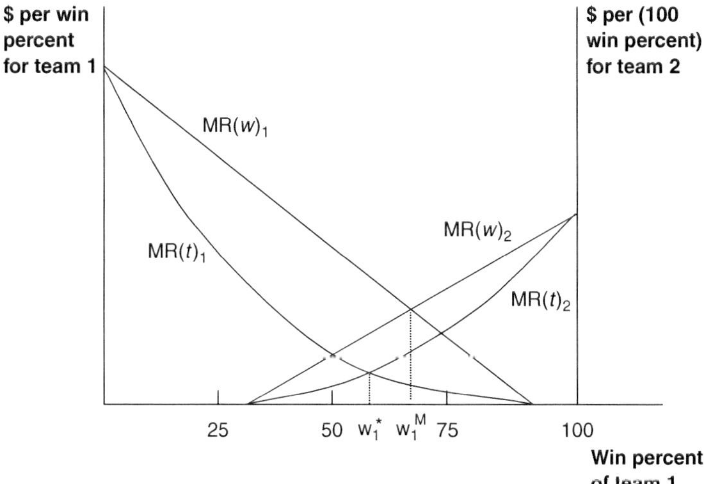

Figure 8.5   Contest-Nash equilibrium and Walrasian fixed-supply conjecture equilibrium

The most important point to note about the Contest-Nash equilibrium is that the intersection of the marginal-revenue curves is to the left of the standard model equilibrium (w_1^* rather than w_1^M). The reason for this can be seen from inspection of (8.1) and (8.7). Marginal revenue with Contest-Nash conjectures simply multiplies the Walrasian fixed-supply conjecture marginal revenue function by a fraction equal to the rival team's win percentage. Because this fraction will be larger for the weak-drawing team in equilibrium (its rival's win percentage will be larger), then its marginal revenue curve will be shifted down by a smaller amount than that of the strong-drawing teams, and therefore its share of wins will be larger than in the standard model.

What then is the implication of the conjecture $dt_2/dt_1 = -1$ in the Walrasian fixed-supply conjecture model? The condition that the marginal revenue of a win is equalized between the teams is a necessary condition for the maximization of joint revenues. Hence, the Walrasian fixed-supply conjecture equilibrium is necessarily identical to the joint profit-maximizing distribution of wins.[10]

Just as the Cournot-Nash equilibrium in the quantity-setting oligopoly model implies more output than maximizes joint profit, so in the Contest-Nash model the levels of effort/investment supplied by the teams are not joint profit maximizing. At the Contest-Nash equilibrium, the marginal revenue of talent is equalized but not the marginal revenue of a win. Each team fails to internalize the externality, which is the reduction of their rival's expected revenue from winning as a result of their own efforts. Because this is an asymmetric model in which one team is stronger than the other, the size of the externalities produced by each are not the same. The small team imposes a larger externality than the strong team, because the strong team generates a larger increment in revenue for a given increase in win percentage. In other words, in the Contest-Nash equilibrium, the marginal revenue of a win is not equalized but is in fact greater for the strong-drawing team than the weak-drawing team. Total revenue would therefore increase if the weak-drawing team had a weaker performance on the field. This is the intuition behind the result that the Contest-Nash equilibrium lies to the left of the equilibrium in the Walrasian fixed-supply conjecture model.

Those who are used to the standard model are likely to object at this point that the conjecture $dt_2/dt_1 = 1$ is correct in the sense that if the supply of talent truly is fixed, then it makes sense to incorporate this assumption in the decision-making process of the owner. This is, however, to turn the static game described here into a dynamic game. This indeed seems to be the intention of Quirk and El Hodiri (1974), although as suggested above (see footnote 1), their model appears to describe a cooperative rather than a noncooperative game. The standard model in more recent times is presented as neither a dynamic game nor a cooperative game, and therefore the static noncooperative Nash concepts, including Nash conjectures, are appropriate.

Gate-revenue sharing and the Contest-Nash equilibrium

Szymanski and Késenne (2004) prove that for any concave revenue function, the Contest-Nash equilibrium in a 2-team model implies that gate sharing will diminish competitive balance. This result can be explained quite simply using the conventional 2-team diagram with both the Walrasian fixed-supply conjecture marginal revenue curves and the Contest-Nash marginal revenue curves, as in Figure 8.5. First, note that when there is no revenue sharing ($\alpha = 1$), the equilibrium is Contest-Nash, whereas for $\alpha = 1/2$, the equilibrium is joint profit maximizing (each team chooses talent to maximize total revenue so that the marginal revenue of a win will be equalized). When $1 < \alpha < 1/2$, each team's choice will be a weighted average of the pure Contest-Nash talent and the joint profit-maximizing quantity of talent. As revenue sharing increases, the equilibrium approaches the joint-profit maximizing level from the left, implying that the win percentage of the dominant team increases. In other words, eliminating the contest externality implies less, not more, competitive balance.

An algebraic example illustrates the point. Suppose we assume the revenue functions as in (8.2) with $a_1 = \sigma > 1$, $a_2 = 1$ (so team 1 is the strong-drawing team), $b_1 = b_2 = 2$, and (without loss of generality) $k_1 = k_2 = 0$. Assuming a constant marginal cost of talent c, we can write the profit functions as

$$\pi_1 = (\sigma - w_1)w_1 = ct_1, \quad \pi_2 = (1 - w_2)w_2 - ct_2. \tag{8.8}$$

This is the standard model with linear marginal revenue curves but with the additional restriction that the slopes are identical, which simplifies the algebra considerably.

In the Walrasian fixed-supply conjecture model, assuming

$$\frac{\partial w_i}{\partial t_i} = 1,$$

we obtain the following first-order conditions:

$$\frac{\partial \pi_1}{\partial t_1} = \sigma - 2w_1 - c = 0, \quad \frac{\partial \pi_2}{\partial t_2} = 1 - 2w_2 - c = 0 \tag{8.9}$$

so that in equilibrium, $w_1^M = (1+\sigma)/4$. With Contest-Nash conjectures

$$\frac{\partial w_i}{\partial t_i} = w_j$$

the first-order conditions are

$$\frac{\partial \pi_1}{\partial t_1} = (\sigma - 2w_1)w_2 - c = 0, \quad \frac{\partial \pi_2}{\partial t_2} = (1 - 2w_2)w_1 - c = 0, \tag{8.9'}$$

so that at the Contest-Nash equilibrium, $w_1^* = \sigma/(1 + \sigma) < (1 + \sigma)/4 = w_1^M$.[11] Now, consider a model with gate-revenue sharing so that the profit functions are

$$\pi_1 = \alpha(\sigma - w_1)w_1 + (1 - \alpha)(1 - w_2)w_2 - ct_1$$

$$\pi_2 = \alpha(1 - w_2)w_2 + (1 - \alpha)(\sigma - w_1)w_1 - ct_2 \tag{8.10}$$

and with Contest-Nash conjectures, the first-order conditions are

$$\frac{\partial \pi_1}{\partial t_1} = \alpha(\sigma - 2w_1)w_2 - (1 - \alpha)(1 - 2w_2)w_2 - c = 0,$$

$$\frac{\partial \pi_2}{\partial t_2} = \alpha(1 - 2w_2)w_1 - (1 - \alpha)(\sigma - 2w_1)w_1 - c = 0 \tag{8.9''}$$

so that at the Contest-Nash equilibrium,

$$w_1 = \frac{1 + \alpha(\sigma - 1)}{\alpha(1 + \sigma) + (1 - \alpha)(3 - \sigma)}.$$

If there is no revenue sharing ($\alpha = 1$), we obtain the solution $w_1 = \sigma/(1 + \sigma)$, whereas if there is equal revenue sharing ($\alpha = 1/2$), we obtain the solution $w_1 = (1+\sigma)/4$. Moreover, the derivative of winning percentage with respect to the revenue sharing parameter at the Contest-Nash equilibrium is

$$\frac{\partial w_1}{\partial \alpha} = \frac{[\alpha(1+\sigma)+(1-\alpha)(3-\sigma)](\sigma-1)-2(\sigma-1)[1+\alpha(\sigma-1)]}{[\alpha(1+\sigma)+(1-\alpha)(3-\sigma)]^2}$$

$$= \frac{(\sigma-1)(1-\sigma)}{[\alpha(1+\sigma)+(1-\alpha)(3-\sigma)]^2} < 0 \qquad (8.11)$$

so that as revenue sharing increases, the winning percentage of team 1 (the large-market team) also increases.

Conclusions

This chapter has shown that when the standard model of talent choice for teams in a professional sports league (here labeled the Walrasian fixed-supply conjecture model) is reinterpreted as a game, any choice of win percentage is a Nash equilibrium. This indeterminacy arises because of the nature of the conjectural variation assumed. Moreover, it is shown that the usual equilibrium identified in the literature is necessarily identical to the joint profit-maximizing equilibrium. The chapter shows that it is possible to identify a unique noncooperative (Contest-) Nash equilibrium once the usual Nash conjectures are assumed. The well-known invariance principle for gate-revenue sharing is, however, shown not to hold at the Contest-Nash equilibrium.

To challenge in this way an orthodoxy that has stood unchallenged for 30 years is bold—some might say foolhardy. The reinterpretation of the model as a noncooperative game provides, however, a framework for thinking about equilibrium in a sports league that is more in keeping with contest theory and with conventional models of industrial organization (see Szymanski, 2003). Some observers have argued that the game theoretic interpretation advanced here is simply a "different model," no better and no worse than the Walrasian fixed-supply conjecture model, in the same way that the traditional Walrasian interpretation of a competitive market stands alongside more recent game theoretic interpretations of the competitive process. It is my belief, however, that the Contest-Nash model and the Walrasian fixed-supply conjecture model cannot coexist quite so harmoniously. At the very least, it must be accepted that the widely used representation of the invariance proposition for a 2-team league makes no sense—competition between two teams cannot reasonably be treated as analogous to perfect competition.

More generally, there is a consistency between Walrasian perfect competition and game theory that is absent here. In the game theoretic

Cournot model of competition, it is clear that the Nash equilibrium tends to the perfectly competitive equilibrium as the number of firms tends to infinity, but this is by no means obvious when comparing the models of sports leagues. In Walrasian perfect competition, firms are price takers, so that whatever output volume they select, they do not influence price directly. When teams choose win percentage, it is hard to see how they cannot influence outcomes (e.g., suppose one team wanted to choose a win percentage of 99%?). However many teams there are, at least one team's choice must always be constrained by adding up—something that is not true of perfect competition.

Even in a league of as many as 30 teams, it is hard to see how it can be argued that all teams are price takers—the Yankees and Manchester United will always move their respective markets through their choices. More generally, the whole interest in studying the impact of redistributive measures within a league is the starting point of asymmetry—some teams exert more influence than others, thus creating competitive imbalance—this is fundamentally inconsistent with any notion of atomistic competition. Under perfect competition, it is not possible to discuss market share—each firm is infinitesimally small relative to the market—but in the Walrasian model of a sports league, it is assumed that each team actually chooses market share (win percentage).

At the very least, it must be the case that the underlying model on which the previous literature has relied requires a more formal justification. It may be, however, that the model just makes no sense. This has important implications not just for those interested in the pure theory of sports leagues but also for practitioners in universities and colleges who teach students the lessons of the Walrasian fixed-supply conjecture model.

Notes

1. Quirk and Fort (1992) state that "an explicit modeling and analysis of team sports leagues using a Nash equilibrium framework appear in Quirk and El Hodiri (1974)" (p. 270). I have, however, been unable to find any use of the name "Nash" in that article (unsurprisingly, because Nash equilibrium had not become such a universal concept in economics by that time), and the proposed equilibrium in fact appears to be cooperative rather than non-cooperative because every team is assumed not only to select a quantity of talent for its own team but also to select a level of talent investment by every other team so as to maximize its own profit (p. 62, equation ii).

2. Here, either w is associated with the expectation of consumers about the percentage of matches won (where demand will depend on consumer expectations) or reflects the outcome of repeated trials.

3. For example, Marburger (1997) factors in a consideration of the demand for absolute quality of the competition between the teams, whereas Késenne (2000) considers the implication of objectives other than profit maximization.

4. This approach was strongly advocated by an anonymous referee.

5. The definition of a game requires the identification of players (here the teams), the set of feasible actions (here, it must be something that the teams can choose independently or else the action set will not be properly defined), the outcomes (here, this will be the amount of talent hired by each team and the associated win percentages), and the payoffs contingent on the outcome (profits).

6. Technically, we can explain the point using the definition of a Nash equilibrium from Mas-Collell, Whinston, and Green (1995):

A compact restatement of the definition of a Nash equilibrium can be obtained through the introduction of the concept of a player's *best-response correspondence*. Formally, we say that player i's best-response correspondence $b_i : S_{-i} \rightarrow S_i$ in the game $\Gamma_N = [I, \{S_i\}, \{u_i(.)\}]$, is the correspondence that assigns to each $s_{-i} \in S_{-i}$, the set

$$b_i(s_{-i}) = \{s_i \in S_i : u_i(s_i, s_{-i}) \geq u_i(s_i', s_{-i}) \text{ for all } s_i' \in S_i\}$$

With this notion, we can restate the definition of a Nash equilibrium as follows: The strategy profile $(s_1, \ldots, s_i)$ is a Nash equilibrium of the game $\Gamma_N = [I, \{S_i\}, \{u_i(.)\}]$ if and only if $s_i \in b_i(s_{-i})$ for $i = 1, \ldots I$. (p. 247)

Suppose it really was possible to have a Nash game over win percentage. Then, we would have to be able to define the best response of team 1 to a choice by team 2 of, say, a 75% win percentage. But any choice other than 25% by team 1 would necessarily alter the choice of team 2 and so would not be a best response to the choice of 75%. One player in a game cannot alter the choice of the other players when identifying its best response; otherwise, the elements of S_{-i} would have to be defined as functions of the elements of S_i, and the correspondence itself would not be defined. Moreover, the definition of a game requires that each of the actions s_i are possible, so that possible outcomes are defined, and it is clearly not possible that both $s_{-i} = 75\%$ and $s_i \neq 25\%$. In other words, each $s_{-i} \in S_{-i}$ has a unique feasible response $s_i \in S_i$ (there are no $s_i' \in S_i$). For example, if $s_{-i} = 75\%$, the only response is $s_i = 25\%$. Hence, team 1 does not have a choice at all. Strictly speaking, 25% is a "best" response, because it is the only feasible response.

7. The issue at this point becomes a trifle philosophical. Can we really define a game in which each player only ever has one response to the choices of the other players? The rationale for game theory in the first place is to explore the logic of choice when decision-makers are interdependent. In this case, the interdependency eliminates choice!

8. Strictly speaking, if the supply of talent is totally fixed, then there are still some constraints on the range of permissible values s_i—for example, if

$S_i \in [0, 100]$ and $s_{-i} = 75$, then the choice of $b_i(s_i)$ is restricted to the interval [0, 25]. This problem is, however, easily avoided if we allow teams to choose a value for a choice variable in some unrestricted range $(0, \infty)$—call this the payroll budget Z measured in \$—and then say that the share of the fixed supply of talent is determined by the share of the aggregate payroll budget

$$t_1 = \frac{Z_1}{Z_1 + Z_2}$$

and $t_2 = 1 - t_1$. In this game, the choice of Z_2 places no restriction on the choice of Z_1. It should be obvious that the Nash equilibrium of the game in which Z is the choice variable is exactly equivalent to the Nash equilibrium of game described in the rest of this chapter in which t is the choice variable because

$$w_1 = \frac{t_1}{t_1 + t_2} = \frac{Z_1}{Z_1 + Z_2}.$$

9. Thus, the common practice in the oligopoly literature of calling the firm's first-order condition a *reaction function* is misleading, because the static model does not permit reaction of any kind.
10. This statement is independent of the determination of the (constant) marginal cost and hence can be considered joint-profit maximizing subject to fixing the wage rate per unit of talent.
11. When supply is fixed, the marginal cost of talent must adjust to ensure that supply equals demand. For the Walrasian fixed-supply conjecture model, this implies that $c^M = (\sigma - 1)/2$ and for the Contest-Nash model $c^* = \sigma(\sigma - 1)/(\sigma + 1)^2 < c^M$.

References

Bresnahan, T. (1981). Duopoly models with consistent conjectures. *American Economic Review, 71*(5), 934–945.

Dixit, A. & Skeath, S. (1999). *Games of strategy.* New York: W. W. Norton.

El Hodiri, M. & Quirk, J. (1971). An economic model of a professional sports league. *Journal of Political Economy, 79,* 1302–1319.

Fort, R. & Quirk, J. (1995). Cross subsidization, incentives and outcomes in professional team sports leagues. *Journal of Economic Literature, 33*(3), 1265–1299.

Késenne, S. (2000). Revenue sharing and competitive balance in professional team sports. *Journal of Sports Economics, 1*(1), 56–65.

Lazear, E. & Rosen, S. (1981). Rank order tournaments as optimal labor contracts. *Journal of Political Economy, 89,* 841–864.

Loury, G. (1979). Market structure and innovation. *Quarterly Journal of Economics, 93,* 385–410.

Marburger, D. (1997, April). Gate revenue sharing and luxury taxes in professional sports. *Contemporary Economic Policy, 15,* 114–123.

Mas-Collell, A., Whinston, M., & Green, J. (1995). *Microeconomic theory.* London: Open University Press.

Neale, W. (1964). The peculiar economics of professional sport. *Quarterly Journal of Economics, 78*(1), 1–14.

Nti, K. (1997). Comparative statics of contests and rent-seeking games. *International Economic Review, 38*(1), 43–59.

Quirk, J. & El Hodiri, M. (1974). The economic theory of a professional sports league. In R. Noll (Ed.), *Government and the sports business* (pp. 33–80). Washington, D.C.: Brookings Institution.

Quirk, J. & Fort, R. (1992). *Pay dirt: The business of professional team sports.* Princeton N.J.: Princeton University Press.

Rottenberg, S. (1956, June). The baseball players' labor market. *Journal of Political Economy, 64*(3), 242–258.

Royal Swedish Academy of Sciences. (1994). Press release: The Sveriges Riksbank (Bank of Sweden) Prize in Economic Sciences in memory of Alfred Nobel for 1994. Retrieved February 5, 2004, from http://www.nobel.se/economics/laureates/1994/press.html

Skaperdas, S. (1996). Contest success functions. *Economic Theory, 7*, 283–290.

Szymanski, S. (2003, December). The economic design of sporting contests. *Journal of Economic Literature, 41*, 1137–1187.

Szymanski, S. & Késenne, S. (2004). Competitive balance and gate revenue sharing in team sports. *Journal of Industrial Economics, 52*(1).

Tullock, G. (1980). Efficient rent seeking. In J. Buchanan, R. Tollison, & G. Tullock (Eds.), *Toward a theory of rent seeking society* (pp. 97–112). College Station: Texas A&M University Press.

Vives, X. (1999). *Oligopoly pricing.* Cambridge, MA: MIT Press.

Vrooman, J. (1995). A general theory of professional sports leagues. *Southern Economic Journal, 61*(4), 971–990.

9

Why Have Premium Sports Rights Migrated to Pay TV in Europe But Not in the US?

Stefan Szymanski

The Business School, Imperial College London

1. Introduction

This chapter is motivated by a simple observation: why is that in Europe most of the most valuable sports rights have migrated to pay TV while in the US the rights have remained available on free-to-air networks? In this context, "most valuable" means live rights, and in Europe the most valuable rights relate to the top national league soccer championships. In the US this typically means the major leagues. In additional the Olympic Games are highly valued by consumers on both sides of the Atlantic, while some other rights attract significant interest in specific regions (PGA Golf in the US, Tour de France in much of Europe, Test Match Cricket in England).

In Italy, the UK, Germany and France the live matches of the national football tournaments are available exclusively on pay TV, often on pay per view. Of the major football markets in Europe only Spain still has some broadcasting of live national league matches on free-to-air TV. The other top club competition in European soccer, the Champions' League, offers a mixture of free-to-air and pay TV programming. Top matches involving national teams, including broadcast rights for the World Cup and the European Championship, would in all probability have migrated to pay TV had not the European Union passed legislation permitting national government to reserve sporting event of critical national significance for free-to-air broadcasters (this applies also to the Olympics). Formula One motor racing is one of the few sports to decide that, rather than sell its rights to the highest bidder, it would continue to make it rights available free-to-air. However, this merely illustrates the point: owners of sports rights in Europe can obtain more cash from pay TV broadcasters.

In the US it is the four major national free-to-air broadcasters who continue to dominate the ownership of sports broadcast rights. CBS holds a share of NFL rights, NCAA basketball and the PGA, NBC holds the rights to the Olympics, and a share in the PGA and the NASCAR championship, ABC holds a share of NFL, NBA, NHL, the PGA and Major League Soccer as well as the Bowl Championship Series and Fox owns a share of NFL, MLB and NASCAR Rights. While many of these rights are re-sold through cable packages, and Major League Baseball teams generate most of their income from selling TV rights locally, frequently through cable broadcasters, it is rare for access to sporting events to be sold as premium pay TV. The only major buyers of sports rights directly for cable distribution have been ESPN (NFL, NBA, MLB and NHL) and recently AOL Time Warner which bought a share of NBA for distribution through Turner Sports. These offerings are sold as a part of cable basic. For example, ESPN currently charges the highest fee for any cable sports channel, at $2 per subscriber. Thus most major sports viewed in the US are watched on free-to-air networks financed by the sale of advertising or as part of a basic cable package. The only significant premium sports events in the US have been pay-per-view boxing, and DirecTV's Sunday Ticket which enables viewers to watch out-of-market NFL games.

The chapter is set out as follows. The next section describes briefly the technology of broadcasting. Section 3 looks at the evolution of national broadcasting policy and the development of sport broadcasting in the US and in the four major European soccer markets (UK, Germany, Italy and Spain). The final section discusses some conclusions.

2.   The structure of broadcasting

The TV industry consists of a set of vertically related markets (Figure 9.1).

Rights holders such as sports leagues provide programming content which is then turned into programming. Typically programmes are bundled into channels (unless sold individually through pay-per-view systems) and channel providers then supply to broadcast platforms which are accessed by the consumers. Until the 1980s free-to-air analogue broadcasting was the dominant platform for the delivery of television services. Since then, however, technological improvements have enabled both cable systems and direct-to-home satellite broadcast systems to offer a competitive alternative. With the arrival of digital

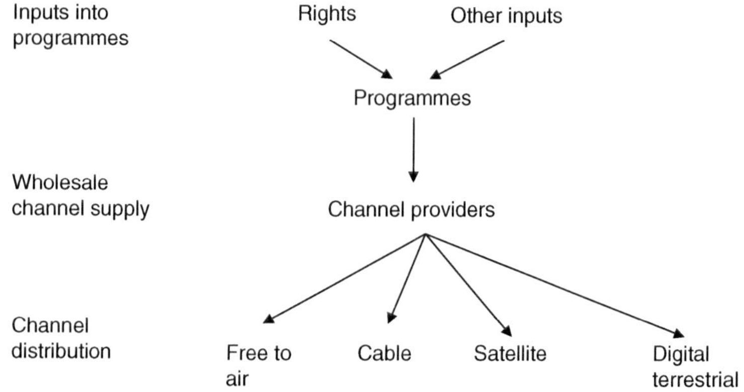

Figure 9.1   The broadcasting supply chain
Source: UK Office of Fair Trading.

services towards the end of the 1990s digital terrestrial TV offered the opportunity to encrypt and therefore charge for over-the-air broadcast signals.

The nature of competition at each stage of the TV industry, like any other, is determined by the nature of technology. In this respect it is developments at the final stage of the vertical chain—channel distribution—which have been the most important. Rights owners and channel providers have been greatly concerned to improve the quality of recording and editing, and these have led to huge advances in the quality of programming material. In the early days such improvements determined the evolution of the market. For example, there was little point broadcasting baseball or cricket on TV until the picture quality was good enough to allow you to see the ball. More recently, developments of cameras for filming in Formula One cars or in helmets of American Football players have enhanced the experience of watching these events. However, these developments have not radically expanded audiences or altered the economic relationships in the industry in the way that the development of broadcast platforms has done.

Free-to-air broadcasting relies on the transmission of signals from broadcasting antennae which, even with booster signals, typically have a maximum radius of 100 miles (Vogel, 2001, p. 176). In the US broadcasting facilities have typically been set up to serve urban areas, which have thus provided the basis for defining the country in terms of 210 broadcast market. In 1999 there were 1616 broadcast facilities serving these markets (Vogel, ibid). Because free-to-air broadcasters concentrated on cities, rural areas often found it hard to receive broadcast signals, and this was the initial impetus behind cable services, which wired households to a well-located receiver. However, as technological development expanded the capacity of these wires it became attractive to connect urban households to cable services. While each cable operator tends to have a limited geographic base, cable networks, at least in theory, have the potential to connect consumers to broadcasters anywhere on the globe—just like telephony. Satellite TV gives an operator a considerably wider reach or "footprint" than any other platform. A single satellite can cover any single European country, and three or four are required to cover the US.

Significant expansion of the television market in Europe and the US ended many years ago. By 1960 90% of US homes had TV, and Western Europe reached similar levels by the 1970s. Expansion in more recent years has been achieved by increasing the availability of channels. Until the recent advent of digital terrestrial TV, most of this capacity expansion has occurred through the development of cable networks and satellite broadcasting. Expanding channel capacity made it possible to increase dramatically the number of broadcast hours available and thereby increase customer choice. This has also been an important factor in driving up the value of rights. When capacity was limited both consumers and suppliers had few alternatives and the controller of the distribution system could extract monopoly rents from control of the bottleneck. Relaxing capacity constraints not only meant consumer choice but also created the potential for competition between channel distributors to bid up the rights. Thus rents have been increasingly extracted upstream by the rights holders. A not unnatural response to this development has been vertical integration. As competition in broadcasting has emerged platform owners have increasingly tried to control content, justifying this on the grounds that financing the overheads implicit in running a broadcast system requires guaranteed access to content. However, critics have frequently been concerned that the desire to control content has been motivated by the desire to pre-empt competition in one way or another. Hence the issue of exclusivity has raised fundamental problems on both sides of the Atlantic.

3. The evolution of broadcasting and national policy

The following is a brief summary of the issues and policy response that have arisen in the development of broadcasting. More detailed analysis can be found elsewhere, e.g. Vogel (2001), Noam (1991), Cave and Crandall (2001), Levy *et al.* (2002).

The United States

The US free-to-air networks, CBS, NBC, ABC and now Fox, emerged between the 1930s and the 1950s. These companies are essentially wholesalers of content (TV channels) to TV stations. Traditionally the stations affiliated to the networks for which they received cash payments to broadcast the network's TV programmes. In this way the station provided an audience for the network, enabling it to generate advertising revenue from commercial breaks. In addition, the networks own their own stations, mostly in the larger cities.

TV has been heavily regulated in the US, primarily through the Federal Communications Commission (FCC), although its decisions are frequently challenged, and overturned, in the courts. The principal restrictions on free-to-air broadcasting have been ownership rules prohibiting any company (network) controlling access to more than a fixed percentage of the population, currently set at 35% of households. In addition the terms on which networks dealt with stations have been closely regulated (ensuring that the networks cannot dictate programming), networks have been obliged to create space for access of alternative programming material and have faced rules on ownership of the content (the "fin-syn" rules), so that content providers could not control the networks. These latter were abolished in the mid-1990s, leading to mergers such as ABC and Disney (see e.g. Walker and Ferguson, 1998).

While the potential for cable broadcasting was recognised as early as 1948, "until the late 1970s the industry was restrained in order to promote the growth of traditional television broadcasting, particularly that by local independent stations" (Crandall and Furchtgott-Roth, 1996, p. 24). These regulations, aimed at protecting free-to-air systems by restricting the range of channels cable operators could provide and ensuring access to local channel suppliers, combined first with tight municipal and then Federal rate regulation based on the premise that cable services are essentially monopolistic. Despite this, cable systems have grown to the point where almost all TV households are passed by cable, and two thirds of households subscribe. Moreover, the Telecommunications Act of 1996 removed most price regulation. Cable companies can typically offer many more channels than free-to-air, and critically, can charge subscription fees to generate income. This part of the broadcast industry is highly fragmented. There are over 10,000 cable systems in operation, although nearly half of these supply fewer than 500 customers, while 279 systems supply 51% of cable customers (Vogel, p. 207).

Satellite broadcasting has developed a remarkable rate in recent years, growing from 0.8m subscribers in 1990 to 18.7m in 2001, 18% of TV households (Levy *et al.*, p. 51). Until very recently, this part of the industry was lightly regulated and indeed cable companies were obliged to grant access to programming material to satellite broadcasters, although no reciprocal obligation was imposed. Now that satellite is becoming a significant competitor, particular in the form of DirecTV (now controlled by News Corporation) pressure for tighter regulation is growing.

Sports programming in the US

The most successful television sport, and the model for most sports broadcasting in the US, has been the NFL. The current 8 year $17bn broadcast contract dwarfs any other in sport. Television has promoted American Football from a minor sport into, arguably, the national sport. Leifer (1995) documents how the NFL was from the beginning willing to alter the game in order to fit in with the TV schedules and advertising breaks. In its early years the NFL was prevented from collective selling of broadcasting rights by the courts (US v. NFL, 116 F. Supp. 310 (1953)) on the grounds that this was deliberate policy of restricting competition. However, the Sports Broadcasting Act of 1961 exempted the collective selling of "sponsored telecasting"—usually interpreted to mean free-to-air broadcasting. From this date on NFL contracts increased rapidly in value: $4.7m in 1962/3 (CBS) increasing to $47m per season by 1970, when the rights were split into three packages—Monday Night Football (ABC), NFC games (CBS) and AFC games (NBC). The fact that these matches drew huge ratings for the networks led to a continuing escalation in rights values. By 1980 they were worth $167m and then from 1990 the contract was split into five packages, three for the networks and two for the cable channel providers ESPN and TNT, although the latter paid only 25% of the total cost of $900m per season. A similar distribution applied in 1994 when the contract was renewed (and Fox replaced CBS) for $1137m per season. However, the 1998 contract, worth $2200m per season, involved only one cable channel, ESPN, who now paid more than any of the networks, although still only just over 25% of the contract value. The most important development in the sale of NFL broadcast rights in recent years has been the Sunday Ticket, costing around $200 per season, which allows viewers to see all NFL matches through the satellite broadcaster DirecTV.

By contrast with the NFL, the national collective broadcast contract for MLB has never been the mainstay of broadcast income. For example, the current contract, split between Fox and ESPN, is worth $559m per year, about $17m per team is exceeded by the amount earned from local broadcast income ($571m). In recent years the local broadcasting contracts have gradually shifted towards cable. In 1996, 41% of local broadcasts were on cable, but by 2003 the figure had risen to 69% of the total. However, the prices charged games shown on cable is relatively low. Even the New York Yankees YES channel is charged at only $1.95 per month per customer in the New York area, and this fee was only agreed after a lengthy dispute with the broadcaster Cablevision.

The United Kingdom

The fundamental difference between broadcasting in the US and Europe, including the UK, is the leading role of the state in establishing, directing and funding European broadcast systems. Thus in the UK the government established the publicly owned BBC as a vertically integrated programme maker, channel provider and broadcast distributor. The advent of commercial television in 1955 offered some competition, but these suppliers were also heavily regulated and as Noam (1991, p. 36) notes, by 1982 a typical New York viewer with cable could watch 23 different channels, whereas a viewer in London could at most watch 3. By 1990 the comparison was 73 channels in New York and 16 in London. Moreover, of London's 16 channels, 4 were free-to-air and 12 were satellite channels—cable subscribers in the UK at this date numbered a mere 100,000 or so.

The BBC has always derived its income principally from a compulsory licence fee that is paid by all TV households. Its activities are overseen by a board of governors appointed by the government and the overall remit of the Corporation is laid down in its charter which subject to occasional revision by Parliament. For much of its existence there has been remarkably little controversy about the role and function of this organisation, its paternalistic mission being accepted by the main political parties and its impartiality unquestioned. However, in more recent years the BBC has become more controversial given the expansion of available channels and the more market-oriented politics of the Thatcher era. Increasingly the BBC has sought to find a role for publicly funded broadcasting that does not simply duplicate what can be produced in the private sector. Currently this has led the Corporation to focus on the development of news and current affairs programming, and to drop out of the bidding for the more attractive, and therefore more expensive sports rights. The BBC has also moved away from full vertical integration, contracting out a large part of its programming to independent production companies.

Commercial channels have, like the US networks, derived their main income from advertising, but in this they have been more heavily regulated (e.g. the number of minutes limited to seven per hour). However, given the restriction on the number of channels licensed, the licensees have been extremely profitable and so have not tended to complain too vociferously about the restraints. Government have also restricted ownership to ensure that commercial broadcasters are British owned. Until 1982 the government licensed only a single channel (ITV), operated by a small number of regional franchises. A second free-to-air channel was licensed in 1982 and a third in 1997.

Cable services also developed much more slowly than in the US. Cable providers did exist for households unable to receive free-to-air signals, but these subscribers could obtain only the four licensed channels, and therefore the cable providers had no incentive to develop their systems. In the early 1980s government began licensing cable channels with the express purpose of broadening the range of entertainment available from TV, but British Telecom, the most plausible entrant was banned from this market while very little cable was laid until 1991 when the government permitted cable franchises to offer telephony. This led to massive programme of cable laying, but also required considerable industry consolidation since the government had, somewhat unrealistically for a population of 23m households issued nearly 100 cable licenses.

Satellite broadcasting had already started in the UK in 1989, well before cable services started to be widely available. Initially there were two competing firms carrying a narrow range of programming, but when they merged to form BSkyB (later renamed Sky) in 1990, largely controlled by News Corporation, the broadcaster developed a strategy based on selling premium movie channels and premium sports channels. To this end Sky set about acquiring a wide range of sports rights in cricket, rugby union and rugby league, tennis, motor sport, golf and so on. However, the single largest expenditure has been the acquisition of English Premier League soccer, which Sky acquired first in 1992 and has retained exclusively until 2001 and in tandem with a pay-per-view service since 2002. Satellite subscribers increased dramatically following the acquisition of Premier League rights. In 1991 subscriber numbers reached just over 1m, and by 1995 had jumped to 3m. Towards the end of the 1990s subscriber growth appeared to slow, but then accelerated again with the introduction of digital services. By 2003 subscriber numbers had reached 6.5m. However, during this period cable subscriptions also grew rapidly, approaching 4m by the same date. However, much of the programming content for cable channels is provided by Sky on access terms overseen by a regulator.

The development of digital TV in the UK also led to the creation of digital terrestrial services. The UK government has pushed heavily for broadcasters to adopt digital broadcasting and most free-to-air broadcasters supply a digital signal. However, a subscription-based digital channel (ITV Digital) was also created in the late 1990s, and attracted a small number of subscribers mainly through its sale of soccer rights, some of which it bought itself and some of which it licensed from Sky. However, the company overpaid for some rights and went bankrupt in 2001.

Sports programming in the UK

Soccer is by far the dominant TV sport in the UK. Throughout the 1990s soccer rights accounted for over 50% of the value of sports programming expenditure. Despite this, soccer was slow to reach UK TV. Live league matches were not shown until 1982, largely due to the absence of competition for the rights. Until that time, the BBC and ITV had a no-compete pact, bizarrely endorsed by the competition authority itself in the 1970s. The broadcasters were prepared to offer very little to obtain the rights, so the members clubs of the Football League refused to make them available. As a result soccer broadcasting was restricted to major international competitions such as the World Cup and special matches such as the FA Cup Final. This was despite the fact that broadcast coverage of other major sporting events was well established. The Football League clubs took the view that small broadcasting revenues would be insufficient to compensate for the large loss of gate they anticipated.

The clubs finally agreed to sell broadcast rights as a result of a financial crisis in the early 1980s. However, the first contract raised a mere £2.6m to be divided among 92 clubs. Competition finally emerged in 1988, when the new satellite broadcaster bid for the rights. Although it didn't win, the BBC/ITV cartel broke down and the latter paid £11m per season for four seasons. However, all of the matches' broadcast involved the top teams of Division One, predominantly five teams, despite the fact that the income was divided among all 92 League members.

Dissatisfaction with this situation led the top teams to form the Premier League in 1992, still connected to the old Football League by the system of promotion and relegation, but selling broadcast rights and generating income only for themselves. Sky won the contract in 1992 paying £49m per season to be divided between the 20 member clubs. The fact that rights had migrated from free-to-air to pay TV led to protests by fans, but this was in part dampened by the fact that Sky showed more matches (60 per season against the 18 shown previously). Sky won the contract again in 1997, paying £180m per season, and again in 2001 paying £422m per season for 66 matches on subscription and 40 available on pay-per-view.

While the migration to pay TV of the Premier League was not challenged in the UK, government concerns that sporting events deemed to be of national significance might migrate to pay TV led to the introduction of "listed events" in the 1990 Broadcasting Act. This list includes The Olympic Games, The World Cup, The FA Cup Final, The Derby, The Wimbledon Tennis Finals, The European Football Championship Finals, The Rugby World Cup Final, Cricket Test Matches played in England, Six Nations Rugby Tournament Matches Involving Home Countries, The Commonwealth Games, The Cricket World Cup, The Ryder Cup and The Open Golf Championship.

Germany, Italy and Spain

While differing in many specifics, the evolution of broadcasting and sports broadcasting in these three countries has much in common with the UK and little in common with the US. Each country has been dominated by publicly controlled and financed terrestrial broadcast monopolies in until the 1970s or even the 1980s. Each has permitted some competition in terrestrial TV in recent years but cable TV has developed only to a limited extent in each country. In each country it is satellite broadcasting that has made the greatest impact in recent years, and to which premium soccer rights have migrated.

As with the UK, one of the key catalysts for change was the 1989 European Union "Television without frontiers" Directive which required all member states to ensure free reception of TV broadcasts from other member states and prohibited the restriction of retransmission. This directive provoked member states into deregulating their own broadcast markets rather than see broadcast services run from outside their own borders. In practice this directive enabled satellite broadcasters to compete in any European state.

Unlike the UK, these countries had a longer tradition of providing extensive coverage of domestic league football, including live matches. Like the UK, soccer rights accounts for over 50% of the value of all sports rights in these countries. In each case free-to-air broadcasters were soon outbid for domestic league soccer rights. In Italy pay broadcasting was introduced in 1993 and in 1999 all league matches moved to pay-per-view. In Germany, live domestic league soccer matches did not start to be shown until 1990 and from the start this was on pay TV. Initially only one match per week was shown, but by 2000 all matches were available. In Spain most of the live broadcast rights to the national league also migrated to pay TV by the end of the 1990s.

Each country also defined a set of listed events, but did not include domestic soccer in that definition.

4.   Why have premium sports rights migrated to pay TV in Europe but not in the US?

There are (at least) four possible explanations:

- Consumer tastes. As far as sports is concerned, Europe is a soccer monoculture. Soccer programming accounts for over 50% of all broadcast rights by value in most European countries. Sporting interest is much more diverse in the US, with no one sport accounting for more than 25% of all sports programming expenditure. The availability of fewer substitutes suggests that the willingness to pay of most European consumers for the programming they are most interested in will be much lower than the willingness to pay of a US consumer.
- Economies of scale. Although the US is defined by Nielsen as 210 distinct broadcast markets, NFL matches have appeal in every segment. The domestic soccer leagues in Europe are essentially national markets, and even the largest of these has only 34m TV households (Germany) compared to 106m in the US. For this reason national free-to-air broadcasters in Europe cannot afford to pay nearly as much in the US to acquire sports rights.
- Contest design. In the US sports leagues have been more willing to adjust the structure of matches to meet the needs of broadcasters, particularly in relation to the timing of commercial breaks, than the governing bodies of European sports. Hence US free-to-air can generate a much larger amount of advertising income per match than their European counterparts, and so can bid more.
- Regulation. In Europe and the US both cable and direct satellite broadcasting have historically been discouraged by regulators from competing with free-to-air broadcasters. However, the decision of the European Union in the 1980s to open TV markets to increased competition ensured that pay TV broadcasters, the only credible

competitors for national free-to-air monopolies, could bid freely and acquire premium sports rights. The US has been slower to allow a significant competitive entry from pay TV providers especially for premium programming.

While each of the first three explanations has some plausibility, it is hard not to believe that regulation has played a significant role. By allowing the development of strong competing free-to-air networks the US government has ensured that these broadcasters can compete with premium pay TV providers for the acquisition of rights in a way that the heavily regulated or publicly controlled free-to-air broadcasters of Europe could not once competition was established. However, the success of DirecTV has begun to suggest that more premium rights will migrate in the US.

One of the striking facts about sports is that the businesses which run them are so tiny given the amount of interest they generate. The Census Bureau reported in 1997 that spectator sports generate a direct income of only $14bn domestically (0.17% of GDP). One reason for this low dollar value is that teams have been unable to extract the rents they generate because mechanisms did not exist either to reach the audience or to charge that audience once it was reached. Free-to-air TV reached the audience, but pay TV offers a much greater opportunity to extract rent. Unless the US adopts a listing system, then a much greater fraction of premium rights may migrate.

Is this in the public interest? Given that fans will always want to watch the one dominant league in any sport (because they prefer to watch the best), and that entry by new leagues will always be difficult, it is not clear that allowing leagues to extract rents provides any social benefit. It might be argued that increasing revenues have funded significant improvements in broadcast quality (picture quality and so on), but it can also be argued that much of the rent has been channelled needlessly to the players. If migration continues, the players could be earning a lot more money in the near future.

References

Cave, M. and R. Crandall, 2001, "Sports rights and the broadcast industry," *The Economic Journal*, 111 (February), F4–F26.

Crandall, R. and H. Furchtgott-Roth, 1996, *Cable TV: Regulation or Competition?* Washington, D.C.: The Brookings Institution.

Leifer, E., 1995, *Making the Majors: The Transformation of Team Sports in America*, Massachusetts, M.A.: Harvard University Press.

Levy, J., M. Ford-Livene and A. Livene, 2002, Broadcast television: survivor in a sea of competition, Federal Communications Commission OPP Working paper series, 37.

Noam, E. 1991, *Television in Europe*, New York, N.Y.: Oxford University Press.

Vogel, H.L. 2001, *Entertainment Industry Economics*, 5th ed., Cambridge and New York, N.Y.: Cambridge University Press.

Walker, J.R. and D.A. Ferguson, 1998, *The Broadcast Television Industry*, Boston, M.A.: Allyn and Bacon.

10

Seizing the Moment: A Blueprint for Reform of World Cricket*

Ian Preston[a], Stephen F. Ross[b] and Stefan Szymanski[c]
[a] *University College London*
[b] *University of Illinois at Urbana-Champaign*
[c] *Imperial College Management School*

Abstract

We argue that the current match-fixing crisis in world cricket has its origin in the economic structure of the game. Cricketers' pay is demonstrably low relative to sports of comparable significance and this is a consequence of the organisation of the game with its emphasis on international representative cricket. We propose and outline details of an international club championship with competition for players' services.

JEL Classification: L83, K49
Keywords: sport, cricket, reform, corruption

1. Introduction: The current crisis and its solution

The crisis in cricket threatens the future of the oldest organised team sport.[1] The revelations of the King Commission (King 2000) in South Africa included the admission by the former South African captain, Hansie Cronje, that he had accepted bribes for fixing matches and suborned the corruption of other team members. The Qayyum Report (Qayyum 1998) in Pakistan found the former Pakistani captain, Salim Malik, to have fixed matches and reported a failure to cooperate with its enquiry by another former captain, Wasim Akram, among others. The investigation by the Central Bureau of Investigation of the Indian Police

---

* (November 2000, revised June 2001)

Force (CBI 2000) pointed to extensive corruption involving among others the former Indian captain, Mohammed Azharuddin, and also alleged the improper involvement of other international players, including former England, West Indies, Sri Lanka and New Zealand captains and players of Australia,[2] with bookmakers. Most recently, the report (Condon 2001) of the investigation commissioned by the governing body of world cricket, the International Cricket Council (ICC), and led by the former UK Metropolitan Police Commissioner, Sir Paul Condon, has failed to draw a line under the current scandals. Referring to a "climate of silence, apathy, ignorance and fear," the comprehensive report suggests evidence of continuing corruption. All of this has seriously undermined the credibility of the international game.

In the short term it is clear that cricket has to deal with the cheats. Given the relatively small number of genuine stars in the game, this process will inevitably prove difficult. The reluctance of national cricket boards to take decisive and immediate action against alleged culprits, even where they have admitted talking to bookmakers, highlights the dilemma of the authorities. Wedded to a not unnatural concern to retain those stars that draw the crowds, there is also genuine sympathy for individuals whose careers may have been distinguished and whose lapses may by comparison have been minor.

In the longer term, there is need to reform the structure of the international game to ensure that the conditions that encouraged cheating to flourish are eliminated. In this chapter we argue that the fundamental problem is the meagre financial rewards received by the top international cricketers. Condon (2001, p. 33) is explicit in acknowledging poor pay of cricketers as a leading candidate explanation for the spread of corruption. Moreover, press reports suggest that this view has already been accepted by some senior figures in the cricket hierarchy. The chairman of the MCC, Lord Alexander of Weedon, reportedly called for cricketers to be paid more so that they are less likely to be tempted by match-fixing offers (BBC website, 17 November 2000). However, the response of the England and Wales Cricket Board (ECB) shows that acceptance is not widespread: "The England and Wales Cricket Board has noted the remarks reportedly made by MCC President, Lord Alexander of Weedon, that international cricketers should be paid more so that they are less likely to be tempted by offers to be involved in match-fixing. The ECB Management Board takes the view that the pay of many international cricketers has increased significantly in recent times and they are now well rewarded for their skill and expertise and that, in any event, there is no justification for any international cricketer to succumb to corruption" (ECB Press Release 18 November 2000). We believe high salaries would be a significant disincentive to cheating, as we believe it is in most other major sports. The incentive to cheat is increased when there is an imbalance between the financial status of the players and the financial returns to the sport as whole. In cricket the top players earn a much smaller fraction of the total revenues generated by their efforts than is the case in other major international sports.

Low pay for international cricketers is the consequence of an organisational structure that uses the revenue from popular international matches to subsidise domestic competitions and that undermines the bargaining position of top players over pay. Removing the cross-subsidy might provide a temporary respite, but since competitions are not capable of generating enough income to cover costs they would have to be severely curtailed. This in turn would limit the supply of new talent coming into the game and hence undermine its long-term future.

We believe that there is an alternative way to deal with the underpayment of professional cricket players. In most sports outside of North America income and thereby professional salaries are boosted by the existence of international club competitions that complement the international representative game. The introduction of international club cricket would in our view add a significant dimension to international cricket that would command spectator and media attention. Competition among international clubs for the best players would be a sure way to bid up the salaries of international cricketers. Such a competition could operate alongside and sustain the integrity and durability of a flourishing Test game.

2.   Cheating in sport

Cheating in sports falls into two categories. On the one hand, when the rewards for winning dwarf the rewards for coming second, third or lower, the incentive of participants is to use every means possible to win. This can lead to a damaging competition among athletes to take performance-enhancing drugs and adopt potentially harmful therapies in the search for excellence. This problem, a consequence of the "winner-take-all" reward structures encouraged by newspapers and media, sponsors and advertisers, is most obvious in the Olympic sports where many believe that illegal doping is rife. However, all the major sports have struggled to control the use of performance-enhancing drugs and cricket has not stood out as a sport suffering particularly extreme problems in this regard.

The second form of cheating is the one we are concerned with here. It is the reverse of the "winner take all" dilemma. If the rewards to athletes are inadequately differentiated, then there is an incentive for those athletes who are good enough to exert a disproportionate influence on the outcome of a contest to use that power to enhance their income, largely through gambling. This is likely to be exacerbated in sports such as cricket where the individualistic nature of the conflict creates opportunities for betting on the performance of particular players.[3] Of course, when athletes' incomes are undifferentiated, it is normally because they are all very low. Match fixers are only interested in sports that command significant public interest. Match fixing in recondite sports such as curling is probably a limited problem even though the best curlers probably make very little money.

Most sports can cite examples of this problem. Perhaps the most famous example is that of "Shoeless Joe" Jackson and the 1919 Black Sox scandal. Jackson, who held the second highest lifetime batting average in baseball (.354) at that date was earning a mere $6,000 a year (less than $50,000 in today's money), unquestionably a small reward compared to the attendance income generated by his efforts. The desire to enhance his income by throwing the World Series was his undoing. An example from English soccer illustrates the same point. In 1965 ten players were jailed for conspiracy to defraud by fixing the outcome of matches on which they had placed bets. Most of the matches concerned took place in the early 1960s, when the average footballer earned less than £20 per week which was in fact the maximum wage allowed until its abolition in 1961. The history of cricket has itself not been without instances of corruption of poorly paid players by bookmakers, with instances particularly well attested in the eighteenth century (see Birley 1999, Craig 2001, and especially Underdown 2000).

Match fixing may be motivated by activities other than gambling. In particular, when one team not in contention for a championship title can influence the outcome by its performance, side-payments or non-monetary arrangements are not unknown. Condon (2001, pp. 27–8) suggests that the "seeds" of the current crisis may have been sown in the atmosphere created by "accommodations" of this kind in the 1970s. However, in any case of match fixing, the fundamental elements of supply and demand must balance. From the point of view of the "buyer", fixing matches is generally only important when there is a high degree of interest in the sport and so a significant return is to be made by controlling the outcome, usually for the purposes of gambling. The potential match fixer must have the capacity to significantly influence the outcome, so that in general only the stars are likely to be approached. On the "selling" side, the players must balance the reward from fixing against the potential cost of being caught. This cost is the probability of being caught multiplied by the penalty for fixing. In almost all sports the most draconian penalty available to authorities is deprivation of sporting income by exclusion from participation in the sport. Raising salaries of the top players is therefore the main way of raising the penalty to cheating. Moreover raising salaries is also likely to diminish the attractiveness of additional illicit income. To put it simply a player on $100,000 a year would find a bribe of $100,000 very much more attractive than the same player earning $1,000,000 a year.[4]

High salaries do not eliminate all forms of cheating, and do not even eliminate match fixing. In particular, if the controllers of the sport are themselves unable to extract a significant proportion of the consumer surplus associated with the sport, then match fixing may be hard to prevent. For example, if 90% of the money spent on the sport is in the form of gambling, while only 10% is generated through the sale of match tickets and broadcast rights, the rewards that someone interested in controlling the outcome of a match or a race may be well in excess of any reward that the event organiser can offer. Any sport that becomes a vehicle for gambling where the gamblers have only a limited interest in the sport itself is at risk. However, high salaries make match fixing less enticing for most players, and mean that those players committed to cheating can be more easily detected since they are a relative minority of the profession.

3. Causes of the cricket crisis and the need for a new competition

It is plain that corruption has made headway in cricket to an extent far greater than other sports of comparable significance. At the level of individual players, no one would deny that "greed and opportunity"— the factors stressed by Condon (2001, p. 35)—are the main factors in explaining why one cricketer will have succumbed to temptation while another will not. However, this is inadequate as an sexplanation for why the sport as a whole should have been so vulnerable. Rather than suggest that cricketers as a whole have a greater tendency to venality of character than other sportsmen, we would argue that the proven susceptibility of the sport to corruption is a product of the incentives provided to them by the economic structure of the sport.

Cheating in cricket can to a significant degree be attributed to the remarkably low rewards that international Test Match cricketers can earn. According to the published accounts of the ECB (1999) English cricket generates an income of around £50m in a typical year and in the recent World Cup year made over £80m.[5] A recent three-year TV deal was said to be worth about £150m. However, the central contracts offered by the ECB to its international players are typically worth something of the order of £150,000 per year,[6] leaving the entire squad with less than 10% of the final take through contracted payments. The principal reason that the clubs receive such a small proportion of the final take is the need to subsidise the domestic game of county cricket. County cricket is a game mostly played over four days, mostly during the working week and so few people can attend, and often those that can attend are on low incomes (e.g., pensioners). The counties simply cannot fund their own expenses, even when the average player receives a wage of only around £30,000. Cross subsidies from the ECB are therefore essential if any young players are to be raised through the county ranks to a Test Match standard. In 2001 each county received about £1.275m from the ECB.

Much the same can be said of the game in other countries. In Australia, currently the dominant nation in world cricket, the Australian Cricket Board has predicted gross cricket related income averaging about A$100m per year over the next four years. The highest paid current contracted Australian player cannot earn more than A$625,000 though the prospect of pay rising to A$1m from 2004 has been mooted. These figures are very low when compared to other major world sports. In North America the *minimum* salaries of major league players negotiated by the player unions are in region of US$250,000 per year (although most journeyman players are likely to earn little more than this). But these are not the stars whom the bookmakers would generally set out to tempt. Stars earn much more—for example in 1998 there were over 50 baseball players who started the season with salaries in excess of US$5m—about 20 times the minimum salary. Even allowing for the fact that there is much more money in North American sports, cricket salaries are significantly out of line when it comes to the gap between the highest and the lowest. A similar story can be told for soccer, where top players will earn many times the salary of the average journeyman. Even in rugby union, which is far less wealthy than soccer or North American sport, top stars can now earn many times the basic wage earned by the regular club player.

Of course, players can earn more than the basic salaries mentioned here because of sponsorship and endorsement deals. Top stars in cricket can earn an annual income many times in excess of the basic retainer. Furthermore, even within cricket, Test Match players can receive bonuses and other rewards related to performance. But even if the test star earns ten times their annual retainer, it must be remembered that a player's career is relatively short and the post career income is highly uncertain. Few cricketers could expect to achieve career earnings in excess of £1m, a sum well below the expected lifetime earnings of even a moderately talented accountant. Cronje's admission that he had accepted US$10,000 to throw a game was as striking for the smallness of the sum (for which, among other misdemeanours, a glittering career was sacrificed) as for its proof of his moral frailty.[7] Could anyone imagine Michael Jordan or Ronaldo accepting such a small sum to throw a game?

Why do players accept these low rewards? The answer must lie in the dominance of the international representative game in cricket. National eligibility rules prevent competition between teams for the services of players, removing the most potent means for players to bid up their salaries. Recent years have seen several high profile contractual disputes between players and authorities over rates of pay—a symptom perhaps of discontent over the weak position of players.

The root of the problem therefore lies in three observations:

(a) International players receive only a small fraction of the income generated by their playing activities—as little as 10% compared to the average of around 50% common in most professional team sports.
(b) The ratio between the salaries of the best international players and journeyman cricketers—typically less than 2:1 compared to more than 20:1 in most professional team sports
(c) Cricket relies almost exclusively on international representative cricket to generate income—club, state or county level income contributes almost nothing.

Our solution lies in solving problem (c) and using the money generated by our solution to solve problems (a) and (b). Domestic competition is hampered not only by the fact that cricket takes a long time to play and a significant fraction of playing time occurs during working hours (baseball to a degree suffers from the same problem). Most domestic matches are not attractive because only a relatively small number of stars appear in the matches. The top players are spread thinly around a large number of teams, and so that in any given match only a few such players participate. Furthermore the best British county players frequently spend most of their time off on Test duty—even more so with the introduction of central contracts. A club level competition that could generate a significant income would have to create a situation where top players regularly faced each other as they do at the international representative level. To achieve this we propose the creation of a new international club competition. This would not replace existing domestic competitions, which are a necessary breeding ground for young talent, but would add an extra tier of club level competition. This competition could involve as few as eight different clubs, based in the major international cricket centres around the world.

These elite clubs would then compete for the services of the top cricket stars—there would be no restrictions on nationality, and perhaps even a requirement to hire foreign players. In this way an active market would be created for services of the stars, a market which is currently missing. As long as the competition in which these clubs participated attracted widespread interest, the clubs that were bidding for the services of the top players would be capable of paying high salaries. In this way the top stars would come to hold a significant financial stake in the development of the game and the likelihood of accepting small bribes to throw matches would diminish. Of course, this scheme cannot guarantee the end of corruption in cricket, and even the wealthiest sportsmen could be open to large enough bribes, but our view is that a thriving international club competition to match the interest in Test Match cricket would not only help to discourage corruption, but would also stimulate interest in the game.

It would be important to coordinate the organisation of such a competition with schedules for Test cricket. The aim is not to challenge the central importance of international five day cricket but to reform other aspects of the game so as to enhance its robustness. The decision of the ICC to endorse a league table for international Test cricket is an important step to contextualise and thereby strengthen interest in Test Match competition. The new competition being proposed here would be a limited overs game and in order to avoid unacceptable additional pressure on players' workloads we would propose that it be arranged in conjunction with a diminution in the number of other one day international games.[8] Condon (2001, p. 34) follows others in pointing to the "large number of One Day Internationals" in which "nothing is really at stake" as a contributory factor in the willingness of cricketers to accept corrupt offers. The growth of the international one day game has occurred largely through a proliferation of small tournaments widely acknowledged to suffer from limited memorability. A club competition of the sort outlined here would be well designed to encourage commitment in one day international cricket, to the general benefit of the game. We would envisage the World Cup remaining as the pinnacle of the one day international game but with a significance enhanced by the reformed context in which it would occur.[9]

4.   The demand for a new competition

We propose the creation of a new international club cricket competition to run alongside Test Match cricket (the most distinguished form of the international representative game). The scope for a new competition is difficult to gauge without a detailed feasibility study, but there are several indicators which suggest that the scope exists. First, perhaps is the notable success of the "World Series Cricket" organised by Kerry Packer, owner of Australian Channel 9, at the end of the 1970s. This breakaway competition was created because Packer was dissatisfied with the Test Match broadcasting deal on offer and therefore he hired the top international stars to play a series of "international" matches. The players received considerably higher salaries to participate in the venture, and the Series introduced a number of important innovations such as night cricket. While Packer ultimately abandoned World Series Cricket after reaching agreement with the cricket authorities, its success with the public in Australia was unquestioned. Our argument is that this kind of "all-star" competition is potentially more interesting to cricket fans than domestic competitions. The sheer number of teams and matches in domestic competition is worth documenting, since it is this fragmentation that limits the scope for interesting competitions.

(a)   Existing domestic competition

Each of the major cricket nations operates to a different system. This in itself prevents the creation of something like a "Champions' League" which is superimposed on domestic competition in European soccer. In Rugby Union, the need to create an international club competition in southern hemisphere, the Super-12 obliged the national rugby competitions to be significantly restructured.

(i)   England

The England season currently runs from mid-April to mid-September. The 18 first-class cricket counties are now divided into two divisions (9 teams each), with promotion and relegation. Teams participate in two leagues—a four day match competition and one-day (Sunday) tournament. In addition there are two Cup competitions played at different stages of the season and which also involve counties below the first-class level (in one competition).

(ii)   Australia

The season runs from October to March. Australia has narrowed down the variety of competition and number of teams at the first-class level to a far greater degree. Thus competition operates at the State level, involving only six teams. Moreover, there are only two main competitions, the Pura Cup for the three-day game and the Mercantile Mutual Cup for the one-day game.

(iii)   India

The season runs from May to February. The main competitions are the Ranji Cup and the Ranji One-Day Cup, which involve 23 teams, mainly representing the states (although there are some others such as the Indian Railways team). The teams are divided into five zones, with zonal champions progressing to a set of play-offs to produce an overall national champion.

(iv)   Pakistan

The season runs from mid-October to January. There are two main competitions, the Quaid-e-Azam Trophy and the Patron's Trophy. These are played at first- and second-class levels. The Patron's Trophy first grade involves nine teams divided into two groups playing both one-day and four-day matches. The Quaid-e-Azam Trophy involves 12 teams in two divisions playing four-day matches leading to a final played between the winners of each division.

(v)   South Africa

The South African season runs from October to March. There are 11 first-class teams representing the provinces of South Africa, and they play in three main tournaments. The Super Sports Series consists of four-day matches, the Standard Bank Series consists of one-day matches and the UCB Bowl involves both three and one-day matches.

(vi)   West Indies

West Indies cricket is complicated by the fact that the region is not a single country, although they play as a single unit at Test Match level. The "domestic" season runs from October to March. The main competitions are the Red Stripe Bowl (including the USA and Canada) which is one-day competition based around ten teams in two zonal divisions and the Busta Cup, which is a four-day competition involving Barbados, Guyana, Jamaica, Windward Islands, Trinidad & Tobago, Leeward Islands, Trinidad, England "A" and West Indies "B".

In total therefore there appear to be in the region of 70 first-class teams in world cricket, most of whom play during the southern hemisphere summer. These figures do not include the teams based in other cricketing nations such as New Zealand, Sri Lanka and Zimbabwe. While the progression from southern hemisphere summer to northern hemisphere summer enables many of the top players to play all year round if they sign contracts with English counties, the fact remains that cricket boasts far more "first-class" teams than any north American sport, and even in Europe it would be hard to argue that there were more than 50 top rank soccer clubs. Given that there is probably a smaller supply of top class cricketers than top class athletes in these other sports, and that the diffusion of these contests spreads the spectator base very thinly, it seems reasonable to suppose that there could be a significant gain to focusing the interest of cricket fans on a narrower range of tournaments and clubs. Whereas soccer, as the dominant international sport, can survive with a fragmented range of competitions, sports such as cricket and rugby, with their smaller revenue base, need to focus the interest of the fans.

(b)   Population, income and city sizes

A successful international club competition will have to satisfy two essential requirements—it must be small enough to ensure that the top stars are regularly pitted against one another, and it must be spread among the largest cricketing nations in order to ensure the maximum degree of fan interest, indeed partisanship. Most cricket nations struggle if, say, their top three batsmen or top three bowlers are injured—suggesting that there are probably few more than a hundred international cricket stars able to compete at the highest level. Assuming that teams require squads of at least 15 players, this suggests the supply of international standard cricketers would support a league of no more than 8 to 10 teams. A league of this size would bring the top players consistently into opposition with one another, and ensure that almost every match contained some exciting confrontations. In essence, the number of clubs should more or less replicate the number of competitive cricketing nations, which again implies somewhere in the region of eight to ten teams.

One weakness of the World Series Cricket was its location in Australia—it was viewed by the other cricketing nations as a largely Australian affair, even if the teams themselves were essentially national teams. In part this reflected the broadcasting arrangements of the competition, which limited the resale of the championship internationally (with digital TV there can be little doubt that the rights could be sold to somebody in the UK, for instance, even if the dominant broadcasters were not interested). To draw the analogy with soccer again, the Italian Serie A is very successful and widely considered the strongest league in the world because of the presence of so many foreign stars, but its viewership figures outside of Italy are negligible compared to genuinely international tournaments such as the Champions League.

We suggest that there are two options for geographical organisation of an international league.

(i) Cities: Adopting a city-based club structure might maximise the interest of a concentrated population. There may be a lesson here from the history of soccer. The authorities of the English Football Association in the nineteenth century envisaged the development of soccer along county cricket lines and established county associations. The fact that club football proved much stronger may in part be due to its foundation on concentrated urban support.

(ii) Regions: Basing clubs around broadly defined regions would allow teams to play at a variety of grounds, picking up revenue by playing occasional matches in areas of lesser support and avoiding feelings of exclusion in areas that would not otherwise have teams.

Given these dimensions, the problem is to decide the location of the clubs. In practice this could be achieved through a franchise system and allowing locations (or entrepreneurs adopting a particular location) to bid. However, since the value of each franchise depends on who else is admitted, it might require a complex and possibly fallible auction design to internalise the impact on other franchises of victory by other particular locations.

In cricket, more than in any sport, the financial backing for the game derives either from very large but very poor populations or from

Table 10.1 Population, Gross Domestic Product (GDP) and GDP per head for the five largest cricket nations (1999)

Country	Population	GDP Billion$	GDP Per Head $
India	995	443	445
Pakistan	136	60	440
United Kingdom	58	1437	24715
South Africa	43	131	3033
Australia	19	395	20695

Source: IMF.

relatively small but very rich populations. Table 10.1, showing the population and gross domestic product per head for the five biggest cricket nations illustrates the point.

India has 50 times the population of Australia, and one fiftieth of the GDP per head. While India's GDP and Australia's population are rapidly growing, it seems inevitable that a large gap will remain for both measures into the foreseeable future. As things stand, cricket is sufficiently popular in Australia that one might expect that a club based in Sydney or Melbourne could generate a larger income than one based in Mumbai or Delhi. However, this need not be the case. The increasingly affluent middle class of India is several times the population of Australia and even if only the richest 2% of the population can afford to attend matches, that still gives a potential support base equal to that of Australia. Moreover, the sale of broadcast rights for an Indian-based team might well produce a large income from such an enormous hinterland.

Similar arguments can be raised in respect of Pakistan, and even South Africa, but it is our view that an international club competition cannot hope to succeed without a presence in each of these five principal cricket nations. On climatic grounds it might also seem attractive to leave the UK out of the picture, as the southern hemisphere have in the case of rugby union, but we believe that the size of the UK market makes such a strategy ultimately implausible.

The choice of locations is inevitably difficult and at this stage somewhat arbitrary. But from an analysis of city sizes it is suggested that the sites should include two from India, two from Australia, two from South Africa, one from Pakistan, either one or two from the UK and possibly one from the Caribbean.[10] These choices reflect not only city sizes but the intensity of support for the game. For example, it is inevitable

Table 10.2 Cities with populations in excess of 2 million people. Eight candidate sites for the World Cricket League starred

World Rank	Name	Population	Country	
6	Mumbai (Bombay)	17850000	India	*
14	Kolkata (Calcutta)	12900000	India	*
16	Karachi	12100000	Pakistan	*
17	London	11800000	Great Britain	*
19	Delhi	11500000	India	
34	Chennai (Madras)	6600000	India	
35	Hyderabad	6500000	India	
36	Lahore	6350000	Pakistan	
40	Johannesburg	5700000	South Africa	*
43	Bengaluru (Bangalore)	5500000	India	
62	Ahmedabad	4150000	India	
68	Sydney	4050000	Australia	*
85	Pune (Poona)	3400000	India	
90	Melbourne	3300000	Australia	*
94	Cape Town (Kapstadt)	3100000	South Africa	*
119	Birmingham	2600000	Great Britain	
121	Rawalpindi	2600000	Pakistan	
130	Lucknow	2500000	India	
131	Manchester	2500000	Great Britain	
134	Kanpur	2450000	India	
149	Faisalabad (Lyallpur)	2250000	Pakistan	
150	Surat	2250000	India	
161	Jaipur	2100000	India	
167	Leeds	2050000	Great Britain	
169	Nagpur	2050000	India	

Source: Th. Brinkhoff: Principal Agglomerations and Cities of the World, http://www.citypopulation.de, 4.6.00.

that Australia, as the world's strongest cricketing nation, and one of its wealthiest, and that India, as the most populous (and the country with the fewest alternative popular sports), will both have an above average number of teams. Whether the UK or South Africa should have two teams seems more debatable. The UK is a bigger market, but support is probably more intense in South Africa (Table 10.2).

(c) Format

To be successful a world league will have to offer a format that attracts spectators, in contrast with most three- or four-day domestic cricket. We think that this inevitably requires the adoption of the one-day version of the game. Games will have to be played at weekends or in the evenings when the fans can attend, but in fact many of these reforms have already been widely accepted within the cricket world. It may be possible to play the longer, more traditional, version of the game for special occasions, long holiday breaks, season openers and so on—but these would be essentially one-offs.

Matches would be played in all cricket playing areas of the world but we believe that for this to work matches played within a region will need always to involve at least one local team. While fans of Karachi may want to see their team play the stars of Australia it is doubtful whether they could be relied upon to attend matches between, say, Sydney and Melbourne played in their city. To the extent that the teams would hire players from all over world, these might indeed include some Pakistani stars, but this could never be guaranteed and would be unlikely to compensate for the direct interest of local fans. Thus we think that a league style "home and away" format will be required.

Scheduling of matches is a critical issue and one important constraint on tournament structure is climate. Cricket cannot be played properly in the rain, and it cannot be played well in extreme cold. Table 10.3 provides monthly climatic data for the eight cities suggested above as potential locations. Scheduling a tournament for such a diverse set of locations will inevitably be difficult. While temperature is not the main problem at most times for most of the proposed locations apart from London, it is necessary to avoid rainy seasons. Temperature considerations rule out London in the northern winter, while rainfall rules out India in the late northern summer.

Again we suggest two options.

(i)   *Rolling format*

It would be convenient to adopt a tournament structure that involved moving from location to location through the season. The competition could start in Australia in November/December during which time the Australian teams would play their home matches against the non-Australasian teams and their local opponents. It could then move to India/Pakistan in January/February, on to South Africa in March/April and conclude in England in May/June (with a possible visit to America if a Caribbean-based team were included). The competition would not need to be drawn out—it could be in four concentrated spells. Perhaps there could also be play-offs and a final in London at the end. Such a scheme would minimise the otherwise massive requirement for travel. It could also encourage mobility between teams since the whole

Table 10.3 Monthly temperature and rainfall for selected cities

City	Variable	Jan	Feb	Mar	Apr	May	Jun	Jul	Aug	Sep	Oct	Nov	Dec
Mumbai	Max temp C	28	28	30	32	33	31	30	29	30	32	32	30
Kolkata	Max temp C	26	29	34	36	35	34	32	32	32	32	29	26
Cape Town	Max temp C	26	27	25	23	20	18	18	18	19	21	24	25
Johannesburg	Max temp C	26	25	24	21	19	16	17	19	23	24	24	25
Karachi	Max temp C	25	26	29	32	34	34	33	31	31	33	31	27
London	Max temp C	7	7	10	12	16	20	22	22	19	15	10	8
Melbourne	Max temp C	26	26	24	20	17	14	13	15	17	20	22	24
Sydney	Max temp C	26	26	25	23	20	17	17	18	20	22	24	26
Mumbai	Min temp C	19	20	22	24	26	26	25	25	24	24	23	20
Kolkata	Min temp C	13	15	20	24	25	26	26	26	26	23	18	13
Cape Town	Min temp C	16	16	14	12	9	8	7	8	9	11	13	15
Johannesburg	Min temp C	15	14	13	10	7	4	4	6	9	11	13	14
Karachi	Min temp C	13	14	19	23	26	28	27	26	25	22	18	14
London	Min temp C	1	1	2	4	7	10	12	12	10	7	4	2
Melbourne	Min temp C	14	14	13	11	9	7	6	7	8	9	11	13
Sydney	Min temp C	18	19	17	14	11	8	7	8	10	13	15	17

Mumbai	Rain mm	4	2	1	4	17	484	616	340	264	65	14	2
Kolkata	Rain mm	9	30	35	45	140	272	125	328	253	114	21	5
Cape Town	Rain mm	15	17	20	41	69	93	82	77	40	30	14	17
Johannesburg	Rain mm	125	90	91	54	13	9	4	6	27	72	117	105
Karachi	Rain mm	13	10	8	3	3	18	81	41	13	0	3	5
London	Rain mm	62	41	49	46	47	50	45	48	60	60	67	65
Melbourne	Rain mm	48	47	52	58	58	50	49	51	59	68	59	59
Sydney	Rain mm	100	111	127	109	98	129	69	80	60	76	83	77
Standard deviation of max temp		7	7	7	8	8	8	8	7	6	7	7	7
Standard deviation of min temp		6	6	6	8	9	10	10	9	8	7	6	5
Standard deviation of rainfall		46	39	43	33	47	163	198	133	101	34	41	40
Average max temp		24	24	25	25	24	23	23	23	24	25	24	24
Average min temp		14	14	15	15	15	15	14	15	15	15	14	13
Average rainfall		47	44	48	45	56	138	134	121	97	61	47	42

competition would travel as a bloc and joining a foreign team would not necessitate spending more time playing abroad than players for teams of their own nationality.

(ii)   Continuous format

An alternative format would concentrate the whole tournament into a single brief period of, say, three months. This could encourage interest in the tournament and the NFL in north America has proven that a very successful format can be played over little more than four months. Inspection of Table 10.3 suggests that the most reasonable prospect of uninterrupted play would be the period March, April and May, although early matches in London could be decidedly chilly and the later matches in Kolkata could be a trifle damp. Overall, however, climate need not be an obstacle to such a concentrated competition. With 8 teams a schedule where each team played each of its rivals 4 times over the three-month period would yield a 28-match schedule and a game roughly every 3 days, leaving time for recovery and travel. Playing squads of around 20 for each team would and a rotation system require each player to appear no more than once a week on average.

5.   Organisational structure and control for a new competition

The motivating thought behind our proposal for a new international club competition is the need to give the top players a greater stake in the game through higher salaries, comparable with other significant international sports. To do this competition between the clubs for the services of the players is essential, since this is the process by which salaries are bid up. The problem with Test Match cricket is that this competition is by definition absent—players play for their country.

Strong clubs must be run as commercial enterprises—they must have incentives to attract fans and generate revenues. Such a league might materialise through the actions of entrepreneurs not currently involved in the administration of cricket if the market is left to its own devices, just as World Series Cricket emerged as a natural reaction to the failure of international cricket to modernise in the 1970s. However, we think it would be better for cricket as a whole if the competition we envisage were introduced under the auspices of the governing bodies of cricket, in particular the ICC with the support of the national associations. There are several reasons for this:

  (i) An independently organised international club league might turn out to be very unbalanced. A degree of competitive balance is necessary to make an attractive competition, but the experience from other leagues shows that a strong central control of the league rules is necessary to ensure that such a balance is maintained. This leading role can be fulfilled by the ICC.

 (ii) To ensure that salaries are in fact bid up through competition it will be necessary to prevent collusion among the owners. This protection can be provided through the sanction of the ICC. The ICC or its representatives might explicitly maintain rules such as a requirement that at least a certain percentage of each team should consist of foreign players, not least to ensure that that players from outside the countries possessing a team have an opportunity to play.

(iii) If the new competition were to sit comfortably beside the current structure of Test Match cricket it would be necessary to co-ordinate time slots and so on. International soccer works well because, by and large, club soccer does not compete with the representative game due to the overall control of the national authorities.

We propose that the structure of the league should be as follows:

(1) The Central Organisation (CO) should be appointed by the ICC to oversee the proposed World Cricket League (WCL). The functions of the CO are:

    (i) To manage the sale of franchises to business interests in the cities selected on the basis of providing a balanced competition.

   (ii) To oversee the sale of broadcast rights and co-ordinate promotional activities for the league (ensuring consistency in merchandising and so on). A significant fraction of these revenues to be allocated as a prize for the winning team, to provide high powered incentives for the participating teams.

  (iii) To impose limited redistribution of income if a significant degree of competitive imbalance emerges. The right to tax on this basis must be strictly limited to some fraction of total revenues in order to ensure that franchise owners have the right incentive to maximise revenues.

  (iv) To withdraw and reallocate franchises in clear cases of failure.

(v) To determine the expansion of the league, either by the addition of new teams to the existing structure or by the creation of a second division with promotion and relegation.

(vi) To ensure that the scheduling of the WCL does not interfere with the scheduling of Test Match cricket and, as far as is possible, domestic cricket competitions.

(vii) To limit the power of clubs to stockpile players—a roster limit of, say, 25 players, might be imposed.

(2) Individual franchise owners will have the following rights:

(i) To retain locally generated revenues (including ticket sales, local sponsorship deals, catering and so on) up to some agreed fraction of the total, probably in the region of 75%.

(ii) To hire players in the market subject to the constraint that at least a certain percentage of players are foreigners. Movements of players between teams to be fixed according to some transfer rules. A transfer window might apply, such that transfers cannot take place during the WCL season.

(iii) To negotiate match schedules with the CO.

We believe that this structure would balance the interests of the players, the national game, the international governing body and the interests of the newly created clubs, without damaging the incentives of the new clubs to create a competitive and attractive league.

6. Conclusions

Cricket is a popular sport, and therefore it has the potential to sustain a successful international circuit such as Test Match cricket as well as domestic competition. However, to realise its full potential requires a structure that draws money into the game. Test Match cricket cannot do this on its own, and we believe the gambling scandals that have been so damaging to the game's reputation are simply a symptom of that failure. Rather than deal only with the symptoms, we propose a way of dealing with the underlying disease, which is the absence of a strong club competition which is a characteristic of all the successful team sports.

We suggest that a club competition limited to a select number of international locations could generate considerable fan interest. Were such a competition to be successful, it would result in increasing competition for player services, higher wages and ultimately give the players a greater personal stake in the future of the game. Moreover, we believe that an international club competition could prove a significant revenue generator for world cricket. In this chapter we have suggested that in an ideal world such a competition would operate most efficiently if sanctioned and ultimately controlled by the ICC. However, if this does not happen, we also think it quite likely that such a competition would generate itself spontaneously.

With cricket in crisis, the ICC holds an effective mandate for reform. By introducing new forms of competition it may be able to wipe clean the taints of the past and strengthen existing forms such as Test cricket.

Notes

1. Most team sports were not formally organised until the nineteenth century, while the rules of cricket were written down in 1744 (Birley 1999).
2. On Australian players' involvement with bookmakers, see O'Regan (1998).
3. Condon (2001, p. 31) points to a wide range of imaginative ways in which players have been alleged to have fixed occurrences within matches for betting purposes—including control of fielding positions, ends of the pitch from which bowling commences and so on.
4. If we take exclusion from the sport as the penalty then the bribe required to corrupt a player needs to make the expected utility under corruption no less than that under honesty. Excluding, for simplicity and without affecting the nature of the argument, considerations of shame and scruples we need $(1 - p)U(y + B) + pU(B) - U(y) = 0$ where y is sporting income, $U(.)$ is utility, p is probability of detection and B is minimal bribe required. The standard assumption of risk aversion implies that B increases with y.
5. "Turnover in 1999 amounted to £83,7212,000 (1998—£50,733,000) including £48,030,000 in respect of the 1999 World Cup" (p. 4).
6. The England cricket captain is believed to earn a higher figure of around £250,000. By comparison the England soccer captain is thought to earn about £5m (though through his club salary rather than payments for his international role).
7. The meagreness of the sums allegedly paid to induce corrupt practice is striking—see, for example, Bose (2001).
8. There may be problems with existing broadcasting contracts. However if broadcasters agree that the reform will generate interest, the rights to broadcast the new competition will offer a profitable attraction.
9. This can be compared to the position in other sports such as football where international representative competitions, such as the World Cup or European Championship, mark an acknowledged high point in the game while the most international competition remains at club level.
10. It is difficult to think of a Caribbean city which could support a team if a city-based structure were adopted. However, on a regional basis the idea would be more attractive, particularly if games played also in North America could attract support from the large expatriate Indian communities there.

References

Birley, D. (1999) *A Social History of English Cricket*, Aurum Press, London.

Bose, M. (2001) "A Game in Shame" in: G. Wright (ed.) *Wisden Cricketer's Almanack 2001*, John Wisden and Co, London, 17–28.

Central Bureau of Investigation (2000) *Report on Cricket Match Fixing and Related Malpractices*, New Delhi.

Condon, Sir P. (2001) *Report on Corruption in International Cricket*, Anti-Corruption Unit, International Cricket Council, London.

Craig, S. (2001) "It's Not Cricket" *History Today* 51, 6, 40–41.

England and Wales Cricket Board Limited (1999) *Report and Financial Statements, 31 December 1999*, London.

King, Judge E. L. (2000) *Commission of Inquiry into Match Fixing and Related Matters: Interim Report*, Cape Town.

O'Regan, R. (1998) *Player Conduct Inquiry Report*, Australian Cricket Board, Jolimont, Victoria.

Qayyum, Justice M. M. (1998) *Report of Judicial Commission*, Pakistan Cricket Board, Lahore.

Underdown, D. (2000) *Start of Play: Cricket and Culture in Eighteenth Century England*, Allen Lane, London.

Index